WHEN
FREEDOMS
COLLIDE

THE CASE FOR OUR CIVIL LIBERTIES

A.ALAN
BOROVOY

LESTER
&ORPEN
DENNYS
PUBLISHERS

To my parents, Rae and the late Jack Borovoy,
for practising what I preach.

FIRST EDITION

Canadian Cataloguing in Publication Data

Borovoy, A. Alan
    When freedoms collide

Includes index.
ISBN 0-88619-189-0 (bound)   ISBN 0-88619-191-2 (pbk.)

1. Liberty. II. Title.

JC585.B67 1988 323.44   C88-094100-6

Printed and bound in Canada by T.H. Best Printing Company Limited
for
Lester & Orpen Dennys Ltd.
78 Sullivan Street
Toronto, Canada
M5T 1C1

PREFACE

One of the frustrations of being general counsel of the Canadian Civil Liberties Association is that virtually everything you say to the public has to be condensed into twelve-second television clips. And, even at that, some of your best *bons mots* wind up on the cutting-room floor. The public rarely gets a feel for the hard thinking that you believe lies behind your media rhetoric. Indeed, the public will likely come to see you as a lot more shrill than you see yourself.

The important issue, however, is not your reputation; it's how you think about things. Unless you manage to get that across, your overall impact is likely to be minimal. The best you could ever hope for are some short-lived victories on those occasions when your rhetoric happened to coincide with some publicly felt need. However, a slight fluctuation in the public mood could rather quickly undo this support. The path to more lasting victories lies in influencing not only the result society arrives at, but also the way it gets there. This means trying to influence how people think about things.

In essence, that's why I decided to write this book. With twelve-second television clips it is not possible to build either a lasting victory or a viable constituency. This does not mean I hold the naïve view that the printed word is a reliable way to communicate and persuade. I have lived in the real world too long to believe so blithely in syllogistic power. My ambitions are less grandiose. As between thousands of television clips and a book, the latter stands a better chance of influencing the thought processes of at least some people.

It is not only our political leaders and the general public that I am trying to influence but also the members and supporters of the Canadian Civil Liberties Association. Very often people join groups such as CCLA because they get "turned on" by the stand that has been taken on one or two key issues. Quite often the reason such people stay with the organization is attributable more to inertia than to anything else. But no less often, numbers of people fall by the wayside or explicitly resign when the organization takes a particularly contentious position. What this illustrates is that, even for longtime supporters and members, there may be little agreement on underlying matters of social policy and analytical method. Not surprisingly, few of the organization's meetings are occupied with such seemingly esoteric questions. Therefore, I wanted to set out more systematically than I ever could on television how we might address the policy underpinnings of certain major civil liberties issues.

Of course, the *raison d'être* of this book transcends the viability of one small organization. Indeed, both the organization and the book are addressed, however modestly, to the most fundamental values of our civilization. The strengthening of our civil liberties is a necessary condition for the very survival of the democratic system. And the deepening of our commitment to the democratic system is also a necessary condition to the strengthening of our civil liberties.

To establish the framework for what you will be reading, it would be helpful to say a word about the fundamental values at issue. At the heart of it all is my commitment to the democratic system.

Democracy is the only form of government in which the people ultimately call the shots. Most of the systems in this world assume that the people are not worthy of so much trust. In many countries, the prevailing view is that what is needed is a wise and benevolent ruler who stands above the selfish passions of ordinary mortals.

The problem, of course, is where to find such a saint. And, even if you do, how can you ensure the survival of the saintly virtues once your candidate takes office? We have seen enough of history to know that personalities are often changed by the experience of power. In fact, a great many of the rulers who have had dictatorial power turned out to be downright vicious and cruel. We need only look at the world around us. In Pinochet's Chile, political dissenters have their genitals subjected to electric shocks and their heads submerged in excrement.

In Khomeini's Iran, thieves are mutilated and religious dissenters are executed. In Zia's Pakistan, adulterers are publicly flogged. And our century has given rise to Hitler and Stalin, perhaps the most savage and powerful despots of all time.

If the twentieth century has taught us anything, it is that we should be most wary of dictatorial power. No ideology—religious, political, or economic—can redeem the exercise of monopoly power. Even the humanitarian rhetoric of socialism was not enough to tame the cruelties of Stalin's gulag, Mao's Cultural Revolution, Ho Chi Minh's re-education camps, and Pol Pot's wholesale slaughters. And, thanks to the powers of modern technology (such as electronic surveillance and computers), it may have become effectively impossible to get rid of certain dictators.

Only democracy provides for the peaceful transition of governors according to the wishes of the governed. This gives us no guarantee, of course, that the governed will act justly. But, in a world without guarantees, which system gives us the *best chance* for some semblance of justice? To opt for democracy does not necessarily require that we have blissful faith in the people. It simply requires that we have *less* faith in anyone else.

The exercise of autonomy is also essential to the experience of dignity. While it is possible that the serf and the slave could be adequately fed, clothed, and housed, it is unlikely that they would ever enjoy a significant measure of self-respect. A sense of dignity requires some control of one's destiny. In democracies secret-ballot elections ensure that the people have the ultimate control. And, in contrast to most other systems, the people are considered equal to each other—if not in ability at least in dignity. This equality, in turn, has increasingly meant one person, one vote, and, ultimately, the majority rules.

But the majorities are composed of mere mortals. What prevents them from abusing all this power? Among the restraints on the majority are the freedoms of speech, press, assembly, and association. These freedoms enable people with grievances to recruit support from the public. In this way, the minority has a fighting chance to influence or even to become a majority. The more victimized a minority feels, the more likely it is to translate its complaints into votes at election time. The votes of the less aggrieved are generally not as predictable. Thus, the politicians will often seek to placate the most aggrieved members of the population. This operates as some deterrent against the mistreatment of minorities.

Another protection minorities have is the rule of law. The power of government to encroach on people is limited to what is authorized by law. Since most laws apply across the board, most of us have an interest in avoiding needlessly oppressive laws. The risks of unfairness are reduced also by the fact that whatever sanctions there are, have to be applied by courts which are supposed to be independent of the political majority. In the common-law democracies, we are further protected by the presumption of innocence. We are not subject to punishment by the state unless the state proves our guilt beyond a reasonable doubt.

This is not to say that democracies can be counted on always to behave according to these lofty principles. It is rather to note that, unlike other systems, democracies have machinery that is especially designed to deter and redress the abuses they may commit. I content myself, therefore, with an essentially modest claim: it is better to have such machinery than not to have it.

In my view, former Canadian social democratic leader, the late David Lewis, spoke with real wisdom a number of years ago when he declared that, despite his deep commitment to socialism, he was a democrat first and a socialist second. Even though he favoured socialistic goals, he gave the priority to democratic means. Whether, therefore, we be anglophones or francophones, federalists or separatists, conservatives or radicals, capitalists or socialists, natives or immigrants, blacks or whites, it behooves us, first and foremost, to defend the democratic *methods* of decision-making.

For the purposes of this book, I speak essentially as an individual and not as the full-time paid representative of the Canadian Civil Liberties Association. I could not undertake to write this kind of book without feeling free to express my personal positions on both the issues and the philosophical principles which guide them. This is a good point at which to express to my CCLA colleagues my deepest gratitude for the gracious way they have indulged my public foray into independent self-expression. On the overwhelming number of domestic civil liberties issues that are mentioned here, there continues to be a complete convergence between the CCLA position and my own. That, of course, is in no small part due to the pivotal role that the organization has given me in the shaping of its policies. I also express here certain views in areas where the organization has not yet taken a position and on other issues that are beyond the organization's mandate. (The latter refers especially to my remarks later in the book on the international implications of our civil liberties principles. Since the CCLA mandate is confined to the domestic arena, this part of the book should create no particular confusion.)

When social activists try to become policy analysts, they invariably encounter conflicting hazards. There is a risk of saying too little for analytical purposes and too much for activist purposes.

The first hazard concerns the limits of intellectual inquiry. It is not possible to say anything without making certain assumptions about facts and values. Those assumptions are properly open to question but they cannot all be questioned at the same time. Our factual and ethical presuppositions have to be addressed consecutively, not concurrently. But if that were attempted, the inquiry would become herculean. Since I am primarily an activist and not an academic, it has been necessary to set substantial limits on the magnitude of the ensuing inquiries. In the first place, my CCLA responsibilities afford me neither the time nor the energy for an interminable exploration of first principles and primary sources. In the second place, a policy discussion of day-to-day issues does not create an obligation to emulate the encyclopaedia. One need not choose between shallow narrative and definitive exposition. It is possible to say something worthwhile without trying to say everything there is.

For activist purposes, it is necessary to build coalitions with wide varieties of people who agree on limited points but who do not necessarily share the presuppositions behind them. In those areas where such presuppositions are explored, there is a risk of fracturing the consensus needed for coalition. A book, however, is not a social action project. In order to do its job, this kind of book must penetrate, at least somewhat, the surface of everyday issues. Regardless of whatever disagreements such inquiries will reveal between me and my various coalition partners, I trust it will still be possible for us to work together in those areas where we can agree. The very essence of coalition involves, after all, collaboration among people whose views are not always compatible.

A book of this size could not be written without the support of many people. In this connection, I am particularly grateful to Toronto lawyer Sydney Goldenberg, Judge Rosalie Abella, and CCLA board chairman Ken Swan for having read virtually the entire manuscript and for having commented so helpfully on it. (Indeed, Goldenberg and Swan also went over several additional versions of certain chapters.) In particular areas I was the beneficiary of similarly helpful comments from

Tony Doob, Owen Shime, Harry Arthurs, Neil Brooks, Marc Rosenberg, Stanley Schiff, Larry Taman, Robert Sharpe, Gilbert Sharpe, Jim Hathaway, Mel Finkelstein, David Draper, John McCamus, David Greenspan, Daniel G. Hill, Judy Ross, and Dawn Cannon. In the case of Dawn Cannon, I am grateful not only for her literary assistance, but also for her unflagging support.

At this stage, I cannot help remembering the encouragement I received from my dear friend the late Millie Shime. Had she lived, I know she would have made available to me the kind of incisive editorial assistance she often provided for other things that I have written. However, she did live long enough to read the first draft of certain key material. I drew considerable sustenance from her comment, "There is a book here."

I began to write *When Freedoms Collide* in September of 1980. Despite the years that have elapsed since then, the actual writing time was relatively short. Most of the book was written during intervals at Christmas and summer when the pressure of CCLA work had somewhat subsided. Even at those times, however, my writing often had to be squeezed into a hectic schedule of CCLA activities. Fortunately, the process was assisted somewhat by the fact that, at least in a few cases, I could revise my previously written essays, newspaper articles, and CCLA briefs.

In midstream I was forced to reconsider the entire project. The 1982 proclamation of the Charter of Rights and Freedoms threatened to revolutionize the Canadian legal system and, perhaps with it, much of what I had already written. I decided, however, to persist as I had begun. This book was never conceived to be a statement of what the law is, but rather a statement of what the law should be. My concern here is not so much with legal technicality as with the social policy behind it. The Charter should not be viewed as the last word on civil liberties but only as a weapon to be used in their promotion. No matter what meaning the courts may attach to the words in the Charter, the most important consideration is what values the people believe should be governing them. Conceivably, some of the laws about which I have written could well have changed by the time of publication. This could be the result of court and board decisions (under the Charter and otherwise), legislative enactments, orders-in-council, and government directives. What has not changed, however, are the central arguments for and against the laws that I favour and those I oppose. That remains the focus of the book.

Nevertheless, I must acknowledge that, in certain critical areas, *When Freedoms Collide* has been a casualty of change. Because of the introduction of a bill to replace the War Measures Act, I decided to omit a chapter that I had written on emergency powers. While I continue to criticize this country's freedom of information and privacy laws, the gap between what they provide and what I propose has narrowed somewhat in some places, making the issue generally more suitable for a brief than for a book. On the other hand, some developments have created civil liberties issues today that did not exist when I began to write. In the fall of 1980, we had never heard of a disease called AIDS. Today, the fear of this disease has created a wide variety of difficult and delicate questions and concerns. In the interests of publishing this book before the infirmities of old age *completely* engulfed me, I simply had to omit certain issues. In any event, the book in no way pretends to be comprehensive.

While there is no attempt here to keep completely up to date on every legal issue that is addressed, there is an attempt through the notes at the back to provide the reader with supportive material, both as to facts and as to law. In this regard, I am particularly grateful to my CCLA staff colleague David Schneiderman, for a tremendous amount of research that made the notes possible. I wrote the book, in the main, without doing fresh research, relying instead on what I happened to remember from general reading and years of CCLA activity (including the research the organization has accumulated). David's job was to verify or rectify what I had already written. The volume of sources and references is a testament to his ingenuity and tenacity. At key points, the notes also contain statements that qualify and explain material in the text. By putting these things in the notes, I sought to maximize accuracy of content while minimizing disruptions to style.

It remains possible that, between sign-off and publication, a major event could intervene that would affect some of my material. But since a book cannot be published if it is subject to perpetual revision, it must be read subject to some cut-off date. For these purposes, I have chosen May 1, 1988. The choice is attributable essentially to two factors (only the first of which is rational). The first of May was about the time that general editing of the book came to an end and copy-editing began. That date also marked the twentieth anniversary of my tenure as general counsel of the Canadian Civil Liberties Association. Events worthy of mention that occur after this date will be acknowledged, if I learn of them in time, in the notes rather than in the text.

As always, the technical support I received from the staff of the Canadian Civil Liberties Association made life bearable for me just as I, no doubt, was making it unbearable for them. In this connection, I am especially grateful to our successive administrative co-ordinators, Helen Cainer and Danielle McLaughlin; my secretary, Pat Caston and her former assistant Yvonne Ho; our former researchers Allan Strader, Erika Abner, and Marie Moliner; and a voluntary researcher, Steven Barret. My writing efforts were also generously supported by grants from the Human Rights Institute of the University of Ottawa, Faculty of Law, and the Ontario Arts Council.

Although he was not involved in vetting parts of the book, former CCLA president J. S. Midanik nevertheless influenced quite a bit of it. For many years, I have sought and received his wise counsel. I know that these exchanges have played a central role in the development of my ideas, even in areas where we disagree. I am also grateful to my editor, Anne Holloway, for many useful stylistic criticisms and suggestions. She helped me to realize that it was possible to reduce the original manuscript by more than one hundred pages without suffering excessive pain. My agent, Beverley Slopen, provided not only intelligent advice but also nurturing support. And my publisher, Malcolm Lester, was helpful and enthusiastic.

I conclude these introductory remarks by acknowledging the debt I owe to the eminent American philosopher Sidney Hook. Those who know his work will see its influence in the pages that follow. I began reading Professor Hook some thirty-five years ago and feel obliged to mention how substantially he has contributed to the way I think about things. This does not mean that there are no important differences between us. Those who know his work will also see a number of such differences here. His impact, however, has been less on the conclusions I have reached than on the methods I have used to get there. What I especially owe to Sidney Hook is the brilliant way he has articulated, refined, and applied the principles of John Dewey's philosophy of pragmatism and instrumentalism.

Nevertheless, only I can take the responsibility for what is written on these pages. I have benefited from the comments and suggestions of many people. But, in the final analysis, I am the only one who will sink or swim with the result.

A. Alan Borovoy
Toronto, May 1988

CONTENTS

Chapter One

THE FREEDOM OF EACH

VERSUS THE WELFARE

OF ALL

The Recurring Fallacies

No doubt, most people have similar feelings about the key periods in their lives, but I continue to believe that there is something special about the past twenty years during which I have served with the Canadian Civil Liberties Association. This period has produced a series of events that has tested, perhaps as never before, the most fundamental assumptions of our democratic way of life.

As a society, we proclaim the importance of civil liberties. But in October of 1970, the overwhelming majority of Canadians enthusiastically welcomed the governmental suspension of civil liberties through the first peace-time invocation of the War Measures Act. Following the kidnappings of British Trade Commissioner James Cross and Quebec Labour Minister Pierre Laporte by the terrorist Front de Libération du Québec (FLQ), Canada became engulfed in fear. The government's solution was to increase the powers of the police to search and seize, arrest and detain, without warrant or bail. It further created the following new criminal offences: membership in the FLQ and the public advocacy of FLQ policies. In this situation, our belief in civil liberties collided with the urgency we felt to ensure the very survival of our system.

We believe in the importance of the rule of law, but we responded with remarkable tolerance to the revelations of unlawful conduct on the part of officials of the Royal Canadian Mounted Police. As long

1

ago as the fall of 1977, we learned that members of the RCMP had participated in burglary, theft, arson, mail opening, assault, and the invasion of tax files. Despite the fact that this litany of wrongdoing spanned more than thirty years and involved hundreds of offences, not one person has even been *charged* outside the province of Quebec. We were told that these illegalities were perpetrated in the interests of national security and law enforcement. Our belief in the rule of law collided with our desire to be protected from spies, terrorists, and dope pedlars.

We proclaim our abhorrence of racial and sexual discrimination. But since the 1960s, a growing number of Canadians have welcomed proposals for "affirmative action" that require employers to hire designated numbers of women and members of minority groups. The point of these proposals is to secure employment for the victims of discrimination in all sectors of our society. But the problem is that a requirement to hire people from some groups could very well lead to a *refusal* to hire people from other groups. Our opposition to racial and sexual discrimination collided with our desire to ensure a more favourable outcome for the traditional victims of such discrimination.

We declare the importance of cultural self-determination. Yet beginning in the early 1970s, many non-native people sought to change a provision in the law which removed Indian status from Indian women who married non-Indian men while granting such status when the situation was reversed. There has been a willingness to impose principles of sexual equality even on some unwilling native communities. Our belief in cultural autonomy collided with our belief in sexual equality.

We proclaim the centrality of freedom of speech. But in 1985 there was substantial support for the false news prosecution of pamphleteer Ernst Zundel, whose publications claimed that the Holocaust was some kind of Jewish hoax. To paraphrase the words of one writer, it wasn't enough for yesterday's Nazis to extinguish six million Jewish lives; their modern sympathizers seek to extinguish six million Jewish *deaths*. Our belief in freedom of speech collided with our belief in racial and ethnic dignity.

Similarly in the late 1970s, feminists who have long opposed censorship began to change their tune because of the "new pornography", which celebrates violence against women and the exploitation of children. Other opponents of censorship experienced an erosion of their tolerance when they read, in the late 1970s, that a gay publication had eulogized the alleged pleasures of sexual relations between men and boys. Our belief in freedom of speech collided with our desire to prevent sexual abuse.

For still others, the Waterloo of their free speech commitments occurred when they read recently of a bizarre court case in the United States. *The Progressive*, an American magazine, was initially stopped by a court injunction when it attempted to publish an article detailing how to make a hydrogen bomb. In a world of more than five billion people, it would take only one resourceful nut to read such material and it could well be game, set, and match for everybody. Our belief in free speech collided with our fear of universal annihilation.

I hasten to point out that these remarks are not intended to divide the world into heretics and true believers. On the contrary, it is my intention to acknowledge that, no matter what beliefs we may profess, we each have our breaking point. Paradox is endemic to the human condition; intelligent decision-making requires that we recognize this inescapable fact.

Usually there is a price to pay for the things we desire. Virtually everything we want will require some sacrifice in something else we want. Everyone has had this experience hundreds of times. If we want more security for our old age, we may have to endure greater privation during our youth. If we want to buy a house, we may have to put off buying a car. If we want more money, we may have to accept less leisure in which to enjoy it. Sometimes the choices are particularly painful. We all know of people who feel trapped in unhappy marriages. They are torn between the misery of the present and anxiety about the future. They may want to leave their spouses but not their children. They may seek to gain more liberty but fear to lose security. Whatever choice they make, they are sure to suffer. What they do not know is which way they will suffer more. This is the phenomenon that American philosopher Sidney Hook labelled "the tragic sense of life". The limitations of human existence are such that inevitably we must face conflicts between good and good, right and right, bad and bad. We are fated to suffer the pain of knowingly having to surrender things we value in order to acquire other things we may value even more.

Here, then, is the theme of this book. It is an inquiry into ways and means of addressing the conflicts and paradoxes that beset democratic societies. The way we handle these conflicts is basic to the survival of the democratic system.

Since the beginning of recorded time, human beings have hungered for a comprehensive way to transcend these tragic dilemmas. To this end, they have turned to fundamentalist religions, sophisticated philosophies, and a wide variety of things in between. Sometimes their "answers" have been found in divine revelation, sometimes in dialectical materialism, sometimes in categorical imperatives. The course of human history is full of attempts to find a workable formula. I have no formula to recommend or panacea to invoke, but I have been able to discern at least six recurring fallacies in the solutions of others. What follows is an attempt to identify these fallacies. Even if they cannot help to transcend or resolve our tragic dilemmas, they may at least sensitize us as to what to avoid.

The Absolutist Fallacy

The First Amendment to the United States Constitution says that "Congress shall make no law...abridging the freedom of speech...." There are no modifications or qualifications. It doesn't say that Congress may abridge freedom of speech sometimes or under certain circumstances; it says simply that Congress may impose *no* such restrictions at all.

Nevertheless, as long ago as the First World War, the U.S. Supreme Court upheld certain congressional restrictions on free speech. Mr. Justice Oliver Wendell Holmes said that there could be no freedom of speech falsely to shout "fire" in a crowded theatre. In such a situation, the likelihood of immediate panic would eliminate one of the essential prerequisites for free speech: an opportunity for the listener to evaluate competing messages. Essentially the court declared that, despite the sweeping language of the First Amendment, free speech was not an absolute. There are at least some circumstances in which exceptions must be permissible.

What could be more essential to the conduct of the doctor-patient relationship than the principle of confidentiality? Would we be prepared, however, to punish the psychiatrist who tipped off the police that a patient was on the way to the airport to hijack a plane? In such event, I believe that our respect for confidentiality would give way to our desire to protect life and limb in imminent peril.

Do such examples make it easy to violate the principles of free speech and medical confidentiality? They shouldn't. To recognize the limits of these principles is not to deny their validity. It is simply to assert that they are not absolutes. Indeed, I cannot conceive of any value or principle to which there could never be exceptions. Perhaps it would be more fruitful to reverse the onus. If anyone knows of an absolute, I defy such person to identify it.

Some people will readily acknowledge the non-absoluteness of values like freedom of speech and medical confidentiality, but insist that there are other more comprehensive and transcendent absolutes by which humans should resolve their conflicts. The obvious example is God. Any commands (or Commandments) that God has issued should, because of their source, be absolutely binding on us.

But how can we finite human beings *regard* anything as divinely willed without becoming enmired in a hopeless dilemma? Once we attribute a command to God, we place it beyond question and challenge. Obviously it is not logical to question perfection. But we humans must admit nevertheless that *we* might be wrong. Since our judgments are finite and flawed, whatever we believe must remain open to question. To deny that is to deny our imperfection. Indeed, it would be like saying that we could not be wrong on the subject at issue. This would transform our belief into an exercise in self-idolatry.

My argument cannot disprove any particular claims regarding the Deity. But it denies our ability to *regard* the objects of our belief as though they came from Him. Conceivably, for example, there may be a God. But even if there is, it is paradoxical to regard with unquestioning reverence what purports to come from Him. In recognition of the fact that we may be wrong, we must admit that any Commandments attributed to Him, individually and collectively, are subject to question and challenge. But, once we admit this, we are effectively denying them the quality of absoluteness. Such Commandments cannot be both beyond and subject to question at one and the same time.

Moreover, how is a mere mortal actually supposed to recognize God in the event of a communication or revelation? There are no scientific principles or logical axioms for making such an identification. Ultimately we have to rely on our finite, subjective, imperfect, and inadequate intuitions. And on what basis can we trust *them* to make judgments of such enormity?

Consider, for example, what happened to Abraham. When he got the command to kill his son Isaac, how did he know the message came from God? Wasn't it just as (or even more) plausible for Abraham to impute such a command to the Devil or even to his own imagination? "Faith" is the answer we get from certain believers. But faith in whom and in what? In order for Abraham to act the way he did, the faith he had to have was not necessarily in God; it was in *himself*. Abraham had to believe in his own ability to identify the source of that horrible command.

There is no way to avoid this problem while we are on earth. Whom can we trust as the authentic recipients of God's word? The pope or the ayatollah? The primate or the rabbi? In view of the disagreements they have with each other, they can't all make equally valid claims. Or, suppose people like Charles Manson, the Son of Sam, and Sirhan Sirhan tell us that they were ordered by God to commit their crimes. On the basis of what do we deny the authenticity of their claims? Normative tradition? Morality? The Ten Commandments?

Such replies simply won't wash. There is no way our moral values can be binding on God. On the contrary, they are supposed to derive their legitimacy because they come from Him. Since He is perfect, He could have good reason to behave in a manner which, to us, might appear inconsistent. He might even have good reason to withhold the reasons from us.

It would be the height of earthly *chutzpah* for humans to try to impose their standards on the Absolute. It follows that there are simply no criteria by which we can test the legitimacy of revelation claims— no criteria other than our finite, subjective, intuitive faculties. And again, we cannot, with consistency, allow them to be the judge of what is absolute.

This is not to denigrate the important role that the world's religions have played in the lives of millions of people. It is simply to put these matters in perspective. I am addressing not the validity of people's beliefs, but the application of their beliefs to the formation of public policy. In a pluralistic society where values are constantly colliding, it is unwarrantedly dangerous to rely on the Divine Will. We have no way of divining the Divine Will without reposing absolutist faith in our own powers of discernment or in the human recipients of claimed revelations. Either way, the exercise is too much for finite mortals.

Similar problems bedevil the secular absolutists. They too are unable to prove that their various positions are absolute. Inevitably, their positions derive from arbitrarily chosen premises or fragmentary observations—a vulnerable source, indeed, for absolutist pretensions.

To whatever extent, therefore, secularists regard their philosophy as an absolute, they are exercising faith, not reason. And, at that point, they would be just as susceptible as their religious counterparts to the charge of self-idolatry. Again, this does not mean that such secularists are necessarily in error about the absoluteness of their respective views. But it does mean that they cannot, with consistency, *regard* their views as absolutes.

The Packaging Fallacy

The way you express a problem can often influence the way you solve it. If, for example, we describe a welfare dispute as a conflict between individual rights and the public interest, we load the dice against the individual. Even though individual rights are seen as important, most people would likely say that the public interest is more important. To say otherwise would seem unjustifiably self-indulgent.

But consider what would happen if the problem were expressed differently. Suppose it were expressed as a conflict between two public interests. Yes, there is a public interest in saving the taxpayers' money. But there is also a public interest in giving people enough money to live in dignity. If we express the problem that way, it is no longer so easy to resolve.

In essence, the fallacy here is question-begging.

The Power-Hoarding Fallacy

It may be hard to believe, but, at the time of this writing, it may actually be an offence in the province of Ontario for a government snowplow-operator or a prison dishwasher to write a letter to a newspaper complaining about the latest federal budget. An Ontario statute prohibits civil servants from making public statements on any matter "that forms part of a platform" of a political party. This is how that province has resolved the conflict between the demands of free speech and those of efficient government.

No one can quarrel with having *some* restrictions on what certain civil servants may say in public. Imagine the confusion if civil servants were allowed to criticize openly the very policies they had to administer. Similar considerations apply to upper-echelon civil servants who are close to government policy-making. If such senior officials could "bad mouth" government policy, the public would be completely confused. Such a situation would ultimately undermine the authority of the elected politicians. Paradoxically, therefore, such unfettered free speech would damage the integrity of the democratic processes. But, at most, this is an argument for some restrictions on the free speech of some civil servants. It can hardly justify the wholesale muzzling of all government employees.

This is what I mean by power hoarding. While there may be a reasonable basis for some acquisition of power over people's freedom, there is a tendency to request and receive more than the circumstances require. These excesses are perpetrated, not by malevolent autocrats who seek to do bad, but by "tunnel-visioned" bureaucrats who seek to do good. Their fixation with their good goals often makes them insensitive to the other interests they affect. The bureaucratic mentality among both politicians and top civil servants likes to play it safe. More than anything else, they dread being caught out on a limb. In order to avoid even the remotest possibility of failure, they seek an expanding level of power to accomplish their objectives. Such power is designed to cover every hypothetical scenario that the bureaucratic imagination can conjure up. The problem, however, is that many additional grants of power for the bureaucrats are acquired at the cost of commensurately less freedom for the citizens.

Examples abound. Canadian police originally sold the public on giving them wiretap powers because such powers were allegedly needed to fight organized crime. In the process, Parliament made it possible for the police to acquire wiretap authority for more than forty offences that have nothing to do with organized crime. Few Canadians would deny the government some level of standby power in the event that a drastic emergency arose with such suddenness that there was no time for Parliament to act. But, while some such level of power may arguably be acceptable, the Canadian War Measures Act has contained virtually no fetters on what the government may do in any situation which *it* calls an emergency.

In the mid-1980s, the Parliament of Canada enacted a new law to curtail soliciting for the purpose of prostitution. It was understandable that such a law be passed. A torrent of uninhibited street soliciting had been unleashed by a court decision that the old law did not restrict prostitutes as many had believed it would. All over the country, home-owners were protesting to government that the prostitute trade was undermining the enjoyment of their property and neighbourhoods. Unfortunately, our politicians were not content to pass a law narrowly addressed to this problem. The resulting law made it a crime for any person to communicate in any way with any other person in any public place—not simply streets—for the purpose of engaging in prostitution or obtaining the sexual services of a prostitute.

Suppose a passenger in a taxi discreetly asked his driver where he might find a prostitute? Or a customer in a drugstore might ask the same question of a pharmacist. Indeed, the scope of the law is so wide that it might catch the conversation of two friends walking quietly down the street or sitting quietly on a park bench. Moreover, a smile, a wink, or a nod might be enough to constitute a prohibited communication.

Particularly revealing in this regard was a television exchange I had at the time with a high-ranking police official. When I pointed out all of the bizarre situations which could be termed illegal under the new law, he pooh-poohed my argument. He confidently assured everyone that the police had absolutely no interest in enforcing the law as broadly as I suggested was now possible. That exchange epitomized the power-hoarding phenomenon: if the police have no interest in exercising certain powers, why in the world should the law make it possible for them to do so?

Power hoarding is a dangerous exercise. The more power is exerted over our fundamental freedoms, the more fragile those freedoms unavoidably become. It is one thing to grant only as much power as is demonstrably necessary and then attempt to devise a number of safeguards to minimize the risk of abuse. It is another thing to grant large amounts of power beyond what has been demonstrated as necessary and then simply to trust that they won't be abused. The latter is the power-hoarding fallacy.

The Either-Or Fallacy

When he was first confronted with the revelations of widespread law-breaking by the RCMP, former Prime Minister Pierre Trudeau disclaimed responsibility on the basis that the minister in charge should not have to know everything that the RCMP is doing.

There was, of course, some merit in Mr. Trudeau's position. If the cabinet minister in charge had knowledge of every police activity, there would be an enormous risk that the police would become thoroughly politicized. But, if the minister had no such knowledge, how could there be any kind of civilian control or accountability?

Despite his impressive intellectual credentials, Mr. Trudeau had committed the either-or fallacy. Why is it necessary to choose between the minister knowing everything or knowing nothing of the relevant police activities? The idea is to ensure that the minister knows something—enough to assume the requisite responsibility but not so much as to politicize police operations. This is not to suggest that it would be easy to strike this delicate balance. It is simply to suggest that, in the real world, we can often avoid having to choose between all or nothing at all.

Similarly, we don't need to choose between the current wiretap powers of the police and no such powers at all, or between the horrendous powers of the War Measures Act and absolutely no standby emergency powers. In all these cases, we could quite reasonably opt for some of the powers at issue without accepting all of them.

For some reason, however, many people become simplistically polarized in their thinking. If we don't like the foreign policy of Ronald Reagan, we must support a policy of appeasement. If we press our criminal justice system to adopt more protections for suspects, this shows a lack of concern for victims. Too many people are either unable or unwilling to appreciate complex distinctions. They simply fail to realize that, on the teeter-totter of life, we are not compelled to choose between the two extreme ends. There is a lot of ground in between where a delicate balance can be sought and sometimes even achieved.

The Pollyanna Fallacy

It is not often that I quote federal finance ministers with approval, but I am impelled to give credit where it is due. During the course of the 1974 Canadian federal election campaign, the then finance minister, John Turner, expressed the essence of the human predicament. He warned the electorate not to compare the prime minister to the Almighty; compare him instead to the alternative. The essence of the Pollyana fallacy is the failure to recognize that most of the time our public policy choices involve unpalatable alternatives. Our goal, therefore, should be to choose which of the alternatives is the less or the least unpalatable.

Take a walk, for example, through New York's Times Square or through the downtown area of a number of other large North American cities. Everywhere you will be greeted by signs of mounting decadence—movies, pictures, and books endorsing sexual perversion, sado-masochism, bestiality, and so on. These are some of the more conspicuous results which have accompanied the easing of our censorship laws. Does this mean that we should resort to a tightening of censorship? Not in my opinion. It simply means we should recognize that, whatever we do in the area of public policy, the dominant outcome is likely to be bad.

We must understand the nature of what is being released when the lid of censorship is lifted. In my view, there is more lechery than beauty in the human psyche. We should not be surprised, therefore, at the proliferation of questionable material. Thus, the most realistic question to ask is which course of action will produce the least bad consequences. For reasons which I will develop later, I happen to believe that the evils produced by censorship generally are worse than the evils produced by lifting censorship. Suffice it for the moment to recognize that either way, we are unlikely to be happy with the results.

We must guard against the temptation to escape into fantasy. Neither God nor socialism, neither the Ten Commandments nor the categorical imperative, can help us to transcend reality. If we are to solve our problems intelligently in the here and now, we must do so within the limits of the unpalatable alternatives available. This does not mean that there cannot be new and creative ways of dealing with our problems. We do not have to be prisoners of yesterday's conventional wisdom. But what it does mean is that few courses of action in public affairs are likely to produce primarily positive results. The realistic goal of looking beyond yesterday's solutions is not the good, it is the less bad. Such recognition is usually a prerequisite to an intelligent solution.

The Redemptive Fallacy

Invariably, there are people who will insist that the foregoing discussion of the Pollyanna fallacy is based upon a needlessly static view of human nature. The human race, they will tell us, is not condemned by nature to be as it appears now—selfish, narcissistic, corrupt. We will be told that our species is capable of radically different behaviour, that spontaneous altruism is within the range of human possibilities. We will be invited to imagine the day when decency will prevail and bureaucracies won't be necessary. All we need to do, they will say, is relax our sexual inhibitions, abolish capitalism, or send our children to Montessori schools.

Such panacea-mongering is what I call the redemptive fallacy. Based as they inevitably are on fragmentary observations or arbitrary postulates, these claims to perfecting human nature are not susceptible of proof. They require instead an exercise in faith. Of course, I cannot deny the possibility that human nature could evolve according to these predictions. What I can challenge, however, is the reasonableness of letting ourselves be guided by these unprovable dreams.

In the first place, they tend to create a defective yardstick by which to evaluate alternative courses of action. How often have we heard, for example, that legislation should be avoided in the field of race relations? The protagonists of this view have warned that coercive legislation is likely to offend people thus rendering less achievable the ultimate goal of universal love. It is better, they say, to educate people to love each other.

The problem is that there is not one stitch of proof that, even if it were possible to reach masses of people this way, education could produce such a state of universal love. In the meantime, minority groups continue to suffer discrimination in jobs, services, and housing. By insisting that all action be measured by the ultimate goal of universal love, these redemptivists effectively undermine our ability to fight discrimination now.

In the second place, redemptivism distorts our thinking about ends and means. For certain redemptivists, the ends never justify the means. The members of this group seek to be redeemed by their every action. As a consequence, they shun the use of any means that may be tainted with impurity. Yet, in our finite world, impure means often represent the only practical way to reduce suffering and injustice. Frequently it is necessary to be nasty and unpleasant. It was the unpleasantness, for example, of economic boycotts, sit-ins, freedom rides, and demonstrations that finally succeeded in racially desegregating much of the American south. Unpleasant injurious strikes, to use another example, have often been needed to elicit liveable wages from recalcitrant employers.

By contrast, there are some redemptivists for whom the ends always justify the means. In this connection, consider the deliberate starvation of millions of Kulaks by Soviet dictator Joseph Stalin. He justified such atrocities on the basis that the next generation would be redeemed in the paradise of socialism. The temptation must be quite irresistible. If you really believed that redemption is the likely consequence of your deeds, what wouldn't you be prepared to do? What horror would be too much? What sacrifice would be too great?

These two types of redemptivists represent opposite sides of the same coin. Many of the religious persuasion are prepared to tolerate a wide range of horrors in order to get themselves up to heaven. And many of the secular persuasion are prepared to *commit* a wide range of horrors in order to bring heaven down to earth.

A third problem with the goal of changing human nature is the inevitable cynicism produced by the collision between aspiration and reality. In some cases, this turns militants into mortgage brokers. In other cases, political activists become religious recluses. Consider, for example, what happened to the "new left" rebels of the 1960s. A good number of them have given up the political struggle. Reality shattered their dreams. Most joined the bourgeoisie; some repaired to caves in order to contemplate the cosmos. A similar fate overtook their predecessors of the 1930s—the Communists, Trotskyists, and other extremists. The harbouring of unrealistic goals tends to erode the ranks of the social reformers.

Fourth and worse still, these hopes of changing human nature have been known to degenerate into destructive violence. When inflated expectations are frustrated, people often become explosively angry. Remember, for example, the Black Power riots in the United States. Remember how soon they occurred after the euphoria that accompanied Martin Luther King's redemptive "I have a dream" speech. To the extent that black people believed in the possibility of realizing King's dream, they must have experienced bitter frustration. Remember too how these riots helped to produce, in turn, a U.S. government less sympathetic to black aspirations than many of its predecessors: the Nixon–Agnew Republican administration.

It is more sensible, therefore, to eliminate these unprovable dreams from our cost-benefit analysis of social problems. In view of the enormous cost these dreams inflict on so many of our vital values, it is only fair to burden their proponents with a heavy onus. If you wish to intrude your redemptive hopes for human nature on our common-sense problem solving, you should have to demonstrate the truth, or at least the probable truth, of your apparently illusory assertions. We are far less likely to go wrong by assuming that reality accords with what we can see, hear, and remember about human behaviour, rather than what we might wish for. While humans have at times indeed behaved like saints, the newsworthiness of the occasions attests to their rarity. We should renounce, therefore, the attempt to create heaven on earth, and focus instead on reducing the hell.

THE CHARGE OF PESSIMISM

I can almost hear the denunciations of my critics: "You are wallowing in needless pessimism. The acceptance of your ideas would paralyse even the quest for improvement. Without redemptive hope, why should anyone struggle and sacrifice for a better world? Unless our reach exceeds our grasp, there is no incentive to progress."

Such criticisms are based upon the fallacious notion that the quest for Utopia is necessary to inspire the effort for improvement. But all around us there is hard evidence that this is not so. Human beings have shown an enormous capacity to be galvanized by less lofty objectives. Consider, for example, the substantial sacrifices made by working people in the course of waging labour strikes. Such sacrifices have entailed the deprivation of income, the risks of discharge and unemployment, at times even the danger of physical beatings and injury. Yet, apart from a few redemptive radicals, the vast majority of strikers hardly expected their struggles to spawn the millennium.

Rarely did these people expect anything more than a reduction in the oppressiveness of their working conditions. Their goals were higher wages, shorter hours, various health and safety protections, longer vacations, retirement pensions, and in the longer term a greater measure of dignity through the entrenchment of collective bargaining rights. Few working people expected their oppressive drudgery to disappear, and few of them expected to be permanently relieved of the need to repeat their costly struggles. They may have realistically hoped that tomorrow's struggles would be less burdensome than yesterday's. But precious few believed that the struggles would end.

Our reach *should* exceed our grasp, but this doesn't mean we need to reach for heaven. Why isn't it enough for us just to keep reaching beyond our current grasp?

Nor is this approach so hopelessly pessimistic. Indeed, in some ways it might be considered a prerequisite for genuine optimism. Once redemptive goals are eliminated, it is finally possible to recognize and appreciate how much progress has actually been made. If we stopped the hand-wringing about universal harmony, for example, we might derive some measure of solace from the fact that our human rights laws have reduced the incidence and hardships of racial discrimination. If we purged from our psyches the vision of a classless Utopia, we might appreciate at last the enormous improvements in working conditions and welfare benefits that have been won by the labour and political struggles of this century.

In short, the anti-redemptive quest for the less bad can both allow us to enjoy yesterday's victories and prod us to engage in tomorrow's battles. We can be encouraged by what we have already done and enlivened by what there is left to do.

There is another reason why the repudiation of Utopia is not really such a pessimistic exercise. Who in the world would want to *live* in Utopia? A society characterized by spontaneous altruism and universal love would have to be the dullest place imaginable. Why should any rational being consciously struggle for a life of such monotony?

AN APPROACH FOR FINITE EARTHLINGS

So where does this leave us embattled human beings? We are still entitled to ideals and we cannot live without values. But such values and ideals must be based upon an explicit recognition that they are limited, fragmentary, and ever subject to exception, question, and challenge.

We can still revere, for example, honesty, peace, and love. But we must recognize that these values are not absolute and they cannot redeem us. Even if we believe in honesty, there are times when it is better to lie. If touchy, homely people ask us how they look, should we tell the truth? Even if we believe in peace, it is sometimes better to fight. Should we have allowed our love of peace to quell our resistance to the barbarism of Hitler? Even if we believe that we should love people, it is sometimes more productive to have genuine contempt for them. How can we simultaneously fight and love the perpetrators of injustice?

In short, we must learn to live with the fact that our most cherished values and our most esteemed goals inevitably will collide. There is simply no reasonable alternative to the perpetual exercise of balancing values and weighing risks. There is no easy or painless way to do it. There is no hierarchy of priorities that can be codified for automatic application to our problems. As circumstances change, so must our priorities. Our task is to be ever on the look-out to adopt the least unpalatable of the unpalatable alternatives available.

One of the advantages of rejecting redemptive absolutes is that we can be liberated at last from the ends-versus-means strait-jacket. The issue is no longer whether the ends always or never justify the means. Such questions should not be resolved in the abstract; they should be resolved in the concrete settings in which they arise. The practical question is what ends will justify what means in what situations. To address these problems in this way is to accept the never-ending exercise of balancing ends and means.

But, if there are no absolutes, how are these value conflicts to be resolved? Where will the standards come from? Will our subjective, arbitrary, irrational tastes then rule supreme? Does a rejection of absolutes mean that might becomes right? The rejection of absolutes need not bring such moral chaos. Whatever our conflicts, we also share a lot. This is an inevitable outgrowth of living in the same society and inhabiting the same planet. The way to resolve our conflicts objectively is to apply what unites us to what divides us.

Suppose, for example, we were attempting to determine a fair wage for auto workers in Toronto. To the extent that we believed market factors should govern, we would probably consider what auto workers earn in other communities and what other workers earn in Toronto. If recourse to such factors still failed to resolve the issue, we would likely look at other market factors. At what wage rate would people leave the auto industry for other jobs in Toronto? And at what point might they leave Toronto for other auto companies? Our arguments would focus on trying to find a wage rate that would strike the best possible balance among all of these market standards.

But these market standards do not thereby become transcendent absolutes. In the context of other problems, the market measure itself could be challenged. Suppose someone came along and recommended a state-directed incomes policy to replace our reliance on the marketplace. At that point, we would likely want to examine such factors as the extent to which economic insecurity would be reduced, the amount of freedom which would be won or lost, the relative viability of state planning, and the size of the resulting bureaucracy. In short, while market mechanisms may constitute the shared values for purposes of solving the first problem, they would be very much open to challenge in the context of the second problem. In order to solve the second problem, we need to apply other shared values.

Potentially the process could be infinite. Realistically, however, this need not concern us. In view of the fact that, in the real world, problems are solved one at a time rather than all at once, there is no practical need for an infinite regression to first principles or absolutes. In practical terms, we live in the middle of history and not at the beginning. We already have shared interests and values on the basis of which we can attempt to solve our problems and conflicts.

The best vehicle we have for solving problems is our intelligence— the ability to draw rational inferences from what is and what can be commonly observed and experienced. Unlike faith and intuition, observation and intelligence are capable of collective scrutiny and verification. The processes of intelligence will not always work satisfactorily but they are the most reliable, objective processes we have. Nor does any of this mean that numerical might is tantamount to ethical right. Certainly there will be occasions when the minority side of an issue has reasoned more validly than has the majority from the relevant shared interests. To such extent, the minority would have a stronger ethical claim.

But being right ethically is of very little consolation if you can't win politically. In a world without guarantees, what kind of political system is most (or least badly) suited to produce results that accord with the shared interests and values of those affected? For the kinds of reasons spelled out in the preface, I believe that democracy best fills this bill. But there is no need to romanticize about it. In the nineteenth century, philosophers believed that the human being was infinitely perfectible and therefore worthy of democracy. On the basis of the twentieth century, I believe that the human being is infinitely corruptible and therefore in need of democracy. In this world, the fear of the worst is a more reliable incentive than the hope for the best.

Chapter Two

THE EXTENT OF DISSENT

The Right to Express Difference
versus the Need to Maintain Harmony

In the fall of 1981, a meeting of the federal prime minister and provincial premiers of Canada produced a decision to dilute certain women's rights and delete certain native rights from the country's new constitution. Within only a few days, the decision was largely reversed; there was an agreement to restore much of what had been removed.

How was it that Canada's powerful ruling elites so quickly and radically reversed themselves? Almost from the moment their initial decision was announced, it was greeted by a storm of public protest—angry demonstrations, picket lines, public meetings, newspaper editorials, radio and television commentaries. The federal and provincial politicians were subjected to a barrage of telegrams, letters, and lobbying efforts. In the face of such widespread and vigorous pressure, our leaders found it prudent to retreat.

The essence of what happened was that the *people* objected to what their governments had done. In democratic societies, the people are supposed to be the ultimate authority. The machinery by which laws are enacted in open sessions and governments are selected through periodic elections is designed to ensure that no laws or governments can long survive without the consent of the people who must abide them.

However, even authoritarian and totalitarian governments often presume to act in the name and with the consent of the people.

18

The people's "consent" in such societies is often achieved through a combination of secret police, storm-troopers, concentration camps, torture chambers, and firing squads. In a number of these societies, even though there are elections in which everyone may vote, there is only one party, one slate of candidates, and one set of policies from which the citizens may choose.

Coerced and contrived consent does not satisfy the standards of democratic procedure. Democrats believe the consent of the citizens must be freely given. This gives rise to one of the most vital principles of democratic society. The right of free consent necessarily implies a right of free *dissent*. Those who oppose existing government policies must have the right to compete openly and publicly with those who support such policies. The citizens must have the opportunity to choose among alternative parties, candidates, and policies. Without open dissent, there can be no effective consent. Without available alternatives, the people cannot effectively exercise their sovereign authority.

The right to dissent does not mean the right to disobey a duly enacted law. It means, rather, the right to oppose passage of the law in the first place, the right to petition for its repeal, amendment, or replacement thereafter, the right to promote the enactment of different laws at any time, and, at the next election, the right to campaign and to vote for alternative candidates to replace the incumbent law-makers.

The chief instruments of dissent are the freedoms of expression, assembly, and association. Democratic principle proclaims that people should be free to speak, write, publish, broadcast, assemble, demonstrate, picket, and organize on behalf of their interests, beliefs, opinions, and points of view. A necessary complement to these freedoms is the existence of many independent mass media of communication (newspapers, magazines, radio stations, television networks) with the right freely to convey to the public news of social controversy as it occurs in our legislatures and in the community.

Of all the fundamental freedoms, the right to dissent may be the most crucial. The exercise of this right enables aggrieved persons to appeal for public support in their quest for redress. The assumption is that the best antidote to unjust government and unjust policies is an atmosphere of free public controversy, which culminates in secret-ballot elections. In this sense, the right to dissent may be strategic; it is the freedom upon which our whole complex of freedoms depends.

As a wise old trade-unionist once noted, this right is the "grievance procedure" of democratic society.

But the right to dissent is even more. It is the vehicle by means of which the quest for truth may be pursued. In science and technology, for example, a plurality of theories and methods may openly compete in order to demonstrate their respective validity. The same holds for religion and philosophy. Ultimate questions concerning the nature and meaning of life are settled, not by governmental fiat, but by individual choice. And the ability to choose is enhanced by the right to explore contesting ideas and to experiment with alternative approaches.

In culture and the arts, the right to dissent, with its accompanying freedom of expression, provides the basis for enrichment. To the extent that all persons have the right to produce and consume as they choose in literature, films, art, music, and dance, they have the opportunity to enrich their own lives and those of others.

Inevitably such vast freedom carries with it enormous risks. Freedom of expression can be used to propagate lies as well as truths, wrongs as well as rights, injustice as well as justice, and junk as well as art. The central question is: where are we prepared to put our trust? In dictatorships, governments arrogate to themselves wide powers to decide how far people may express themselves and be exposed to the expressions of others. The assumption is that those in power are sufficiently wise and benevolent to make such decisions on behalf of everybody. Democracies, on the other hand, are fearful of reposing so much trust in their leaders. It's not that democratic societies necessarily have blind faith that the masses of people will always choose wisely. It's that they have considerably *less* faith in anyone else.

Indeed, the power to encroach on public communication carries with it a substantial risk of tyranny. The exercise of such power can decide the outcome of almost any conflict. Deny tenants the right to distribute their organizing materials and you could ensure victory for their landlords. Stop striking employees from picketing and you could guarantee the domination of their employers. Take opposition viewpoints off television and you could hand the next election to the government.

In science, philosophy, and culture, the exercise of comparable tyranny is likely to abort creativity. To the extent that governments impose orthodoxy in those fields, the risk increases that scientific innovations will decline, intellectual activity will atrophy, and the arts will wither. While openness may not be a guarantee of vitality, repression is a guarantee of aridity.

Democracies prefer to run the risk of error through the free competition of viewpoints rather than to run the risk of tyranny through curtailing what the people may say, see, and hear. If there be error, the answer to it generally is not less but more communication.

While the right to express difference is a prerequisite of democracy, the need to maintain harmony is a prerequisite of society—*any* society. Co-existence is simply not possible without at least a minimum level of communal harmony. People need some reasonable guarantee of social peace, order, and security. They have to be assured that their homes, streets, schools, and places of business are safe and sound. They must be able to believe that they can conduct their affairs in peace and dignity. At some point, the right to express difference has to collide with the need to maintain harmony. For those who seek to avoid the either-or fallacy, the issue is not whether, in the abstract, we are for the right of dissent or for the maintenance of harmony. The issue is in what concrete situations these interests must give way to each other and by how much.

I have long believed that Canadian law contains a number of measures that needlessly and excessively inhibit the right of effective dissent. In Canada the problem with encroachments on the right to dissent is not wholesale invasion, it's piecemeal erosion. The danger is that an accumulation of legislative enactments and judicial pronouncements will serve, not to eradicate, but to emasculate the right of dissent.

In a number of key areas, there are disquieting signs of such emasculation. While the right to dissent receives homage in our constitutional documents and official rhetoric, it is beset by a host of impediments to its practical realization. What follows is an attempt to identify some of the more important of these impediments and to indicate in what directions reform might lie.

THE EFFORT TO LIMIT UNPLEASANT DISRUPTION

Measures against Demonstrations and Picket Lines

Canadians will not soon forget the months-long Gainer's strike during 1986 in Edmonton, Alberta. It was a classic. The setting was a meat-packing plant where the wages were low and the working conditions were hard. The contestants were an employer who was seen as a rich playboy—Peter Pocklington—and a group of employees who were constantly under pressure to make ends meet. Both sides were determined to win. The employer recruited new employees and the strikers set up picket lines to dissuade them.

Virtually every morning, strikers and new recruits would collide. Pocklington resorted to transporting the recruits across the picket line by bus and with police escorts. The pickets nevertheless attempted to stop them. Nasty violence was a frequent occurrence, as were arrests and the laying of criminal charges. The scenes were played to the nation almost every night on the television news.

At times the pickets numbered as many as three hundred and the police escorts were at least two hundred strong. Picket-line tactics varied. They included throwing missiles and sometimes Molotov cocktails. There was even an attempt to organize prayer meetings at the plant gate. Periodically the buses of strikebreakers were blocked. Other times they got through. The arrest rate, however, continued to climb. During one week, as many as two hundred people were arrested in picket-line confrontations.

Of course, the Gainer's strike was the exception and not the rule. Very few demonstrations and picket lines are accompanied by the kind of violence that characterized that unhappy conflict. Nevertheless, demonstrations and picket lines are often experienced as unpleasant disruptions. To a place of business, a picket line is a disruption of the very activities for which the business was established. The pickets may be urging employees and customers to keep out, or at least to avoid dealing in certain products. If demonstrations are large, they can also disrupt traffic. In such event, motorists, pedestrians, and perhaps shoppers can be seriously inconvenienced. And, if a demonstration or picket line is sufficiently hostile, it can also threaten physical violence.

In consequence, numbers of restrictions and regulations have been imposed upon the right to conduct demonstrations and picket lines. But such restrictions often provoke bitter controversy. While a restriction or regulation may minimize the disruption for some, it reduces the impact of protest for others. The less affluent members of society particularly are dependent upon such instruments of pressure. They don't publish newspapers or even newspaper ads; they don't own radio or television stations or even purchase broadcast time. If they can't organize a conspicuous demonstration or picket line, they will not be able, with much effectiveness, to impress their views or interests on the body politic.

Historically, Canada has had too low a tolerance for the disruptive impact of picket lines and demonstrations. Time and again, the right to demonstrate and picket has come off second best in its collision with other values. To a great extent, our priorities appear to have been influenced by an inadequate appreciation of the realities involved. Our legislatures and courts have often been insensitive to the requirements of effective dissent.

A classic illustration of this phenomenon occurred in the Supreme Court of Canada. In the late 1970s, the court considered the constitutionality of a controversial Montreal by-law that had been enacted in the late 1960s. In response to a number of violent demonstrations on behalf of the cause of French unilingualism for Quebec, the city of Montreal enacted a by-law empowering its executive committee, under certain circumstances, to prohibit "for the period that it shall determine...the holding of any or all assemblies, parades or gatherings" on all or part of the public domain of the city. Despite the fact that the then chief justice of Canada described this by-law as "draconian", the majority of his colleagues upheld it as constitutionally valid. What is remarkable is the way the court dismissed the notion that a ban on demonstrations involves an infringement of free speech: "Demonstrations are not a form of speech, but of collective action. They are of the nature of a display of force rather than of that of an appeal to reason...."

Since when does free speech have to appeal to reason? People in the real world are persuaded most often not by reason, but by pressure. Politicians hungering for position will respond more to political tension than to logical syllogism. Workers hoping for higher wages will find it more useful to threaten their bosses with strikes than to subject them to sermons.

Of course, this is not to justify the abandonment of reason in public affairs, it is simply to recognize its limitations. Pressure without reason is irresponsible, but reason without pressure is ineffectual. To be sure, the range of acceptable pressure cannot include the commission or threat of physical violence. But it must be able to entail varying levels of political, economic, and social injury. And freedom of expression, to be effective, must be able to include the threat to inflict such injury and the attempt to recruit the support of others for it.

Consider, for example, the demonstration of 100,000 people who gathered in Ottawa during the fall of 1981 to protest high interest rates.

When such a large, angry crowd is prepared to incur the inconvenience of travelling to Ottawa on a stormy November Saturday, a pointed message is conveyed to the government. It was clear that this was not primarily "an appeal to reason". The government already knew and had rejected the arguments of its critics. The demonstration was essentially a dramatized threat to deprive the government of the votes it needed for re-election. Where argument had failed, the protesters were hoping that pressure would succeed. They were effectively saying, "shape up or ship out". Why can't *that* qualify as an exercise in expression?

To confine the right of free expression to appeals to reason is to load the dice against the "have-nots" of society. The "haves" use the pressure of money to advance their interests: they grant and withhold economic benefits. Why can't the "have-nots" use the pressure of numbers to advance *their* interests? By assembling in the streets, they threaten to grant and withhold political benefits.

As I have already acknowledged, freedom of expression cannot be an absolute. Indeed, the Charter itself says that the rights and freedoms it contains are to be subject to "such reasonable limits…as can be demonstrably justified". Even freedoms as fundamental as that of expression are susceptible to certain trade-offs. The problem, however, is to what extent the courts will put demonstrations into the trade-off hopper. The courts may too readily define this necessary weapon of the disadvantaged as beyond the range of the Charter's protections.

Unfortunately, this unreality about freedom of expression appears well ingrained in Canadian legal thinking. Thirty years ago, the late Mr. Justice Ivan Rand, on behalf of the Supreme Court of Canada, attempted to set out the limits of permissible behaviour for lawful picket lines.

> There is a difference between watching and besetting for the purpose of coercing either workmen or employer by presence, demeanour, argumentative and rancorous badgering or importunity, and unexpressed, sinister suggestiveness, felt rather than perceived in a vague or ill-defined fear or apprehension on the one hand; and attending to communicate information for the purpose of persuasion by the *force of rational appeal*, on the other [emphasis added].

The judge was attempting here to construe a section of the Criminal Code which applies to picketing. To the extent that these remarks are considered a valid interpretation, the law itself should be changed.

Why should "argumentative and rancorous badgering" be proscribed? Of course, pickets should not be able to employ or threaten physical violence or obstruction. But why shouldn't they be able to use unpleasant social pressure? In short, why shouldn't they be free to embarrass and censure those employees and customers who enter the affected premises? Suppose, for example, picket-line interlopers are greeted with epithets such as "scabs", "finks", or "traitors"? Since the proprietor is free to use economic benefit to entice people across the picket line, the pickets should be free to use social pressure to try to keep them away. To restrict the pickets to rational persuasion is to bias the rules in favour of the proprietor.

This demand for appeals to reason has produced some questionable practices in this country. When courts have faced evidence of violence or disorder on labour picket lines, they have frequently issued injunctions restricting the number of pickets to not more than three or four at a gate. What might have begun as a powerful expression of vital grievances often wound up looking like a pathetic advertisement to "Eat at Joe's". According to the judges, such emasculation of picket lines could be justified on the basis that greater numbers are not necessary for the purpose of communicating information—that is, for appeals to reason.

Such judgments reveal a striking insensitivity to the realities of picket-line conflicts. Picket lines are not meant to be exercises in polite, reasonable discussion; they are instruments of unpleasant social pressure. A picket line shorn of numbers and bound by the canons of Emily Post weakens the pickets' ability to generate the necessary pressure. Large demonstrations happen to carry greater moral weight in our community than do small ones. Token picketing tends to convey an appearance of half-hearted or non-existent support.

It was not until the advent of legislative intervention that the courts stopped perpetrating these unacceptable inequities, at least in certain jurisdictions. To its credit, Ontario, for example, now requires considerable evidence of both danger and of a police inability to handle the situation before it will permit the courts to undermine by injunction the integrity of a labour picket line.

But, even in some places that have such legislation, certain picket lines are not safe from such judicial interference. With few exceptions, provincial labour laws will regard "secondary picketing" as unlawful in itself. Secondary picketing refers to situations in which people involved in a dispute with one party try to increase the pressure on their adversary by picketing the premises of another party, usually a supplier or customer. In most Canadian jurisdictions, secondary picketing will likely be prohibited in its entirety by injunction. There will be no question of simply reducing the numbers.

The leading Canadian case on this issue occurred in Ontario during the mid-1960s. A striking clothing workers' union decided to launch a boycott against an employer's products. Some of the products were being sold at a retail store in a little Ontario community. The union set up a small picket line in front of the store; its signs simply identified the goods in question and declared that they were not union made. There was no attempt to discourage general public patronage. Yet the proprietor of the store sought and secured a court injunction removing all of the pickets from the vicinity of his premises. According to the Ontario Court of Appeal, the right to trade is carried on for the benefit of the entire community, but secondary picketing is carried on only for a limited class of people. On this basis, the court declared that "the right...to engage in secondary picketing...must give way to [a merchant's] right to trade...."

Why should the right to trade in shirts, socks, and shorts be considered more holy than the right of secondary picketing? I could understand such a value preference if there had been evidence that the people in the targeted community were being denuded by the boycott. But, so long as adequate clothing was readily available in other places, there was no valid basis for regarding haberdashery transactions as more beneficial to the community than picketing. Moreover, the pickets could not *force* the public to boycott the premises or the goods. All that was involved here was an attempt to *persuade* the public to boycott the goods. As long as the object of the boycott is not unlawful, how far is it appropriate for the *courts* to compare the social benefits between traders and pickets? Might there not be an argument for letting the public choose for itself between the salesmanship of the merchant and the admonitions of the pickets? Alternatively, if one of these interests is generally to be preferred over the other, perhaps the elected legislatures rather than the appointed judiciary should be required to make the choice.

Yet, without the benefit of any guiding legislation, Canadian supporters of the California farm workers have also suffered the judicial destruction of their picket lines. On a number of occasions, picket lines were set up at large Canadian retail stores to discourage the purchase of California grapes. This was part of an international movement, which began in the 1960s, to support the efforts of several thousand very poor and often migrant farm workers in California to win union bargaining rights from their powerful employers. Fervently dedicated to the principles of non-violence under the leadership of the saintly and charismatic Cesar Chavez, the farm workers' union attempted to pressure their employers by launching an international boycott against the grapes that their employers produced. While there was some indication that customer patronage did decline at those Canadian stores that were picketed by the farm workers and their sympathizers, the employees of the stores generally continued to work. Indeed, it was the express policy of the farm workers and their supporters that work stoppages in Canada should be avoided. Notwithstanding this solicitude, a number of these picket lines were prohibited by injunction.

Admittedly, these injunctions preceded the era of the Charter of Rights and Freedoms. In consequence, the issue of free expression was not specifically addressed in many of these judgments. There are clues, however, that the judiciary was unable to perceive the implications for freedom of expression in such picket lines. Consider, for example, the comments of the Quebec Superior Court when it issued an injunction against farm-worker picketing at Montreal's Dominion Stores: "If the Respondents had limited their campaign to a plea to the public to support the boycott of California grapes...without centering their activities at or near Petitioner's stores, and without assailing Petitioner for refusing to support the boycott, Petitioner might not have grounds for complaint."

The implication is clear. Of course the pickets were entitled to freedom of expression to make their case. They could have published advertisements, purchased radio or television time, even hired a hall. In short, they could have appealed to reason. What they could not do, in the words of the court, was "picket Petitioner's stores in order to alienate or estrange Petitioner's customers". In short, the supporters of the grape boycott could do all sorts of things to advance their cause, *except what might be inexpensive and effective.*

It is of some interest that the Quebec court did not once refer to this picketing as "secondary". A similar case, which produced an injunction in Toronto, did refer to the farm workers' picketing as "secondary". Indeed, the Ontario Supreme Court judge in the latter case pointed out "that secondary picketing is prohibited and for very sound social reasons...to do otherwise is simply to import into our province the social and economic battles of other people, the end of which one could not possibly foresee."

Remember, the primary dispute here was not in Ontario but in California. Of course, the court might have wished to immunize Ontario residents against the impact of foreign struggles. But the implications of such an approach appear rather far-reaching. On the basis of the court's reasoning, would injunctions be issued against those who picket premises where South African wine or Soviet-made cars are being sold? Would a picket line in such a situation also be perceived or defined as devoid of free speech implications?

There is some indication that these judicial reservations about picketing have survived into the Charter era. In the course of upholding an injunction against a threatened secondary picket line in a local labour dispute, the British Columbia Court of Appeal recently held that such picketing could not claim Charter protection as "freedom of expression". The judges quoted with approval the following statement of an American writer: "A labour picket line is thus not so much a *rational appeal* to persuasion as a signal for the application of immediate and enormous economic leverage, based upon an already prepared position. As such it must, under ordinary circumstances, be classified as action, rather than expression [emphasis added]."

Once more we are told that the prerequisite for free expression is an appeal to reason. Fortunately, the Supreme Court of Canada expressed some disagreement with the British Columbia court about the constitutional status of picketing. But our feeling of encouragement may be premature. While the Supreme Court did acknowledge that there is "always some element of expression in picketing", its judgment does not explicitly address the issue of how far picketing may depart from appeals to reason. The Supreme Court made it clear, of course, that acts and threats of violence would not be protected. But the court did not consider the scope and limits of the non-violent conduct that will be permissible. The judgment does not say, for example, how far pickets will be permitted to shower their adversaries with invective. Nor does it indicate how far pickets may assemble in large numbers if, in doing so, they create some interference with interests such as commerce and traffic.

These, of course, remain critical issues. While I have to appreciate the court's acknowledgement that *some* elements of picketing are entitled to constitutional protection as "freedom of expression", my disquiet will not be significantly relieved until I know to what extent other interests will be subordinated to those of the pickets.

My disquiet is fuelled by certain other holdings of the Supreme Court of Canada in this case. The judges ruled that, in any event, the Charter did not apply to the circumstances at issue. This was because the case involved only private parties and the common law; neither the government nor the terms of a statute were involved. The Charter is supposed to concern itself only with the behaviour of government, not with that of private parties. While I am generally sympathetic with the idea of keeping the Charter out of private-sector interactions, we must remember that this case dealt with an injunction imposed by a judge. That is hardly the act of a private party. Judges are appointed by the government and their orders are enforced by the coercive power of the government. I cannot agree, therefore, that a judicial order restricting free speech should be immune to Charter scrutiny.

This case seems to have given rise to a strange incongruity. To the extent that a *statute* restricts free speech, the court acknowledges the Charter would apply. But in the case of a *judicial* restriction on free speech, not authorized by statute, the Charter could well not apply. In the result, elected, accountable legislatures will be more subject to Charter scrutiny than unelected, less accountable judges.

The case represents a classic illustration of giving with one hand and taking with another. In the early part of its judgment, the Supreme Court of Canada says that picketing is a form of expression subject to constitutional protection. In the latter part of its judgment, the Court effectively declares that, in most situations where picketing actually occurs (the private-sector disputes of labour and management), the constitutional protection might well be rendered stillborn.

This denigration of picket lines has emerged in completely non-labour contexts as well. In November of 1982, for example, a planned peace demonstration was undermined by certain actions of law enforcement authorities. The Metropolitan Toronto Police established a blockade so as to prevent the demonstrators from coming within half a mile of Litton Industries, a company that manufactures guidance systems for the cruise missile. Presumably this action was influenced by a protest bombing that had occurred there a few weeks earlier.

Lacking access to the specific information that triggered this police action, I am in no position to pass judgment on whatever justification may be offered for it. My focus instead is on the lack of adequate legal machinery for resolving such conflicts between demonstrators and police. The problem is that the police had been given the legal power to adopt this extraordinary measure. Moreover, both police and government appeared insensitive to the important interests they had jeopardized in the process. As far as they were concerned, a demonstration half a mile away was quite capable of conveying its message to the public. In short, it could still appeal to reason.

Unfortunately, however, the demonstrators were prevented from exerting a number of their legitimate pressures. In order to be minimally effective, certain kinds of demonstrations must have some opportunity to confront those who are engaged in the activity under attack. In the case of places like Litton Industries, the targets would include the management, the employees, and even the customers whose patronage helped to bolster cruise missile production. One of the objects of such a demonstration is to generate social pressure on those who are going in and out of the premises. The idea is to create in these people a sense of guilt, shame, or at least a feeling of censure. While the demonstrators must not be allowed to use or threaten physical violence, they must be as free as possible to inflict such social pressure. It is obvious that this cannot be done from half a mile away.

While there may be some situations in which the interests of public safety require the separation of demonstrators from the targeted premises, it is not proper to repose in the *police* the unilateral power to make such decisions. The police interest in the conduct of demonstrations is to keep the peace and to ensure an orderly flow of traffic. But such functions, as important as they are, must be weighed against the interest of the demonstrators in staging a conspicuous event. To allow the police the power of imposing such limits on the demonstrators is to make the police the umpires of their own ball game. No matter how fair the decisions of the police may be in fact, they may well not *appear* fair. Indeed, they will often provoke suspicion that the restrictions they impose are motivated less by the objective needs of the situation than by the desire of the police to ease the burdens of their job. I believe, therefore, that such decisions should generally be made by an independent agency, on application from the police.

It is obvious that the political prerequisite for such a transfer of power is the recognition that the existing arrangements are unfair. So long as the only expressions of dissent that are seen as worthy of protection are those that appeal to reason, there will be no incentive to change the law. There will not be a sufficient appreciation of the fact that a Litton type of blockade represents a substantial encroachment on the effective freedom of expression.

Similar problems have arisen in the case of municipal by-laws. In the late 1960s, for example, a group of Vietnam war protesters sought a parade permit to march down Toronto's busy Yonge Street on a Saturday afternoon that coincided with the annual international day of protest against the war. Instead they were offered a permit to march down Bay Street and University Avenue. I don't know how many of my readers have been on Bay Street or University Avenue on a Saturday, but if they have, they probably were the only ones there. In certain parts of Canada, we don't ban demonstrations, we re-route them. The demonstration becomes, as one writer put it, not an exercise in freedom of communication, but an exercise in freedom of soliloquy. You can say anything you like in your backyard or your bathtub. The problem arises when you seek access to a live audience.

At the time, there was a by-law in Metropolitan Toronto enacted—curiously—by the Police Commission. The by-law prohibited parades and demonstrations on normally busy streets unless they had been occurring annually for ten consecutive years prior to October 1, 1964. This undermined the proposed Yonge Street march. Unfortunately for the protesters, the Vietnam war had not been going on that long.

The by-law created what lawyers call vested interests. The Santa Claus Parade and the Orange Parade, which had been staged annually in Toronto for decades, were such vested interests. Political protest, however, usually arises contemporaneously with its provocation. One is not likely to find, for example, continuing parades against Mackenzie King's conscription policies. Meaningful political protest could be rendered virtually impotent without ready access to a busy street and an available audience. Indeed, under such conditions, it might very well lack the newsworthiness even to attract attention from the media.

The Toronto by-law provided another exception. The chairman of the Police Commission and the chief of police could grant a busy-street parade permit under "unusual circumstances of municipal, provincial or federal importance". The precedents for applying this exception turned out to be simply fascinating. On one occasion, a visiting convention of the Fraternal Order of Eagles secured a Yonge Street parade permit on a Friday afternoon—a time often busier than Saturday. The parade was allowed to tie up this main artery for five hours with five thousand marchers and thirty-five marching bands. On the occasion of Richard Nixon's second inauguration, also a Saturday, another group of Vietnam war protesters attempted to march on Yonge Street and again there was a refusal to grant a parade permit. Yet a few months later those same portions of Yonge Street were made available on a Friday for another parade, to an organization whose name was so exotic that it has embedded itself in my psyche: The Mystic Order of the Veiled Prophets of the Enchanted Realm.

While the Toronto parade by-law has been improved, the decision-making machinery remains flawed. The power to enact such by-laws remains in the hands of a largely appointed body: the Police Commission. The power to apply such by-laws to particular cases remains in the hands of a largely interested party: the Police Commission. The right to march on city streets deserves a more equitable system of legislation and adjudication.

Even if picket lines and demonstrations don't appeal to reason and even if their prime function is to exert unpleasant pressure, they may nevertheless lay claim to being legitimate instruments of dissent. As such, they should be entitled to a high level of constitutional protection and community deference. But, since freedom of dissent and expression are not absolute, they may sometimes have to be modified in order to accommodate certain other values and interests. That's not now in issue. What is now in issue, however, is the dismissal of so many demonstrations and picket lines as lying outside the field of protected expression. If this attitude persists, there will be no need to examine and weigh the competing values involved. The stage will be set for the unwarranted suppression of one of the most vital vehicles by which disadvantaged people can impress their interests on their adversaries and the general community.

Measures against Seditious Speech

There is little that could be as disruptive to society as the prospect of revolutionary violence. Understandably, therefore, the law, even in democratic societies, seeks to discourage any possible resort to physical violence as a vehicle for social reform. Moreover, it is felt that the power of the state should not have to languish in helpless paralysis until the violence actually occurs. The fear of disruption creates an incentive to equip our law enforcement authorities with powers of prevention.

In consequence, our law prohibits not only acts of violence but also a certain amount of speech which precedes them. The sedition section of the Criminal Code renders punishable a person who "teaches and advocates...the use, without the authority of law, of force as a means to accomplish a governmental change within Canada."

Again the law goes further than necessary to protect society's legitimate interests. The issue is at what point in the continuum between the thought and the deed it is appropriate for the law to intervene. Speech likely to result in imminent violence is arguably dangerous enough to warrant legal intrusion. On the other hand, speech not likely to culminate in this way does not warrant such intervention.

The risk created in the sedition section is that the words "teaches" and "advocates" are sufficiently wide and vague to encompass the soapbox orator who has no followers and the theoretician who seeks no followers. A person who expresses the desirability of overthrowing the government by force is not necessarily a threat. A person who philosophically justifies revolution or violence is not necessarily a threat. The threat is the call to action by someone who has followers. The law properly intervenes at the point where speech is likely to precipitate immediate action.

To leave the law in its current state is to run the risk of punishing the impotent preacher along with the dangerous demagogue. The Criminal Code should be amended to confine the offence of sedition to the incitement of violence against government in situations where there is a clear and present danger that the incitement will be acted on.

THE EFFORT TO BAN OFFENSIVE MATERIAL

To a great extent, offensive material undermines our sense of dignity. People will go to great lengths, therefore, to immunize themselves against the impact of what offends. They will even seek resort to the power of legal prohibition. At the same time, freedom of expression must include the right to say not only nice, but also nasty, things. Since one of the pragmatic functions of free expression is to create the conditions by which we can redress our grievances, we must have the right to condemn as well as to approve. At what point does one person's right to utter nasty criticisms outweigh another person's right to be immunized against offensiveness?

Similar considerations apply to cultural matters. Often the same material will produce opposite reactions: some will be pleased, others will be hurt; some will be enriched, others outraged. Which group should the law protect?

It is rarely possible to express, for legal purposes, the relevant distinctions between acceptable criticism and unredeemed offensiveness, between the worthwhile and the worthless. I conclude, therefore, that in general the law should avoid the attempt. Subject to few exceptions, it is better to risk exposure to insult than to allow an interference with society's "grievance procedure". By the same token, it is usually better to permit a piece of trash than to suppress a work of art.

Scandalizing the Courts

In the fall of 1986, radical lawyer Harry Kopyto was banished from Ontario courts until he apologized for telling a reporter that the courts are "warped in favour of the police". In the fall of 1987, the Ontario Court of Appeal reversed this judgment and acquitted Kopyto. In the opinion of the appellate judges, the Charter guarantee for freedom of expression protects even the kind of nasty remarks that were made by Kopyto. For the time being, therefore, the criminal offence that formed the basis of this charge has become extinct in the province of Ontario. We don't yet know whether the appellate courts in the other provinces will follow suit. And, of course, we don't yet know what position the Supreme Court of Canada will take on the matter. In view of this uncertainty and the fact that Kopyto's offence has been part of our legal system for centuries, it would be wise to reflect a little further on the controversy and the law that produced it.

The radical lawyer reportedly made his contentious remarks as he emerged from a small claims court, having lost his latest attempt to sue certain RCMP officers. In the early 1970s, RCMP officers reportedly had composed and then circulated, within a Trotskyist organization, a letter which was made to look as though it had been written by one of the Trotskyist leaders. The letter contained embarrassing information about the psychiatric condition of another of the organization's leaders. The RCMP objective was to foment irreparable splits within the radical movement.

Some years later, government commissions of inquiry disclosed and criticized these "dirty tricks". In the wake of the revelations, Harry Kopyto was retained by a Trotskyist leader to seek redress for this misconduct. Kopyto went both to the criminal courts and to the civil courts. Every tack he tried proved unsuccessful. On the occasion in question, a small claims judge had dismissed his application for civil compensation.

Upon being approached by a reporter from the *Globe and Mail*, Kopyto made the remark in question and it appeared in print the next day. For this outburst, the attorney-general laid a criminal charge against him. The offence? Scandalizing the courts. This refers to public statements (outside of court) that bring the courts, the judges, the proceedings of particular trials, or the administration of justice into public contempt, ridicule, and disrepute. While such prosecutions have not been frequent, they have also not been rare. One of the more controversial involved a ten-day jail sentence imposed upon a New Brunswick university student, in the spring of 1969, for having written in a student publication that a certain trial was a "mockery of justice" and that the courts were "instruments of the corporate elite".

The offence of scandalizing the courts, a hold-over relic from the British common law of contempt of court, was designed to protect the administration of justice. According to the theory, judicial authority in the community could be undermined by intemperate public criticism. Indeed, the fear of a hostile public opinion was so great that the courts were able to send offenders to jail until the judges were satisfied that the contempts had been purged.

But this power was spawned in another era, before the evolution of modern democracy. The problem is how such a power can be squared with modern notions of free speech. After all, freedom of expression is supposed to protect nastiness as well as pleasantries. In fact, according to democratic beliefs, our institutions are supposed to function best in an atmosphere of free public criticism.

For years the courts have been quick to point out that they too believe in freedom of expression. It's all right, they have said, to knock the courts. But such sniping should avoid "invective and abuse, and the imputation of...corrupt...motives" to the judges. The only problem with this is that a publication devoid of invective is likely also to be a publication devoid of readers. When, for example, was the last time you saw a line-up to buy the *Canadian Bar Review*? In the real world, verbal vinegar is often necessary for social impact.

To be sure, invective against judges would often be unfair and irresponsible. But there are also times when it would be completely justified. York University President Harry Arthurs once summarized the problem succinctly: "Unless you assume that judges can't be venal or biased, there must be a right to say so."

There is also a procedural problem. How far should the targets of criticism be allowed to set the limits of that criticism? Just about everywhere else in the law, the courts are impartial referees. Not so in this situation. They have had the power to punish what they see as undue injury to their own institutional reputations. Those accused of contempt are not even entitled to a trial by jury. Small wonder that, at the turn of the century, the British House of Commons passed a resolution describing the contempt power of the judges as "practically arbitrary". Yet those same "arbitrary" powers were adopted by the Canadian Parliament and applied by the Canadian courts.

Moreover, on a number of occasions, the courts' actual use of these powers has revealed a remarkable touchiness. In 1954, for example, journalist Eric Nicol wrote a bitter article against capital punishment in the Vancouver *Province* newspaper. In allegorical style, he portrayed all society as the accused before the Bar of Heaven for allowing legal executions. In making his point, he described the jury in a certain British Columbia capital trial as "the people who planned the murder" and the judge as the one who "chose the time and the place and caused the victim to suffer the exquisite torture of anticipation".

It is clear that Nicol's scorn was directed not against the judge or jury in that particular case but against capital punishment in general. Despite the fact that the references to judge and jury were obviously allegorical, Eric Nicol and the *Province* were convicted of scandalizing the administration of justice. Although writer and newspaper were fined only $250 and $2500 respectively, the judge pointed out that, had it not been for the apology tendered and the newspaper's respected record, he would have imposed "severe penalties".

Such thin-skinned judgments can only erode our faith in the courts' ability to draw the line when *they* are the ones under attack. To be fair, there are many cases in which the courts have resisted the impulse to punish their detractors. But that just confuses the issue. Since the courts have been both tolerant and intolerant about attacks on their reputations, it becomes harder to know where you stand. Consider, for example, the following statement made about a judge in a case from Australia, a jurisdiction whose judgments our courts often cite: "...Mr. Justice Higgins is, we believe, what is called a political judge, that is, he was appointed because he had well served a political party. He, moreover, seems to know his position, and does not mean to allow any reflection on those to whom he may be said to be indebted for his judgeship...."

Remarkably, in this case, the court acquitted the writer of scandalizing contempt of court. Yet, how can any rational person say that this comment was less offensive than what Eric Nicol wrote? The inconsistency and confusion in the cases contribute little to the protection of freedom of speech. The consequence is that lawyers who wish to advise their clients how to stay out of trouble would likely urge caution when it comes to criticism of the courts. In the result, we could expect an excess of unwarranted *self*-censorship.

Some people say that curtailing this contempt power would trigger the decline, perhaps even the collapse, of our judicial system. On the contrary, the *use* of such power would be much more likely to impair the prestige of the courts. Moreover, the courts may have become the only institution in our society still protected in this way. Barring an incitement to violence, it is generally not unlawful to speak such ill of any other government agency. This may even be true of the many administrative tribunals—such as the provincial labour relations boards, liquor licensing boards, and welfare appeal boards—which, like the courts, exercise a wide range of judicial functions. If such a contempt power has ever been used to protect their reputations, you would have to turn the law books upside down to find an example of it. Yet there isn't the slightest sign that our system of administrative justice is crumbling. What, then, entitles the courts to this special coddling?

The courts are different, say some people, because the judges can't protect themselves. Their tradition and position make it improper for them to answer attacks or to sue for defamation. But why shouldn't the same restraints apply to administrative adjudicators? Indeed, it would be a rare event to see one of them answer abuse with a lawsuit or a polemic. Remember too that judges are already protected more than most people. They enjoy a unique kind of job security. Until they die or reach a ripe old age, it would take a virtual cyclone to remove them from office. In any event, this contempt power was never designed to protect the personal reputations of the judges. It has to stand or fall on whether it's a necessary safeguard for the judicial system itself.

It is worth noting that the administration of justice in the United States does not appear to have suffered any significant erosion of its authority despite the lack of comparable contempt powers in that country. In this connection, I remember well the sight of large "Impeach Earl Warren" billboards conspicuously posted in the South during the 1960s. Moreover, there was literature suggesting that the U.S. chief justice was a pawn of the Communist Party. Yet both Earl Warren and the court over which he presided managed to survive intact.

For these purposes, I can think of no better authority than a much neglected court judgment from the turn of the century. The highest appeal court in the British empire, the Judicial Committee of the Privy Council, declared that contempt of court convictions for "scandalizing the court...[had] become obsolete" and that the courts could "leave to public opinion attacks or comments derogatory or scandalous to them". This expresses the essence of our society's commitment to freedom of speech. At base, there must be a willingness to trust the people or at least to mistrust them less than the elites. Surely it's more democratic for our courts and judges to preserve the respect they enjoy, not through the awesomeness of their powers, but through the quality of their justice. I hope, therefore, that the rest of the country follows the intelligent lead of the Ontario appellate court.

Defamation

During the winter of 1969, an underground newspaper in British Columbia sustained a criminal conviction for publishing an article that awarded "the Pontius Pilate Certificate of Justice" to a particular Vancouver magistrate. This case resurrected the criminal offence of defamatory libel from the grave of obscurity in which it had been languishing for a generation. The offence inflicts the punishment of the criminal law upon a person for making a statement "that is likely to injure the reputation of any person [not only a judge] by exposing him to hatred, contempt, or ridicule".

The original rationale for this offence grew out of the danger that "libellous" statements could provoke breaches of the peace. Yet the Criminal Code is overflowing with offences which incite or tend to incite breaches of the peace—counselling the commission of an offence, attempting to commit an offence, causing a disturbance, watching and besetting, obstructing, and so on. In view of the multiplicity of prohibitions against behaviour that could cause breaches of the peace, defamatory libel has been virtually confined to the protection of injured reputations.

But why should there be *prosecutions* to vindicate reputations? Why does the state have a greater interest in the reputation of some people than in the free speech of others? It is one thing for those who feel victimized to launch civil actions for damages if they believe that others have libelled them. But it is quite another matter to threaten the alleged libellers with prosecution, conviction, and possible imprisonment. The vindication of personal reputation hardly warrants the awesome power of incarceration. The section ought to be repealed.

Yet even civil defamation creates some unwarranted risks to legitimate freedom of expression. In the late 1970s, for example, the British Columbia minister of human resources successfully sued a newspaper for publishing a cartoon that portrayed him gleefully tearing the wings off a fly. The judgment of the court sounds almost like a satire on itself.

> After consideration I have reached the conclusion that considered symbolically, allegorically or satirically, as it should be and because, in the natural and ordinary meaning that viewers would attribute to it, it meant and would be understood to mean that the plaintiff is a person of a cruel and sadistic nature who enjoys inflicting suffering on helpless persons, said false pictorial representation adversely affecting and lowering his reputation and standing in the estimation of right-thinking members of society generally by exposing him to hatred, contempt or ridicule, and disparaging him in his office as Minister of Human Resources, and upon the evidence I find that the cartoon was not objectively a fair comment on facts.

Remarkably, the judge managed to squeeze all of this into one sentence. Gilbert and Sullivan couldn't have done better.

While the Court of Appeal subsequently overturned this judgment, the case illustrates the lengths to which the law may go to vindicate a fragile ego. In this case, the fragile ego belonged to none other than William Vander Zalm, the man who subsequently became premier of British Columbia. The episode prompts an irrepressible question: to what extent have the cartoonists and columnists in that province been intimidated by the demonstrated litigiousness of their premier?

At the very least, the litigation rights of public personalities should be reassessed. The viability of the democratic processes requires a very broad right to challenge, criticize, and even satirize the wielders of power and influence. The thin skin of a leader should not be able to impair the free speech of a critic. Moreover, the effective right to criticize stands to be jeopardized if, in the midst of a heated issue, the fear of a lawsuit fetters the spontaneity of debate or muzzles the utterance of what is reasonably believed. In general, our defamation law could give supporters of the status quo a considerable advantage over dissenters. As a practical matter, not everything that emerges in public debate can be exhaustively researched beforehand. Thus, there is an argument for restricting the defamation claims of public personalities.

Besides, involvement in public life is usually a matter of voluntary choice. As Harry Truman once warned, "If you can't stand the heat, stay out of the kitchen." Moreover, those in public life can often command access to the media in order to reply to any attacks they may have sustained. In this regard, the American law may be instructive. In that country, public personalities have to prove malice in order to recover damages.

Hate Propaganda and False News

During the first six months of 1985, the Canadian public endured a grotesque spectacle—the back-to-back trials of pamphleteer Ernst Zundel in Toronto, Ontario and of high school teacher James Keegstra in Red Deer, Alberta. Zundel was charged with spreading false news for having published material denying the truth of the Nazi Holocaust against the Jews. Keegstra was prosecuted for a violation of the anti-hate law for having preached to his high school classes about the alleged evils of international Jewry.

Day after day, these trials were major news events in the Canadian media. We were subjected to detailed cross-examinations of concentration camp survivors. They were asked how they knew that their fellow prisoners were gassed and even how they knew that those prisoners were dead.

In the Zundel case, there were interminable discussions regarding the properties of the gas that was used and the nature of the facilities involved. Time and again, the defence told us that our history books are wrong; mass gassings could not possibly have occurred. And we were subjected to the bizarre testimony of defence witnesses who not only denied the historically documented accounts of the Holocaust, but also claimed that many of the Jews were actually happy in the concentration camps. For much of his twenty-six days of testimony in the hate trial, Keegstra invoked Scripture in support of his anti-Jewish arguments.

It would be hard to imagine an obscenity that could parallel the deliberate denial of the genocide suffered by the Jews of Europe. And it would be hard to imagine the enormity of the affront which such denials inevitably must inflict on those who were lucky enough to survive the Holocaust. It is easy to sympathize with the pain of those who, having suffered such horrors, are now told that *they*, not their tormentors, are the enemies of Western civilization. Understandably, therefore, many people experienced both joy and relief when Zundel was finally convicted and sentenced to eighteen months in prison. But these emotions quickly soured when the Ontario Court of Appeal, for a number of technical reasons, ordered a new trial. No one, except perhaps Zundel himself, welcomed the prospect of a rerun. The Keegstra case is also on hold. He was convicted and fined $5000 and, at the time of writing, he was awaiting judgment from the Alberta Court of Appeal.

No matter what results finally obtain, these cases have raised questions that go to the very roots of our legal system. Should freedom of speech extend to those who are prepared to perpetrate the kind of malevolent indignities that have characterized the pronouncements of Ernst Zundel and James Keegstra? To what extent is a court of law the proper forum to redress such insults? How is a judge or jury supposed to resolve questions of historical accuracy? What are the implications for situations involving genuine historical controversies?

These searching questions are the outgrowth of decisions which were made in the mid-1960s. That period marked the effective beginning of the campaign for legal redress against racist speech. The precipitating factor was the emergence of new political groups that called themselves Nazis. Donning uniforms and displaying swastikas, these fledgling groups began to resurrect the anti-semitic and racist invective of the Hitler era. White Christians were admonished to be on guard against mongrelization by inferior blacks and against subversion by an international Zionist-Communist-banker-Jewish-Freemason conspiracy.

The brazen *chutzpah* of this propaganda provoked widespread revulsion. In Canada the revulsion found further expression in special demands that new laws be enacted to stop the propagation of racial hatred. The demands came from Jews who had survived the horrors of the Nazi concentration camps, blacks whose memories embraced the lynch mobs of the Ku Klux Klan, veterans of the Second World War, and many, many others who sought simply to maintain racial and intergroup harmony in their communities. By the end of the 1960s, the Parliament of Canada had enacted an amendment to the Criminal Code making it illegal to espouse publicly certain forms of racial, religious, and ethnic hatred.

The theoretical arguments for such legislation are rather alluring. Racists would not allow free speech for others, so why should they enjoy it? It's one thing to tolerate legitimate differences of opinion on racial matters, but it's another thing to tolerate outbursts of sheer hatred. After the Holocaust, racism is simply beyond the pale.

Even if such arguments sound persuasive, problems arise when the focus shifts from theoretical considerations to practical ones. The question then becomes how to articulate a prohibition which is precise enough to curb this neo-Nazi propaganda without running an excessive risk of catching in the same net a lot of other material that it would be clearly unconscionable for a democratic society to suppress. The amendment in question wound up prohibiting the public communication of statements "which wilfully promote hatred" against people distinguished by race, religion, and ethnicity. There can be no reasonable objection to a law that purported to prohibit the incitement of racial *violence* in situations of imminent peril. But "hatred" is a much more nebulous and, therefore, dangerous concept. Our experience tells us that freedom of speech is often most necessary when it creates some level of tension or unrest. The late Martin Luther King, Jr., for example, referred to his own tactics as an exercise in "constructive tension". The problem, then, is: how does a blunt instrument like the criminal law distinguish between destructive hatred and constructive tension?

While few genuine racists have thus far been convicted under this section, others have certainly suffered from it. In the mid-1970s, the police used the anti-hate law to arrest some young people at a Toronto Shriners parade for distributing leaflets bearing the words "Yankee Go Home". Although the crown attorney had the good sense subsequently to withdraw the charge, these young activists suffered the suppression of their legitimate protest and some of them spent two days in jail.

In the late 1970s, the anti-hate law was used in a bizarre case to prosecute and convict two French Canadian nationalists who had distributed anti-French material in order to create pro-French sympathy. This incident grew out of a controversy in Windsor over the public funding of French education. The accused were hoping their material would turn the tide in favour of the French position. While their convictions were reversed on appeal, consider the price in money and anxiety that had to be involved. Although these victims of our anti-hate laws were hardly deserving of medals, they should not have been subjected to the ordeal of prosecution. It must be clear that they bear no relationship whatever to the intended racist targets of the legislation at issue.

The anti-hate law has also provoked questionable investigations. The Ontario attorney-general investigated the fact that Toronto libraries were carrying the pro-Zionist novel *The Haj* by best-selling author Leon Uris because, in the opinion of an Arab organization, the book "slurs and maligns Arabs". For more than a month, Canada Customs held up the admission to Canada of a film sympathetic to jailed black South African leader Nelson Mandela. And federal officials conducted a probe of the anti-Communist Hollywood film *Red Dawn*. Although I have not seen these materials and therefore cannot comment on their merits, it seems apparent that they are not of the kind that the law was designed to suppress. This is not necessarily to say that the contents are devoid of anything which might be racially or ethnically offensive. It is simply to say that they are not likely to fall into that category of unredeemed racial invective which prompted Parliament to enact this law. Even though no charges were laid in these cases, official investigations tend to create a chill over the robust exercise of freedom of expression.

We have already noted how the similar wording of our laws on criminal defamation and scandalizing contempt of court supported criminal convictions for the "Pontius Pilate" award, the allegorical references to the role of judge and jury in the "murder" of a condemned man, and the denunciation of the courts in a campus newspaper as "instruments of the corporate elite". Since these dubious consequences were made possible by the existence of legal prohibitions such as those against promoting "hatred", "contempt", "disrepute", and "ridicule", they underscore the dangerous potential of the anti-hate law.

Remarkably, many of the key defenders of Canada's anti-hate laws have not even addressed the risk of catching the wrong people. In the course of his judgment upholding the law's constitutionality, Mr. Justice Quigley of the Alberta Court of Queen's Bench had occasion to point out that our anti-hate law "is not a proscription against the freedom to publicly criticize any of our nation's fundamental values or institutions". He insisted that the law simply "deals with" the right of racial, religious, and ethnic groups "to be protected from wilfully promoted hatred at the public level". The judge has accurately stated the *intent* of the legislation, but the *effect* of such laws often exceeds their intent.

A 1986 working paper of the Law Reform Commission of Canada assures us that "hatred is enmity" and "promoting enmity is clearly dysfunctional to society". Perhaps so, but nowhere does this working paper attempt to assess the risk that legitimate expressions of conflict will be suppressed as illegitimate expressions of hatred. In view of the inherent vagueness of the word "hatred" and some of the regrettable experiences this country has already had with the existence of such words in the law, it is not reassuring to be told by the Law Reform Commission's working paper that the anti-hate law will catch "only the most serious kinds of hatred".

The same defects have characterized certain presentations of the Canadian Jewish Congress. In its 1969 brief to the Senate committee on the bill that ultimately became law, the congress simply assumed the adequacy of the proposed definition of prohibitable hate and went on to argue for the importance of the bill's objectives and the fairness of its safeguards. Hardly a word was addressed to the number of *non*-Nazis the bill was likely to catch. Hardly a word was addressed to whether this was a risk worth taking. To what extent did the number and potency of the Nazis warrant this risk to the free speech of non-Nazis?

Many of the supporters of our anti-hate law have derived undue consolation from the law's safeguards for free speech. The Canadian Jewish Congress, for example, noted with approval the defences an accused person might invoke against a possible charge—the truth of the statements at issue, a reasonable belief in the truth of such statements, and the relevance of the statements to the public interest. The following is an extract from the congress' remarks about these defences:

> If statements are true, we are fully content that they be made without let or hindrance; if discussion of such statements is in the public interest and if it be found that the speaker or writer had reasonable grounds to believe them true, we are satisfied that there should be no interference with them. These are the defences that are already present in the Criminal Code in respect of defamatory libels and we do not quarrel with their inclusion in this legislation.

At first blush this may look like a concession to free speech, but it is not a very substantial one. Where political polemics are concerned, the defence of truth is not very helpful. Most political controversy deals with matters of opinion, not of provable fact. Imagine, for example, trying to prove in court that English Canadians have unfairly exploited French Canadians. The defence of reasonable belief in the truth is not much more helpful. It's one thing to ask a court to evaluate the reasonableness of believing in the truth of rather narrow allegations, such as whether person X robbed the corner store. But it's another thing entirely for a court to evaluate the reasonableness of various political theories, such as whether the English, French, or even the Catholic Church must bear the responsibility for some of society's problems.

And how is a court to determine what public discussion is relevant to the public interest? Is a court to ask whether, as a matter of fact, the public is interested in the subject at issue? Or is a court to determine, as a matter of value, whether the public *should* be interested in the subject at issue? If it is the first, the test is too restrictive. People should have the right to expand the range of public interests at any given time. If it is the second, the courts would be acquiring excessive powers to control the ambit of public discussion. On the basis of what and whose value judgments is an appointed, politically non-accountable judge supposed to limit the range of permissible discussion?

Finally, I am saddened by the consolation which the Canadian Jewish Congress derived from the idea that these questionable defences were already available for the Criminal Code offence of defamatory libel. Within months of this congress presentation, the underground newspaper mentioned earlier was nailed for defamatory libel because of the "Pontius Pilate" article. The free speech defences so eulogized by the Canadian Jewish Congress proved of no help to the free speech of that publication.

Some defenders of the anti-hate law have argued that there is a certain amount of vagueness in *all* legislation. According to them, arguments such as mine make the case, not against the hate law in particular, but against all law in general. There is, of course, an element of truth in this contention. It fails, however, to address the priority role of free speech in democratic societies. What is put at risk here is not simply a value like driving a car or handling money. It is the grievance procedure of democracy. Even if other important values undergo certain risks at the hands of inevitably vague laws, *this* value has to be treated with special solicitude.

Significantly, many supporters of our anti-hate law have attempted to extend rather than restrict its scope. Understandably frustrated over the paucity of successful prosecutions, many people have called for the deletion of the "wilful" requirement. This change is designed to eliminate the need to prove a "specific intention to promote hatred". But that requirement is there in order to reduce the risk that this law might be used against over-eager speakers who become carried away while delivering a legitimate polemic. Suppose, for example, in a fit of anger over a land-claims dispute, a native representative blamed Canadian whites in general for the poverty of the Indian people. While such a statement might well be improper, it should certainly not be unlawful. Democratic debate cannot coexist with such a demanding obligation to bite one's tongue.

Indeed, such an amendment arguably might imperil communications media such as the CBC for including, in a newscast, film footage of a hate-monger making a speech. Without a requirement of wilfulness, there is an argument that showing such a film would make the CBC liable to a conviction for "communicating" the hate-monger's message. Moreover, the deletion of "wilful" would have caught the French Canadian nationalists in the case to which I referred earlier. The original conviction was thrown out on appeal because it was held that the communication had not been wilful.

There has been some indication also of an attempt to remove the safeguards for certain religious discussions. While this change might make it easier to take action against racist sermonizing that periodically occurs, it also creates a serious risk. How far, for example, would such a deletion increase the vulnerability of a group like Quebec's Jehovah's Witnesses for repeating today the nasty things they said about the Roman Catholic Church during the late 1940s and early 1950s? Believing as they did that the Church hierarchy was behind the persecution they suffered at the hands of the Duplessis regime, the Witnesses published a stream of anti-Catholic material. The response of the Duplessis government was to charge the group's leaders with seditious libel. The Supreme Court of Canada was widely praised for dismissing the charge on the grounds that, by itself, the creation of inter-group ill will was not an offence. Ironically, some of the very constituencies that hailed that judgment as a landmark protection for civil liberties have been recently advocating amendments that could undo its effect.

There has also been a proposal to delete the requirement that certain prosecutions must have the consent of the attorney-general in the affected province. Again, this change would expose more people—not just genuine racists—to the ordeal of prosecution. The consent requirement acts as a potential buffer against the abuse of these awesome powers.

A further irony is that there may be a real danger here to one of the groups on whose behalf many of these changes are being sought—the Jewish community. There is a chance, for example, that Canadian sympathizers with the Palestine Liberation Organization might lay anti-hate charges against Canadian Zionists on the basis of the PLO's dubious slogan that Zionism equals racism. Even if a conviction was unlikely, the charge itself could cause enormous distress.

This point cannot be stressed often enough. Freedom of expression is undermined not only by the convictions that are ultimately registered, but also by the prosecutions that are initially threatened. If we cannot engage in public debate without the fear of facing a criminal prosecution, we are not enjoying freedom of expression. This is the phenomenon that certain American courts have so sensitively labelled "the chilling effect". The risk of having our speech chilled increases with the vagueness of the prohibitory legislation that might apply. In order to avoid the possibility of prosecution, people might be impelled to ensure that their speech steered as far as possible from the prohibited zone. Very often, the likely casualty of such self-censorship would be perfectly legitimate speech.

While I normally avoid the argument of the "slippery slope", it has some regrettable application to our experience with the anti-hate law. Yesterday's restrictions on free speech have made it easier, in fact, to propose tomorrow's restrictions. This helps to explain, for example, the relative ease with which so many reputable people and organizations have urged the repeal of the free speech safeguards in the anti-hate law. Unfortunately, there are further examples of this phenomenon which are even more disquieting.

Consider, in this connection, the 1986 working paper of the federal Law Reform Commission. In the opinion of the authors, it is not enough for our anti-hate law to protect those who have been harmed by hate material in the past—such as racial, religious, and ethnic groups. They warn us that "others might be harmed in the future—for example, the mentally handicapped or the elderly." On the basis that the Charter protects against discrimination by reason of "colour, race, ethnic origin, religion, national origin, sex, age, or mental or physical disability", the authors of the working paper insist that "it is entirely reasonable that groups characterized by the same criteria be protected by the criminal law when they are subjected to vicious expressions of hatred."

Whatever happened to the "clear and present danger" test? Here we have eminent legal analysts telling us that freedom of speech can legitimately be restricted, not simply because of a current threat but also because of what *might* happen in the future. No need for any evidence of the threat. Speculation and conjecture will now suffice. At one time, it would have been unthinkable for people of this calibre to make such proposals. History, however, has eased the problem. Sometimes there really is a slippery slope.

Moreover, there is good reason even to doubt how well the cause of racial dignity is served by the anti-hate law. In some important respects, the requirements of a hate prosecution are at odds with the canons of common sense. From the standpoint of common sense, it is usually wise to avoid debating the merits of a malevolent obscenity. As Toronto Rabbi W. Gunther Plaut once astutely observed, if someone calls your mother a whore you don't debate the subject. To do so is to give the allegation an aura of legitimacy. It also perpetuates the indignity.

But, when you prosecute, you must treat accused people and their pronouncements with seriousness. Consider, for example, what happened during the false news prosecution of Ernst Zundel. There were solemn debates in court over the monstrous claim that Auschwitz was a Jewish country club rather than a Nazi death camp. The prosecutor, not the defence, called a Gentile banker to the stand and asked him whether he was in the pay of a Jewish conspiracy. This is not necessarily to blame the prosecutor for using those tactics. Understandably he felt he had to meet every element of the accused's defence. It is simply to recognize that the risk of farce is endemic to the very nature of the proceedings.

Nor should we overlook what a criminal prosecution can do for a hitherto obscure propagandist. Outside of Jewish circles and a few government offices, Zundel had been a virtual unknown. By the time his trial was in full swing, he had become a household name. The media carried major headline stories in which he could trumpet his obscenities to the entire country. Similar notoriety resulted from the anti-hate trial of Alberta's James Keegstra, whose lunatic theories of a Jewish conspiracy were broadcast to the world. I do not raise this issue of publicity because of any fear that the trials will attract a significant following for the hate-mongers. I simply regard the trials as an affront to our dignity and common sense.

To what end are we asked to incur these risks to freedom of speech and common sense? If the hate-mongers in this country posed some kind of imminent peril to the well-being of our society or the groups within it, there might be an argument for taking these risks. In this connection, the government-appointed Cohen committee made some rather strange remarks in its 1968 report which advocated the enactment of our anti-hate law.

> However small the actors may be in number, the individuals and groups promoting hate in Canada constitute a "clear and present danger" to the functioning of a democratic society. For in times of social stress such "hate" could mushroom into a real and monstrous threat to our way of life....

It's hard to fathom how the Cohen committee could view a situation as a "clear and present danger" because of what *could* happen in times of social stress. I would suggest that the committee's two sentences simply cannot coexist. If hate-mongering is a "clear and present danger", we must already be living in the apprehended times of social stress or at least on the brink of them. But nowhere does the committee report say this. Indeed, it candidly admits that our hate-mongering problem should not be described "as one of crisis or near crisis proportions". If the committee was acknowledging, on the other hand, that we are not living in the apprehended times of social stress, how could it regard the hate-mongering danger as clear and *present*? Remarkably, in the course of upholding the constitutionality of our anti-hate law, Alberta's Mr. Justice Quigley quoted with approval these contradictory statements in the Cohen report.

A more realistic assessment of hate-mongering was made by Daniel G. Hill, the first director of the Ontario Human Rights Commission: "The Canadian public is relatively immune to extremist, anti-semitic, and other 'hate' materials". I have never seen any concrete current evidence that rebuts or seriously challenges Dr. Hill's statement. This is not to say that Canada lacks serious racial problems. But it is to say that such problems do not emanate from the extremists.

Consider the state of Alberta's Social Credit Party, which, unlike the British Columbia party of the same name, accepted the likes of James Keegstra as a candidate despite the reports of his anti-semitic activities. In the 1984 federal election, that party contested fifteen ridings. It ran last in eleven. Where it didn't run last, it was rescued from such disgrace by the Libertarian, Communist, or Rhinoceros parties, all aspirants to electoral oblivion. In the aggregate, the Alberta Social Credit Party polled only 0.6 per cent of the total vote, just squeezing by the official practical jokers, the Rhinoceros Party, at 0.4 per cent.

Those who favour the anti-hate laws frequently remind us that Hitler too was once insignificant. They urge the prosecution of even marginal propagandists on the grounds that they are all potential Hitlers. These arguments overlook not only the vast political differences but also the striking legal similarities between pre-Hitler Germany and today's Canada.

Remarkably, pre-Hitler Germany had laws very much like the Canadian anti-hate law. Moreover, those laws were enforced with some vigour. During the fifteen years before Hitler came to power, there were more than two hundred prosecutions based on anti-semitic speech. And, in the opinion of the leading Jewish organization of that era, no more than 10 per cent of the cases were mishandled by the authorities. As subsequent history so painfully testifies, this type of legislation proved ineffectual on the one occasion when there was a real argument for it. Indeed, there is some indication that the Nazis of pre-Hitler Germany shrewdly exploited their criminal trials in order to increase the size of their constituency. They used the trials as platforms to propagate their message.

This is not to suggest that what was unworkable in Germany is bound to be unworkable in Canada. Indeed, I share the views of Daniel Hill and others that the Canadian public is relatively immune to extremist invective. On this basis, there is reason to hope that the anti-hate law in Canada would not likely backfire the way it did in Germany. But, if that is so, the anti-hate law is not likely needed in Canada the way it was in Germany. If the social and political climate here is not particularly receptive to hate propaganda, why should we incur all of the other risks that accompany the use of the legal sanction?

The other Canadian law that has been used recently against hate-mongers is the false news section of the Criminal Code, under which Ernst Zundel was prosecuted. In the course of upholding the constitutionality of this section, the Ontario Court of Appeal made much of the requirement for the prosecution to prove beyond a reasonable doubt that the accused had *knowingly* lied. Speech of this kind is seen as the antithesis of seeking truth; it does not aid the working of parliamentary democracy; it does not further self-fulfilment. In short, the court sees the deliberate lie as falling outside any sensible rationale for freedom of expression.

In the abstract it would be hard to defend the right to tell deliberate lies. In the concrete, however, the attempt to ban such lies could endanger a lot of everyday discussion. Consider how often people in political situations accuse each other of falsehood, and how often there is some justification for the charge. Such people often tend to exaggerate their own claims and minimize the claims of their adversaries. If these exaggerations and minimizations led to threats of criminal prosecution, imagine the impact on freedom of expression. If Ernst Zundel can be convicted for denying the Holocaust, to what extent are pro-Communists now vulnerable for denying the atrocities of Stalin, or pro-Catholics for denying the enormity of the Inquisition, or pro-Zionists for denying Israel's nuclear clout, or pro-Palestinians for exaggerating the threats posed by Israel?

Even if such advocates were ultimately cleared because of inadequate proof that they had *knowingly* lied, the damage would have been done. One of the most critical dangers to freedom of speech is the existence of laws that impel us to look over our shoulders for engaging in normal democratic discourse. The people most likely to be intimidated are those with unpopular or unconventional ideas. Unless they were particularly imprudent or extraordinarily courageous, they could well decide that it is better to be quiet than to risk going to court. This is why public opinion, rather than legal coercion, should decide the truth and falsity of most allegations relating to public policy issues.

Of course, not all conceivable false news laws would create such a threat to legitimate discourse. There could be no reasonable objection, for example, to a law which prohibited the spreading of false news in situations where there was an imminent peril to life or limb. By way of illustration, legal sanctions might be appropriate against a radio station for falsely broadcasting that Soviet missiles were on their way to strike Canadian cities. But the false news section is neither this narrow nor this specific. Nor does it mention the Holocaust or racial tolerance. It makes unlawful the spreading of *any* false news that is likely to injure *any* public interest. And nowhere are the words "public interest" defined.

In the absence of such a definition, how are speakers to know when their inevitable exaggerations and minimizations encroach on the taboo area? Of course they can't know. The best way they can protect themselves, therefore, is to confine their speech to non-controversial matters that avoid as much as possible issues of public interest. Hardly a state of affairs compatible with freedom of expression.

While the false news section has not given rise to many prosecutions, it has nevertheless produced some questionable ones. After the sedition prosecution of the early 1950s failed to convict the Jehovah's Witnesses for their anti-Catholic material, the Quebec authorities attempted to nail them for spreading false news. Again, there was an acquittal. But what a message this must have conveyed to Quebec's Jehovah's Witnesses and other dissenting minorities. If you insist on attacking the Quebec and Catholic establishment, beware! This was another case in which the ultimate acquittal would not have been adequately consoling. The charge itself must have chilled the free speech of the aggrieved minorities. The very existence of the false news law contributed to the resulting oppression.

In the early part of this century, an American was actually convicted of spreading false news for a sign he had posted in connection with the closing-out sale of his business. The sign declared that Americans were not wanted in this country. I would have thought that this man's statement was essentially an expression of opinion rather than an assertion of fact. How is a court supposed to evaluate the truth of the claim that Canadians have been inhospitable to Americans? How far, therefore, will the false news law authorize the state to punish our expressions of opinion?

The case of the hapless American also serves to highlight the dangers of leaving the words "public interest" undefined. In that case, the court found that the man had injured our public interest in attracting more American immigrants. Suppose, however, that it had been Canadian policy at that time to discourage such immigration? Would this mean that, despite the man's "lie", he would have been acquitted? In our time, suppose a "dove" minimized Soviet atrocities at a time when it was Canadian policy to increase our military arms program? Conversely, suppose a "hawk" exaggerated the Soviet threat at a time when it was Canadian policy to promote détente? Can the "public interest", for these purposes, change from day to day? Must a court depend upon the policies of government or is it supposed to probe for more fundamental values?

The failure of a statute even to address such issues should be seen as fatal to its attempts to restrict free speech. The failure of the Ontario Court of Appeal in the Zundel case to analyse the issue this way creates some pessimism about the future of the Charter in this crucial area.

In any event, hate-mongers can be fought without incurring the risks that accompany our anti-hate and false news laws. A wise strategy must distinguish between racists who have status in the community and those who don't. It is generally foolish to take strong public action against relatively unknown bigots. That would make such people look more important than their activities warrant. I hasten to point out that I don't advocate ignoring the fringe extremists in our midst. Of course they bear watching, lest they acquire at some point a clout which they now lack. In general, however, our best response to such people would be indirect. It would involve the continued improvement of our laws and actions against the really serious racial problems in this country— in jobs, housing, and so on. The fallout from a stronger program against racist *deeds* is likely to weaken further the impact of racist *words*.

The racist speech of more prominent individuals should generally provoke a counter-attack at the political level. If such people vilify Jews, blacks, or other minorities, they should be made to suffer political and social censure, including their removal from relevant positions of influence. This is not to discount the dangers and difficulties of public censure. (To be sure, many delicate distinctions will have to be drawn—between demagoguery and scholarship, between relevant and irrelevant employment, and so on.) It is simply to note that, unlike prosecution, public censure in such situations can be both legitimate and effective.

Following the reports of James Keegstra's anti-semitic preaching in Alberta's schools, for example, public censure triggered action. The educational authorities discharged him as a teacher for abusing his pedagogical trust. The voters ousted him as mayor for disgracing his representative role. Once such people lose their positions of influence, they should be left to wallow in the obscurity which they so richly deserve. In such circumstances, prosecution becomes pointless. The important lesson of the Zundel and Keegstra trials is the need to develop a strategy that is at once less dangerous to freedom of speech and more effective against racism than is criminal prosecution.

Pornography

I have seen...women's naked and mutilated bodies suspended upside down on barbed wire fences, a woman spread-eagled and forced to have relations with a dog, brutal and sadistic gang rapes...spikes hammered into vaginas, nipples hacked from the breasts of a woman pinioned with a leather bit in her mouth.

This statement made in the early 1980s by former Ontario film censor Mary Brown describes the kind of "entertainment" reportedly provided by certain modern films. A number of feminists and moderates, as well as fundamentalists and conservatives, are demanding that such material be banned. It's hard not to sympathize with their concern. The justified revulsion over such portrayals has given the power of legal suppression new respectability.

We should distinguish, however, between moral condemnation and legal prohibition. While the former may appear easy, the latter is fraught with difficulty. Again, the legal problem is one essentially of definition. Even if it were conceded that we should suppress the kind of stuff mentioned in Mary Brown's statement, the tough question is the same as it is with hate propaganda: how to do it? How is the law to formulate a standard that will prohibit this vile pornography without simultaneously catching in the same net a lot of other material which it would be unconscionable to suppress? So often our obscenity laws have wound up nailing the wrong material.

In the 1970s, for example, arguably artistic and educational works, such as the film *Last Tango in Paris* and the book *Show Me*, had to undergo prolonged and expensive court battles before they were ultimately vindicated. In *Last Tango*, a down-and-out middle-aged widower was shown having anal intercourse with a lovely young woman. *Show Me*, a book designed to explain sex to youngsters, featured a number of drawings that many people found offensive. In the opinion at least of a number of prosecutors and police, these works fell within the Criminal Code definition of obscenity—"the undue exploitation of sex".

But what in the world is an "undue" exploitation? For that matter, what is a "due" exploitation? The answer, we are told, is to be found in community standards. But how are these to be discerned? Not infrequently, numbers of experts have offered conflicting opinions as to whether a particular work violates community standards. How are the triers of fact supposed to choose? Indeed, our judges have often been at diametric odds with each other over the interpretation and application of this terminology.

Consider these cases. In the early 1960s one trial judge, three appeal court judges, and four judges of the Supreme Court of Canada found that *Lady Chatterley's Lover* was obscene within the above definition. However, five judges of the Supreme Court carried the day in a declaration that the book was not obscene. Despite the acquittal, the judicial head count was eight to five in favour of a conviction. During the same period the book *Fanny Hill* was found to be obscene by a trial judge and two appeal court judges, and not obscene by three other appeal court judges. Here the judicial head count wound up in a three-all tie.

If the most eminent legal experts in the community disagree so sharply about what constitutes an "undue exploitation of sex", how is the lay citizen supposed to make such judgments? Unlike the situation with most other criminal laws, those who are subject to prosecution for obscenity often have no way of determining in advance if they are committing an offence. A person who picks up a gun to rob a bank knows beforehand that such conduct will run afoul of the criminal law. But a person who writes, publishes, or distributes a particular book may not know that the book in question will ultimately be considered an "undue exploitation of sex". Unless they avoid all material with realistic sexual content, publishers, film-makers, authors, and booksellers must experience considerable insecurity as to whether they are in compliance with the obscenity laws.

Moreover, it is often the *police*, not the courts, who make the effective judgments as to what is obscene. Faced with the possible threat of prosecution or arrest, few publishers, theatre owners, distributors, and booksellers are likely to defy police instructions to discontinue a film showing or to remove certain literature. Thus, in numbers of cases, censorship decisions are made without any involvement of the courts. There are times also when the distributors of material feel obliged to withhold it, even without instruction to do so by the police. Although distributors of magazines or films, for example, bear no responsibility for what has been produced, they may become criminally responsible for its dissemination. This situation has imposed upon innocent third parties an obligation to act as pre-censors. Their vulnerability is exacerbated by the differences of legal opinion in interpreting such a vague and subjective definition.

A brief history of recent attempts by our legislators and interest groups to develop an improved definition will convey the pitfalls awaiting those who favour legal prohibition in this area. An initiative in the late 1970s and early 1980s by the federal Liberal government would have defined, as obscene, material which has as a dominant characteristic "the undue exploitation of...sex, violence, crime, horror or cruelty, through degrading representations of a male or female person or in any other manner". The essence of this proposal was to move the definition of obscenity beyond the subject matter of sex. This, however, would be likely to *increase* the dangers to legitimate communication. Indeed, this definition might be broad enough to suppress the eleven o'clock news.

To what extent, for example, might pictures of Vietnam war casualties or the mass suicides at Jonestown be considered "undue" exploitation of violence or horror? How far might descriptions or commentary concerning executions, kidnappings, floggings, and gas chambers be construed as "degrading representations of a male or female person"? To what extent, therefore, might editors and commentators be subject to legal sanctions for the realistic portrayal of the news? Even if charges were not laid, there could well be a chilling fear of them.

In the early 1980s, the National Action Committee on the Status of Women (NAC) proposed a narrower definition—"any printed, visual, audio or otherwise represented presentation, or part thereof, which seeks to sexually stimulate the viewer or consumer by the depiction of violence, including, but not limited to, the depiction of submission, coercion, lack of consent, or debasement of any human being". For the purpose of this definition, NAC would make the depiction of sexual activity by anyone portrayed as being under the age of sixteen sufficient to stigmatize the material as pornographic.

While the NAC approach contains fewer dangers than do some others, it is nevertheless seriously flawed. Among those flaws is the risk that it could prohibit important political commentary. Suppose, for example, that a film-maker wished to dramatize some of the sexual horrors that occurred at Auschwitz? Such a portrayal could be very much in the public interest. By reviving and making vivid this despicable epoch in human history, the contemplated film could help to fortify viewers against the evils of racism. Yet such a film arguably could fall within the NAC definition.

If enacted into law, this definition could also wind up suppressing such works of art as the famous rape scene in Ingmar Bergman's classic film *The Virgin Spring*, or a passionate love scene between the ostensibly teenaged Romeo and Juliet. Indeed, the history of literature is full of material that might fit the NAC definition. Greek mythology portrays the rape of the beautiful Leda by the god Zeus in the form of a swan. The progeny of this union turns out to be the even more beautiful Helen of Troy. In Ayn Rand's *The Fountainhead*, the strong individualistic will of the hero leads him to sexual assault. This action is depicted by the author, without apology, as an expression of the hero's exemplary individuality.

Undoubtedly, partisans of the NAC approach would argue that none of this material deliberately seeks "to sexually stimulate", therefore none of it would be prohibited. But who can be so sanguine about the ability to impute sexual intentions to authors? The very subjectivity of the exercise increases the risks of fallacious findings. In any event, to the extent that the material did in fact cause sexual stimulation, the law might well infer that this was intended. The law already contains a presumption that people intend (and are therefore responsible for) the natural consequences of their acts. This inference would be rendered all the more likely when the material is accompanied by pictures or expressed in film.

Moreover, the NAC argument has to rely primarily on the literary and cinematic judgment of the courts. It reveals no disrespect for our judges to point out that, in matters of art, literature, and films, everyone's power of discernment is infected with subjectivity. What could appear to be a serious political or psychological statement to one viewer could well look like sexual exploitation to another. (Remember how our judges have already differed.) And, even if some of the NAC leaders were disposed to place a higher level of trust in the courts on this subject, would they feel the same way about the police, who are often the effective decision-makers on issues of obscenity?

The NAC proposal represented an attempt to formulate a legal distinction between erotica, which the group would allow, and pornography, which it would outlaw. The former involves voluntary sex acts between men and women participating as equals. The latter involves coercive sex acts imposed by dominant men over submissive women. It is easier, however, to make such distinctions in abstract theory than to apply them in concrete law.

It is particularly disquieting to read some of the arguments that have been marshalled behind such legislative proposals. Consider, for example, the views of Professor Lorenne M. G. Clark, who for a number of years spoke on behalf of NAC on this issue. An advocate of prohibiting the depiction of coerced sex, she made some questionable arguments: "If it is wrong to engage in sexual activities which violate the injunction against causing harm to others...then it is also wrong to condone the manufacture, sale, and distribution of materials which depict such behaviour...." Plainly and simply, this is a *non sequitur*. Professor Clark's conclusion just does not follow from her premise. The fact that it is wrong to commit murder, robbery, treason, or theft hardly makes it wrong for literature or films to *depict* such conduct. In this one sentence, Professor Clark would ban many of the best books that have ever been written or films that have ever been made. After all, most fiction is about conflict and much of this conflict involves depictions of wrongful conduct.

Such faulty analysis bedevils much modern commentary on the subject of law and pornography. Journalist Susan G. Cole, for example, expressed the censorship conflict as follows: "As feminists we consider our own rights more important than the civil liberties of propagandists for male domination." But what does Ms. Cole have to say about the rights of all the other people whose interests would likely be imperilled by the censorship exercise? What about the rights of Ingmar Bergman and those men *and* women who wish to see his films? What about those who wish to produce and those who wish to see explicit news reels on current events or realistic historical dramas? It may be comforting for Ms. Cole to believe that the censorship she advocates will intrude only on the pornographers she condemns. The reality, however, is likely to be otherwise. The victims of censorship are likely to include a variety of persons and materials that have nothing to do with the objects of Ms. Cole's indignation.

Similarly questionable arguments have appeared in support of this position in the daily press. Consider, for example, the many articles on pornography published by former *Toronto Star* columnist Lynda Hurst. Writing approvingly of the stand against pornography taken by one of her colleagues, she asked the following question: "We restrict manufacturers who pollute our air and water, my newly enlightened colleague informed me when she returned from assignment, so isn't it time we regulated the folks who are trying to pollute our minds?" Ms. Hurst's metaphor is not only fallacious, it is also downright dangerous. Chemical analysis is capable of providing some measure of objective assessment of how various substances in the air and water are likely to affect our bodies. What comparable standards are available for the materials that can affect our minds? Physical pollutants can be defined and described with a large measure of precision, reducing the likelihood that our anti-pollution laws will be misapplied. As indicated, mental pollutants are not at all susceptible of such precise articulation.

A few years of such polemics led to the creation, in the early 1980s, of a special government committee on pornography, known as the Fraser committee. Unfortunately, however, this group was also unable to extricate us from the definitional quagmire. Indeed, if the recommendations of the Fraser committee are adopted, this country could wind up prosecuting librarians for lending classical literature to members of the public. The conduct the Fraser committee would make illegal includes the distribution of material that describes or depicts "incest" and "bestiality". Remember the classic Greek tragedy *Oedipus Rex*? The hero, separated from his parents during infancy, subsequently falls in love with his own mother. Isn't that incest? And couldn't the rape of Leda by Zeus in the form of a swan be considered bestiality?

The Fraser committee would make "artistic merit" a defence to such a pornography charge. But artistic merit frequently depends upon the taste buds of the beholder. And these could be as varied as the number of beholders. In view of the fact that artistic merit has long been a mitigating factor in the law of obscenity, the differences of opinion among the judges and the number of decisions to prosecute in questionable cases serve to remind us just how unreliable such a defence can be.

Significantly, there is another Fraser committee recommendation under which even artistic merit could not be invoked as a defence. The committee would stigmatize as pornographic any material that "advocates, encourages, condones, or presents as normal the sexual abuse of children". For these purposes, "sexual abuse" refers to sexual relations which are already prohibited by our law. This might be wide enough to catch the modern classic *Lolita* by Vladimir Nabokov, which portrays the sexual passion of an adult man for an under-aged girl. Despite the author's sensitivity and literary skill, the book might be said to encourage or at least to condone the illicit relationship that it depicts. Without a defence of artistic merit, such a book would be more vulnerable to criminal condemnation.

While it incorporated a number of the Fraser committee recommendations, the first pornography bill under the Mulroney Conservative government went miles further. Introduced in the spring of 1986, this bill's proposed prohibitions included "any visual matter showing vaginal, anal or oral intercourse, ejaculation, sexually violent behaviour, bestiality, incest, necrophilia, masturbation, *or other sexual activity* [emphasis added]." While the existing law suffered from vagueness, this bill achieved absurdity. During the past several years, many first-rate films have sensitively portrayed various forms of sexual intimacy. Conceivably, the provisions of this bill could imperil these films and any Canadian theatre-owner who sought to show them. To what extent, for example, would the portrayal of anal intercourse bring the film *Last Tango in Paris* within the scope of this bill?

When asked such questions, the then minister of justice, John Crosbie, pointed to another section of the bill under which "artistic merit" would constitute a defence. As already shown, this concept is too subjective to be reliable. In any event, the prospect of an ultimate acquittal is simply not good enough. The threat of prosecution, by itself, can chill the exercise of artistic freedom.

And what are we to make of the concluding words "...or other sexual activity"? I used to think of myself as worldly but, for the life of me, I have been unable to figure out what sexual activity these words include that does not appear in the rather detailed list that precedes them. A number of commentators have conjectured that, if enacted, the bill could prohibit the showing of hugging, kissing, or perhaps even holding hands. Was there ever a more magnificent example of the power-hoarding fallacy?

While the bill introduced by Mr. Crosbie's successor, Mr. Hnatyshyn, in the spring of 1987 removed this contentious phrase, the result was only marginally more satisfactory. Mr. Hnatyshyn sought to improve the definitions by making them a lot more explicit. Unfortunately, his bill was also deeply flawed.

Consider, for example, the prohibition in the Hnatyshyn bill of "any matter...that...promotes, encourages or advocates...a degrading act in a sexual context, including an act by which one person...ejaculates onto another person". In 1986 the Institute for the Advanced Study of Human Sexuality published a book entitled *Safe Sex in the Age of AIDS*. On page 55 there appears the following advice: "Obviously, there is no danger of infection as long as no bodily fluids are exchanged. Even if the man should ejaculate, there need be no risk as long as the semen does not come in contact with any orifice or cut or break in the skin.... *Thus, the man may ejaculate on the woman's back or between her breasts* [emphasis added]." Quite clearly, this material promotes, encourages, and advocates what the bill calls "degrading acts in a sexual context".

In response to the criticism that such material could be banned, Mr. Hnatyshyn noted that his bill contains not only the defence of artistic merit but also defences for "educational, scientific or medical purpose". Perhaps these latter defences might involve less subjectivity than the one for artistic merit, but there are problems with them too. Indeed, many of the arguments regarding the book *Show Me* focused on whether it was educational. An impressive array of experts appeared on *both* sides of the question. No self-respecting democracy should expect the creators and distributors of *Safe Sex in the Age of AIDS* to depend upon the fragile defences provided by Mr. Hnatyshyn's bill.

Unfortunately, even these defences would not be available if a person were charged in connection with "child pornography". Moreover, the breadth of the sections on child pornography are simply inexcusable. They would make it an offence to deal with material that, among other things, encourages or advocates most forms of sexual activity for persons under the age of eighteen. Thus a philosophical work like Plato's *The Symposium* might run afoul of the bill because of the speeches it contains which approve of sexual relations between men and boys. The same fate could be suffered by classic literature such as *The Decameron* and *The Satyricon* because of the comments they make about sexual activity among children. Perhaps most notable in this regard are some of the works of Dr. Spock and certain other modern clinicians who candidly advise parents that masturbation is healthy for their children. For some bizarre reason, masturbation was specifically included on the bill's taboo list of sexual activities.

Under the terms of Mr. Hnatyshyn's bill, those who produced or distributed such material could well be guilty of a criminal offence; they would have no recourse to the defences of artistic merit, educational, medical, or scientific purpose and they could face up to ten years in jail. It would take an exceptionally fertile imagination to conceive of an outcome as absurd as this.

When the librarians launched protests against the bill, the best that Mr. Hnatyshyn and his cohorts could offer them was an assurance that it was "extremely unlikely" that they would ever be charged. Perhaps so. But librarians and others can be forgiven if they don't want to run the risk. Governments in democratic societies are obliged to offer their citizens something more than an admonition to trust the authorities. Quite apart from philosophical considerations, there are practical problems with such advice. Even if our existing law enforcement personnel deserved complete trust, we could make no such judgments about their successors.

In any event, as indicated earlier, the enforcers of our existing obscenity laws have not behaved with uniformly good judgment. But, lest I be accused of berating the authorities in perpetuity for their misdeeds of the 1970s, 1960s, and earlier, I regret to assure the reader that there are more recent examples. As late as the fall of 1987, a police force in Alberta raided the offices of an *anti*-pornography group and seized its materials. Then the police announced that they were considering prosecution. In the mid-1980s, Ontario officials censored the anti-porn film *Not a Love Story*, made by the National Film Board. And in 1983 customs officials seized a film dealing with male masturbation even though the intended recipient of the film was the University of Manitoba Medical School. In order to recover the film, the medical educators had to initiate court action. A request for trust is no way, therefore, to overcome a defective definition.

Considerations of space preclude an exhaustive examination of the definitions which have surfaced on this subject. Suffice it for now to indicate that I have never seen one devoid of the kind of difficulties I have been describing. Indeed, I don't think such a definition is possible. Our language simply lacks the precision to make the requisite distinctions. Thus, the key question is which of the competing risks is the least dangerous to incur. Is it better (or less bad) to risk the suppression of works of art and important political statements? Or is it better (or less bad) to risk the greater proliferation of unredeemed trash?

At this stage of history, I believe it is more sensible to opt for the latter danger over the former one. In part, of course, this preference is based upon the need to protect, as much as possible, the concomitants of freedom of expression. It is also based upon considerable doubt about the harm that flows from even the vilest forms of pornography.

Many of the current claims concerning the harmfulness of pornography are based upon recent laboratory research in which men who were exposed to certain kinds of violent pornography responded more aggressively to women than did those men who were not so exposed. The problem with such research is that the comparisons are necessarily confined to the aggression which the experiment subjects have been specifically invited to commit in the laboratory setting, such as pressing a button to administer certain mild shocks. There is a world of difference, however, between invited aggression in the laboratory and uninvited aggression in society. There is some indication that violent hockey players, for example, are generally no more violent than anyone else in "real life". Moreover, there has been little measurement of the cathartic effects of exposure to pornography. For how many men does such material serve as an instrument to sublimate their aggressive propensities?

On the basis of his review of the research literature, Professor Jonathan Freedman, chairman of the psychology department at the University of Toronto, appended the following statement to a 1984 brief of the Canadian Civil Liberties Association:

> ...the particular work that has been done on the effects of pornography is fraught with problems and, in my opinion, tells us little about how exposure to pornography affects aggression or sexual crimes in the world outside the laboratory.... The basic situation is that we do not have sufficient scientific evidence to draw any clear conclusions...there is no evidence that pornography is harmful to women or to our society.

Psychologist Edward Donnerstein, whose research is often quoted by pro-censorship crusaders, has stated, "We can show a causal link between exposure to porn and effects on attitudes; but no one can show a causal link between exposure to porn and effects on behaviour."

While attitudes can influence behaviour, we don't live in a vacuum. All material is invariably subject to the competing influences of other material. Indeed, democrats have long believed that, in general, the answer to bad material is not suppression, but rather good material. Only in limited situations such as those involving a "clear and present danger" is there any basis to consider restricting freedom of expression for such purposes. If we could suppress material merely because of its detrimental impact on male attitudes towards women, what about other potentially harmful attitudes? Could we suppress Communist propaganda for undermining our attitudes about the value of preserving democracy? Could we suppress certain feminist material because it might arguably create negative attitudes about the institution of marriage? On this basis there might even be an argument to suppress the Bible. Couldn't the Inquisition, for example, be regarded as at least somewhat attributable to the attitudes created by generations of exposure to Scripture?

While pornography cannot in general be categorized as physically injurious, there is no difficulty describing it as aesthetically offensive.

We know, of course, that many people are repelled by sexually explicit material. Since they have just as much right to use the streets as those with stronger stomachs, the law might consider some measures to protect their sensibilities. In this connection, we should examine the distinction between public and private obscenity which was recommended by the Law Reform Commission of Canada. It suggested that the law might regulate what sellers could display in public but not what adults could consume in private. One of the most trenchant explications of this distinction emerged in an essay by American literary critic Irving Howe.

> If you want to go into one of those joints for five dollars and see what you see and do what you do there, I don't propose to stop you. But I see no reason why I or my kids should be *forced* to look, when we walk along the streets, at the stuff which delights you and disgusts me. Go to the porn movie but don't oblige me to look at its stills just because I'm walking by. Get your *Hustler* in a brown paper wrapper, but don't oblige me to be hustled by it just because there is a newsstand around my corner.

It is significant that, in the same essay, Professor Howe makes the following statement: "At this point in history, after all we have tasted of the age of totalitarianism, how can anyone suppose that the possible benefits of censorship could outweigh the probable dangers?"

Thus far, I have dealt with material in which the impugned sexual activity is *simulated*. The films or books simply depict the offensive behaviour. In recent years, however, an even newer form of pornography has emerged which reportedly involves the actual, not simulated, abuse of real people. The "snuff" films are said to feature real tortures and killings. Some "kiddie porn" is supposed to involve real children in actual sexual encounters.

To the extent that certain particularly repugnant crimes are committed for the purpose of titillating a potential audience or readership, there is an arguable case for a legal prohibition of the resulting film or literature. Indeed, this may be a variant of the "clear and present danger" exception. The knowledge that the films or pictures will enjoy a legally accessible market might serve as an incentive to the commission of the initial crime. In that sense, there could be a direct relationship between the distribution of the material and the criminal assault on the particular individuals. When such assaults are committed *for the purpose* of producing distributable material, there is an argument for making it unlawful knowingly to engage in such distribution. But, for the reasons indicated, it would be more dangerous to proscribe than to permit material involving *simulated* sexual abuse. Where such material is concerned, therefore, legal prohibition should not be attempted.

One practice that should clearly be eliminated is film censorship. Prior restraint—requiring things to be approved before they can be seen by the public—is a more pervasive intrusion than subsequent prosecution. It is one thing to render people accountable for the things they publish and show. But it is quite another matter to force them to have their material cleared before they are allowed to make it public. Nor is there a need for such prior restraint. The power of subsequent prosecution is a potent enough weapon. Its mere existence is likely to deter the greatest number of potential offenders. Anyone who is not so deterred is not likely to be significantly more deterred by the need to go to a censorship board.

The situation in Canada with regard to prior restraint is absurdly anomalous. The disclosure of the most delicate of defence secrets is subject only to criminal prosecution. There is no obligation on any of the media to clear such material with a censor before publishing it. Yet, in some jurisdictions, sex-related films are subject to pre-censorship. Does this mean, therefore, that sex is potentially more dangerous to society than a breach of national security?

Apart from legal weapons, there are political weapons such as those that were recommended against the purveyors of race hatred. Moreover, governments should explore alternative mechanisms for reducing the influence of pornography. If pornography is seen as encouraging violence against women, there are certain activities that discourage it—the counselling of rape victims to charge their assailants, the provision of shelter and assistance for battered women, the campaigns for laws against sexual discrimination, the lobbies for improved daycare facilities, and so on. The combined effect of these activities is to impress the dignity of women on the psyche of society, without significant risk to freedom of expression. Government should undertake, therefore, to increase its support of such activities.

In the fight to curtail the influence of pornography, education is probably the most over-stressed and under-used response. While education is often invoked as a facile panacea for the world's problems, it is often inadequately applied. Experience tells us that the right kind of education can make a significant impact on people's behaviour. It appears, for example, that the reports of the U.S. Surgeon General on nicotine and cancer may have actually brought about a significant reduction in smoking. Psychologist Edward Donnerstein has also told us that certain debriefing exercises appear to have reduced the belief, in the minds of many men, that women enjoy being raped. There is no reason why government could not undertake a much bigger effort to educate the community about the rights and dignity of women and children. This could be done by advertising in the media and instituting special programs in the schools. For such purposes, a little imagination and a healthy budget could go a long way.

Chapter Three

NATIONAL SECURITY

INTELLIGENCE

Prudent Precautions
versus Chilling Surveillance

In the summer of 1987, Ted Finn suddenly resigned his position as the first director of the newly created Canadian Security Intelligence Service (CSIS). The precipitating event was the revelation in a British Columbia courtroom that CSIS had used improper material for a wiretap warrant it had obtained during its investigation of the June 1985 Air India plane disaster. More than three hundred men, women, and children died when an Air India jet, bound from Canada for India, exploded mysteriously over the Atlantic Ocean near Ireland. The calamity was widely believed to have been an act of terrorism perpetrated by Sikh extremists seeking an independent state on the Indian subcontinent. The investigation led indirectly to the arrest, in 1986, of members of the British Columbia Sikh community for another offence entirely. But the disclosure of the improprieties in the CSIS wiretap warrants triggered the immediate release of the Sikh suspects and the staying of the charges against them.

While this incident was decisive in terminating the short-lived regime of Ted Finn, it was by no means the only controversy plaguing the new agency during the summer of 1987. Just a few weeks earlier, the watchdog Security Intelligence Review Committee (SIRC) had published its annual report, in which it criticized CSIS for "intruding on the lives and activities of too many Canadians". In SIRC's view, "CSIS over-estimates the likelihood of violence by some groups". The

67

review committee went on to cite the case of a CSIS target, a group that publishes a magazine dealing with a wide range of topics including the arts as well as social policy issues, from a "far left point of view". While acknowledging that some members of the group who have advocated violent action might rate investigation as individuals, SIRC argued that it was improper to target the group itself. (The significant thing about SIRC is that it was especially created by Parliament to monitor the activities of CSIS. As such, it enjoys access to a wide range of secret CSIS materials. Tripartisan in composition, SIRC is perceived as impartial and unbiased. Thus, its criticisms of CSIS forced Solicitor-General James Kelleher to promise action.)

The summer of 1987 also produced another scandal, this time involving a CSIS informant who was charged by the Quebec authorities with participation in the planting of bombs during a labour dispute involving the Confederation of National Trade Unions (CNTU). To top it off, the informant pleaded guilty.

A mere three years after its creation, CSIS showed signs of becoming immersed in the kind of hot water that had engulfed its predecessor, the RCMP Security Service. As long ago as the fall of 1977, Canadians learned that the security service of the RCMP had been involved in widespread illegalities including burglary, theft, arson, mail opening, and the invasion of tax files. And we were told that the encroachments perpetrated by our national security officials extended far beyond the realm of any genuine security threats. Among the reported targets of RCMP security surveillance were the following: the Canadian Union of Public Employees, the former Waffle faction of the New Democratic Party, the Parti Québécois, the National Farmers Union, and the National Black Coalition.

Of the foregoing targets, I am unaware of any that are foreign-controlled, terrorist, or totalitarian. According to no less an authority than former federal Solicitor-General Warren Allmand, the RCMP definition of "subversion" was wide enough to include "being militant against the status quo...on the left rather than on the right".

Indeed, there is some indication that these dubious propensities of the RCMP have their counterparts in other "national security" operations. During the turbulent 1960s, the American Federal Bureau of Investigation was involved in massive surveillance and disruptions of lawful civil rights and anti-war activity. Reputations were tarnished and lives were ruined. So pervasive were these FBI encroachments that even civil rights leader Martin Luther King, Jr. was subjected to electronic bugging. His well-known commitment to democracy and non-violence did not spare him these grotesque intrusions. On all these occasions, "national security" was the government's justification.

In the United Kingdom the national security agencies, M.I.5 and M.I.6, have frequently been hit by scandal. Similar reports concerning Australia's counterpart agency produced a massive royal commission in that country. The national security agency in Israel has been accused of misconduct and then committing perjury to cover it up. In the mid-1980s, it was revealed that French national security officials had sunk a boat belonging to the controversial Greenpeace Foundation. An innocent victim died in the encounter.

At this point, it is important to address some of the underlying assumptions which relate to this issue. In the troubled and dangerous world of today, it is not sensible to object to the performance of security and intelligence functions on behalf of the Canadian people and their institutions. A combination of Soviet expansionism, international terrorism, and our own unhappy experience with made-in-Canada terrorism has rendered foolish any suggestion that this country has no need of a national security service.

But the endorsement of the goal does not carry with it *carte blanche* for the means. The lessons of history both recent and past demonstrate all too well the ease with which national security has been invoked improperly to curtail personal liberty. Sometimes such invocation has served the interests of self-seeking despots; sometimes it has merely concealed the judgments of well-meaning zealots. Whatever the motives, the results have often meant a needless loss of liberty.

In Canada the federal government created a royal commission, under the chairmanship of Alberta superior court judge David McDonald, to conduct a probe into what went wrong with the RCMP's security service and what changes should be made to avoid such problems in the future. The commission deliberated from 1977 until 1981. It heard from scores of witnesses and examined mountains of files at a cost to the Canadian taxpayers of some ten million dollars. At the end of the road, the government accepted the commission's central recommendation. A new security service, CSIS, was created outside of the RCMP. And, unlike the RCMP, CSIS would be a civilian agency with no law enforcement responsibilities. Its sole function would be to gather and analyse intelligence.

To this day, there has been little disagreement with this approach. After the emergence of so many scandals, the RCMP came to be regarded as too recalcitrant to reform. It was seen as an unwieldy bureaucracy too set in its ways to respond to progressive ideas. Hence the widespread conviction that it would be better, once and for all, to divest the RCMP of these responsibilities.

The idea of a civilianized security operation generated the hope that intellectually sophisticated university graduates would be recruited to do the work. No longer bound by the entrenched military traditions of the RCMP, CSIS would be free to develop flexible selection programs. It could go to the universities to encourage their graduates to volunteer for service. Security intelligence work would cease to be the monopoly of those with a right-wing police mentality. Civilians could be trusted more than police to make the delicate distinctions that are so often required between subversives and dissenters.

And, in the event that CSIS was tempted to overstep the boundaries of its mandate, it would be held in check by a combination of safeguards. The role of the solicitor-general was clarified to include direct responsibility not only for the broad policies under which CSIS operates, but also for the application of those policies to its day-to-day activities. The most intrusive forms of surveillance would require CSIS to obtain judicial warrants. And there would be a committee (SIRC), independent of both the government and CSIS, which would conduct comprehensive monitoring to determine whether CSIS was behaving both lawfully and reasonably. The committee would be given access to a wide range of CSIS secrets and it would report its findings publicly to Parliament. The combined impact of civilianization, increased ministerial supervision, judicial warrants, and the independent review committee was supposed to usher in a new era of responsible activity in the arena of national security.

What went wrong? Why didn't the reforms work the way they were supposed to? SIRC has suggested that one problem was the slow pace of civilianization: CSIS relied heavily on officers who had served with the RCMP Security Service. In SIRC's view, these officers carried their habits with them when they transferred to the new agency. McDonald commission research director Peter Russell has suggested that, since the creation of CSIS, solicitors-general have not been in office long enough to assert themselves effectively over the new agency.

Remarkably, few observers have focused on civilianization itself. The central concept has managed to survive relatively unscarred from these recent controversies. I propose nevertheless to call it into question as a possible exacerbating factor. There are two aspects to the issue of civilianization which should be examined: functions and powers.

FUNCTIONS

CSIS was created in order to provide Canada with an early-warning system against dangers to its national security. The animating philosophy is the old adage that an ounce of prevention is worth a pound of cure. Better to head off spies, terrorists, and revolutionaries than to suffer the damage they can cause. According to an author quoted in the McDonald commission report: "The primary objective of an efficient intelligence service must be to prevent any insurgency or terrorism developing beyond the incipient stage. Hence a high quality intelligence service is required *long before the insurgency surfaces.*"

A civilian intelligence agency essentially gathers intelligence. It does not make policy or enforce the law. That is for politicians and police respectively. Virtually all of the investigations the CSIS Act contemplates are designed to serve intelligence rather than law enforcement purposes. Since the goal of an intelligence investigation is to assess, understand, and predict, the idea is to discover almost everything there is to know about the targets, including their most intimate habits and beliefs.

The problem is that it is very difficult to conduct such pervasive surveillance without casting a chill over political liberty and personal privacy. At the very least, many people are likely to *feel* that they are under surveillance. This will particularly apply to those who have unconventional opinions and ideologies. If such people think their organizations are infested with spies, they will not speak freely at their meetings. If they think they are being followed, they will not attend certain functions. Thus, there could be a substantial reduction in their enjoyment of their fundamental freedoms. A viable state of civil liberties requires not only the reality of their existence, but also the experience of their enjoyment.

By contrast to an intelligence investigation, a law enforcement investigation is a more limited exercise. It is designed essentially to collect evidence for the purpose of prosecution. Its scope is limited to gathering evidence of crime; its duration is limited to the period before trial. As a consequence, the law enforcement investigation is much less threatening to civil liberties.

The further security surveillance is removed from the discipline of law enforcement, the greater the risk of blurring the line between improper subversion and legitimate dissent. The virtue of the law enforcement approach, for these purposes, is its focus on gathering evidence of relatively definable crime. So long as illegal conduct is the subject of investigative activity, there is less risk of snooping on legitimate dissenters. But when security surveillance is divorced from law enforcement, investigations are more likely to involve vaguer, broader, and less definable matters. This is what could imperil legitimate dissent.

Small wonder that an agency divorced from law enforcement would run into the kind of trouble that CSIS has recently attracted. A law enforcement agency would be less likely than a purely intelligence-gathering agency to employ improper materials for obtaining wiretap warrants. Law enforcement agencies must anticipate intense scrutiny of their material by partisan defence counsel in open court. They would never expect comparably rough treatment by impartial judges at the in camera hearings for their warrant applications. The defence lawyer would be trying to discredit the agency's material; the judge would simply be reviewing it. Moreover, the defence counsel would likely know a lot more about the case than would a judge. For all of these reasons, the anticipated use of material for subsequent prosecutions would help to restrain the snooping agency from engaging in conduct that would blow their case.

Such considerations could well apply also to the case of the CSIS informant who was involved in the bomb conspiracy during the Quebec labour dispute. Had CSIS been using this informant in order to acquire evidence for a prosecution, it might have been far more careful to ensure that there would be no embarrassing disclosures. Indeed, SIRC specifically criticized CSIS for its insensitivity to this man's "potential...to become involved in illegal activities". The problem is that intelligence-gathering unrelated to a prosecutorial outcome is less likely to be concerned about the appearance of propriety. In short, the agency does not as readily expect to be found out.

This is not to say that such improprieties do not occur within the framework of law enforcement operations. Obviously, they have. My point simply is that, as between a law enforcement and an intelligence-gathering operation, the latter is more likely to attract such troubles because it has less incentive to avoid them. Indeed, that's why the CSIS scandals are so significant. Despite four years of public hearings into RCMP illegalities, there still wasn't enough care taken to avoid such problems. Unfortunately, neither SIRC nor the minister even considered to what extent civilianization might have been an exacerbating factor.

The advocates of civilianization have argued that it would have been folly to leave the security service within the very RCMP that had committed so much misconduct. Even if the security service had been largely dissociated from the criminal investigation branch, neither had managed to avoid serious impropriety. As an institution, the RCMP was considered too large and rigid to be entrusted with the job of reform. But these arguments overlooked what was likely the main reason that Mountie misconduct survived as long as it did. For many years, the RCMP had been such a sacred cow that few would have dared to restrain or control it. In the wake of the McDonald revelations, however, there was reason to hope that this situation would change. A significant factor contributing to this hope was the useful set of proposals made by the McDonald commission for the supervision and control of security operations—such as the requirement for judicial warrants, the expanded level of ministerial involvement, and the establishment of an outside review committee. If such safeguards had been imposed upon the RCMP, it might no longer have been the same institution.

Following the revelations of all the abuses committed by the RCMP's American counterpart, the FBI, the U.S. authorities moved in the diametrically opposite direction from what was done in Canada. Instead of creating a civilian security agency divorced from law enforcement, the Americans amalgamated the FBI's domestic security investigations with its general criminal investigative division. The "express purpose" of this move, in the words of the then FBI director, was to handle domestic security investigations as much as possible "like all other criminal cases". The narrower focus of criminal investigations was seen as less likely to intrude on lawful dissent.

While trouble may be inherent in the very nature of security and intelligence operations, it is significant that the security intelligence activities of the FBI were relatively scandal-free for about seven years after the reforms of the early and mid-1970s. By comparison, the problems plaguing CSIS appear to have existed almost from the time the agency was created. This contrast becomes all the more striking when we consider that, because of America's pivotal position in the world, its intelligence agencies must have been under much more intense pressure than their Canadian counterparts to employ dubious tactics. These experiences suggest that Canada might have been better off to have moved intelligence work and law enforcement closer together rather than farther apart.

In any event, we never had to choose between leaving these functions in the RCMP or giving them to an all-civilian agency. There remain alternatives to both these solutions. Perhaps, for example, CSIS might acquire law enforcement functions for security-related offences. If that were done, Canada would have two federal police forces—one handling security matters such as espionage, sabotage, and terrorism, and one handling more regular criminal investigations relating to such areas as customs, excise, and drug violations. An alternative approach might entail leaving the domestic security work within the RCMP, but, like the situation with the FBI, integrating it more fully with the criminal investigation branch. If that were done, CSIS would function only in a tightly defined area of counter-intelligence against foreign-controlled security threats. Whatever approach is favoured, recruitment could still change in order to attract more qualified personnel.

At this point, I am obliged to acknowledge that, in the case of security threats emanating from foreign powers, such as espionage, there is an argument for a certain amount of intelligence-centred surveillance that does not culminate in prosecution. A criminal trial could undermine the viability of our counter-intelligence operations. It could uncover what needs to be undercover. And it would do so without commensurate benefit. The jailing of a few Soviet spies, for example, would hardly dent the Soviet capacity for espionage. Foreign diplomats—a frequent target of our counter-intelligence efforts—are, of course, immune from prosecution.

Such considerations do not as readily apply to other security threats beyond espionage. Terrorists and revolutionaries are much more vulnerable than spies to the therapy of law enforcement. The prosecution and incarceration of a few FLQ terrorists, for example, could and did inflict mortal wounds on that organization's activities. While there is sometimes an intelligence component even in more conventional criminal investigations, the goal, sooner or later, is to prosecute. Significantly, the regular criminal law appears to apply intrusive techniques such as wiretapping and electronic bugging for law enforcement rather than for pure intelligence purposes. But the CSIS Act nowhere makes such a distinction. Home-grown revolutionaries are subject to the same intelligence-centred focus as KGB agents.

Although there is a need for greater flexibility in responding to certain foreign-controlled security dangers, the agency handling them should also have law enforcement functions. Even if the agency focuses generally on tactics other than prosecution, the fact that it may have to prosecute at some stage could diminish some of the propensities to take questionable shortcuts. This would be in the interests of civil liberties.

POWERS

The goal of civilianization is preventive intelligence. The means is the capacity to spy. This has led to the creation of powers so broad that Canadian citizens are lawfully vulnerable to electronic bugging, surreptitious searches, mail opening, and the invasion of their confidential records even when there isn't the slightest suggestion of any illegality.

Under the Act, CSIS is potentially entitled to use all of these intrusive surveillance techniques to monitor "activities...in support of acts of serious violence for the purpose of achieving a political objective within Canada or a foreign state." Those words are broad enough to have permitted intrusive eavesdropping on Canadian citizens who raised money for the state of Israel following the Yom Kippur invasion. It could similarly imperil those who send financial help to the rebels in El Salvador or Namibia, or even the Contras in Nicaragua. Even if such "activities" are lawful, open, and free of foreign control, the law makes those who conduct them potentially vulnerable.

By virtue of another sub-section, the CSIS Act could permit all of these intrusive surveillance techniques for "activities...intended ultimately to lead to the destruction or overthrow by violence of the constitutionally established system of government in Canada." How in the world are the CSIS operatives supposed to get evidence of "ultimate" intentions? Can the word "ultimately" deal with any point between now and the end of time? It is obvious that this language could encourage speculation about the hereafter, rather than evidence from the here and now, to serve as the prerequisite for intrusive surveillance. These words could well encourage CSIS to make extravagant predictions of future violence. The problem is that the more speculative the exercise becomes, the greater the risk of intruding on completely lawful behaviour.

Intrusive surveillance can also be used to monitor "foreign influenced activities...that are detrimental to the interests of Canada and are clandestine or deceptive". "Influence" covers a lot of territory. If the Canadian Civil Liberties Association draws inspiration from the American Civil Liberties Union, does this mean that the CCLA is "foreign influenced"? What are the limits of "detrimental"? Suppose certain Canadian citizens were employed by a foreign corporation involved in commercial negotiations with the government of Canada. Since it might be in the interests of Canada to sell high and buy low, would any opposite interest be considered "detrimental"? Could those serving such interests have their conversations bugged, premises searched, mail opened, and records invaded? The requirement that the targeted activities be "clandestine or deceptive" may not adequately diminish the danger. There is an element of the "deceptive" in many commercial transactions.

Moreover, there are real doubts whether these dangers are sufficiently diminished by the subsequent exemption for "lawful advocacy, protest or dissent". It is not clear if lawful activities such as fund-raising or commercial negotiations would be covered by this exemption.

With such vague and broad powers that exceed any genuine security threat, it is not surprising to learn from SIRC that CSIS is "intruding on the lives and activities of too many Canadians". The breadth of its surveillance mandate virtually invites CSIS to spy excessively.

This is not to overlook the action taken in late 1987 by Solicitor-General James Kelleher on the recommendation of a special committee he had established to review SIRC's damaging report. To his credit, Kelleher abolished the counter-subversion branch that CSIS had been operating. This branch had been the one involved in much of the dubious surveillance. While we should welcome Mr. Kelleher's action, we must also question whether it goes far enough. Even if this branch no longer exists, the powers it had remain available to CSIS as a whole. It is important, therefore, to examine not only the details of certain operations but also the central philosophy from which they spring.

Some supporters of the central philosophy in the CSIS Act have acknowledged that preventive intelligence gathering does create risks to civil liberties. In their view, however, the risks are worthwhile. The damage inflicted by a breach of security can be so devastating to the peace of the community and even to the enjoyment of civil liberties that prevention is seen as the best of the available options.

But how much security is actually provided by all this preventive intelligence gathering? The experience of the FBI is instructive here as well. Comprehensive audits of the FBI performed by the independent General Accounting Office (GAO) of the U.S. Congress found that, despite a relatively unencumbered mandate, "generally the FBI did not report advance knowledge of planned violence". In 1974, for example, the GAO estimated that the FBI obtained advance knowledge of its targets' activities in only about 2 per cent of all its investigations. And most of this knowledge related to completely lawful activities such as speeches, meetings, and peaceful demonstrations. According to a member of the U.S. Senate Intelligence Committee, "the FBI only provided...a handful of substantiated cases—out of the thousands of Americans investigated—in which preventive intelligence produced warning of terrorist activity". And a former White House official who had relevant experience declared that "advance intelligence about dissident groups [was not]...of much help" in coping with the urban violence of the 1960s.

These findings induced U.S. law-makers to restrict the scope of the FBI's preventive intelligence gathering. Where certain foreign influences are concerned, a statute enacted in 1978 stipulates that electronic bugging against citizens and resident aliens within the United States requires probable cause to believe that their activities "involve or are about to involve" a federal crime.

Since 1972 U.S. bugging operations against essentially indigenous security threats have been conducted entirely under a general criminal law which requires probable cause to believe that certain *actual crimes* are involved. When intrusive surveillance requires evidence of current misdeeds rather than predictions of future ones, it is less likely that legitimate dissenters will be victimized. American experience suggests also that national security would not be significantly endangered.

The U.S. Supreme Court did declare, as long ago as 1972, that a broader bugging power could be constitutionally sustained for domestic intelligence purposes, but Congress has declined to act. Even more significant, not a single president since 1972 has even requested a broadening of this bugging law. In this respect at least, the government of Canada has achieved something remarkable. It has made Ronald Reagan look like a civil libertarian!

While not all intrusive surveillance has been equally circumscribed, there is a discernible trend towards imposing such restrictions in the United States. In an increasing number of situations, Americans cannot be subjected to intrusive surveillance unless illegality is indicated. In view of such developments in the leading country of the Western alliance, it ill behoves Canada to adopt the kind of posture reflected in the CSIS Act.

In my opinion, intrusive surveillance should not be permitted against Canadian citizens and permanent residents unless, at the very least, a serious security-related *breach of the law* is involved. Since law-breaking involves not only completed acts but also attempts, counselling, aiding, abetting, and even conspiracies, this should afford enough preventive scope to the intelligence-gathering exercise. Indeed, there is considerable risk that the inclusion of conspiracies could still cast too wide a net. Perhaps, for such purposes, intrusive surveillance should require evidence not only of a conspiracy but also of some overt conduct in furtherance of it.

The stipulation "serious" is designed to avoid the potential trivialization of security surveillance. Suppose, for example, there were a plan to throw rotten tomatoes at the prime minister. Or a conspiracy to pour discolouring fluids on the parliamentary carpet. While such activities may well warrant a law enforcement response, they hardly justify the intrusive surveillance of a security operation. For such purposes, the targeted misconduct should involve serious security-related law-breaking such as sabotage, espionage, or serious violence impairing the operations of government. While some forms of intrusive surveillance against citizens and permanent residents should require even additional conditions, none should be allowed on the basis of anything less.

There are some situations where the standards for surveillance need not be as high. The legal status of the proposed target is a relevant consideration. This country owes its greatest protections to its citizens and permanent resident aliens. It need not incur the same obligations to those who are visiting temporarily as it does to those who are staying indefinitely. There may also be practical reasons for a difference in investigative thresholds. Visitors could well be here for only brief periods—weeks or perhaps even days. That might not afford enough time for our security agents to acquire the kind of preliminary evidence of unlawful conduct that I believe should be required for intrusive surveillance of citizens and permanent residents. Moreover, experience indicates that, compared with citizens and residents, a significantly higher proportion of visitors is involved in foreign intelligence activity.

It is important to resist the tantalizing arguments of those who urge a false egalitarianism. Some have suggested, for example, that it is unfair to make distinctions between residents and visitors. Their solution is to propose low standards for *everyone*. Such an argument was advanced, for example, by the senate committee that made recommendations on the government's first security bill (C-157). Yet the committee did not abide by its own argument. Its report proposed that citizens and permanent residents be exempted as targets for the collection of certain intelligence relating to the activities of foreign states.

Lower standards are also permissible for less intrusive techniques of surveillance. Where methods such as watching, trailing, interviewing, and source-checking are involved, less exacting standards could apply.

Apart from those forms of surveillance that require judicial warrants, the statute does not specify what level of authorization is needed for the various levels of investigation. Since any state surveillance involves some level of encroachment on the vital values of privacy and liberty, the decision to engage in it should not be left so completely to the exercise of bureaucratic, and possibly arbitrary, discretion.

The standards for surveillance should also be influenced by the purpose for which the surveillance is exercised. Potential informants, for example, may have to be subjected to some form of investigation in order to establish their credibility. But it would obviously be inappropriate for them to be susceptible to the amount and duration of surveillance that might be employed in the case of those who are actually suspected of misconduct. Different standards might also be applied in the case of security checks for those applying to hold classified government jobs. In such cases, of course, the applicants might be asked to consent to the investigation.

The Techniques of Intrusive Surveillance

Without question, electronic surveillance is one of the most intrusive of the investigative techniques. Unlike the physical search of premises, the electronic bug cannot readily discriminate. It tends to overhear everyone within earshot—the guilty, the suspected, and the innocent alike. Elsewhere I note the statistics on the amount of innocent privacy which is invaded by law enforcement bugging. In the area of security and intelligence, the dragnet character of the technique is even greater.

While federal law enforcement bugs from 1968 until 1970 in the United States lasted an average of 13.5 days and overheard an average of 55 people and 900 conversations, the average national security bug during the same period in that country lasted from 78.3 to 290.7 days and overheard somewhere between 5,500 and 15,000 people per year.

Unfortunately, the Canadian statistics do not include the number of people and conversations intercepted. But they do reveal the length of the bugging operations. Here too a similar pattern emerges. In 1978 the average duration of a law enforcement bug was 73.5 days, and, in 1983, 68 days. In the case of federal security bugs, the surveillance lasted as long as 244.7 days in 1978 and 253 days in 1983.

In view of this enormous capacity to intrude, we should ask to what extent the security benefits derived are worth the privacy costs incurred. In security matters, the impact of bugging is especially difficult to measure. Unlike normal law enforcement, the prosecution and incarceration of offenders are not often the object of the exercise. Thus, there are few tangible bench-marks by which to judge these eavesdropping techniques. What we do have are the opinions of several experts. Significantly, a number of them have expressed considerable doubt about the necessity of security bugging. Morton Halperin, a former member of the U.S. National Security Council, made the following statement: "In my judgment, such surveillance has extremely limited value and can in no sense be called vital to the security of the United States...the American government has many other sources of information of significantly greater value." Former U.S. Attorney-General Ramsey Clark contended that, if all security bugs were turned off, the impact on security would be "absolutely zero".

In the event that the involvement of these two commentators with the American Civil Liberties Union generates some skepticism about their judgments, we should note the similar assessments from people at the other end of the ideological spectrum. Consider, for example, the remarks of former FBI Director J. Edgar Hoover:

> I don't see what all the excitement is about. I would have no hesitance in discontinuing all techniques—technical coverage (i.e., wiretapping), microphones, trash covers, mail covers, etc. While it might handicap us, I doubt they are as valuable as some believe and none warrant FBI being used to justify them.

Mr. Hoover's associate who was in charge of these matters, the late William Sullivan, recommended a few years ago that all security bugs and taps be turned off for a period of three years in order properly to assess their value. He would not likely have made such a proposal if he thought that the results would create a serious danger to American security.

In this connection, there is on the public record a remarkable statement made by the man whose own surveillance activities helped to drive him from the most powerful office in the world, former U.S. President Richard Nixon: "They [the taps] never helped us. Just gobs and gobs of material: gossip and bullshitting.... The tapping was a very unproductive thing. I've always known that. At least, it's never been useful in any operation I've ever conducted."

In view of the misgivings expressed by these experts, it is especially disquieting to examine the breadth of the security bugging power in the CSIS Act. Why should citizens and permanent residents be subject to a greater bugging power, for security purposes, than what is already contained in the Criminal Code? At the moment, the Code potentially permits electronic surveillance for the investigation of more than forty criminal offences including high treason, intimidating Parliament, spying, sabotage, hijacking, murder, wounding, arson, possession of explosives, kidnapping, robbery, extortion, and even conspiracies to commit these offences both in Canada and elsewhere. It would be hard to imagine a serious threat to our national security that has been omitted from the list. On the contrary, it might be argued that, in many ways, the bugging power in the Criminal Code exceeds the bounds of demonstrated necessity. But where citizens and permanent residents are concerned, what is the need for anything more?

Surreptitious entry is a particularly insidious form of intrusion. It is designed essentially to permit the conduct of an intelligence probe. The security officers rummage around the premises in search of information. Unlike the law enforcement bugging operation and the search-and-seizure exercise under the Criminal Code, the target of a surreptitious entry is unlikely to learn what has happened. The goal of the operation is rarely the prosecution of offenders; it is usually the acquisition of intelligence.

Although it is difficult to compare the intrusiveness of certain techniques, there are some respects in which a surreptitious entry for the purpose of a search is more dangerous than one which is committed to install a bug. In the latter case, the intruders can minimize the length of time they spend on the property. As soon as they plant the bug, they can leave. In the former case, however, they may have to linger for substantial periods until they find what they are seeking. But the longer they linger, the greater the risk of a confrontation with the owner or occupant. Such a confrontation could well go beyond the invasion of privacy. It could imperil life and limb.

In my view, the only argument that might currently be made for so insidious and dangerous a power against citizens and permanent residents is in circumstances where there are reasonable grounds to believe that a serious security-related breach of the law is being directed by a foreign power. Since it would often be unwise to prosecute those who are involved in international wrongdoing, there might be some justification in such situations for Canada to have some flexible powers of surreptitious intelligence-gathering. Against essentially indigenous or domestic security threats, however, it is much harder to make a case for such a power. Where they are concerned, the power of entry should more often be designed to gather evidence for prosecution, by way of either electronic bugging or search and seizure. In the domestic cases, however, the targets should generally be told about the surveillance.

Again, my views are sustained by the American experience. American law does not now permit surreptitious entry, for intelligence purposes, against an essentially domestic threat. Nor has there been any concerted attempt to enact such a power in that country.

Until the CSIS Act, mail opening in the course of post was prohibited almost entirely. Although it is now allowed for security intelligence purposes, the controversies that preceded the new law continue to nag at us. How far can *any* mail opening power be justified?

On the strength of its extensive probe into past mail opening activities, the McDonald commission concluded that the intelligence produced by these operations was of "only marginal value". In view of the fact that the RCMP had admitted to hundreds of illegal mail openings over at least thirty years, this was hardly the stuff on which to base a new power of surreptitious surveillance.

While the law had already permitted forms of surveillance more intrusive than mail opening, this could not constitute a basis for yet another encroachment on civilian privacy. Even though the CSIS Act may represent Canada's first comprehensive legislation in this area, our society does not have the luxury of starting from scratch. We are in the middle of history and not at the beginning. Since the operative standard of democratic government is no additional encroachment without justification, the onus remains on the proponents of mail opening to demonstrate its necessity. If anything, the existence of more intrusive techniques might occasion some valid arguments against such techniques, but this alone cannot justify the creation of a new power.

Nor do I overlook the argument that emerged a number of years ago. Why is it permissible to obtain a search warrant to seize a letter immediately after its delivery to the intended recipient, but not moments before while it is in the course of post? The answer is that the investigation of delivered mail is more likely to be known to the targets. It will require a personal visit to their premises. Their likely knowledge of the investigation will serve to reduce the incidence of abuse. Undelivered mail, however, is much more susceptible to surreptitious interception.

In view of the intrusiveness of mail opening and the failure to demonstrate a need for it, there is a strong argument for having no such power in our society. Again, however, a fear of international hazards creates a more cautious response. Even if yesterday's benefits were only marginal, tomorrow's could be greater. While I would generally repudiate such conjecture as a basis for increased police powers, I am aware of how our dangerous world can create novel situations with unexpected suddenness. Thus, there is an argument for having in place a sufficient panoply of statutory powers in order to meet the unanticipated crises of the international order.

On this basis, I can conceive of one security situation in which there might be an argument for a power to open the mail of a citizen or permanent resident—where there are reasonable grounds to believe there is a serious security-related breach of the law directed by a foreign power. But whatever the arguments about foreign threats, and apart possibly from dangerous substances and contraband, it is hard to justify the mail opening power which the Act permits against essentially domestic threats.

In order to plan intelligently and to provide a complex level of services, the government collects mountains of information about us—assets, debts, income, employment, aptitudes, health, ancestry, and so on. So vital are these data to government operations that the law often requires us to furnish the facts the government seeks. In many such situations, the balance between personal privacy and the government's "need to know" is a legal obligation on the data collectors to keep confidential the contents of individual files. We are assured that the use of the information will be confined to the purpose for which it was collected.

However, the Privacy Act generally permits government agencies, at their own discretion, to turn over personal information in their custody to those who are conducting unrelated investigations. This gives CSIS and all other investigative agencies a substantial ability to invade citizen privacy. At the very least, such access to this information should require a judicial warrant. It is surprising that the consequent incongruity has attracted so little attention. Our law requires a judicial warrant to invade residential privacy but not informational privacy.

Fortunately, the Privacy Act does carve out some important exceptions. The power to turn over personal information to investigative agencies does not apply to particularly sensitive subjects such as the material in unemployment insurance and income tax files. But the CSIS Act opens even this door. It creates an opportunity for CSIS, on judicial warrant, to get at most of the information which is blocked by the Privacy Act. Again, I believe that even the custodians of our national security should not be allowed such access to the personal information of citizens and permanent residents without, at a minimum, reasonable grounds to believe there is a serious security-related breach of the law involved.

There is some personal information in the hands of the government which is so delicate that, even in the circumstances of such law-breaking, it should be withheld from the security service. The McDonald commission recommended, and the Act adopted, such an immunity for census information. The commission made a particularly persuasive case for this exemption:

> While such [census] information may not be more personal than that found in some other federal data banks, the tradition in this country has been very strongly in favour of complete confidentiality of census returns. The unqualified guarantee of confidentiality helps to overcome the reluctance of Canadians to respond to inquiries about personal matters....

There is a strong argument for applying this reasoning also to the Income Tax Act. In order to levy a proper tax upon us, the revenue authorities must have the opportunity to probe deeply into our circumstances. In order to keep these intrusions to a tolerable minimum, the Act requires us to complete an annual return in which we take the responsibility for disclosing what is relevant. By and large, this works well to limit the involvement of the revenue agents in our daily lives. But a key reason for this success is the taxpayers' confidence that the data they reveal are not generally available for anything but tax purposes. Indeed, such a restriction has existed in the law since the inception of the income tax.

It is not difficult, therefore, to understand the public indignation which was provoked by the revelations of RCMP access to tax data for non-tax purposes. These intrusions were considered nothing short of a breach of faith with the Canadian taxpayer. According to the Mc-Donald criteria, there is no reason why tax data should be substantially more accessible than census data. No adequate case has been made for a statutory power of surreptitious access to tax records for non-tax purposes. The RCMP intrusions reportedly yielded no security benefits great enough to outweigh the obvious civil liberties costs. Any breakdown in the tax system of confidential self-assessment is likely to precipitate a larger measure of government intrusion in our private lives, as more people falsify their returns in order to hide information they do not want revealed to other authorities. That is why it is so crucially important for taxpayers to believe that their returns will be treated in confidence.

A Word about Informing and Infiltrating

Although they represent perhaps the most prevalent of the surveillance techniques, secret informants are especially threatening to personal privacy and political liberty. Unlike physical searches and electronic bugs, informants not only spy but also participate. If they are sufficiently charismatic, they can distort the political activities of the groups they infiltrate. Indeed, they might even provoke some of the very illegalities they have been assigned to detect.

Apart from professional police undercover agents, informants are often unstable and disreputable. For example, Sara Jane Moore, who attempted to assassinate former U.S. President Gerald Ford, was an FBI informant. The untrustworthy character of many informants has led the intelligence agencies to assign several to the same place without their being aware of each other's identity. In the result, much of their work has involved spying on each other. At one time the FBI infiltration of the American Communist Party was so extensive that there was 1 informant for every 5.7 genuine members.

In those cases where money is the chief incentive, informants may be tempted to distort and exaggerate in order to maintain their value. If nothing much is happening, the intelligence agency is not likely to go on paying them. Financial rewards also create an incentive for informants to become *agents provocateurs*.

Despite all these dangers, the CSIS Act is remarkably devoid of attempts to regulate the activities of informants. No doubt the defenders of the status quo will be quick to adopt the reasoning of the U.S. Supreme Court: "The risk of being...betrayed by an informer...is the kind of risk we necessarily assume whenever we speak". At most this argument might militate against the amount of regulation over informants as compared to other forms of surveillance. But it cannot justify the virtual absence of regulation.

It is anomalous for the Act to specify that judicial warrants are needed for some forms of intrusive surveillance while it contains virtually nothing on approving the use of informants. A technique at once so intrusive, threatening, and in need of such political sophistication should be accompanied by statutory requirements as to whose approval will be needed to allow it and under what circumstances. Even if the law does not require the permission of a judge, it should require approval from identifiable officials at the highest level. There is simply too much at stake to leave to the vagaries of bureaucratic discretion.

The difficulties in targeting are matched by the difficulties in determining how to respond to the questionable behaviour of covert informants. In order to gain the trust of the targets, the informants may feel impelled to commit unlawful acts. Yet, if they succumb to such pressures, we will have a situation in which the government is subsidizing illegal behaviour. The CSIS Act is silent on the question of misconduct by informants. This could create the impression that informants will be treated no differently than anyone else if they commit unlawful acts. But those who live in the real world simply won't believe it. We know that, in exchange for information, people are often let off the hook for some of their misdeeds. Thus, the issue is not whether informant misconduct might be excused, but rather what conditions and criteria will influence the judgment. Today these decisions are being made in the bowels of the security service and government either arbitrarily or on the basis of guidelines that have not become the subject of public scrutiny and debate. The dangers to civil liberties and the rule of law require a different approach to this thorny problem.

Such issues should not be left so completely to bureaucratic discretion. If informant misconduct is to be excused by the exercise of prosecutorial leniency, the most stringent, publicly accessible criteria should apply. Acts of violence should elicit the most severe response and, to whatever extent there is a question of non-violent illegalities, the informant should be judged more harshly for instigating them than for merely joining in.

There also has to be some system for measuring relative harms. In order for infiltrators to be excused, their misdeeds should be of a clearly lesser magnitude than what they have been assigned to watch and detect. Obviously, laws involving moral turpitude would require more sacrosanct treatment than regulatory ones. Driving over the speed limit, for example, would not create the same kind of difficulty as participating in a break-in.

By the same token, there should be much stricter standards in those situations involving a victim. Perhaps consideration might be given to excusing an infiltrator's participation in illegality when there is a particularly strong basis to believe that, if the victims knew, they would consent. Such a possibility existed recently, for example, when a police infiltrator in a racist organization allegedly helped to smear swastikas on the properties of some black and Jewish people. If the property owners had known that the infiltrator's participation in the vandalism was designed to apprehend their racist tormentors, and if compensation had been available, they might well have consented.

In any case, there should be specific prohibitions against undue interference with the lawful activities of the persons and groups which have been targeted for infiltration. Just as electronic bugs should not be intercepting privileged communications, so too should informants not be intercepting them. In the event that informants unavoidably become privy to such a communication, they should be prohibited from disseminating it. If they become witnesses in criminal prosecutions, the crown attorney should be obliged to reveal to the court their role as informants, together with an accounting of the money paid to them for such purposes. In that way, the jury would be able to assess the weight of their testimony and the accused would be able to seek redress for any wrongful injury the informants might have caused.

It is time also that Canadian law created a clear defence of entrapment that would acquit accused people whose misconduct was provoked by undercover agents in circumstances where there was a reasonable doubt that the offence would otherwise have been committed. The creation of such a defence might serve to deter informants from acting as *agents provocateurs*. If nothing else, a defence of entrapment would reduce the damage which government-supported illegality inevitably inflicts on the administration of justice.

The Follow-up to Surveillance

Even the most cynical Canadians were shocked when the McDonald commission revealed that the RCMP Security Service had files on 800,000 people. The sheer volume staggered our imaginations. It was hard to believe that so much material was required for genuine security purposes. It was much easier to believe that the RCMP had been spying extensively on the private lives of innocent, law-abiding Canadians.

The revelations had to provoke paranoid reactions in many people. What did the Mounties have on us? Our extra-marital affairs? Those indiscreet marijuana parties? What did they know about those respectable people who have been trying to hide their radical past or homosexual present?

It is difficult for the intelligence-gathering exercise to discriminate between what material is important and what is not. Once an authorized investigation begins, there will be a tendency for the security agency to accumulate all of the information it can. Moreover, since the investigators cannot always assess the relevance of every piece of data, they will be tempted to retain everything they acquire. Very likely, therefore, vast amounts of irrelevant personal information will find its way into the agency's files. Yet, as the American Civil Liberties Union has observed, such information may well be "the single most effective tool for political manipulation at the disposal of the government".

Beyond the question of political manipulation, there is the question of elementary fairness. Human dignity is diminished to the extent that facts about people pass out of their control. Periodically the question is asked, "If you have nothing to hide, why worry?" In the first place, those who have nothing to hide are probably leading awfully dull lives. In the second place, the very question is improper. It assumes the permissibility of intruding on people unless some reason can be found for not doing so. For democrats, however, the position must be reversed. People should be protected from intrusion unless a valid reason is provided for allowing it.

For these reasons, I regret the relative absence of effort in the CSIS Act to restrict the retention of information. While there are restrictions on what may lawfully be disclosed, there is an unavoidable risk that what comes in could get out. The Act should be amended to include criteria for the retention of surveillance material. Such criteria should articulate a test of relevance for whatever intelligence or law enforcement functions might be appropriate. Moreover, there should be time limits on such retention (a shorter period for domestic than for foreign purposes), and an explicit requirement for the destruction of the material and, where appropriate, entire files that are not necessary or relevant for such authorized purposes. Since computers render information instantly retrievable, the statute should contain the minimum criteria for how the material should be stored, who might have access to it, and how such access should be allowed.

Suppose a surveillance operation revealed that the targets were, or were soon likely to become, involved in a serious security-related breach of the law. Obviously there must be a power to counteract such misconduct. Of course, there is always the power to arrest and prosecute. But there are times when these responses might not be considered appropriate. The evidence might not be sufficient to produce a conviction in court, or the government might prefer to wait until the security agency could penetrate to even higher echelons of the conspiratorial operations. An early prosecution could blow the cover of informants and infiltrators.

Not surprisingly, the 1975 government mandate to the RCMP Security Service included a directive to maintain internal security "by...deterring, preventing, and countering individuals and groups" when their activities fell within the specified criteria. In practice, this mandate served as authority for some pretty sordid "dirty tricks". There is evidence, for example, that the notorious RCMP break-in against L'Agence Presse Libre du Québec was designed to create disruption among the FLQ and its sympathizers. We also know now that it was an RCMP official who issued the supposed FLQ communiqué denouncing former FLQ ideologue Pierre Vallières. In an earlier renunciation of violence and terrorism, Mr. Vallières had urged his followers to join the more moderate and democratic Parti Québécois. But the RCMP feared that an influx of potential terrorists and Marxists would undermine the democratic and law-abiding character of that party. In another situation, the RCMP circulated among members of a Trotskyist group some psychiatric data about one of their leaders. The material was supposed to discredit him and thereby sow dissension within the Trotskyist organization.

In these situations, the RCMP was acting not simply as investigator but also as judge. It was deciding guilt and imposing sentences. Moreover, it was tampering with the democratic political processes. While the fake communiqué was targeted at Mr. Vallières and his former FLQ associates, it may also have affected the membership roster of the legally innocent and politically democratic Parti Québécois. Even if some Trotskyists were involved in unlawful activity (as yet not proven or even suggested), the dirty trick perpetrated against them must inevitably have affected their lawful activities as well. Significantly, more than thirty-five years of FBI investigations into the American Trotskyists failed to produce a hint of law-breaking in the security area.

The RCMP apparently suffered few qualms of conscience about these tactics. The officer who concocted the fake communiqué said, "I believe that there is every reason to consider using it again if ever a situation arises in which it would be likely to make a useful contribution". When asked about the dirty trick perpetrated against the Trotskyists, former Solicitor-General Warren Allmand expressed his endorsement. And Allmand was one of the more *liberal* members of the Canadian government.

It appears that such dirty tricks found their sustenance in the federal cabinet's 1975 mandate to the RCMP, which was embellished in subsequent documents. One internal memorandum, for example, talked about "disruption, coercion, and compromise". Despite the history and supporting evidence of misdeeds, the CSIS Act says virtually nothing about this vital issue.

The issues posed by these dirty tricks have to be more squarely faced. How far is it appropriate for a security agency to foment dissension among targeted constituencies? If not otherwise unlawful, may it compose and circulate fake materials? To what extent may it resort to deliberate falsehoods in order to mislead and confuse? In short, what options, if any, are available to the security service in addition to merely collecting and reporting on intelligence?

It is not enough for the Act simply to omit deterring, preventing, and countering from the functions and duties of the security agency. Such issues must be handled in explicit terms. Otherwise there may be an argument that the agency is entitled to do whatever it is not explicitly prohibited from doing. The Act should be amended so as to address these questions. It should contain either outright prohibitions or detailed guidelines setting out the permissible limits of what the security agency may do to combat whatever security threats it encounters. The history of the past few years has rendered unacceptable continued statutory silence in this area.

SAFEGUARDS AND REVIEW MECHANISMS

Even if all my foregoing proposals were adopted, I would not expect the millennium in security and intelligence to have arrived. Illegalities and excesses could well be committed no matter what the law provided. As indicated, the temptation to break laws and take short-cuts is inherent in the very nature of security and intelligence work. In view of all the previous security-related misconduct, what confidence can the public have that there won't be a repetition?

Ministerial control of the security agency is one important safeguard. But there is reason to believe that, as a matter not only of practice but also of philosophy, past ministers did not exercise the requisite control. According to former Prime Minister Pierre Trudeau, the minister in charge should not even have a right to know what the police are doing in their day-to-day operations. In his view, the minister should be responsible only for policy guidelines but not for daily activity. Shortly after the first revelations of RCMP wrongdoing, Mr. Trudeau was quoted as follows: "...it is not a matter of pleading ignorance as an excuse. It is a matter of stating, as a principle, that the particular minister of the day should not have a right to know what the police are doing constantly in their investigative practices...."

The prime minister's theory was addressed to the danger of a politicized police force. One way to reduce this danger is to ensure that the minister does not exercise day-to-day control over police and security activities. But the problem with the theory is that it creates an insoluble conundrum. How can the minister be assured that the troops are observing the policy guidelines unless there is *some* knowledge of their day-to-day operations? Moreover, why is it necessary to choose between the minister knowing everything or nothing of the relevant operations? Why, in short, must we fall prey to the either-or fallacy?

The fact of the matter is that there simply cannot be effective ministerial control without some ministerial knowledge of day-to-day operations. There may be valid arguments concerning how much knowledge ministers should have and by what means they should acquire it. But a faithful application of the Trudeau theory would create a security agency that was a law unto itself.

Fortunately, the CSIS Act seems to have resolved the problem in favour of more rather than less ministerial supervision and control. Despite the policy of the Act, however, a key component of this problem will remain. Many ministers will make an effort not to know things that would make their jobs more difficult. The more a minister knows, the greater the prospects of conflict with upper-echelon security officials. Thus, even for a minister who does not subscribe to the Trudeau doctrine, ignorance may be desirable. It is important, therefore, to consider additional safeguards and review mechanisms.

For these reasons, we should welcome the requirement in the CSIS Act for judicial warrants in the case of electronic bugging, surreptitious entry, mail opening, and the invasion of confidential records. No court would be likely to refuse a warrant in a compelling case. But, being more independent of the political process, a court is likely to be more demanding than the government as to the purpose, duration, and terms of the warrants it issues. There is also reason to believe that the mere requirement of judicial permission could serve to deter the government from even requesting surveillance warrants in some unjustified cases.

But judicial warrants cannot compensate adequately for defects in the statute. To whatever extent a set of circumstances were to fall within the statutory criteria, the judges would be reluctant to with-hold warrants. Since even legal surveillance could be unreasonable, further safeguards are necessary. Fortunately, the Act has provided for an independent Security Intelligence Review Committee (SIRC) whose personnel is drawn from outside the security agency and the government service. There is even a requirement that the government consult the major opposition parties about the selection of committee members.

To the extent that it has access to the files of the security agency, the review committee can give the minister a "window" on the agency's daily operations. Where there is some indication that the agency is violating the law, policy, or good sense, the committee can draw this to the minister's attention. This should make it increasingly difficult for the minister to invoke ignorance as an excuse for inaction. If the system is to function properly, the minister will face the competing demands of the security bureaucracy and the review committee. Thus, there will be strong pressures for a level of supervision and accountability that has been so lacking in the past.

Despite the significant improvement that the establishment of such a committee implies, the situation is nevertheless inadequate. The term of office for committee members is only five years. Because it is the government which decides whether anyone's term will be renewed, members may be tempted to curry favour with the government, or at least they could be susceptible to such a perception. Moreover, the Act expressly provides that the review committee can be denied access to a key source of information about potential government misconduct: cabinet documents.

These flaws should be corrected. The term of office should be extended and made non-renewable. It should also carry financial benefits sufficient to enable the members to live comfortably after their terms of office. The committee should have access to *everything* relevant in the possession of the security service and the government, including cabinet materials. There is simply no valid basis to provide the committee with access to nuclear secrets, for example, but deny it cabinet documents. Complete access is the prerequisite of public confidence.

Who watches the watchdogs? There is a risk that, even with these changes, the review committee would increasingly identify with the security agency, as has often been the case in the relationship between regulatory agencies and the businesses they regulate. In these circumstances, secrecy increases the risk. The McDonald commission made a most useful recommendation that an additional monitoring role be played by a small parliamentary committee composed partly of opposition members. The introduction of such a perspective could help to reduce the risks of an excessively cozy relationship.

The importance of these control mechanisms cannot be exaggerated. Just as weak controls can distort a strong statute, so can strong controls improve a weak one.

Chapter Four

THE AMBIT OF

POLICE POWERS

Safety for the Public

versus Safeguards for the Suspects

In the spring of 1974, a police drug raid on a small Fort Erie hotel made national headlines and provoked a fierce public controversy. During the course of the raid, the police physically searched virtually all of the 115 patrons they found on the premises; in the case of the 35 women present, the police had them herded into washrooms, stripped, and subjected to vaginal and rectal examinations. Despite all of the searching, stripping, and inspecting, the police found nothing more incriminating than six ounces of marijuana, and most of it was found, not on articles of clothing or within body orifices, but rather on the floor of the lounge. Only three people were charged with drug-related offences.

The ensuing public outrage forced the government of Ontario to create a special royal commission to assess the propriety of the raid. After listening to the evidence of the police, the patrons, and other interested parties, the commission issued the inevitable verdict. The intrusive aspects of the raid were described as "foolish" and "unnecessary". But, cautioned the commission, they were not unlawful.

Under the Narcotic Control Act as it then stood, if there were reasonable grounds to believe that places other than private dwellings contained illicit drugs, the police would be entitled, without warrant, to enter forcibly and conduct a search. Apparently all parties conceded that in this case, it was reasonable to suspect there were drugs in the hotel. It was not considered reasonable, however, to suspect so many of the patrons. But, according to the commission's interpretation of the Act, the police in such circumstances could search *everyone* found on the premises whether or not there were reasonable grounds to suspect each of the persons so searched. All it would take to render a person lawfully vulnerable to such an encroachment was the coincidence of being innocently present on suspicious premises.

The provisions of this remarkable statute invite flights of fantasy. On the basis of the Narcotic Control Act, if marijuana were reasonably believed to be somewhere in the Canadian National Exhibition stadium during a Toronto Argonaut football game, as many as 60,000 spectators would be legally subject to a compulsory genital examination. When I indicated this possibility during a panel discussion I was involved in some years ago, a witty police officer shot back, "If the police actually did that, it would make for the greatest half-time show in history."

To the extent that the Fort Erie raid was both "foolish" and "lawful" there must be serious questions about the reasonableness of the law itself. How can a reasonable law permit such unreasonable police conduct? The answer is that the law gave the police more power in this area than they reasonably needed. This is a beautiful example of the power-hoarding fallacy. Even assuming a power of personal search could be justified in circumstances such as those at Fort Erie, why would it have to be dragnet in scope? Why would it not suffice if the only persons susceptible to this power were those under reasonable suspicion? Of course, every such restriction could increase the number of offenders who escaped detection. But how great would be the risk, and how many would be involved? Are the additional benefits of the existing search powers worth these additional risks to innocent people?

The laws we support depend upon the risks we prefer. In Canada there is a tendency to seek an exceptionally high level of protection from crime. This has produced a willingness to trust the police with a level of power out of all proportion to the crime threats involved. Although the record of police abuses is not serious in comparison with police records in other countries, we must remember that until recently Canada was a rather small, provincial, and not very urbanized society. Now that it is becoming larger, more complex and heterogeneous, the prospects for social conflict are increasing. And increased social conflict, even when healthy, will enlarge the opportunity for contact and conflict between citizens and the police. In such a climate, the risk is greater than ever that an excess of police powers will create an increase in police abuse. No less important, this situation threatens to expand considerably the number of people who may be subjected to surveillance and encroachment. What is at issue, in other words, is the freedom of the individual.

But how about the reverse side of the coin? If we reduce the powers of the police, do we not correspondingly increase our exposure to crime? Such issues cannot be resolved on the basis of abstractions. They require an examination of specifics. What interests are likely to be imperilled in what ways by the reduction, enlargement, or preservation of which police powers?

As I write, the Canadian law in this area is in a state of flux. Already, the new Charter of Rights and Freedoms seems to be having an impact. The "Fort Erie" search power, for example, has been largely reduced by a court decision on the Charter's protection against "unreasonable search and seizure". But not all the over-broad police powers are open to challenge in this way. Since Canada has long been subject to legislative pressure for an ever-widening level of police powers, we should consider the justification for such powers and the effectiveness of the safeguards against them.

The Power to Bug Conversations

One of the most frightening images in George Orwell's *Nineteen Eighty-four* is the deployment in every home of a special television screen by which Big Brother is able to monitor all private conversations. The revulsion evoked by Orwell's fantasy grows out of the importance our society attaches to personal privacy. Even when "objectively" there is nothing to hide, people in our society seek an inviolable retreat from scrutiny where they can express, without intimidation or embarrassment, their hopes and fears, their joys and pains.

The increased police employment of electronic surveillance threatens to revive the images of *Nineteen Eighty-four*. The technology is sophisticated enough now to invade our most intimate retreats.

An important insight into the bugging phenomenon is yielded by the American experience of the past several years. An examination of the U.S. data reveals that to date some 1,500 people have been convicted of criminal offences arising out of 1969 and 1970 investigations involving the use of electronic bugs. During the course of this bugging, however, the American authorities overheard more than 40,000 people in more than half a million conversations. Clearly, the overwhelming number of these people were innocent of wrongdoing. Indeed, apart from cases of gambling, the great majority of intercepted conversations were designated by the authorities themselves as non-incriminating— more than 75 per cent in narcotics investigations and 84 per cent in theft-related matters. The trouble, however, is that electronic bugs cannot readily discriminate. They tend to overhear everyone within earshot—the guilty, the suspected, and the innocent alike. Virtually everyone and everything is swept up in the electronic net.

As such surveillance increases, it is inevitable that more innocent people will have their privacy invaded and more people will come to believe they are being overheard even if, in fact, they are not. This, in itself, will represent a major setback. One of the most important components of privacy is the subjective experience of it. While privacy, like everything else, is not an absolute, it is nevertheless central to democracy. Electronic bugging should not be allowed, therefore, except in a situation where there is no other means to counteract an evil that unquestionably outweighs the evil posed by the surveillance itself.

Apart from the thorny area of national security, organized crime is the evil most often invoked to justify the electronic bugging powers of the police. I am prepared to acknowledge that much of organized crime is every bit the insidious cancer on our body politic that it has been alleged to be. Moreover, the argument is frequently made that the criminal syndicates are so well protected by subordinates, intermediaries, and cooperative customers that it is virtually impossible to secure evidence against them. Many police intelligence authorities claim, therefore, that only electronic surveillance has the capacity to penetrate the protective walls surrounding these underworld operations.

The evidence, however, falls short of the claim. Consider again the American experience. While the U.S. authorities cannot boast decisive victories against organized crime, they often appear to have had as much success without the bugs as with them.

In the mid-1960s, the FBI was ordered to stop its growing practice of electronic bugging in the arena of domestic crime. Yet, from 1966 until 1969, without any bugging at all, there was a reported increase in convictions and a tripling of indictments against members of the syndicates. Indeed, the FBI declared that 1968 "was a year of striking accomplishment against the bulwark of the hoodlum criminal conspiracy—La Cosa Nostra". Law enforcement claimed this success *without* the use of electronic surveillance.

It is significant also that in the late 1960s, the President's Commission on Law Enforcement and the Administration of Justice paid special tribute to two cities for continuing "to develop major cases against members of the criminal cartels". The two cities so mentioned were New York, where the police were bugging extensively, and Chicago, which was subject to Illinois's total ban on such activities.

Despite the grant of special wiretap powers by a 1968 statute of the American Congress, there has been a mixed response from the special strike forces which had earlier been created to fight organized crime. One strike force co-ordinator, for example, made the following statement about electronic surveillance: "It has not often been applicable. We have been able to make a case without it and we have had more indictments and convictions than any Strike Force in the country."

A few years ago, Cornell law professor Robert Blakey, a steadfast American supporter of police bugging, pointed out that in the little under a decade after U.S. federal law validated this practice, approximately fifty-five Cosa Nostra members were being convicted per year. But, Blakey admitted, only 10 per cent of these cases involved electronic surveillance.

Thus, in the fight against organized crime, the most that can be said for electronic bugs is that sometimes they may have been helpful. This is hardly an impressive record for a technology that simultaneously invades the privacy of countless innocent people.

To what extent is the amount of protection secured through this form of surveillance worth the enormous price that we must pay in personal privacy? The proponents of police wiretapping have failed completely to make a persuasive case. Even in the area of organized crime, where some of the strongest claims have been made, the supporters of electronic bugs have failed to demonstrate that, without them, society's vital interests would be seriously imperilled. But, in the domestic criminal area, Canadian law does not even limit electronic bugging to organized crime. These intrusive devices are legally available, on judicial warrant, for more than forty offences that have nothing to do with organized crime. Until recently, the list included such grave dangers to the public safety as threatening the dog, cat, or bird of another person.

Remarkably, there have been times when the government of Canada has attempted to go even further. In the late 1970s, for example, the government introduced a bill which would have made it legally possible for the police to obtain bugging warrants for any offence that carried a jail sentence of five years or more. This could have included such trivial matters as the mere possession of marijuana.

In response to the inevitable criticism provoked by such proposals, the best the police could do was to assure us that they would have neither the time nor the inclination to use electronic surveillance for such minor matters. In short, the police were asking for trust. According to the critics, however, there was simply no need to repose this level of trust in the police. The critics insisted on knowing why the police should have any intrusive power beyond what was demonstrated as necessary. These contentious provisions of the bill were finally dropped, but the mind-set that produced them persists.

Apart from the national security area, are there then any circumstances in which police bugging can be justified? Suppose there were a kidnapping and there were reasonable grounds to believe that X knew the whereabouts of the hostage. Imminent perils to life and limb create arguable exceptions to general rules. Thus there would be a case for allowing the police, on judicial warrant, to bug X in order to find and save the hostage. But, beyond such emergencies and certain security matters, the need for this surveillance has not been demonstrated.

The peculiarly surreptitious character of electronic bugging has prompted support for special safeguards. Despite the objections of the minority federal government, opposition parties forced the passage in 1974 of an enactment requiring the police, within ninety days of such surveillance, to notify the target of their bugging, whether or not charges ensued. This safeguard was designed to introduce an element of accountability into an otherwise completely secret practice.

The idea was to enable an innocent victim to seek redress in the event of improper surveillance. The safeguard was also to act as a deterrent against needless bugging. Since everyone under such surveillance at some stage must discover what had happened, the police might not be as likely even to seek wiretap permission unless, in the circumstances, it was essential. The prospect of having to contend with a growing constituency of angry surveillance victims might serve to restrain much of the impulse to bug.

From the outset, however, this safeguard was the subject of considerable controversy. Police authorities argued that, since notification could alert criminals that they were under surveillance, investigations would be undermined. The then justice minister, Otto Lang, described this opposition amendment as "goddamn stupid". Thus, by 1976, a majority federal government had proposed the complete repeal and then a substantial dilution of this controversial safeguard.

But the government and police arguments overlook the fact that the 1974 law empowered the courts to delay the notification if, in their judgment, early notice to the target would jeopardize an investigation. This was designed to protect the interests of both law enforcement *and* personal privacy. In attempting to remove this safeguard with its accompanying judicial scrutiny, the government was asking once more for a needless level of public trust in police performance.

If anything, this safeguard should be tightened even further. While targets must currently be told that they have been bugged, they need not be told why. The current law seals the lips of the police and the packets of documents upon which their bugging applications are based. Virtually the only time when such information is forthcoming is on those occasions when the wiretap evidence is used against an accused in court. This situation creates a strange paradox. The persons accused of offences are likely to find out why they were bugged. The persons who are never charged will not. To enjoy this safeguard, therefore, it is better to be charged than to be cleared.

This is unacceptable. There is no reason why the law could not create a right for the targets of bugging to learn not only what but also why. Indeed, they should be entitled to whatever information they would need to pursue their legal remedies in the event that the invasion of their privacy was unlawful. In anticipation of widespread apoplexy in our police departments, I hasten to point out that this right should be presumptive, not conclusive. In those circumstances where such disclosure of information could jeopardize ongoing criminal investigations, the police should be permitted to apply to a court for a suspension of their obligation to notify.

But the power to decide should be reposed in the courts, not in the police. This is the very least of the changes that should be made in our bugging laws. Without it, we have the untenable situation in which the law provides a wide panoply of safeguards and remedies but then forecloses on the practical possibility of using them. In its current form, the law virtually invites the disrespect of the community it is supposed to serve.

There is even a good case for a further extension of the notification obligation. Recent reports reveal that police in this country have been involved in twice as many bugging operations as their American counterparts. The United States, of course, is ten times the size of Canada and its crime problem is infinitely worse. It is reasonable to suspect, therefore, that there is a lot of needless bugging in this country.

One way to reduce this practice here is to require the police to notify not only the targets of their bugging but also all other participants in the intercepted conversations whose identities can be reasonably ascertained. The more people that learn of such invasions to their privacy, the more people that will raise hell. And the prospect of such reactions could well serve to deter the police from bugging when it isn't really necessary. Unless the target of such surveillance winds up charged, I cannot argue for a concomitant right on the part of all participants in the overheard conversations to acquire the kind of information I advocate for the target. But such participants should have a right at least to learn that some of their conversations have been bugged.

Even though these people might not learn enough to pursue their legal remedies, they might be enabled nevertheless to exert political pressure. While the targets of a bugging operation might be reluctant to complain lest they be stigmatized as suspects, the people whose conversations are inadvertently intercepted would not likely harbour such inhibitions. Many of them could be expected to complain loudly. Moreover, since the police could anticipate such a development, they, in turn, would be expected to be a lot more circumspect about undertaking bugging operations. And this is precisely the result we should desire.

Under the current law, the federal and provincial governments must publish annually a series of reports indicating the offences for which they have bugged, the charges they have laid, and the convictions which have been obtained. Unfortunately, however, there is no requirement to report on the privacy costs. For every person who is convicted, how many others have had their privacy invaded? And at what financial cost? Canadian law should be amended in order to require a much fuller public account of costs and benefits. Proper public scrutiny should be regarded as the minimum prerequisite for such pervasive intrusions on the privacy of the individual.

The Power to Intercept and Open Mail

Apart from national security matters, there is virtually no legal power in Canada to intercept and open first-class mail in the course of post without the consent of the intended recipient or sender. Yet, of all the unlawful activity associated with the revelations of RCMP wrongdoing, mail opening appears to have been the most brazen. For many years, it was official RCMP policy to authorize mail opening in conscious defiance of the law. In contrast to much of their other impugned conduct, such as surreptitious entries, the RCMP made little attempt to defend this practice as lawful. Indeed, the upper echelons of the force centralized the authorization procedure on the precise ground that it was not lawful and was not likely to become so.

Although Canada's then prime minister, Pierre Trudeau, was far from apologetic about the general revelations of RCMP misconduct under his administration, he was openly contemptuous of those who criticized the illegal mail opening. Since none of the other Western democracies lacks a mail opening power, he asked, why should Canada? Without taking any forthright steps to prosecute or discipline the wrongdoers, the Trudeau government initiated instead a move to legalize the wrongdoing.

During the 1978 Parliament, first and second readings were given to a government bill for the legalization of mail opening. Although the bill ultimately died on the order paper, there have been many subsequent indications that Canada has not seen the last of such efforts. Prime Minister Trudeau never recanted his position. One of his longest surviving solicitors-general, Robert Kaplan, still a "front bench" Member of Parliament, declared himself in favour of such a power. And the report of the McDonald commission on RCMP wrongdoing contained a supportive recommendation, as did a 1986 document authored by the Police Powers Project of the Federal Ministry of the Solicitor-General and Ministry of Justice.

As a possible model of things to come, it would be instructive to examine how the bill proposed to deal with the power it sought to create. Apart from the area of national security, the bill provided for mail opening on judicial warrant to seize certain drugs and intercept communications with respect to such drugs.

In principle, I would have a hard time objecting to a power of inspection and seizure where contraband is concerned. But it is not necessary to read a letter in order to determine whether it contains contraband. Indeed, it may not be necessary even to open the letter. In many cases, modern technology might well be able to detect the contraband in sealed envelopes. To the extent that this can be done, letters should not be opened unless they have been first found to contain the substances at issue. In those cases where the technology cannot perform this task, there would be an argument for opening letters reasonably suspected of containing contraband. Even in those situations, however, steps should be taken to minimize the reading of any letters that are found subsequently *not* to contain the illegal substances.

The proposed power to intercept communications raises different problems. The only way to determine whether a communication is relevant to the investigation of a criminal offence is to read it. But the very act of reading it constitutes an encroachment on personal privacy. Moreover, the intercepted communication may never reach its intended recipient.

Often only the communications of one side will be monitored. The replies, if any, are not as readily subject to interception. Of course, mail surveillance would be conducted generally on what is received rather than on what is sent. Thus, people could attract police surveillance even if they were the unwitting and unwilling recipients of unilaterally incriminating communications from someone over whom they had no control. Conversely, guilty recipients could implicate innocent senders. The broader the terms of a warrant to open mail, the larger the number of innocent letters which would be subject to such intrusion.

On the other hand, as a weapon to enforce narcotics legislation, the power to read mail communications is of limited value. What even partially sophisticated drug dealer would be likely to write incriminating statements in letters? A similar point was made at the hearings of the McDonald commission by one of the RCMP's experts in these matters. Here is an instructive extract from the testimony of Chief Inspector T.S. Venner:

> In very few of these parcels or letters, or whatever, that are opened, is there any communication found therein. What we are talking about here is parcels or letters containing drugs; very seldom messages or communications.... I think it is important, because again, I think there is a widespread belief that it is our intent to interfere with the privacy of communication, more so than with getting a hand on the contraband substance itself. And it is simply not the case.

Even though the RCMP and the McDonald commission claimed that, for narcotics purposes, mail opening could be limited to the seizure of contraband, the government was prepared to create an additional power to intercept communications. Another example of the power-hoarding fallacy.

The Opportunity to Commit Abuse

Periodically there are complaints of police brutality. Increasingly they have been the subject of royal commissions, court cases, media stories, and legislative debate. Despite the differences in the circumstances surrounding these complaints, a common theme has nevertheless emerged. In the greatest number of cases, the allegations of abuse refer to situations of custodial confinement.

This should not be surprising. To whatever extent police officers are tempted to exert excessive force, they are not likely to do it on the city hall steps at high noon. There is another reason that these allegations tend to originate in the custodial setting. What is usually at issue is the quest for information, evidence, or a confession.

The particular perils of the custodial situation have produced a number of special safeguards governing police procedures on arrest and detention. One of the longest-standing of these safeguards addresses the issue of custodial interrogations and confessions. In order to introduce into court any statement made by an accused person during a custodial interrogation, the police must first prove that the statement was voluntary.

As helpful as this safeguard could be, pre-Charter jurisprudence set some critical limits on it. A man arrested on a charge of murder confessed his guilt while the police improperly detained him incommunicado. Despite the possibility that his confession might otherwise have been inadmissible, the Supreme Court of Canada ruled portions of it acceptable as evidence because they correctly revealed where the police could find the murder weapon. This decision demonstrated that, in key ways, the safeguard against involuntary statements was more concerned with ensuring the reliability of the statement itself than with discouraging the police misconduct that produced it.

The safeguard against involuntary statements recognized that many people would do or say anything—even to the point of making a false confession—to avoid a physical beating. But, if the contents of the confession are confirmed by the subsequent discovery of tangible evidence, there is no longer a sound basis to consider the confession false. On the strength of this analysis, the court restricted the scope of the safeguard against involuntary statements. But the court's analysis could give rise to a disturbing lesson. In order to nail their suspects, the police might be advised not simply to assault them but to beat hell out of them. The police might have to inflict enough pain to induce their suspects to reveal the whereabouts of tangible evidence.

Another problem with this safeguard is the difficulty of proof. Usually the only witnesses to any coercive pressure are the several police officers who are accused of inflicting it and the one suspect who claims to have suffered it. In court, the credibility of the police officers will usually be more compelling than that of the suspect, a person who may be already tarnished by a criminal record and unsavoury reputation. Thus, even though the burden of proof with respect to the statement is on the police and not on the suspect, they will enjoy a considerable advantage in their ability to persuade a court.

Moreover, the custodial setting—jailhouse, station, cruiser—is inherently so oppressive that numbers of suspects might feel pressured to cooperate with the police even though no additional coercion is applied. Yet the court could well rule that there was nothing "involuntary" about the resulting statements and they should therefore be admitted into evidence. By itself, the experience of arrest and confinement is so harrowing for many people that they will go to great lengths to curry favour with their captors. This might produce a fully admissible custodial statement that plays havoc with the truth. In the frightening circumstances of confinement, many people could be tempted to say or do things which make themselves look guilty when they are not, or guiltier than they are.

This raises the further concern of police harassment. In certain sectors of society, particularly among the disadvantaged, people not infrequently are "invited" into a cruiser or to the police station for questioning. If judicially analysed, numbers of these "invitations" might well be designated as unlawful arrests—that is, for example, persons went unwillingly in circumstances where there was neither a warrant nor a sufficient basis to believe that they had committed or were about to commit an indictable offence. But the requisite judicial scrutiny is unlikely to occur; such people are among the most reluctant litigants in our society. And, in a significant number of cases, these people will be released without having to face charges. Once they talk or convince the police that they have no relevant information, the incident is brought to a close. But, in the meantime, improper pressures may have been used for which there will never be an adequate accounting.

I expect, of course, to be reminded about the right against self-incrimination. There is generally no legal obligation to answer police questions or indeed to say anything, but many arrested people simply don't know that they have such a right, and many of them who do know lack the courage to exercise it.

Both the Diefenbaker Bill of Rights of 1960 and now the new Charter of Rights and Freedoms contain another safeguard which could be more helpful: the right of arrested people to "retain and instruct counsel without delay". To the extent that this safeguard is observed, it could be a potent antidote to improper pressure. The early introduction of a lawyer could provide the arrested person with intelligent strategy and psychological support in a setting so devoid of emotional foundations. In a number of cases, counsel might help to eliminate the interrogation completely by persuading the police to forgo it, or by negotiating a faster release from custody. In other cases, legal advice might give prisoners both the courage and the wisdom to maintain their silence, if it is in their interests to do so. Moreover, the mere prospect of having to deal with counsel might reduce any police propensity to abuse their powers of arrest in the first place.

It may be, however, that few arrested people have exercised this right. In the decade before the adoption of the Charter, the Canadian Civil Liberties Association conducted a number of surveys in an effort to determine the experiences of arrested people. In all, several hundred such persons were interviewed. A substantial majority (at least 70 per cent) said that they had been interrogated by the police while they were in custody. Incredibly, only one person claimed to have consulted a lawyer before being questioned. Of those who requested access to the telephone, only a minority reported that the request was granted immediately. In the greatest number of cases, access to the telephone reportedly was denied outright or delayed until after questioning took place. These surveys dealt only with arrested people who were subsequently charged. We can only speculate about the number of effective arrests that occur without charges being laid. It is extremely doubtful whether a greater number of those people exercise their custodial rights to counsel.

At this point, there is some indication that the beefed-up provisions of the new Charter of Rights and Freedoms might be making a difference. Ultimately, the critical factor will be the nature of the sanctions that are triggered by police misconduct.

Our Limited Sanctions against Police Misconduct

Suppose one or more police officers broke the rules we are talking about. Suppose, without warrant, they bugged conversations or opened mail. Or suppose they arrested certain suspects in circumstances where there was no lawful authority to do so. And suppose once they took their prisoners into custody, they denied them access to counsel and began to pummel them. The offending police officers would be subject to criminal prosecutions, civil lawsuits, and departmental discipline. Unfortunately, however, these sanctions are beset by a number of impediments.

Criminal prosecutions are handled usually by the crown attorney's office, which is also involved in daily cooperation and association with the police. Thus, there is reason to fear that prosecutions *of* police will not be as vigorously pursued as prosecutions *by* police. And, when the accused is a police officer, it is not expected that fellow officers will perform the kind of conscientious investigation that characterizes their other work. And how much more true would this be in a case where the victim of the police misconduct is an underworld figure or someone who is often in conflict with the law!

The Toronto experience prior to the reforms of the late 1970s fuels these concerns. From 1969–1973, 301 criminal charges were laid against police officers by aggrieved civilians. By 1974 only two convictions had been registered. All others had been either dismissed or withdrawn. And one of the two convictions was under appeal.

Nor do civil court actions for damages appear to be a satisfactory avenue. Civil litigation is expensive, time consuming, and emotionally taxing. Negotiations for settlement, examinations for discovery, innumerable motions, trials, and appeals could take years to produce results. Few people have the resources to investigate the facts, engage counsel, withstand pressure by the police, and handle the many expenses. Between 1969 and 1973 only seventy-nine law suits had been launched against Toronto police officers. By 1974, thirty-three had been dismissed and thirty-four were still pending (thirteen of them since 1972). One had resulted in a court judgment for the complainant, but in the amount of only $1,000 plus costs. There had been about ten settlements with an average compensation of only $1,000 each.

While disciplinary complaints may be processed more expeditiously, the concern is that they will be handled less impartially. Since a finding of misconduct against a police officer could adversely affect the public relations of the entire department, such procedures are vulnerable to the suspicion of "cover-up".

A factor common to all of these sanctions is that practically speaking the initiative rests with the complainant. Invariably, most of the grievances against the police arise from among the least accepted sectors of society—criminals, suspects, and the disadvantaged. Even if their complaints are justified, such people rarely have the confidence to challenge the police. Indeed, a number of surveys conducted by the Canadian Civil Liberties Association among such aggrieved people revealed that more than 85 per cent refused to take subsequent retaliatory action. When asked about their reluctance, most replied flatly, "It would do no good."

The Need for Independent Investigation and Review

The bottom line is that we can't rely on police departments to investigate their own officers.

So long as the only publicly subsidized investigations are conducted by colleagues of the implicated officers, the system will be unable to enjoy the requisite confidence of complainants, other police officers, and the public. As far as complainants are concerned, the investigations will be susceptible to the suspicion of cover-up. As far as the accused police officers are concerned, the investigations will be susceptible to the suspicion that intra-departmental rivalries will prevail over the interests of scrupulous fact finding. As far as the public is concerned, all of these factors will taint the appearance of fairness. It makes sense, therefore, to push for the speedy adoption of an independent mechanism to investigate and review civilian complaints of police misconduct.

Such a system will never work, according to certain politicians and police authorities. They maintain that only members of the police department will be able to enlist the requisite cooperation in order to get the necessary evidence. However compelling this argument may be in theory, it has already been refuted in practice. The most important Canadian public inquiries into police misconduct, the McDonald commission into RCMP wrongdoing and the Morand commission into police practices in Toronto, successfully brought in outsiders to handle their investigations. Another argument made by opponents of independent systems is that, with few exceptions, their counterparts have failed in the United States. This argument overlooks some of the tremendous differences between the U.S. and Canada. As serious as many of our problems are, there is no parallel to the racial polarization that has plagued the large American cities. In that kind of political situation, civilian review could and did become a convenient scapegoat for reactionary demagogues.

In a few police departments such as the RCMP and that of Toronto, new systems have been adopted. Complaints are investigated internally but reviewed externally. While this represents an improvement over the old system where everything was handled internally, I believe that the front-line investigations should also be independent. So long as such investigations are handled by officials who have departmental or even general police interests to protect, the system will likely discourage many aggrieved people from making their complaints known. The Canadian Civil Liberties Association has encountered this problem time and again, particularly among minority racial and ethnic groups. These people were simply not prepared to confide their complaints about police officers to other police officers.

A recent incident in Toronto serves to dramatize this problem. A police officer was "cold shouldered" by members of the department because his testimony in court helped to convict and jail a fellow officer for a serious assault on a suspect. The treatment was so severe that the testifying officer wound up resigning his job. In the light of such experiences, potential complainants can have little faith that Toronto police officers will fairly investigate their allegations. It is important, therefore, that *all* civilian complaints be investigated externally by those who have no departmental interests to protect or collegial relations to sustain.

Independent investigators should not simply respond to complaints. They should also initiate them. Indeed, with certain rights of access to police files and premises, they should conduct ongoing audits of police operations. The findings from these audits could form the basis of complaints and the subject of periodic reports to the minister in charge.

In that way, the minister's involvement in daily operations could focus on those cases in which the independent officials reported that there were apparent violations of law or policy. Instead of facing only the pressures emanating from the police, the minister would have to deal also with the competing pressures from the independent officials. The resulting tensions would help to keep the minister from taking the path of least resistance. The independent officials should report periodically to the legislature the existence, if not the details, of any outstanding differences between their office and that of the minister.

Moreover, the knowledge that such officials had certain powers of access to jailhouses and detention areas would act as a deterrent to many forms of custodial misconduct. A great advantage of this approach over the existing system is that it would be much less dependent on initiatives from aggrieved people. At the same time, however, the independent arrangements might encourage more aggrieved people to come out of the woodwork in search of redress.

The Exclusion of Tainted Evidence

Another possible sanction against police misconduct might involve the adoption of some form of exclusionary rule which would deny to the police the use in court of evidence acquired unlawfully. Until the Charter, Canadian law allowed very few such exclusions of evidence. Under the Charter, this remedy is now officially part of our law, but we don't yet know how far it will be applied. Such a sanction has the advantage of requiring no special initiatives from other police officers or from the aggrieved party. Defence counsel could simply challenge the admission of any evidence that resulted from the questionable activities of the police. This would force an inquiry at the trial into the legality of the police tactics.

Perhaps even the mere knowledge that evidence so obtained could not subsequently be used would also act as some deterrent against the contemplated misconduct. In this connection, consider a recent statement (pre-Charter) made by an Ontario crown attorney following the extraordinary trial of two Toronto police officers accused of using illegal tactics to obtain a confession from a suspect. According to this prosecutor, so long as illegally obtained evidence is admissible in court, "these things are bound to happen".

Admittedly, however, certain studies in the United States have cast doubt on this proposition. That country has long provided for the exclusion of tainted evidence from criminal trials. On the basis of the American experience, some of these studies have questioned just how far the exclusionary rule really does deter police abuse. The evidence seems to be divided on this issue. In any event, opponents of the rule argue that it is wrong to allow a guilty civilian to go free just because a police officer has also transgressed. In this view, *both* law-breakers should be punished.

The problem with this argument is its basis in unreality. It would be impossible to fill a thimble with the number of charges laid or disciplinary measures imposed against police officers whose unlawful methods succeeded in nailing suspects that their departments wanted to get. Police departments are highly reluctant to punish their officers for successful investigations. Without some form of exclusionary rule, therefore, there is a great risk that too little will be done about police abuse. The one thing that the law cannot afford is an appearance of tolerance or indifference towards police misconduct. For these reasons, I have long supported the adoption of a broader exclusionary rule for Canada.

When this matter was debated at the time of its inclusion in the Charter of Rights and Freedoms, some hyperbolic statements were made by certain law enforcement authorities. They charged that a broader exclusionary rule would import into Canada the terrible crime problem of the United States. They dangled before the Canadian public the spectre of street violence and bloodletting.

In order to accept this argument, however, we would have to believe that the police in this country were disposed to rampant law-breaking. If Canadian police were not guilty of significant law-breaking, what difference would it make to the crime rate if we had an exclusionary rule? At the time of the debate, I amused myself by declaring publicly that I had more faith in the willingness of Canadian police to obey the law than they apparently did themselves. Furthermore, acquittals in American courts that result from the exclusionary rule are relatively infrequent. How, then, can it be seriously argued that there is a causal relationship between the exclusionary rule and the existence of a serious crime problem?

But, in response to the perception that trivial police mistakes have produced some absurd acquittals in the United States, Canadian politicians determined that police illegality would not lead *automatically* to the exclusion of evidence in this country. Instead the Canadian Charter provides that evidence acquired in violation of the rights and freedoms it contains will be inadmissible in court in those circumstances where its admission would bring the administration of justice into disrepute. This would appear to pave the way for admitting evidence in the event of mere technical oversights. We are only beginning to learn how far other criteria will influence the Canadian courts.

The pre-Charter debates impel me to make a recommendation on this issue. In order to ensure conspicuous sanctions for police wrongdoing, I propose that the court should inquire whether, by the time of the trial against the suspect, the delinquent police officers have been charged or disciplined. To the extent that they have, this factor might dispose a court to admit the tainted evidence against the suspect. On the other hand, where no such action has been taken, the courts should lean against admitting the evidence. Such an approach is designed to meet some of the key objections to the exclusionary rule. According to my proposal, the rule would be less likely to be applied in those situations where the police are prepared to police wrongdoing by the police. This standard need not be exclusive or necessarily determinative, but it should be one of the criteria which the courts use to decide what will bring the administration of justice into disrepute.

A special word is needed about the Charter provision that arrested people are entitled to retain and instruct legal counsel without delay. Unfortunately, the counterpart section in the Diefenbaker Bill of Rights did not inspire the courts to exclude evidence taken in violation of it. The Charter provides the further requirement that the police *advise* arrested persons of this right. Compliance with these safeguards is such a crucial counterweight to custodial pressures that special sanctions are called for. Indeed, civil libertarians should press both the courts and Parliament on this issue.

Unless there is some imminent peril to life or limb, the police should be effectively barred from conducting custodial interrogations until the arrested person has either consulted counsel or, having been advised of the right to do so, has waived the opportunity. In the event of a police failure to comply with any of these obligations, all of the fruits which derive from the interrogation (such as statements and tangible evidence) should be rendered inadmissible as evidence in court. Even if tainted evidence will not be excluded in all situations, the rules should be tougher where *custodial* misconduct is involved.

Suggestions of this kind often evoke shrill denunciations from many police authorities who complain bitterly that such rules and sanctions would effectively handcuff them in their pursuit of criminals. The experience of other jurisdictions refutes these objections. In some respects, Scottish law contains greater protections for arrested people than those I have recommended here. Custodial interrogation is discouraged: statements obtained that way are banned from court. Nevertheless, Scotland has demonstrated an ability to solve crimes which compares favourably with the record in Canada. Moreover, the conviction rates in the two countries have shown no significant differences.

Data from the United States point in the same direction. Since the famous *Miranda* decision of 1966, American law has made custodial access to counsel a condition of the admissibility in court of custodial statements. Although there has been a decline in the rate of confessions in some places, reliable studies have shown no significant reduction in the rate of suspects convicted or crimes solved since the *Miranda* decision. In short, the increase in custodial safeguards and sanctions did not decrease the ability of the police to do their job.

The easier it is to make accused people talk, the greater might be the number of arrests on inadequate evidence. The police could be tempted to arrest on mere suspicion in the hope that an intimidating interrogation would produce the missing link in their case. Surely, however, democratic values seek to protect innocent people not only against criminal conviction, but also against the ordeal of arrest and prosecution. That is why the law should do its utmost to ensure that the police have substantial evidence *before* they arrest and prosecute. Interrogations made easy undermine this objective. Even at that, it is not the police interrogation *per se* to which I am now taking exception. It is, rather, the *custodial* interrogation *without the benefit of legal advice*.

There is some indication from early decisions on the Charter that the superior courts are moving in a direction similar to the one I have advocated here. I hope this trend continues.

Due Process for the Police

The quest for due process should apply to the police as well. Civilians are more likely to receive fairer treatment *by* police when there is fairer treatment *of* police. In my view, police in Canada have a number of legitimate grievances concerning the way they are treated.

In many places today, police officers do not have the minimum kind of job security enjoyed by most unionized employees. These constables are not entitled, as of right, to outside arbitration when discipline or discharge emanates, not from a civilian complaint, but from police management. In these jurisdictions, if police officers wish to challenge such discipline, they could be confined to appeals within the police structure. The highest they have a right to go in Ontario, for example, is to the Ontario Police Commission. That is like asking an auto worker from General Motors to appeal to the Chamber of Commerce.

Most provinces have removed from the police the most potent instrument of self-help, the right to strike. Elementary equity requires that, in view of the demands made and the rights removed, our society should ensure to police officers the minimal protections available to most unionized employees. At the very least, therefore, police officers should be given the right to independent arbitration of all their discipline and discharge grievances.

Chapter Five

DISCRETIONARY

LAW ENFORCEMENT

The Interests of Leniency
versus the Standards of Equity

In early February of 1981, two hundred Metropolitan Toronto police officers conducted the largest single law enforcement operation Canada had experienced since the FLQ crisis of October 1970. In a single night, more than three hundred people were arrested. Their crime? Not terrorism or murder or kidnapping or dope peddling. The overwhelming number of those arrested were charged with nothing more than being found-ins on the premises of common bawdyhouses. Their "crime" involved having sex with other consenting adults in rooms which they had rented for such purposes. The rub is that all of the sexual participants were men. The "bawdyhouses" were bathhouses frequently attended by members of Toronto's homosexual community.

The raid provoked a storm of protest—demonstrations, parades, picket lines; delegations to the municipal council, police commission, and provincial solicitor-general. The police were accused of "gay bashing", using excessive force, and engaging in overkill. Not so, insisted the authorities. According to them, the police were merely enforcing the law. Police officials and elected politicians alike told the protesters that, if they didn't like the bawdyhouse laws, they should petition the Parliament of Canada to change them. It was the job of the police and the prosecutors to enforce the law as it stood On the eve of the second anniversary of the raid, Ontario's Attorney-General Roy McMurtry sang the same tune in response to Opposition questions: "It will be very difficult for any police force anywhere to take the position that, because it involves an issue that is bound to provoke some public controversy, they [sic] are therefore going to ignore this law breaking."

But police don't merely enforce the law. They make choices, and they have always made choices, as to what laws they will enforce under what circumstances, and how they will do it. Imagine, for example, the deployment of two hundred police officers to crack down on illegal jaywalking! The fact is that the police simply cannot give every law the same amount of attention. No society, least of all a democracy, has enough police for a job like that. Inevitably, therefore, choices must be made and priorities must be struck. Some laws will get more attention than others. Some crimes will get harsher treatment than others. The issue is not whether there should be such differences in law enforcement, but how such differences are determined and who does the determining.

Even if the police felt an obligation to lay some charges in connection with the bathhouses, why was it necessary to go about it in the way they did? Why, for example, did they have to terrorize more than 250 found-ins who were doing nothing more than having sex with each other? As long as those found-ins were not inflicting their sexual activities on unwilling participants, unwilling observers, or children, their conduct, even if unlawful, hardly represented a threat to the public interest. If such a threat could have been said to exist, it came from those who operated the bathhouses, not from those who used them. Why couldn't the police simply have issued a few summonses to the proprietors?

The ultimate results in court reinforce these misgivings. By the time of the raid's second anniversary, 278 of the men charged as found-ins had had their day in court. As many as 241 were completely cleared, by way of either acquittals or withdrawals of the charges at the request of the Crown. Of the 37 who either pleaded or were found guilty, not a single one went to jail, and most received either conditional or absolute discharges. In the legislature, Attorney-General Roy McMurtry explained the high rate of acquittals and withdrawals on the basis that, after so long, the police were simply unable to identify many of the accused people.

In the course of explaining the results of the raid, McMurtry unwittingly impugned the reasons for it. The issue is not whether the police could identify the accused but *why* they couldn't. If the people scooped up in the raid had been suspected of selling dope rather than having sex, it is inconceivable that the police would not have made it their business to identify them. The results suggest, therefore, that the entire undertaking was essentially an exercise in "trivial pursuit". But an exercise, it must be remembered, that created pain and suffering for a good many of its victims and their families.

Since it was open to the police to handle the matter differently, the question is why they didn't. What policies guided their choices? Who made those policies and how were they made? We know that there is anti-gay feeling in segments of the police force and the public. We know also that gays are a particularly vulnerable minority without the political clout of other constituencies. These factors give rise to a suspicion of bigotry and favouritism in the methods of law enforcement. Unfortunately, there appear to be other examples of the same phenomenon.

The mention of police video surveillance generates images of the most serious threats to our society: espionage, terrorism, organized crime. In Ontario, however, this sophisticated technology has been used to crack down on buggery, fellatio, and masturbation. Thanks to the wonders of video surveillance, more than 130 men in that province have been arrested since 1983 because they were having sex with each other in public washrooms. In Orillia, Welland, Kitchener, St. Catharines, and Guelph, periods of video surveillance were followed by mass arrests which, in turn, triggered headlines and major news stories. While this sexual misconduct was not seen as sufficiently serious to justify jail terms or any other heavy penalty, the accompanying publicity devastated the lives of many of the accused and their families. In one case, there was even a suicide.

The controversy provoked irrepressible questions. Why did washroom sex warrant such large and costly police operations? Why did it warrant the humiliation and torment that would inevitably accompany the laying of charges? Perhaps even more significant, how could it justify such intrusive snooping on completely innocent washroom users? Indeed, to what extent did innocent excretion occupy police surveillance? And what was the effect of this on police morale? How has the role of voyeur squared with the self-image of the officers who had to perform these assignments? When they were criticized for this lavatory overkill, the police invoked again their favourite argument: they don't make the law; they merely enforce it. But one doesn't need the worldliness of a James Bond to imagine far less damaging and intrusive methods by which the police could have controlled the situation in those public washrooms.

Reactions to gays do not exhaust the areas in which law enforcement methods have provoked suspicions of bias. Towards the end of 1979, police officers were dispatched to investigate an incident at Toronto's Contact School, an experimental institution for high school students. The subject of the investigation was a speech made earlier at the school by Dudley Laws, a black community leader with a reputation for radicalism. What business did the police have investigating a speech in such a setting? Their mere involvement could cast a chill over the practice of academic freedom at the school.

In response to an inquiry by the Canadian Civil Liberties Association, the lawyer for the police department provided an explanation that exacerbated these uneasy feelings. He said there was some concern that Mr. Laws had made "very intemperate and inflammatory statements" to the students about a recent incident in which two Toronto police officers were facing charges in the shooting death of a black man. Here is part of his explanation about the possible legal basis for the investigation: "From what I could make out the case appeared possibly to involve...a contempt of court with respect to the rights of accused persons awaiting trial as a result of the shooting incident."

Contempt of court in this context was concerned with the right of the accused police officers to a fair trial. Once a charge has been laid, it is impermissible to publish or broadcast remarks that would be likely to bias a jury against the accused. In this situation, however, it is simply preposterous to believe that such interests could have been seriously imperilled by a speech to high school students. In any event, how many *civilians* have had the benefit of such police assistance after *they* have been the targets of a speaker's invective?

When police resources are used with such apparent selectivity, suspicions are triggered about police motives. The investigation began to look like an attempt to intimidate a black leader who had long been unpopular with the police, and to help a couple of beleaguered colleagues. No less, it created the impression that the police were trying to deter educators from inviting radicals to speak to their students.

Such suspicions about police motives are likely to be fuelled by the monumental insensitivity Canadian police have periodically shown towards the rights of other accused people awaiting trial. Not only is it rare for Canadian police to help, but they have also been known to hurt, the prospects for a fair trial. On a number of occasions we have witnessed the spectacle of police officers convening press conferences where they disclosed the most awful things about arrested suspects.

In early 1983, for example, the RCMP, the Vancouver police, and the British Columbia attorney-general's office held a joint press conference following the arrest of five people in connection with a number of bombings on the west coast. In the course of describing the circumstances leading to the arrest, one RCMP spokesman is quoted as saying that "the suspects had guns in their duffel bags". Another RCMP spokesman reportedly embellished this disclosure by telling the press conference that "several large calibre guns and rifles were found in [the suspects'] vehicle, as well as hundreds of rounds of ammunition". When asked whether the suspects were professionals, he is quoted as saying that they were "skilled in their activities".

During the course of the press conference, the police allegedly stood before a table containing four handguns, two semi-automatic rifles, one machine gun, shotguns, hunting rifles, and camouflage jackets. If a vitriolic speech to a group of high school students could be seen as a threat to a fair trial, what could be said about these disclosures to the mass media?

As contentious as these interviews were, it is even worse to make such public comments in the middle of a trial. Yet this is just what Ontario Attorney-General Roy McMurtry did. During the trial of a stock promoter on a weapons charge, Mr. McMurtry publicly called the accused "a known con man". When he made this statement to a group of reporters, the jury in the case was not sequestered. Its members were able to read these comments in the daily press. Such a slur, bearing the imprimatur of an attorney-general, could well have influenced the jury's deliberations. Yet the incident triggered neither a police investigation nor a ministerial apology.

Another area where police conduct has provoked suspicions of bias is in the handling of labour strikes. On several occasions, law enforcement policy has appeared something less than even-handed. Consider, for example, the bitter Boise Cascade strike that occurred in north-western Ontario towards the end of the 1970s. During the course of this violence-ridden conflict, numerous strikers were arrested as a consequence of ugly encounters on one or more of the picket lines. In a large number of these situations, the strikers spent hours and sometimes even days in jail until "show cause" bail hearings ordered their release. The reason for this special treatment of people who were thought to be generally law abiding and respectable was that the police and prosecutors were seeking special conditions for bail. They wanted the courts to order the accused strikers to stay away from the picket lines until after they had their trials. Most of the time, the bail courts obliged. In the result, the picket lines were decimated.

When the authorities were accused of helping management, they replied that this tactic was necessary to keep trouble-makers from breaching the peace. Despite its seeming plausibility, this answer simply didn't wash. Researchers were unable to find a single case in which such conditions had been imposed upon *non-strikers* charged with picket-line misconduct. Indeed, I came upon the case of a non-striking employee who was released without conditions even though he was accused and later convicted of pulling a knife on one of the strikers, while restraint conditions had been imposed upon strikers charged with—and later acquitted of—nothing more than breaking car windows.

When the Canadian Civil Liberties Association complained of this disparity in pre-trial treatment, the then solicitor-general of Ontario, Roy McMurtry, replied as follows: "I understand that the non-striking workers tended to be more placid in their behaviour than their fellow workers who were on strike. This may be the reason why the striking workers felt that leniency was being shown by the police to non-strikers." This statement provoked the following CCLA rejoinder:

> Even if non-striking workers were generally more placid than the strikers, that would hardly account for the leniency which was shown in the case of the non-striker who was specifically mentioned in our letter. You will recall that he was ultimately convicted in court for pulling a knife on a striker. Such behaviour hardly qualifies as "placid". Indeed, it was considerably more serious than the conduct which led to detentions and bail hearings for so many of the strikers.

McMurtry responded by sending the CCLA a transcript of the hearings where these issues had been discussed before a committee of the Ontario legislature. The transcript revealed a number of references to the non-striker with the knife, but time ran out on the discussions before there was any resolution or reply from the government. When the CCLA wrote once more to McMurtry, seeking an answer to its earlier questions, he replied that he had nothing further to add.

Nowhere has the issue of favouritism in law enforcement appeared more blatant than in the official responses to RCMP wrongdoing. As long ago as the end of 1977, it became public knowledge that members of the RCMP had been involved in the commission of hundreds of unlawful acts including burglary, theft, arson, mail opening, and unauthorized invasion of tax files. Not a single charge has yet been laid outside the province of Quebec. From the very beginning, the governmental response reeked of double standards. Instead of laying charges and launching prosecutions in the normal way, the government dumped everything onto the lap of the McDonald commission, which was created to investigate RCMP wrongdoing. There the whole matter remained bottled up for more than four years.

Why, it must be asked, was it necessary for a royal commission to tell us whether or not members of the RCMP, like everyone else, have to obey the law? The McDonald commission might well have been used to probe and report on what the law *should* be in some of the thorny areas involving national security. It might even have been used to monitor the integrity of possible government prosecutions against the RCMP. But the government used the commission, not to bolster ordinary law enforcement, but to replace it.

After the passage of four years, the expenditure of some ten million dollars, and the accumulation of mountains of testimony, the day of reckoning finally came. The McDonald commission reported and the ball was returned to the government's court. The then federal minister of justice, Jean Chrétien, managed to wait for about a year before deciding what to do about all the RCMP misconduct within his enforcement jurisdiction. Not surprisingly, he decided to do nothing. He announced that there would be no prosecutions for offences at the federal level such as mail opening and the violation of confidential files. Incredibly, he relied heavily on the fact that the limitation periods had expired under some of the relevant statutes. He even had the *chutzpah* to make the point that such limitation periods were "running during the nearly four years" of the McDonald commission. This recalls the old joke about the man who murders both of his parents and then pleads for mercy on the grounds that he is an orphan.

It would be hard to find a document as replete with lame excuses and double standards as the full text of Chrétien's "no prosecution" statement. While he acknowledged that not all of the limitation periods had expired even under the statutes which have them, he refused nevertheless to prosecute in such situations. He said that it would be improper to distinguish between those who would now be protected by the lapse of time and those who could not claim such a benefit. This is simply incredible. In a comparable situation, civilian wrongdoers would not likely receive such leniency. Suppose, for example, certain civilian members of a criminal conspiracy escaped to another jurisdiction. Can you imagine a government refusing, out of "fairness", to prosecute their co-conspirators who remain in our jurisdiction?

For crimes which have no limitation periods—such as mail opening—Chrétien again cited the length of time that had elapsed. Most of the mail openings had reportedly ended in 1972 and he said that none had been carried out since 1976. But civilians have been prosecuted for misdeeds as old as these. Why should the age of an offence operate so uniquely to the Mounties' advantage?

Chrétien also argued that, among members of the RCMP, the mail openings had acquired an aura of legitimacy. This simply does not square with the sworn testimony of high-ranking RCMP officers who said they knew very well that the practice was illegal. Indeed, they had centralized control of mail opening precisely because they had not anticipated its early legalization. In any event, how far has ignorance of the law ever excused civilian wrongdoers?

Chrétien argued further that the RCMP mail-openers were not motivated by personal gain. But isn't it likely that at least some of them acted to curry favour with their superiors and political masters? In any event, how different are these Mounties from many civilians who have been prosecuted despite lofty motives? At the time of the unlawful postal strike of 1978, for example, it was generally believed that Canadian Union of Postal Workers President Jean Claude Parrot was largely motivated by a sincere desire to improve the lot of his union members. Nevertheless, the government of Canada chose to prosecute him and even to urge that he be jailed. Why should the issue of unselfish motives spare Mounties but not posties?

Chrétien based some of his reluctance to prosecute on the fact that the McDonald commission had recommended a limited legalization of mail opening. But such considerations have not routinely immunized civilians. The recommendations of the LeDain commission, for example, never stopped the federal government from prosecuting thousands of civilians for the very offence LeDain would have abolished—the simple possession of marijuana.

To top all this off, Chrétien argued that the government simply did not have enough evidence to prosecute in particular cases. For such purposes, it would be necessary to launch hundreds of investigations.

But why hadn't this already been done? As far back as November 1977, the Canadian Civil Liberties Association had written to the prime minister requesting that the government "launch immediate investigations...into the allegations of illegal conduct in the post office [and other federal agencies]" with a view to laying charges in appropriate cases. The prime minister rejected this recommendation on the basis that it would mean unnecessary duplication of effort. In his view, "the mandate of Mr. Justice McDonald extends to just such investigations".

Similar statements were made by other government spokesmen during the same period. When asked why no charges had been laid in connection with the illegal mail openings, for example, the then justice minister, Ron Basford, replied as follows:

> ...for the very simple reason that any facts or reports I have seen do not contain the precise type of information that is required in the laying of charges against specific officers or constables. That is one of the precise purposes of the hearings of the McDonald inquiry, to put before them facts with sufficient precision so that if charges can be laid, they will be laid.

Yet, apart from a few special matters, the McDonald commission never conducted such case-by-case investigations. Even when it became apparent that the commission had no intention of doing so, the government still did nothing. How far can this record sustain public confidence in the equity of Canadian law enforcement?

Despite this appearance of favouritism and bias, Chrétien's successor as justice minister, Mark MacGuigan, refused to change the policy, arguing that it would be inappropriate to alter the position of his predecessor. But cabinet ministers often alter the policies of their predecessors and they have done so even where prosecutions are concerned. A few years earlier, for example, federal officials let it be known that they would not prosecute native Indians for hunting on unoccupied Crown land in breach of a certain conservation statute. A few years later, however, the policy changed and an Indian man was prosecuted for the very conduct which was supposed to have been immune. If that no-prosecution policy could be changed, why not this one? There was even a stronger basis to resist change in the case of the Indians. The Indian accused, unlike the potential RCMP accused, committed his misdeed *in reliance* on the no-prosecution policy.

None of this is to suggest that there should have been wholesale prosecutions of RCMP wrongdoers. It is simply to question this wholesale immunity.

Apart from Quebec, the provinces have shown no more interest in even-handed justice on this matter than has their federal counterpart. In the case of Ontario, however, the double standards reached exalted levels. Not only did Ontario take no action, but it also stopped private citizens from taking their own. A private citizen attempted to lay charges against certain RCMP officers for allegedly circulating a phony document within a Trotskyist organization. The document, containing some confidential psychiatric information, purported to discredit one of the Trotskyist leaders. Instead of allowing the justice of the peace to decide in the usual way whether the allegations of the citizen justified the criminal process, Ontario Attorney-General Roy McMurtry took the rather unusual step of filing a stay of proceedings. The practical effect was to deprive this citizen of his right to prosecute.

Yet, little more than a year later, the same Roy McMurtry solemnly told the Ontario legislature that it would be improper for him to interfere in the event that private citizens attempted to lay charges with regard to the abortion clinic Dr. Henry Morgentaler was planning to open in Toronto: "If a justice of the peace, exercising unfettered discretion, decides that there is sufficient evidence for the charge to proceed, *it is then and only then* that the Attorney General, acting in open court, may intervene to stop the prosecution [emphasis added]." But, in the RCMP case, McMurtry acted *before* the justice even had a chance to consider the evidence.

It makes a difference. One of McMurtry's reasons for taking such action is that a police investigation had failed to turn up the requisite evidence to support a charge. But, with all due respect to McMurtry, all we have is his word for it. The point of allowing a justice to make the decision first is that the whole matter is reviewed by someone who is presumably outside of the governmental and police entourage. While McMurtry had no trouble respecting this procedure in the case of Dr. Morgentaler, he thought it should be by-passed in the case of the RCMP.

Unfortunately, this short-cut did not exhaust Ontario's resort to double standards and dubious reasoning on the issue of RCMP wrongdoing. Consider the remarkable memorandum which McMurtry filed in support of the stay of proceedings. The memorandum pointed out that the "dirty trick" which the officers were accused of perpetrating in this case formed part of a general RCMP operation known as "Checkmate". What these officers were supposed to have done was no worse than what was allegedly involved in other Checkmate situations. And it was certainly no worse than what was imputed to their seniors and superiors in this very case. But a dearth of evidence with respect to the others precluded prosecutions against them. It would be unfair, argued the memorandum, to single out these officers.

This was a most remarkable proposition. On the basis of McMurtry's reasoning here, it would be improper for the police to prosecute a junior member of a criminal conspiracy while senior members remained at large and unidentified. When was the last time such extravagant mercy was extended to civilian wrongdoers?

The memorandum also argued that it would be unwise to run the risk that the accused officers might be acquitted. If that were to happen, the RCMP misconduct would be perceived by the public and the police as either lawful or, if unlawful, at least acceptable. On this score, surely it would have been better to sustain an acquittal than to avoid a prosecution. While there may be a risk that an acquittal might appear to vindicate the misconduct at issue, a failure to prosecute compounds this risk. It creates the impression that the *government* condoned the wrongdoing.

The memorandum stated that future misconduct was more likely to be deterred by a clear governmental statement in clarification of the law than by an unsuccessful prosecution. On the contrary, a failure to prosecute tells posterity that the government is afraid of a confrontation with the RCMP. But a prosecution, even if unsuccessful, would have conveyed the message that the government would not tolerate such behaviour. Tomorrow's officers would have been made to realize that they might well have to face the unpleasantness of a prosecution and some risk of a conviction if they broke the law.

According to the memorandum, it would be unfair to prosecute individual officers in those cases where the law-breaking was a matter of official RCMP policy. On the basis of this argument, what was primarily at issue was not the personal guilt of those who performed the acts in question but the official policy upon which they were based.

Surely, however, this was not an either-or proposition. One of the effective ways to change a wrongful policy is to prosecute those who unlawfully implement it.

The memorandum also relied heavily on what it called the "inherent contradiction" that allegedly had plagued the RCMP Security Service for years. Essentially this "contradiction" involved breaking the law in order to protect the interests of national security. Despite many attempts, the RCMP complained that it had been unable to obtain federal government guidance on how to resolve the contradiction. McMurtry said that it would be unfair to permit such prosecutions against RCMP officers until there was more definitive evidence on the role of the federal government in their wrongdoing.

Rarely has the invocation of a red herring been accompanied by such piety. To whatever extent federal cabinet ministers might have failed to give the requisite guidance, or even if they had knowingly tolerated RCMP law-breaking, they should have been politically censured or possibly even prosecuted themselves. But how could this excuse the unlawful conduct of any RCMP officer? Like the ordinary citizen, or surely to an even greater extent, police officers are presumed to know the law. They cannot be absolved simply because they have superiors who are more guilty. Indeed, since Nuremberg at least, even obedience to a direct order of a superior will not excuse a subordinate for the commission of an offence. Had a more uniform standard of law enforcement been applied in this situation, we might have seen charges laid against certain officers and then withdrawn in exchange for evidence that might have helped to finger some of their superiors up the line.

The chief problem with McMurtry's reasoning is its insistence on treating police officers by a more lenient standard than is applicable to everyone else. Such an approach has the potential to erode public respect for the rule of law. Consider, for example, the position of the Canadian Labour Congress during the autumn 1978 strike of the Canadian Union of Postal Workers. Despite a common and bitter opposition to the special Act of Parliament terminating the strike, the CLC declined to support CUPW at the point when the latter's action became unlawful. CLC President Dennis McDermott was publicly attacked for his stand by significant elements of his own constituency. What will this country say to its Dennis McDermotts the next time they face such pressure to defy the law? Indeed, so long as RCMP wrongdoers remain immunized, what *can* anyone say?

Other constituencies are bound to be similarly affected. There is every reason to expect the proliferation of conflict and tension among the various interests in our society. Civil servants and their unions are reacting bitterly to the wage restraint efforts of many governments. Native people are planning further efforts to vindicate their long-neglected land claims and treaty rights. The abortion issue continues unabated, perhaps exacerbated by the escalation of "right to life" demonstrations and the planned expansion of Dr. Henry Morgentaler's special clinics. The increasing and welcome heterogeneity of Canada's population has led naturally to a certain increase in dissidence. So long as Mountie law-breakers can be excused, there is a great danger that many other groups will consider themselves no less worthy. What credibility can a government hope to have if it enforces the law in an arbitrary and conspicuously unfair manner?

The memorandum's most plausible argument was that, on the facts and the law, the case was simply inadequate. Since I have neither seen the report of the police investigation nor attempted to negotiate the conflicting interpretations of the Criminal Code, I am unable to either support or rebut this conclusion. I believe, however, that such considerations would apply primarily to a decision by the *government* not to prosecute. They cannot as readily support such interference with the right of a *citizen*. It's not for the attorney-general to decide whether a citizen has an adequate case to prosecute. That's what the justice of the peace is supposed to do. In short, McMurtry had no business by-passing the procedure which he insisted on for Dr. Morgentaler. While the Supreme Court of Canada finally overturned this stay of proceedings, the case remains troubling for what it reveals about the fairness of law enforcement policy.

The issue of police and prosecutorial discretion has become crucial. People's confidence in the democratic system depends heavily on how law enforcement is seen to be exercised. Does it appear biased or fair? Are some groups treated with privilege while others are subject to prejudice? Preferences and priorities are unavoidable. We wouldn't want the same level of police activity for every law. Liquor violations, for example, should not command the same attention as kidnappings and murders. Nor would we want to have charges laid in every case where there was evidence to do so. In real life, there are all sorts of extenuating circumstances.

In view of the apparent bias in many law enforcement decisions, it is no longer acceptable to continue handling this issue as we have in the past. There is now no systematic disclosure to the public of law enforcement policy. We don't know who are making some of these key decisions and on what basis they are doing so.

Consider the bathhouse raids again. What motivated the exercise? Why was such a large contingent of police officers removed from other duties to participate in this one? Was it because the sex in the bathhouses was somehow considered more serious than the other matters that the police had to handle? Was the whole thing simply an exercise in gay-bashing? Were members of the public complaining about the bathhouses? If so, how many and over what period of time? Who made the key decision to launch the six-month investigation and then the raid? Was it made by middle or upper management? When did the chief find out? To what extent, if at all, did the decision-makers believe that their choices reflected the consensus of values in the community? And by what methods was such consensus discerned?

Guidelines for the exercise of discretion should be spelled out and made public. They should become the subject of legislative and community debate. Depending on the subject matter, they might emerge ultimately in various forms. Some might be appropriate simply in the form of rules at the department level; others might more wisely appear as by-laws of local police commissions or municipalities. Still others could become the subject of ministerial directives, cabinet regulations, or, in some cases, even provincial or federal statutes.

By way of illustration, consider again the problem of sex in public washrooms. So long as the sexual acts are not inflicted on children or on unwilling adults, they should generally be regarded, not as a serious matter, but, at worst, as a nuisance. The guidelines should specify that the goal is to prevent the acts rather than to torment the actors. Thus, they should require a number of preliminary measures before there is any question of laying charges. Such measures could include the posting of warning notices and periodic patrols by uniformed officers. Moreover, the guidelines should explicitly prevent the use of video cameras except in response to the most serious threats to the peace and security of the community. At the very least, the use of such equipment should require a regime of legal controls no less exacting than what the law now provides for audio surveillance.

It isn't necessary to agree with the details of my proposed guidelines for public washrooms or video surveillance in order to support the principle of having some guidelines for these and other matters. The public should be satisfied that the policy choices are the outgrowths of the broadest possible discussion and debate. And we should reduce, as far as we possibly can, the opportunity to be arbitrary. Nor is there any particular reason to believe, as some have suggested, that such published guidelines would undermine the independence of the police. Beyond the law and the guidelines, there need be no additional political dictation regarding the selection of people to investigate, the tactics to be employed in such investigations, or even ultimately the charges to be laid. The guidelines would operate as general statements of policy which the police would interpret and apply in particular cases. Of course, the police could subsequently be held accountable for any questionable interpretations of the guidelines. But such a process would not necessarily interfere with their day-to-day operations.

It is possible that published guidelines might jeopardize certain strategies the police use to fight crime. In some situations, they might unduly alert law-breakers about police tactics. At most, however, this is an argument for withdrawing some of the guidelines from public scrutiny. It is not an argument for the amount of non-disclosure which is currently practised.

To what extent would public guidelines undermine the authority of Parliament? How can respect for the rule of law co-exist with guidelines which announce that certain laws will be enforced only under certain circumstances? The fact is that we *already* have discretionary law enforcement. The only difference between the status quo and what I am proposing is that today such decisions are autocratic and my proposals would make them more democratic.

Chapter Six

PUBLIC INQUIRIES

AND PRE-TRIAL PUBLICITY

Knowledge for the Public
versus Fairness for the Parties

The Powers of Public Inquiries

Public inquiries—particularly those convened to assess blame—undermine the right against self-incrimination. Such inquiries subvert the normal rules that people in general don't have to talk to the authorities and that accused people in particular don't have to testify at their trials. At inquiries, virtually anyone can be forced to testify, even those under suspicion. How far, if at all, therefore, can such inquiries be justified in our society? There is one situation long recognized as an exception to our society's general disinclination for these kinds of public inquiries. I refer to the case where wrongdoing has been suspected in a police department or in the upper echelons of government.

In such circumstances, normal investigative procedures could not command sufficient public confidence because they would be subject to the control of interested parties. What confidence could we have, for example, in a police department investigation of corruption among its own members? Such investigations would be so vulnerable to the suspicion of cover-up that there is a special argument for having an inquiry do the job. This explains the ready public acceptance of such commissions as those headed by Mr. Justice David McDonald and Mr. Justice Donald Morand into the RCMP and the Metropolitan Toronto Police, respectively.

Unless there are public inquiries into such matters, the public could be rendered helpless to challenge the misdeeds of powerful bureaucracies. The bureaucrats would be in a position to stall, stonewall, and cover-up. There might well be no way of obtaining the evidence necessary to call malefactors in high places to account.

The justification for a public inquiry in such a situation is simply that it may be necessary in order to ensure ultimate control by the people over the institutions which govern them. In short, it may be necessary for the exercise of effective popular autonomy—a prerequisite of democracy.

In view of how such public inquiries affect the very viability of the democratic system, it is difficult to attach a higher priority to the right against self-incrimination. In this regard, however, our society has taken an important step. It has immunized people from having their coerced testimony used against them at any subsequent trials or hearings. In this way, we trade immunity for information. If we force you to give self-incriminating testimony at a public inquiry, we can't use that testimony against you if you are ultimately charged with an offence.

But, it may be asked, why bother with a public inquiry if we can't use the evidence it gathers? The answer is that our rules don't bar any and all evidence from subsequent use. They simply provide that people are immune from having their *own* testimony used against them in the event that they become the accused in a criminal trial. We are certainly free, however, to use all the other evidence in a prosecution against them.

In the early 1980s, the government of Ontario set up an entirely different kind of public inquiry—the controversial Grange commission into the mysterious baby deaths at Toronto's Hospital for Sick Children. In 1980–81 thirty-six babies died apparently from overdoses of the heart drug digoxin. The police reached the conclusion that the situation involved murder. After a short investigation, several charges of murder were laid against Susan Nelles, a member of the nursing team that had been attending the babies. After more than twenty days of a preliminary hearing, Ms. Nelles was discharged for lack of evidence.

Public frustration became unbearable. The government simply had to do something. What do governments so often do when they have to do something? They create a public inquiry. Accordingly, Mr. Justice Samuel Grange of the Ontario Court of Appeal was named a commissioner to perform essentially two functions: phase one was to find out "how and by what means" those babies died, and phase two was to assess the way the police and prosecutors handled the case of Susan Nelles. Phase two, of course, represented a traditional public inquiry. It was concerned with possible wrongdoing in high places. Phase one, however, involved a new ball game entirely. It appeared to extend the special powers of public inquiries to the identification of wrongdoers *outside* of government.

How then could there be an acceptable justification for the inevitable violations of the right against self-incrimination? In the case of wrongdoing inside of government, the justification is based on the requirements of effective public autonomy. But when the wrongdoing is outside of government, it's much harder to produce a similar justification. Indeed, the commission hearings began to look like an extension of the failed police investigation. If the normal procedures of a police investigation could not find the killer, the special powers of a public inquiry might do the job.

Small wonder that the phase one hearings of the Grange commission triggered an unprecedented wave of criticism in editorials and media commentary across the country. Small wonder too that it provoked articles in respected newspapers outside of Canada, such as the *New York Times*. And small wonder that the powers of the Grange commission were attacked and finally clipped by the Ontario Court of Appeal. In a unanimous judgment, the court barred the commissioner from naming whatever persons he might find were implicated in the deaths at issue.

Yet might there not be a rare category of circumstances where an argument could be made for the powers of a special inquiry to find a wrongdoer outside of government? I refer to a situation in which there is a continuing danger to a particularly sensitive public interest. Suppose, for example, wrongdoing were suspected in a nuclear facility. To what extent could this country accept such a continuing peril to the national security? In such circumstances, there would be enormous pressure for the special powers of an inquiry in order to identify wrongdoers, at least for the purpose of removing them from positions where they could cause harm. If there appeared to be no other practical way to clear the facility of the danger in question, it is inconceivable that such a grant of power would be denied.

To what extent, then, could a similar argument be made about the tragedies at the Hospital for Sick Children? As a result of the baby deaths, numbers of parents might well have been afraid to submit their children to the care of the hospital. For all those parents knew, there were wrongdoers in that hospital who would continue to have access to their babies. Arguably, therefore, the restoration of public confidence in that vital facility could have required the identification and removal of any such continuing danger.

Some argued at the time that it would be enough for such a commission simply to indicate *how* the deaths were caused. The public record of the evidence would then be available for concerned parties to draw whatever conclusions they wished concerning *who* was responsible. Thus, the police, crown attorneys, hospital, and professional licensing bodies could consult the record in order to take whatever action they felt was warranted. According to this argument, there simply was no need for the commissioner to take that additional and dangerous step of naming those he believed were implicated. To these critics, the naming of names was the ultimate fruit of poisonous roots—a violation of the right against self-incrimination.

The difficulty with the "no naming" solution lay in the fact that it threatened to leave a vital public interest inadequately protected. By the time the Grange commission was appointed, the responsible authorities no longer enjoyed sufficient public confidence to assess responsibility for the wrongdoing. The fact that so many babies died in unexplained ways reduced public confidence in the hospital. The fact that charges were laid against an apparently innocent person reduced public confidence in the prosecutors and the police. Thus, the judgments of the authorities were likely seen as unduly tainted by self-interest. That is why it was reasonable to believe that the public preferred to have the considered opinion of someone who was disinterested and independent. While no one would have been legally obliged to accept the judgment of the commissioner, those in authority would have been politically impelled to deal with it.

In some ways, the image of the Grange commission may have been doomed from its inception. The government failed to provide an adequate articulation of precisely what purposes might justify the kind of inquiry it had created. In his speech to the Ontario legislature announcing the establishment of the commission, the then attorney-general, Roy McMurtry, pointed out how the proposed inquiry was "in the interests of the parents of the [dead] children, the dedicated personnel at the hospital...and the administration of justice generally." Significantly, McMurtry's statement made no mention of the most important constituency for these purposes: the present and future users of the hospital. Only *their* interests could possibly have excused the kind of powers that were unleashed during phase one of the inquiry. Yet it was virtually impossible to find a clear statement to this effect.

To a great extent, the controversies at the commission were attributable to this lack of clear purpose. To much of the public, the commission hearings acquired the appearance of an extended police investigation. Indeed, they became universally perceived as a prelude to prosecution. No doubt this impression was fuelled by McMurtry's assurance when he established the commission that "if evidence ever becomes available to warrant the laying of additional charges, the public can be assured charges will be laid and a vigorous prosecution pursued." While the attorney-general did point out that there must not be trial by inquiry, he left open the implication that the inquiry might well assist whatever trial might ensue. Moreover, lawyers for the attorney-general's office and the Metropolitan Toronto Police enjoyed full standing to cross-examine witnesses during phase one and they did so aggressively.

The unique uses of the extraordinary powers which it created required from the government a clear indication that prosecution was *not* the purpose of the exercise. Indeed, the prerequisite for using such powers in this way is a willingness on the part of the government to forgo prosecution if necessary. In short, the legitimate goal of an inquiry of this sort is not to charge potential wrongdoers; it is to stop possible wrongdoing.

To whatever extent the restoration of public confidence in the hospital could justify the kind of powers involved, the decision should have been made and articulated that, even if prosecution could not be pursued because of unfairness, that was a risk worth taking. It would be hard to find such a caution in the government's statements. On the contrary, the government behaved as though a key function of the commission was to pave the way for a possible prosecution. On the other hand, there might be a problem in creating an automatic immunity from prosecution for those named as wrongdoers by an inquiry. Since most inquiries are aimed at wrongdoing in high places, this could be tantamount to adopting a policy of leniency for government officials. But, while prosecution might not irrevocably be ruled out, it should at least be encumbered.

The attorney-general should be required to explain publicly whether, in the circumstances, it is fair to prosecute. Have the hearings at the inquiry made a fair trial possible? Have the potential accused been subjected to an undue amount of interrogation and harassment?

Conversely, would the *failure* to prosecute operate effectively as an unfair immunity for certain types of officials? Of course the courts would still retain the discretion to dismiss, for unfairness, any charges that might come before them. But the idea is to force any government that wants to use the powers of an inquiry in this way to face the very real prospect that it may have to abandon prosecution. Such an approach is necessary in order to reconcile any public need for information with the right against self-incrimination.

Many of the critics of the Grange commission focused unduly on the issue of naming names. Their victory in the Court of Appeal could well have proved to be a pyrrhic one. Since the commissioner was barred from saying "who done it", he may have found himself effectively unable to say who *didn't* do it. Thus, he may have become powerless to remove from the genuinely innocent whatever cloud of suspicion was hovering over them. In recommending that the government compensate Susan Nelles for her earlier legal expenses, the commissioner did help to clear her of lingering suspicion. But suppose there had been other suspects who hadn't incurred such expenses and he wanted to absolve them. The court decision appears to have left all of the important interests in jeopardy. The reputations and fair trial rights of certain parties had already been hurt *and* the users of the hospital might have been prevented from learning enough to feel safe.

One of the key arguments against the commission's naming names was that the identification of such possible wrongdoers is a function of a court of law, not a commission of inquiry. This argument is based upon the assumption that courts necessarily treat people more fairly than do other tribunals. The rules of criminal court are directed, of course, to the outcome that can be visited upon those who are found guilty: a loss of liberty. A proper commission of inquiry, however, generally involves a less onerous outcome, such as injury to reputation or loss of position. There is no doubt, of course, that such outcomes are serious, but it is not clear that they require the precise protections that exist in the criminal courts.

In any event, there is no need to choose between the ultra-tight controls of the criminal courts and the much looser procedures of many commissions of inquiry. There is a lot of room in between. Certainly there is nothing to prevent a commission from devising viable protections even if they are not exact replicas of what is available in the criminal courts. Indeed, there are many tribunals, other than courts, in our society that have managed to strike an admirable balance between the requirements of sound adjudication and the canons of procedural fairness: for example, the labour relations boards, the municipal boards, and the human rights boards of inquiry. If the procedural rules of a commission are not adequate, the answer is not to truncate its legitimate functions. The answer is to change its defective procedures.

For all of these reasons, the criticisms of the Grange commission should have emphasized not the naming of names but the safeguards that must accompany the process. A lot more could have been done to protect the reputations of the innocent and the fair trial rights of anyone ultimately charged.

As a consequence of this experience, it would be wise to begin addressing the kinds of safeguards that might be adopted for future inquiries. In this connection, consider the role of the attorney-general and the police during phase one. They were not needed to help a commission such as this identify the source of wrongdoing. But, because of their involvement with law enforcement, they must have been seen as using the commission's special powers to build a case for prosecution. While the proceedings of a commission may possibly trigger criminal charges, this is not what they should have been designed for.

There should also be some attempt to set tougher guidelines for admissible evidence. While an inquiry may well permit more latitude than a court, it should not allow the kind of scope exercised by this commission. On a number of occasions, for example, witnesses were asked and allowed to testify about their groundless suspicions concerning named individuals. While there is some indication that this was an unintended by-product of a decision made for other purposes, the rules should be clarified so as to minimize the risk of recurrence. Future inquiries should be explicitly required, at the very least, to exclude testimony whose prejudicial impact is great but whose probative value is slight.

Significantly, some of the controversial procedures and testimony at the Grange commission were not disputed by counsel for the parties concerned. While counsel likely had sound tactical reasons for handling those situations as they did, the question this raises concerns the appropriateness of the traditional adversary process for this kind of inquiry. Should we rethink the proper role, for example, of the commissioners and their counsel in such circumstances? Is there an argument for the addition of some other constituency, such as a special public interest counsel or perhaps even a human rights or civil liberties group, in order to increase the likelihood that some of these "due process" considerations will be more adequately addressed?

It has also been suggested that some of the damage caused by such inquiries can be significantly reduced by holding their hearings in camera. According to this argument, adequate public scrutiny can be achieved by releasing the transcripts of all the evidence with the commissioner's ultimate report. In that way, accusations against persons would not go undefended for long periods of time. Allegations and their responses would be available together so that members of the public might evaluate them at the same time.

The real world, however, is rarely as neat as the theoretical models. It is quite conceivable, for example, that media representations of transcript material might miss or de-emphasize some important details of a witness's subsequent reply to an earlier allegation. There is also a possibility that a ruling of the commissioner might have interfered with the ability of certain witnesses adequately to defend themselves. Indeed, closed hearings could effectively deprive the parties of a vital safeguard against the unfair conduct of an inquiry.

The knowledge that the public is watching as things happen can serve as deterrent and remedy against high-handedness and misjudgment on the part of those entrusted with such special power. For these purposes, it must be remembered that not every decision of such an inquiry can lawfully or practically be appealed. On the other hand, some critics of the Grange commission in particular argued that openness proved of little help to the parties there. Indeed, it was perceived as one of the causes of the harm. What is hard to measure, however, is whether in camera hearings might not make such situations even *worse*.

Another possibility for reducing the damage caused by public inquiries is a combination of openness and withdrawal. Consider, for example, open hearings with media coverage deferred (if this were constitutionally permissible), as is the case with preliminary hearings in criminal matters. On this basis, the media could attend the hearings and take notes but such material would not generally be published or broadcast until, let us say, any consequent trials had been completed. Alternatively, there could be openness and media coverage but no media cameras in the hearing room. There are pros and cons to all these questions that require the most careful examination.

In any event, we should consider adopting a special safeguard for those future inquiries which are allowed to finger wrongdoers. In order to protect the fairness of any possible trials, it would be wise to ensure that the public does not learn who has been named by a commissioner until after the trial of any persons charged or a specified period elapses without such charges being laid. It is unavoidable in open inquiries, of course, that unpleasant things will be said about named individuals. It is significantly more damaging, however, for a person to be accused by the commissioner than by another witness.

According to such a moratorium proposal, the public would still find out as usual the names of those under charge. But it would not learn at that time whether the persons charged are the ones the commissioner identified. A moratorium along these lines would help to ensure that potential jurors would not be influenced by the commissioner's findings. Significantly, the McDonald commission on RCMP wrongdoing recommended a similar measure.

It is to be hoped that inquiries such as phase one of the Grange commission will be an extremely rare event in our society. Nevertheless, we may have to recognize the possibility that the complexities of modern life may some day produce another situation needing such treatment. It is important, therefore, to extract the long-term lessons from this experience. To whatever extent there is felt to be an overriding public interest for using special powers in a similar manner, the government should articulate that interest in very clear terms. It should make clear also its willingness, if necessary, to forgo prosecution. The procedures of such inquiries should be tailored to their legitimate purposes. And workable safeguards should be adopted for the protection of the parties. Such an approach cannot guarantee, of course, an ideal balance between the public's need for information and the parties' rights against self-incrimination. Alternative approaches, however, are likely to produce something discernibly worse.

The Problem of Pre-trial Publicity

"Trial by media" has become a pejorative epithet in our society. The feeling is that adjudication must occur in the dignified setting of a courtroom, not in the sensationalized representations of the media. A number of rules, customs, and practices have evolved in order to keep the media from jeopardizing due process.

The law of contempt of court threatens to punish anyone who engages in undue public commentary about a case that is pending before the courts. Evidence given at preliminary hearings in criminal matters is subject to a "no publication" ban until the actual trial of the accused person. And, as I indicated above, at least one public inquiry—the McDonald commission—recommended suspending publication of those parts of its report that identified possible wrongdoers. Some law reformers have gone so far as to call for a new law barring the media from publishing, until trial or conviction, the names of accused people.

It's one thing to provide that *governments* desist from publishing those parts of a public inquiry report that identify wrongdoers. It's another thing, however, to propose legislation that would restrict the legal rights of the *media* to publish certain matter. Indeed, I believe that, in some respects at least, the law may already be excessively restrictive of the freedom to comment publicly on pending court cases.

During the fall of 1983 alone, there were three separate incidents in which such freedom to speak and to publish were threatened with possible legal attack. In December of that year, the then chief justice of Canada, Bora Laskin, rebuked Ottawa lawyer Lawrence Greenspon for participating in a number of media interviews involving his upcoming Charter challenge of cruise missile tests over Canadian soil. In arguing his case outside of court before arguing it inside, Greenspon, in Laskin's view, had come "close to contempt of court".

It's hard to fathom the judge's reasoning. Indeed, the lawyer's interviews might have made a positive contribution to the public interest. They might have helped to inform the public about the complicated issues in the case, so that more people would be more able to follow what happened when the matter got to court. To restrict such pre-hearing commentary is to make the public excessively dependent on press reports of the incomprehensible legalisms that are often uttered in court.

Moreover, why shouldn't Greenspon's client have been entitled to his advocacy skills in media interviews? His client in this case was Operation Dismantle, a peace organization that had an interest in trying to persuade the public about the merits of its cause. Even though the case at that time was before the courts, the issue of cruise missile challenges was also very much before the government, Parliament, and the public. The democratic processes required the full participation of everyone who was knowledgeable on the subject. Why should involvement in such a court case have restricted anyone's participation in the accompanying political debates?

In any event, how could Greenspon's public pronouncements possibly undermine the court processes? In no way was he dealing with matters of evidence whose disclosure could prejudice a potential jury. He was dealing essentially with legal and policy issues that were slated for consideration by professionally trained judges. When such issues are involved, the adjudicators are not confined, as they may be on questions of evidence, to what they hear in the courtroom.

Indeed, I question how far such pre-trial restrictions should apply even to matters of evidence. In October of the same year the panelists at an Ontario Press Council forum were given a lawyer's letter cautioning them about any statements they might wish to make on the subject of the controversial Susan Nelles case. Since Nelles had begun a lawsuit against certain law enforcement officials, the panelists were warned to be particularly careful not to say anything that could influence a potential member of the jury. If it were alleged, for example, that the police had been out to "get" the young nurse, the speaker might be found in contempt of court.

As important as it is to protect the right of fair trial for all parties involved in court cases, should this right operate as such a broad restriction on freedom of speech and the press? Why should a private lawsuit of the kind Nelles launched deprive the public of an important and timely debate about the police handling of her case? The entire public has an interest in determining at the earliest possible moment whether the police may have misbehaved.

It simply will not suffice to tell the public, as some courts periodically have done, that freedom of speech on such matters is not being denied, it is simply being delayed—until the end of the trial. Such replies are hardly consoling. This kind of litigation could go on for years. If there was indeed misconduct in the police investigation, might it not be repeated against other people? Moreover, several years after the event, there will be much less inclination for a vigorous debate. The passage of time has a way of eroding political enthusiasm. Where issues of such public importance are concerned, why can't the legal and political processes run concurrently? Why should the courts be allowed to exercise this kind of monopoly over whatever issues are brought before them? In short, I question why the judicial process should enjoy such an automatic priority over all of the other processes in our society.

In any event, if the chief harm is the undue influencing of potential jurors, this might be addressed in the jury selection process. Or we might even ask the provinces to dispense with the right to trial by jury in some civil cases. I assume that our society would be prepared to trust its judges to resist the influence of a public debate. Indeed, this is the kind of trust we repose in them all the time. Judges are often expected, for example, to exclude from their consideration some evidence they have ruled inadmissible. If we depend on our judges to disabuse themselves of something they may have heard within the last two minutes, why can't that apply to something that they may have read within the last two months? Despite the importance we attach to trial by jury, its preservation in civil disputes cannot outweigh the right of the public to a full and timely scrutiny of its vital institutions.

I have more sympathy with the attempt to curtail public comment about impending criminal trials. This is designed to reduce the risk that innocent people will be railroaded into jail as a consequence of sensationalizing by the media. Yet, even in criminal matters, the law of contempt may go too far.

In September of 1983, a former Toronto alderman, accused of indecently assaulting a juvenile, convened a press conference to answer the charges against him. The *Toronto Star* report of the press conference omitted some of the alderman's most crucial arguments. Perhaps the omission was explained by the *Star*'s rather remarkable comment that much of what the accused and his supporters had to say could well be a contempt of court. How bizarre! A law whose prime function is to protect the accused winds up suppressing what he says in his own defence.

It's not clear how far, if at all, any of the above matters would actually have been found in contempt of court. But when the *Toronto Star*, an eminent Press Council lawyer, and the chief justice of Canada raise the contempt issue in relation to such matters, it becomes apparent that the law itself has to be changed. A viable democracy cannot afford to create such an aura of doubt about the legality of legitimate debate.

But, even if it were conceded that the law was too restrictive of free speech in the foregoing respects, we would still be obliged to consider the other restrictions which have been proposed, such as the ban on naming accused people. In this regard, the case of Susan Nelles aroused a lot of controversy across the country. The young nurse's ordeal triggered a soul-searching and painful debate. Should the mass media have been allowed to disclose her identity when she was charged? Despite her discharge, will she ever really be free of public suspicion? Is this an acceptable consequence in a society that believes people should be presumed innocent until their guilt is proved beyond a reasonable doubt?

For these purposes, I assume that the proposal for a ban on naming accused people has nothing to do, as some have suggested, with the right to a fair trial. Since there cannot be pre-trial publication of most evidence, how can the mere publication of an accused's name affect the right to a fair trial? By the time the case comes to court the jury will know the name anyway. How much difference would it make to the mind-set of the jurors if they heard the name earlier? The interest to be protected in such a publication ban is not the right to a fair trial; it is the enjoyment of a fair reputation. How far, if at all, does this interest support the proposed prohibition?

On the other side of the ledger, there is freedom of the press and the public's right to know. The arrest of a person represents a public act of a public official in the course of a public duty. Members of the public should have a right to know, therefore, what has been done on their behalf, to whom, and why. The powers to investigate, arrest, and prosecute are awesome. As much as possible, a democratic society must ensure that such powers are exercised without favour or bias. Full and free disclosure enables the public at large to perform this monitoring function. Indeed, the knowledge that investigative and prosecutorial decisions are subject to public scrutiny could also operate to deter improprieties in the administration of justice.

Consider, for example, the Watergate scandals in the United States. If there had been a ban on identifying accused people at the time charges were laid, the American people would have been unable to monitor the exercise of prosecutorial discretion when it was important to do so. They would have been obliged to wait months and sometimes years until trials began or convictions were imposed. Even then, their knowledge would have been incomplete. To learn who has been convicted does not reveal who has been charged. Until all the cases are disposed of, the possibility remains that other names will come to light. By that time, of course, the issue will have lost its political impact.

Some commentators have suggested that a distinction be drawn for people in public life. While acknowledging the importance of the public being able to monitor prosecutorial decisions with respect to public people, these commentators have argued that this need not hold for private people. But how shall such a distinction be drawn? Suppose, for example, a cousin or friend of the attorney-general were charged with a criminal offence. Obviously the public would have an interest in knowing that the law enforcement authorities were prepared to go after such a person. Yet the accused might well be a person who had never opted for public life. How could a legal test possibly be formulated so as to apply here but not to other private people?

Some have suggested that it would not be necessary to publish the name of such an accused person. The disclosure of the relationship to the attorney-general would suffice. But would this be fair? If one of the attorney-general's twelve cousins or five close friends was charged, what would the publicity say? A cousin was charged? Or a close friend? Publicity of this kind would engulf *all* of the twelve cousins and five friends in a cloud of suspicion. Why would this be better than naming the specific person who had been charged?

Some who favour such prohibitions on disclosure concede the difficulty in making these distinctions. Nevertheless, they argue that the public only needs this kind of information in a small percentage of the cases where charges are laid. Better, therefore, not to allow publication in *any* cases. I believe this reasoning is fallacious. The fact is we simply don't know how often prosecutorial decisions may reflect on the integrity of the administration of justice. People interact with government in an infinite variety of ways. And these interactions are not susceptible to prior prediction. Even if such situations represent a minority of the charges laid, they might still provide a significant barometer of government conduct.

Consider the following hypothetical people: a silent contributor to the governing political party, one of the opposition parties, or a particularly troublesome pressure group; a business proprietor the government is attempting to entice into making a substantial investment; a business proprietor who has irrevocably refused to make such an investment; influential members of a union that is involved in delicate negotiations with either government or key industries in the community; influential members in rival unions; members of religious cults or established churches; members of the dominant white Anglo-Saxon majority or of a non-white ethnic minority. For every one of these people, it might well be in the public interest for the public to know whether there had been a decision for or against prosecution. The examples go on and on. Favouritism and prejudice have unlimited opportunities to exert their influence.

There may even be situations where, at the time of publication, the press simply do not know the relevant facts that could have influenced the decision for or against charging an accused person. The publication of the name might provoke some follow-up activity on the part of certain readers. Suppose, for example, certain readers identified the published names as being associated with a political party, business operation, trade union, religious cult, or ethnic minority. While these associations might have had no apparent relevance to the charge, they might nevertheless provoke someone to investigate the possibility of a pattern of harassment. Of course, unless the connection were apparent, it might be improper for a media story to include such associations. By now, few newspapers would be likely to publish gratuitously the religious or ethnic identities of accused people.

If there were a prohibition against naming those charged, it could conceivably extend to those who were merely under investigation. If that were to happen, the public would lose another valuable barometer for holding the administration of justice to account. In an earlier chapter I mentioned an investigation the Toronto police conducted into a speech which black community leader Dudley Laws had delivered at an alternative school. Mr. Laws' reputation as an anti-police activist provoked the Canadian Civil Liberties Association to call on the police authorities to explain the purpose of the investigation. The civil liberties organization knew about this incident from reports in the press. If there had been a ban on naming people in such situations, the police might never have been called to account for what appeared to be unwarranted intimidation. It doesn't take much imagination to envision a situation where the victim of the harassment in question is someone a little more publicity-shy than Mr. Laws.

In early 1983, the press publicized a raid which the Toronto police carried out against the Church of Scientology. Despite the fact that the police seized mountains of the church's material, no charges were laid for more than a year. It is important that the police be required to account for such an intrusion even if the Scientologists might have preferred that the raid not be publicized. Regardless of the church's wishes, it may nevertheless be in the public interest to know what the police did. Suppose the police had been involved in wrongfully harassing an unpopular cult? Disclosure would make possible a public response which could protect everyone else's interests.

The same is true of the many victims of RCMP security surveillance. Through the media, the public learned of the improper investigations which had been conducted against such lawful dissenters as the Parti Québécois and the Waffle faction of the New Democratic Party. The media also carried allegations of RCMP surveillance against civil rights lawyer Clayton Ruby and the president of the National Farmers Union. If the permission of the targets had to be secured as a pre-requisite to publication, we cannot be sure that it would have been forthcoming. Some of these parties might have feared that disclosure would irreparably imperil their political or other fortunes.

Nevertheless, it was in the interests of *many others* that these matters become public. Disclosure served to alert the public to the possibility of improper surveillance by the RCMP. In that way, other constituencies could take political action to contain the RCMP.

The publicizing of such matters also serves as a deterrent against improper cover-ups. Suppose, as was feared, the Scientologists had infiltrated the police and the government. If the raid hadn't been publicized, improper pressures could more easily have been exerted against laying any charges. The matter could more readily have been covered up so as to immunize those suspected of criminal behaviour.

There is another valid purpose served through a policy of publication—self-protection. Susan Nelles had held a position of del-icate public trust. The disclosure of the charge against her acted as a warning to others—hospital administrators and private parties who may have considered employing her as a nurse. If the police thought there was enough evidence to justify charging her with mur-der, shouldn't others be warned about the dangers of reposing so much trust in her?

Many of the proponents of prohibiting such publication argue that this is one of the very consequences we should seek to avoid. Susan Nelles was entitled to be presumed innocent until she was proved guilty. It is unfair, therefore, that she carry a stigma of guilt simply because she was charged. But the presumption of innocence was never intended to be an all-purpose doctrine. Its major function is to protect people from state-imposed incarceration unless there is the requisite proof of guilt. It was not designed to protect reputation or employment.

The exacting standard of proof—beyond a reasonable doubt—grows out of the high priority our society attaches to physical freedom. But we don't require that standard of proof in order to assess people for employment. The more delicate the responsibilities may be, the lower the standard of proof we require. Mere membership in the Communist Party, for example, might presumptively disqualify a person from holding a government position in which there is access to secret defence information. This disqualification can be defended even if there isn't an iota of evidence that the impugned person has been guilty of actual misconduct. It just doesn't make sense to protect a person's right to a job simply because misconduct has not been proved beyond a reasonable doubt. Indeed, suppose a person charged with a relevant offence were acquitted at trial. The fact of acquittal cannot automatically guarantee the restoration of the job. Suppose, for example, there had been substantial evidence of guilt and the acquittal was attributable primarily to a technicality? In such circumstances, it would be hard to argue for the person's automatic reinstatement.

In the early 1980s, an Alberta husband and wife were charged with criminal offences involving the abuse of children in a hostel they operated for wayward youngsters. In many cases, their clients were parents who sent their children to the hostel in the hope of improving certain behaviour problems. Shouldn't these parents have a right to know that the people they were entrusting with their children had been charged with abusing those children? Wouldn't it be improper to keep those parents in the dark about the fact that the police and prosecutorial authorities believed there was substantial evidence of criminal abuse of their children?

Suppose a food distributor were charged with selling substandard meat. Would there be some virtue in withholding such knowledge from the consuming public until the matter came to trial several months later? Remember, charges are not supposed to be laid unless there are reasonable and probable grounds to believe in the guilt of the accused. While that may not be a high enough standard to justify physical incarceration, it is enough to justify a warning to potential consumers. If it subsequently emerged that the police did not have the requisite grounds to lay the charge, there should, of course, be hell to pay. The officers should be disciplined or even charged themselves. At the very least, compensation should be forthcoming to the person who was wrongly accused. Such considerations explain the high level of public sympathy for the idea of compensating Susan Nelles following her discharge at the preliminary hearing and the proceedings of the Grange commission.

Some people have recommended a compromise measure in which the courts would be empowered, in certain circumstances, to impose on the media an order banning the names of those under charge or investigation. The difficulty with this approach is that it would likely enshrine a number of double standards in our legal system. The courts would be more likely to order such a ban in the case of middle-class people who would more readily be seen as having reputations which could be damaged. Yet it is most important for the public to learn how the authorities are treating both the reputable *and* those of lesser standing.

The conflict between the protection of reputation and the public need for information is a particularly painful one for civil libertarians. Whichever choice we make, we are undermining an interest to which we are deeply committed. For all of the reasons indicated, I believe that it is generally less bad to permit than to restrict publication. This does not mean, of course, that every name of every accused person must, in fact, be published. It means simply that the names must be publishable. That fact itself operates as some deterrent to potential misconduct on the part of the law enforcement authorities. Nor does it mean that there couldn't be some individual exceptions to the general rule such as, for example, certain prohibitions against publishing the names of accused juveniles.

Further measures might be adopted to reduce the dangers to personal reputation. Perhaps the media could be persuaded or even pressured to ensure that the ultimate vindication of an accused person receives a level of publicity comparable to what was given at the time of the original charge. And our contempt-of-court laws might be amended or clarified in order to ensure accused people a clear right to speak out in their own defence before their trials are held. That might help at least somewhat to dissipate the cloud of guilt which so often accompanies the publication of a charge.

Of course, none of these measures is adequate. There simply is no adequate solution to this painful conflict. What I suggest, however, is that the approach recommended here represents the least inadequate of the available alternatives.

Chapter Seven

THE REGULATION
OF THE ECONOMY

The Quest for Communal Equity
versus the Right to Commercial Liberty

According to an influential sector of North American public opinion, an essential element of democracy is the freedom of the marketplace: the right to buy, sell, and rent one's services, produce, or land. In the opinion of those who subscribe to this philosophy, it is unrealistic to talk about political or personal freedom unless this includes a right to acquire and control the disposition of property. In those systems of government where the state owns or controls most of the property and wealth, no one feels independent enough to challenge the powers that be. The centrality of economic motives in people's lives makes them susceptible to the will of those who control their access to the things that money can buy. To whatever extent this control extends to food, shelter, clothing, and health services—in short, the necessities of life—the prospects for independent action are reduced. Since the ability to act independently is what makes a democratic opposition possible, we can expect less democracy where there is more control of property by the agencies of the state.

That's why, according to this philosophy, the contemporary enemies of freedom include not only the totalitarians (Fascists and Communists) but also those who advocate democratic socialism and more welfare-state measures. Regardless of the *intent* of the social democrats and welfare-state liberals, the *effect* of what they advocate is seen as promoting the conditions of statist control. In consequence, there has been a growing movement in North America to roll back much of the welfare state—to transfer certain utilities from public to private ownership and control, to reduce many of the government regulations over business activity, and to cut the scope and number of government services.

The proponents of this philosophy in the United States include economists Milton Friedman and Friederich Hayek, well-known writers and media performers William F. Buckley, Jr. and George F. Will, influential senators Barry Goldwater and Jessie Helms, the religious proselytizers of the Moral Majority, and even President Ronald Reagan. In Canada their confrères can be found in a number of constituencies: the National Citizens Coalition, the British Columbia Social Credit Party, the Libertarian Party, the *Sun* newspaper chain, and key sectors of the right wing of both the Conservative and Liberal parties. While many of these people claim that their proposals represent sound economics and social policy, they also argue that what they advocate is essential for democracy and civil liberties. It is the latter claim which should be addressed here.

In the first place, we should dispose of the either-or fallacy that infects much of the free market philosophy. Practically speaking, there never has been and likely never will be a completely free or state-planned economy. For people who live in the real world, the critical questions are how much and where, not whether, the market should be free or planned.

In the second place, not every state-imposed regulation of market activity diminishes the freedoms of all the participants. Indeed, it may well be argued that some state restrictions operate so as to enhance the freedoms of many affected parties. Consider, for example, the impact of our labour laws. At one time, there were no laws requiring employers to pay minimum wages or to observe maximum hours of work. The overwhelming majority of working people were paid a pittance even though they regularly toiled day and night. There was almost no leisure time and what little there was could not be enjoyed because virtually all of the workers' stipend had to be allocated for the necessities of life. Not surprisingly, the life span of most workers was significantly less than what it is today.

According to the theory of the marketplace, those workers were always free to quit their jobs and seek more suitable employment elsewhere. The problem, of course, is that this freedom was more theoretical than actual. For the greatest number of working people, there was no suitable employment elsewhere. Effective freedom in the marketplace depends essentially on the bargaining power people can wield. And this bargaining power, in turn, depends on a number of factors over which many people simply have no control—for example, just plain luck. In reality, only a handful of workers had the kind of skills that enabled them to bargain effectively for better working conditions. Thus, the overwhelming majority of the labour force had to accept a condition of wage slavery in order to obtain the barest necessities of life.

Between that day and ours, a host of laws has been enacted restricting many of these marketplace freedoms. Today there are strict limits on the number of hours that many employers can require or even permit their employees to work. Employers are also required to pay at least a certain scale of minimum wages and to provide for vacations and vacation pay. If a certain percentage of a particular work force wishes to be represented by a union, the employer can be compelled by law to recognize that union and engage in collective bargaining with it.

Current law also requires employers and employees to make payments for the purposes of unemployment insurance and workers' compensation. In the event that lay-offs or injuries cause unemployment, these funds will provide the victims with varying levels of income. Following the adoption of these and other restrictions, the overwhelming number of workers in our society have a lot more money and leisure time than their counterparts of a mere half-century ago. While it may be true that other factors have influenced this development, it's hard to resist the conclusion that some combination of these reforms made at least a contribution.

Have these compulsory benefits reduced our overall freedom? It is true, of course, that many employers have considerably less freedom than they did a half-century ago. But how can that be said about their employees? Doesn't the increase in leisure time and money mean more effective freedom for *them*?

To perceive today's marketplace simply in terms of freedom versus restrictions is overly simplistic. It is more valid to see much of it in terms of freedoms versus freedoms. By restricting certain freedoms of employers, we have created new freedoms for employees. Thus, the only meaningful questions are *which* freedoms and *whose* freedoms are to be enhanced or diminished.

To press the point a little further: I have never met, and, indeed, do not know of, any free marketeer who believes that our society should not have criminal laws and police departments to enforce them. These free marketeers have no difficulty understanding that the freedoms they prize would be rendered meaningless in a state of anarchy. If you have to spend most of your life looking over your shoulder and building defences against criminal attack, your freedom will not be worth very much. Restrictions on criminal activity are seen as a way of enhancing rather than reducing the state of our freedom.

Why can't this reasoning be applied to the economic area as well? Just as we feel the need for certain state-imposed protections from physical assault, so too do many of us feel the need for certain state-imposed protections from economic assault. In short, an economic state of anarchy can be just as debilitating to the enjoyment of freedom as a physical state of anarchy.

In the third place, the marketplace has always been governed by rules and regulations. Unless there were physical anarchy, it could not have been otherwise. Thus, the free marketeer is simply exercising a preference for the old rules over the new ones. There is no reason why many of the old rules are any more consonant with freedom than their modern counterparts.

At one time, for example, the rule between sellers and buyers was *caveat emptor*: unless a contract otherwise stipulated, "let the buyer beware". How does this rule better serve the cause of freedom than the modern rules that require, among other things, honest advertising from sellers? Many sellers are in a better position than buyers to know the defects of their products. In the absence of a precise agreement to the contrary, why shouldn't *they* bear the primary responsibility if the product turns out to be something other than what they had every reason to believe the buyers intended to purchase?

In order to avoid the perils of *caveat emptor*, many consumers would need to retain experts to inspect the items they were about to buy. Such precautions would clearly be beyond their practical ability. Why should it be considered an intrusion on freedom to relieve consumers of this anxiety? Of course, the seller's freedom may be diminished but again the question is not whether freedom *per se* is reduced but which freedom and whose.

Consider, for example, the relationship between restaurateurs and customers. Who is in the better position to know whether the food is healthy, defective, or foul? If *caveat emptor* applied, what should the customers do? Should they draw up contracts on entering restaurants describing in very precise terms the quality of the food they are contracting to eat? Alternatively, should they seek access to kitchens so that they and their experts may carry out proper inspections of the facilities? The response of the modern welfare state has been to enact legislation imposing certain standards on the sellers of food in favour of the consumers. In that way, restaurant customers can have a reasonable level of confidence that the food they are about to order has been prepared under acceptable health conditions.

Now, why are these rules favouring the consumer any more intrusive of freedom than *caveat emptor*? Every rule restricts *someone's* freedom. The only issue is whether these rules ought to favour sellers or buyers.

To be sure, there are many equities on both sides. There is also a host of economic factors that have to be weighed. Perhaps distinctions should be drawn for certain buyers and certain sellers. Perhaps neither *caveat emptor* nor a system of "sellers beware" should apply universally. It is not my function here, of course, to prescribe a set of rules for the market relationship between sellers and buyers. I am simply making the point that freedom can rarely be the decisive factor in these matters. The approach of the welfare state is that there is no reason to allow yesterday's wisdom to rule in perpetuity. Modern legislatures should not feel inhibited about reassessing how previous generations may have struck the balance between the affected parties.

Consider also the landlord-tenant relationship. In many situations, the common law courts used to require tenants to pay what their leases specified, even if the leased premises became unliveable. If the place were completely destroyed by flood, fire, or other mishaps of nature, the tenants still had to pay. The only way tenants in these circumstances could be spared was to ensure, in advance, that the lease contained a special provision exculpating them from liability in the event that the premises were destroyed.

Again, there is no reason to believe that the interests of freedom are more effectively served by burdening rather than relieving the tenant of such liability. Since there has to be a rule governing what happens in those situations about which the lease is silent, why can't such a rule favour the tenant instead of the landlord? Why shouldn't the modern state feel free to rework the equities according to its own, rather than its predecessors', concepts of right and wrong?

Fourthly, there is the issue of accountability. When private parties make market decisions, they are accountable essentially to themselves. Decisions are made on the basis of what is likely to enhance the wealth of the decision-makers. The theory of the free market is that most people will benefit from this process. Investment will be directed towards those economic activities that satisfy the wants and needs of consumers because that is the best way to make money. On this basis, most, if not all, will live happily ever after.

Unfortunately, experience has revealed a sizeable gap between theory and reality. During those periods when the marketplace was the primary source of authority, the interests of large numbers of people were simply neglected. The much touted law of supply and demand is somewhat misnamed. It should be renamed the law of supply and *effective* demand. The consumers whose needs and wants determine what will be produced and distributed are those who have purchasing power—that is, money.

In one of his inaugural addresses as president of the United States during the depression of the 1930s, Franklin Delano Roosevelt declared that he saw one-third of his nation "ill-housed, ill-clad, and ill-nourished". He also contended that, as long as the key economic decisions were made in the marketplace, such destitution would continue. Builders, food processors, and clothing manufacturers lacked the requisite incentive to house, feed, and clothe the destitute of America. The potential buyers did not have enough money to enrich the potential sellers. Thus, the marketplace could be expected to neglect Roosevelt's one-third in perpetuity.

In varying degrees during the last half-century, governments in the Western democratic world have responded as Roosevelt did. They have adopted devices for influencing the decisions of the marketplace sellers and directing more money to the less well off buyers. In short, they have begun to engage in an increasing exercise of state planning of their respective economies. In order to encourage low-cost housing, governments have made low-cost loans to builders and guaranteed the mortgages of buyers. Tax incentives have been made available to those who engage in many other economic and business activities that government has considered to be in the public interest. In order to ensure that the uncoordinated decisions of entrepreneurs did not lead to premature and depressing surpluses, governments have imposed production quotas in some sectors and have required that certain marketing be done through specified agencies. In order to reduce many of the costs of other necessities of life, governments have regulated certain prices (such as in rent control) and have imposed restrictions on how certain services are to be delivered (for example, medicare).

Another way of influencing market decisions has been the assumption of direct ownership by government of many economic enterprises. Today in Canada, for example, the public owns outright an airline, a railway, a medium of mass communication, and certain sources of electric power. Moreover, government also makes available to certain constituencies of people direct amounts of money through unemployment insurance, workers' compensation, family allowances, and general welfare benefits.

Presumably, one of the consequences of all this government intrusion in the marketplace is the creation of a level of democratic accountability for many crucial economic decisions that affect the entire community. Since agencies of government and the public are now making these decisions, the people affected have more say over such decisions. Ultimately, of course, the people assert their interests by the way they vote at election time.

Again, it is not my function to say how far, if at all, this government involvement is good for the economy. All I am arguing, at this point, is that it is hard to characterize government involvement in such economic decisions as *per se* undemocratic. Indeed, to the extent that such involvement renders the crucial decisions of daily life reviewable by those who are affected by them, such arrangements may well be *more* democratic.

It might still be argued that if government were to control virtually all economic decisions, the situation would be undemocratic because there would be no independent power centres to exert countervailing pressures on government. While no one state-planning measure could validly be seen as damaging in this way, the accumulation of many incremental measures could produce in time an anti-democratic impact. For reasons which I will indicate shortly, I believe that Western societies are a long distance from such a point today. In any event, these are fair questions to raise in trying to sort out today's issues. It is fair to ask how much freedom will likely be won or lost by the cumulative effect of the measures that we are being urged to adopt. There is no reason why such considerations cannot consciously be faced, issue by issue. My point simply is that there is no justification for any assumption that the adoption of such additional measures would *necessarily* reduce the aggregate freedom in society. Indeed, as I have already indicated, some such measures might even increase and enhance the range of many people's freedoms.

The fifth factor concerns the ethics of redistributing wealth. In order for government to assume public ownership, regulate economic transactions, and provide benefits, it needs a tremendous amount of money. Where will such money come from? There are two possibilities—voluntary subscription and mandatory subscription. In certain right-wing literature, vigorous arguments are made in favour of a voluntary tax system. In the opinion of this literature, the compulsory tax system is a form of theft that involves "stealing" from one to give to another.

The problem with the metaphor of theft is that it assumes the moral acceptability of yesterday's rules governing economic transactions. Much private wealth is attributable to such phenomena and just plain luck. If modern society questions the morality of accumulating wealth under such conditions, why shouldn't it be free to make changes? And, if such changes are going to cost money, why shouldn't modern society also be free to impose the requisite taxation?

Some free marketeers argue, however, that yesterday's rules acquire their legitimacy, not from their inherent morality, but from the fact that they happened to be in effect when certain transactions occurred. What amounts to theft, or at least unfairness, is taking from people the money they made if, at the time they made it, they were observing the rules then in place. In all fairness, it must be acknowledged that there is some merit to this argument. Yesterday's rules do deserve *some* deference. But so do today's needs. In a world without absolutes, reasonable people have to avoid slavish adherence to such market principles. Thus, neither the precedents of yesterday nor the exigencies of today are entitled to invariable priority. As always, the idea is to strike the best balance we can among all the values we revere.

On this basis, it is not appropriate to impugn any and all taxation as theft. One might attack certain tax measures as economically or even morally dubious, but one cannot validly impugn the very essence of the taxation exercise. The *status quo ante*, unlike the Ten Commandments, is not etched in stone.

Moreover, on empirical grounds, there is simply no basis to believe that voluntary contributions would produce the requisite amounts of money. Prior to the emergence of the welfare state, private charities were expected to do the kind of job that the government now does. Few would doubt that such charities were atrociously under-funded for the tasks they had undertaken. And, while similar statements might be made about the treasuries of modern governments, we know, as a matter of financial fact, that there is simply no comparison in the kind of resources that have been made available through taxation as opposed to donation. Before the advent of the welfare state, numbers of North Americans literally faced starvation. While poverty persists, enormous improvements have occurred. Thus, the onus has to be on those who argue for voluntary subscription to demonstrate that the needed money would likely be forthcoming. It is fair to say that, to date, this onus has yet to be discharged.

Of no less weight is the impact of voluntary subscription on the ability to plan allocations for welfare programs. Not only would such a system not raise enough money, but it would also increase the difficulty of determining, from year to year, how much would likely be raised. Thus, it could become harder to treat the payments for beneficiaries as a matter of legal right.

In my view, one of the most important gains of the welfare state concerns the growing effort to treat the beneficiaries with dignity. Great uncertainty as to how much would be available and therefore how much could be paid detracts from the dignity of the recipients. Surely the attempt to treat these people with dignity is more commensurate with democratic values than the lack of such attempt. Moreover, the person who can effectively count on a specified minimum income has to have more effective freedom of choice than the one who cannot. On both these counts, therefore, it is fair to conclude that mandatory conscription with specified allocations is, at the very least, no less democratic than voluntary subscription with less certain allocations.

A related question concerns how much people may legitimately be taxed. While some free marketeers are prepared to concede a small amount of compulsory taxation, they insist that the tax burden should be shared on the basis of equal proportions. They vigorously repudiate any system of progressive taxation whereby people are taxed on the basis of their ability to pay.

According to this approach, a person with an annual income of five thousand dollars pays the same percentage in tax as a person whose annual income is one hundred thousand dollars. Unless the amounts to be paid were minuscule, such a formula would devastate the poor. They would simply be transferring money from one pocket to the other. Whatever they paid in taxes would render them so impoverished that much of the payment would have to be returned in the form of welfare benefits. On the other hand, if the amounts were minuscule, they could never raise enough to do the job required.

Numbers of free marketeers have readily acknowledged this problem and have recommended that the very poor not pay any taxes. Some have even suggested that the people at the bottom end of society be put on a form of negative income tax whereby the state would pay them to whatever extent their incomes fell below a specified minimum. Others have suggested that larger amounts of people's incomes be exempted from taxation and that the surpluses be taxed on the basis of equal proportions. The significant feature in all these proposals is that they accept some form of taxation based on the ability to pay. In principle, therefore, some form of progressive taxation may no longer be debatable among those who accept as valid the existence of taxation. It is not the function of this book to sort out the difficult issue of who should pay what. For my purposes here, it is enough to make the point that some form of progressive taxation is perfectly compatible with democratic freedom.

The sixth argument addresses equitable considerations. A critical factor that influences people's ability to make money is the stability of the community from which they make it. Industrial peace, social harmony, low rates of inflation, opportunities to advertise, high general productivity, all contribute immeasurably to the success of business. Why shouldn't the community that creates these conditions be entitled to exact some price from entrepreneurs in return? That price might take the form of taxes that are recirculated to others, or restraints to ensure that others are not unduly injured. Again, this argument does not resolve either the amount of the tax burden or the nature of the restraints. It simply says that the community is entitled to some such measures in return for what it has contributed.

Seventhly, there is an empirical argument. As a matter of *fact*, most of our fundamental freedoms have enjoyed greater protection in most Western democracies since the advent of the welfare state than prior to it. On almost any barometer, this appears to be the case. Political participation? During the past fifty years, there has been a tremendous increase in labour unions and their involvement in politics. Millions of industrial workers have been able to exert a level of pressure on the body politic that was hardly contemplated in an earlier era. Hitherto disenfranchised people—women, native people, blacks— have become enfranchised. There has also been a proliferation of organized pressure groups representing a number of hitherto unorganized constituencies—industrial accident victims, tenants, welfare recipients, consumers, mental patients, and even prisoners.

Protections for the individual against the state? Paradoxically, during the era of expanding welfare-state power, there has been an increase in the legal rights of the individual to challenge the power of the state. A host of precedent-making court cases in the United States has engulfed those accused of crimes with many hitherto unrecognized safeguards. Arrested people must not only have the right to consult legal counsel, but they must also be told of this right and, in some situations, be subsidized in exercising it. Any evidence gathered in violation of such rights is not admissible against the accused at their trials.

In Canada the federal Parliament and a number of provincial legislatures enacted bills of rights to apply in their respective jurisdictions. Such efforts culminated in the adoption of a constitutional Charter of Rights and Freedoms in 1982. The Charter has already been used to strike down a statute that shifted certain burdens of proof from the state to the accused and another statute authorizing a general search warrant. Parliament has banned corporal and capital punishment. A number of provincial legislatures have made it harder to commit people to mental institutions.

The examples go on and on. I do not suggest, of course, that the welfare state was necessarily responsible for this increase in the protection of other freedoms. However, it would be hard to impugn the welfare state as a barrier to them. Of course, it might still be argued that, if the welfare state had not emerged, the general level of our freedoms would have been even greater. I think it is fair, however, to impose upon the advocates of such a proposition the onus of demonstrating it. Thus far, at least, this onus has not been met. Welfare-state intrusions on free-market decisions have coexisted with the greatest expansion of democratic freedoms known to the human race.

Argument number eight throws one of the arguments of the free marketeers right back at them. If, as they believe, democracy requires a level of economic independence from government, it also demands that people enjoy a certain level of economic independence from *each other*. Just as susceptibility to economic control by the state can undermine the independence to act, so too can susceptibility to economic control by other citizens—employers, landlords, mortgagees, food processors, doctors, clothiers, and so on.

In establishing a panoply of economic protections, the welfare state has tried to create an economic floor below which citizens cannot fall. The idea is to ensure that all people have enough of the necessities of life to reduce their vulnerability to control by *anyone*. Whether that floor should be raised, lowered, or maintained, is largely an empirical question. But, so long as the free marketeers argue that some measure of economic independence is a prerequisite for democracy, they cannot object *in principle* to a collective effort at establishing such a floor.

Thus, free marketeers, *laissez-faire* capitalists, and rugged individualists cannot claim that they alone are on the side of freedom. On questions of economic regulation, the contest almost invariably will be, not between freedom and restriction, but between freedom and freedom. The issue will be whose freedom and which freedom should be protected or curtailed in which situations. To see the questions from this perspective is to eschew the kind of hyperbole that erodes the fibre of democratic debate. It is also to see the world as it really is.

Chapter Eight

THE ADMINISTRATION

OF PUBLIC WELFARE

The Integrity of the Purse
versus the Autonomy of the Person

Even though the welfare state does not necessarily violate our fundamental freedoms, it has created some novel civil liberties issues. The following is an excerpt from an affidavit which was sworn in the 1970s by a Toronto mother, separated from her husband and living on welfare:

...a [welfare official] came to my door, showed me a card indicating that he was from the department...and said that this was a routine investigation. He said that he wanted to see the apartment and then began to look around. Upon opening a closet in the living room, he discovered some beer bottles and said, "I don't give a shit what you do with your cheque; what I want to know is whether you're good for those kids." Then he asked me for a picture of my husband and as I was searching for one in my purse, he went into the bedroom without asking my permission. He opened the closet in the bedroom and found...my boyfriend...who had hidden there when he heard the knock on my front door. He had hidden there in order to avoid trouble between the welfare authorities and myself. [The welfare official] said that he no longer needed a picture of my husband because he had discovered my husband in the bedroom. I advised the [welfare official] that the man in the cupboard was not my husband. [The welfare official] asked my boyfriend a number of questions relating to our relationship. [The welfare official] said that my "sex life" was my own business and that it had nothing to do with my receiving welfare cheques. Thereupon he left my premises. [A few days later], when I telephoned the welfare office to inquire whether I could attend there to collect my cheque, my [regular] welfare worker...advised me that [the welfare official who had visited me] had informed them that because he had found a man in my apartment, I could not collect my cheque until that man attended at the office...and answered some questions.

Some people say that public welfare is administered in a more humane fashion today than it was when this affidavit was taken. Others argue that many of these core problems remain. For my present purposes, these different perceptions do not need to be resolved. It is enough to recognize that the power to grant and withhold financial benefits can create an enormous source of control over those who seek such benefits. Civil liberties issues arise whenever the state attempts to condition the granting of benefits on the surrender of vital freedoms—a recurring problem in the modern welfare state.

Such issues are laden with profound consequences for the viability of the democratic system. Millions of people receive major portions of their income in direct state payments: unemployment insurance, family allowances, old-age pensions, medical services, housing, and so on. For many people the state is also a source of substantial indirect wealth through measures such as licences, contracts, franchises, and tax deductions. There is hardly anyone who is not dependent upon some kind of government activity.

To whatever extent the state could condition the provision of assistance on a surrender of freedom, it could potentially erode key features of the democratic system. The economic facts are such that few people could escape. The consequent danger is the growth of a new form of authoritarianism. In such a development, personal freedoms would not suddenly be repealed; they would gradually be purchased. The preservation of a viable democracy requires, therefore, the imposition of some limits on the power of the state to restrict personal liberties in exchange for financial benefits. Because of the pervasive character of modern government assistance, such limitations on the state will need to apply not only in those areas where the citizen has a right to a benefit, but even in those areas where the benefit is discretionary. People's vulnerability to control depends more on the intensity of their wants than on the enforceability of their claims.

Unavoidably, however, *some* power will need to be exerted by the state with respect to persons who seek public help. In view of the limits on public funds, not everyone who wants assistance will be able to get it. As soon as restrictions are enacted, there will have to be some way of distinguishing those who are eligible from those who are not. This creates the need for the state to have some powers of investigation and control. Just as certain freedoms of the individual are subject to restriction by the police in the interests of protecting public safety, so too are certain freedoms subject to restriction by other state agencies in the interests of protecting public money. The fundamental principle of civil liberties in the assistance situation, as in all other situations, is that the state should intrude upon the vital freedoms of the individual no further than is reasonably required by an overriding public interest.

Those who seek welfare are for the most part poor. This condition makes them among the most vulnerable to manipulation and control. When government assistance is permitted to erode personal freedoms, the people seeking welfare are hit the earliest and the hardest. A society professing to believe in equality before the law could hardly reduce the level of people's freedoms according to their financial dependence on the public trough. The problem is to determine which public interest in which situations should be regarded as overriding and how far such public interests, in fact, necessitate intrusions on individual freedoms.

Only recently have civil libertarians begun to perceive state benefits not only as a boon but also as a threat. And only recently have the poor begun to surface as a discernible constituency. In consequence there has been a dearth of effort in Canada to evaluate welfare policies from the perspective of civil liberties. What follows is such an attempt.

Encroachments on Personal Privacy

In a Toronto case during 1987, a woman on welfare faced an untenable situation. Her husband kept moving in and out of their apartment. When he moved in, she would dutifully report his presence and thereby lose her welfare entitlement. Unfortunately, the husband also failed to give her money. Her plight was exacerbated by the fact that he regularly beat her. On one occasion when he moved back, she decided that, since he gave her no money, she would be better off not reporting his presence. During this period he beat her so severely that criminal charges were laid. This compounded her problems. If she testified against her husband, she increased the risk of being found out for her failure to report his return to the marital home. This meant that she could face charges for welfare fraud.

While the dilemmas confronting people on welfare are not generally this severe, they frequently require a significant encroachment on some important value that the rest of us take for granted. Often, what is at issue is personal privacy.

Consider the case of women on welfare—single mothers, deserted wives, and wives separated from their husbands—perhaps the largest category of welfare recipients. It has been the policy of a number of Canadian welfare departments to pressure these women into taking their husbands to court for support money. It is not clear how far some departments are prepared to cancel payments for women who won't cooperate. In some cases, there has been little doubt that this will happen. In other cases, there may be a greater willingness to consider extenuating circumstances. In any event, how many women in such a position would be prepared to challenge the expressed wishes of the department that was providing them with subsistence income? Many women simply could not know whether, in the crunch, their department would follow through on its actual or implied threats. What they do know is that a refusal to cooperate would probably make them unpopular with their welfare workers on whose good will they depend.

It is not hard to understand why welfare departments want women to chase their defaulting husbands. In law, spouses have the primary obligation to provide financial support for each other and their children. Thus, many people believe that it is only fair to make the spouses fulfil their obligations. Why should the public purse be drained while the delinquent spouse is spared?

On the other hand, this policy can intrude on the privacy and dignity of women whose spouses fail them. Some of these women find it difficult to discuss with lawyers, judges, and social workers the intimate and often painful events surrounding the break-up of their homes and families. Others, of course, are afraid of their husbands; they prefer to avoid any contacts or encounters. Still others feel that court action is a needless imposition; they know very well that their husbands lack the funds to support them. Perhaps most significant are those women who wish to avoid court battles because of the personal affection they continue to harbour for their husbands. They believe that there is still a chance for reconciliation. A court action, apparently instigated and prosecuted by the wife, could well shatter these hopes. To impose upon these women an obligation to sue is to contravene our society's general commitment, whenever possible, to save marriages and preserve families. It could also be cruel.

Why not compromise? Welfare departments should lose the power to base the provision of welfare on the wife's willingness to sue her husband, but they might gain instead the power to sue him in their own right. Under such a scheme, the department would be required immediately to provide for the wife but allowed subsequently to recover from her spouse. This is analogous to the system of subrogated rights that insurance companies acquire when they pay a claim.

In those cases where the relevant facts are not in dispute, it might be stipulated that such departmental court actions could be conducted without even involving the wife. In cases where, because of evidentiary conflicts, the wife needs to be involved, she might be called and paid as a witness in a suit that would clearly not be her own. Such a system could be adopted with no additional expenditures of public money or evasions of spousal duty.

For those cases where even these measures might not be enough to protect the legitimate interests of the family members there are additional possibilities. The wife might be given the right to petition the welfare authorities not to proceed against the husband even though they are supporting her. Perhaps the law might provide that the department may not go after him when there are reasonable grounds to believe, among other things, that such action would imperil the prospects of reconciliation between the spouses. There should also be an opportunity to appeal before the state could even begin the process against the husband.

This is not to set out a comprehensive scheme for handling these situations. It is simply to indicate the practical possibility of improving upon the status quo.

Canadian welfare departments have committed other intrusions on the marital relationship. In one Toronto case, a husband had reportedly attempted to get welfare assistance for himself, his wife, and his two children. But his application was refused because he had recently quit his job under circumstances which the department found unacceptable. Thus the wife and children were rendered ineligible to receive assistance. Since this situation threatened to inflict destitution on the wife and children, the man abandoned the marital home. His departure meant that his wife could receive welfare benefits for herself and the children. Unfortunately, however, their marriage suffered in the process.

According to the report of another case, a wife attempted to obtain assistance for herself and her two children despite the fact that her estranged husband was living in the same residence. The husband paid only rent money and contributed nothing to the support of the wife and children. Although she had asked him to leave, he had refused. She told the department that she and the children would like to move but they couldn't because she lacked the money. The welfare worker agreed to give her food and rent money for one week so that they could move, but the woman was warned that, if she stayed with or returned to her husband, there would be no further assistance. While most of our laws aim to preserve the marital relationship, the welfare law can accelerate its dissolution.

How far might it help to provide that husbands and wives could apply separately for welfare assistance? Under such an arrangement, one spouse and the children could receive help even if the other spouse was declared ineligible. Separate eligibility would serve in many cases to make women less dependent on the idiosyncratic behaviour of their husbands. One of the difficulties with this idea is that while the family shared the same home they could be pressured to share the same meagre benefits. In such circumstances, there might be an increased risk that the needs of the children would go wanting.

On the other hand, how far do we want the *welfare* laws to intervene in the internal relationships within a family? At the moment, lack of attention to children, whether rich or poor, is handled by our *child-care* laws. How far is it appropriate for the poor to be governed by standards so different from those which apply to the rest of the community?

This policy of regarding a cohabiting man and woman as a family for welfare purposes has applied not only in the cases of legal marriage, but also in those situations where men and women are living together "as though they were husband and wife". They too have not been able independently to obtain welfare assistance. Often this has meant no benefits for women if there was a male presence in the home. Such provisions have set the stage for additional encroachments on people's privacy. Precisely what does it mean for unmarried people to live together *as though* they were married? How far may the welfare departments penetrate the intimacies of domestic relationships in order to make this determination?

Few welfare issues have provoked as much controversy as the "man in the house" rule. Small wonder. It is a veritable invitation to intrusive investigation. And there have been plenty of reports that such investigations, in fact, have occurred. It is alleged that, on numbers of occasions, welfare officials have rummaged through the homes of their clients, looking in drawers and under beds for signs of a male presence. Even upturned toilet seats have been known to trigger interrogations. Departmental investigations have attempted to discern the nature of the relationships obtaining between the cohabitating men and women. Do they sleep together and, if so, how often? Does the man nurture and/or discipline the children and, if so, how often and in what ways?

Since the early 1970s there has been a raft of reported cases in Ontario in which welfare departments cancelled assistance to women because of alleged cohabitation with unrelated men. (While it appears that men in such situations are now also subject to the rule, the numbers affected are relatively few.) Almost every time the welfare appeal board has sustained the department's judgment. In many of these cases, there was no evidence at all that the man, in fact, was supporting the woman. There was simply a combination of cohabitation, sexual relations, and occasional financial help.

There have also been issues about how to interpret the evidence. In a number of cases, the men and women have flatly denied that they were even living together. According to their version, the man would stay overnight from time to time but he was not a permanent resident in the woman's home. This has led to inspections of his employment and tax records. The appeal tribunal has often preferred the circumstantial and hearsay evidence contained in the written reports of the bureaucrats to the direct testimony of the parties. Often those reports contained the observations of people who were not available to be cross-examined at the appeal board hearing. In some situations, the appeal tribunal impugned the credibility of the testifying parties and witnesses without bothering to explain why it did so.

It wasn't until the courts got into the act that this jurisprudence underwent some challenge. As early as 1974, the Divisional Court of the Supreme Court of Ontario held that money rather than sex is the key determinant of whether a couple is living together "as though they were husband and wife". And, as late as 1985, the same court talked about "the disturbing frequency with which claims appear to be rejected on nothing more than 'mere suspicion'...." Despite these judicial admonitions, welfare departments, with the approval of welfare appeal boards, have continued to disqualify women in these circumstances. There is reason to believe that these cases represent only the tip of the iceberg because most welfare recipients lack the fortitude to appeal to the boards, let alone to the courts.

The resulting situation is simply unacceptable. For the women, their families and friends, the "man in the house" rule has produced unwelcome intrusions on personal privacy. For the welfare officials, the rule has required costly and unpleasant investigations which disclose uncertain results. For the administration of justice, the attempt to apply the rule has produced a tarnished reputation.

The rule should be substantially revised. Unless a man living on the same premises as a woman has a legal obligation to support her and her children (because they are legally married or involved in certain lengthy or child-bearing unions), the welfare law should treat the situation no differently than one where she is cohabiting with another woman. In such situations, there might be some question about the *amount* of the applicant's entitlement (if it could be established that the cohabitant was paying something to live there), but there would be no question of the applicant's *eligibility*. Unless the welfare administration could demonstrate that she, in fact, was receiving the level and continuity of support that spouses are legally obliged to provide for each other, there would be no question of denying or cancelling her assistance. Why should it make any difference if the woman is living with a man friend rather than a woman friend?

Indeed, the different treatment which the welfare law has accorded these situations might well be considered discrimination under the equality rights section of the Charter of Rights and Freedoms. In order to satisfy the requirements of the Charter, it might be argued that the welfare law should consider, not the sex of the cohabitant, but the economic realities and legal obligations of the relationship. Conceivably, the current law might even be considered discrimination on the basis of sexual orientation. Here we have the extraordinary situation in which a homosexual relationship might attract more protection than a heterosexual one.

Moreover, in the absence of explicit evidence, it is not reasonable to assume that a man living on the premises would be providing the kind of support that spouses must provide for each other. Both parties would often be in the economic under-class of society. Frequently both would be survivors of broken marriages. It is likely, therefore, that many of the men involved would already be liable to make support payments to their first families, and their poorly paying jobs would not enable them to pay for a second family.

Nor can the rule be justified on the basis of sexual morality. At this stage of history, there is no reason why the bedrooms of the nation should be any more open to welfare officials than to police officials. In any event, such an intrusion would be highly selective: it would apply only to poor people. Similarly, the rule cannot be justified in order to promote the proposition that men who reap the benefits of marriage should be compelled to bear the costs. This rationale would inflict punishment upon the woman and her children because of the delinquency of her cohabitant.

Furthermore, it's hard to take seriously the argument that, if both parties stand a better chance of getting welfare assistance while they are single, they won't bother to marry. In view of the many ways that welfare law already undermines the viability of marriage, this argument simply lacks credibility. In any event, the question of marriage between a cohabiting couple would not be likely to arise until they had established a somewhat durable relationship. At that point, they might well have acquired a legal obligation to support one another and would, therefore, be regarded as a family unit for purposes of my proposed rule.

In 1986 the Women's Legal Education and Action Fund (LEAF) launched a Charter challenge in court against the Ontario "man in the house" rule, and the Canadian Civil Liberties Association organized a delegation to the Ontario minister of community and social services. In 1987 the government of Ontario amended its regulations so as to implement a certain amount of what I have advocated here. But, in much of the rest of the country, the rule has remained intact.

The converse of the "man in the house" who is believed to be supporting the woman and her family is the absentee man who is *not* supporting them but should be: the unknown putative father of her children. The unwed mother may be claiming welfare assistance from the state in circumstances where there is a man who has a prior obligation to provide support.

In my earlier discussion of the situation with the deserted wife, I suggested that the welfare department be obliged to pay her and then be allowed, on its own, to chase her legally liable husband. In principle, there is no reason to distinguish the two situations. The welfare department should also be obliged to pay the needy unwed mother and then allowed, on its own, to sue the putative father. Alas, however, life is rarely so easy. In the case of the deserting husbands, there is little difficulty in proceeding this way. Even if we don't know where the deserting husband is, we are likely to know who he is. The existence of marital relationships is usually traceable to public records. Not so, of course, with putative fathers. In order to find out who they are, it is usually necessary to obtain the cooperation of the women involved.

Some women in such situations are reluctant to identify the fathers of their children. The father may be a married man with a family of his own. Other unwed mothers may simply prefer to keep their private lives confidential. Some women don't want the father even to know that there is a child, fearing that he will attempt to assert some claims or control. Again, we have a classic conflict of values. How far should the interest in protecting the public purse warrant such an intrusion into the privacy of these sexual relationships?

In many situations women have suffered the denial of benefits because of their refusal to finger the putative father. In Ontario this policy was upheld as recently as 1985 in a situation where a woman refused to identify the donor of the sperm by which she had been artificially inseminated. According to the Ontario Divisional Court, "this invasion into the privacy of the applicant is authorized by statute because she had applied for a benefit."

If this is what the statute authorizes, the statute should be changed. The economic benefits of compulsory disclosure are not worth the privacy costs. Few experiences in a person's life are as intimate as those involving sex. Few experiences have as much potential, therefore, to be accompanied in their exposure by incalculable pain and suffering—not only for the immediate parties but also for their respective families. Moreover, since we are dealing primarily with the poor, the prospect of recovering an adequate amount of money is often tenuous at best. In any event, even without this compulsion, it is reasonable to believe that voluntary cooperation would always be forthcoming from a significant number of women. Why, then, should there be such harsh rules?

The residential privacy of welfare claimants has also been susceptible to unwarranted intrusions. Much of the law on this subject has been loose, broad, and vague. Strictly speaking, of course, welfare recipients have the same legal rights as everyone else to the privacy of their homes. But, if the exercise of such rights can result in the valid termination of their assistance, the existence of such rights will be denuded of its significance. The practical question is, how far may welfare departments demand entry as a condition of granting assistance?

Most Canadian welfare laws have either allowed or required welfare officials to visit the homes of welfare recipients in order to assess their circumstances and eligibility. But what do such visits include? Must they be pre-arranged or may they be unannounced? And may the officials explore the premises, or are they confined to superficial observations? Many welfare laws also require the departments periodically to review the recipients' circumstances. Do such periodic reviews include subsequent visits to the recipients' homes? And, if so, how frequent may they be, and how extensive or restrictive are the powers of inspection on such occasions? Regrettably, the relevant laws too often are silent on these crucial issues.

Unannounced departmental visits have hardly been a rarity. From the spring of 1986 until the winter of 1987, for example, the Quebec welfare authorities triggered an explosive controversy by systematically conducting more than 100,000 home visits. Even though the officials who carried out this assignment had been especially trained and equipped with a code of ethics to protect the rights of the recipients, there was widespread protest over the government's action. The investigators were denounced as "welfare police". And the government was challenged to use similar tactics against rich people who evade taxes. It is significant that the home visits revealed no wrongdoing in 80 per cent of the cases.

Ironically, those persons who are accused of the most heinous crimes often enjoy more discernible protection of their domestic privacy than do the innocent recipients of public welfare. At the very least, these inequities should be reduced. The welfare law should attempt to match the performance of our other laws. It should spell out in clear terms the safeguards for privacy and the conditions of encroachment. Our professed commitment to equality before the law demands nothing less.

Encroachments on Freedom of Choice

The presence or absence of conscripted labour distinguishes the free from the slave society. In a free society, no legal power can force the citizen to work at a task, in a place, or at a time that he finds disagreeable. When free citizens work at unpleasant jobs, they do so through choice, motivated usually by the desire for adequate or additional money. While this motive can be very powerful, the citizen is legally free to resist it. Except for emergencies, the democratic state may not properly impose the choice of work upon its citizens.

In this area too, the payment of public welfare assistance creates for the democratic society some rather perplexing problems. While the government may not validly compel people to engage in work, the question arises: why should it *subsidize* their refusal to work? Put another way, why should industrious taxpayers be required to share with self-indulgent non-taxpayers the fruits of their labour? But to deny welfare assistance to destitute people who are unwilling to work is to make the democratic state, at least indirectly, an agent for the effective conscription of labour.

Most Canadian jurisdictions have resolved this dilemma by withholding welfare assistance from unemployed persons unless their unemployment is due to circumstances beyond their control and they are making reasonable efforts to correct the situation. What, however, constitutes "reasonable efforts"? What jobs may a recipient validly refuse or abandon? In short, how far does the payment of welfare entitle the democratic state to encroach upon this fundamental aspect of the citizen's personal autonomy? While I cannot provide a comprehensive picture of how welfare departments, appeal tribunals, and the courts are answering these questions, I can identify a few significant problems.

In the mid-1970s, the Ontario Social Assistance Review Board dismissed the appeal of an applicant who had declined to submit to medical treatment. In the words of the board, "...if she is temporarily unemployable and this will be remedied by medical treatment, then she must seek the treatment...." While the dismissal of this appeal was based also on the woman's failure to complete a form on her medical condition, the stated reasons included her refusal to take treatment. Apart from a casual mention of what was involved as "minor", the report of the facts does not disclose the specifics of the treatment she had been asked to take. Indeed, it is not even clear whether the tribunal was told. The judgment simply refers to the fact that an earlier report of the welfare administrator had described the treatment as "minor". We have no way of knowing whether the tribunal questioned or simply accepted the administrator's opinion.

We do know, however, that social attitudes on the question of medical treatment are highly varied and subjective. What might be minor to one person could be traumatic to another. In the absence of further facts, it is difficult to know how far the tribunal would be prepared to extend this line of reasoning. In the meantime, we have to be concerned about the sweeping nature of the tribunal's remarks.

There is a wide-spread belief that persons who are not well groomed and properly dressed probably reduce their chances to obtain employment. Understandably, therefore, many welfare departments have attempted to pressure recipients to make themselves more suitable in these respects. But how far may they go?

In one of the early cases, the Ontario Social Assistance Review Board heard an appeal relating to a young man who had been denied welfare assistance because of his refusal to shave his beard and cut his hair in order to obtain a job as a security guard. The board dismissed the claim on the grounds that the appellant's "unemployment could not be considered due to circumstances beyond his control...as a matter of cutting one's hair or shaving surely lies in the control of an individual."

This reasoning represents an extremely literal interpretation of the applicable law. Does it follow from this case that absolutely nothing that lies within the control of individuals will excuse them from compliance with an employer's job requirements? Suppose, for example, employers required their employees to move to certain districts of the city, eschew membership in certain organizations, and join yoga classes after hours. Since compliance with such instructions lies within the control of most people, would those who were denied employment for refusing to comply become ineligible for welfare assistance?

It would be more difficult to quarrel with the denial of welfare assistance in a situation where an applicant refused to do something—not immoral or dangerous—that was reasonably related to the functions of the job. Indeed, this was the very argument which had been advanced to the board in the above case. The appellant argued that beardlessness and short hair were irrelevant to the proper performance of a security guard. Unfortunately, the board's judgment nowhere addressed this issue. This part of its decision was based solely on the appellant's refusal to do something within his control. How far, therefore, will the legal powers of our welfare departments underwrite the whims and prejudices of recruiting employers?

Welfare officials have often been called upon to assess whether the recipients behaved reasonably in refusing to accept certain conditions of work. In one case, they disqualified a claimant for quitting a job which required him to perform roof work. The record disclosed that he had protested his inability to work in high places since suffering an injury from a fall at some time in the past. Although he had indicated his willingness to work at ground level, the Ontario Social Assistance Review Board dismissed his subsequent appeal on the grounds that he "offered no substantial reason for leaving his employment".

According to the report of the case, the appellant was not present at the board hearing. If the board was simply ruling that, because of his absence, the appellant could not satisfy the onus on him, the judgment would be less contentious. Or if the board had chosen for some valid reason to disbelieve the man's story, there might be no serious controversy about this decision. These possibilities, however, are not clear from the report. As it stands, the judgment appears as authority for the more dubious proposition that the fear of high places cannot justify resignation from employment.

And what constitutes "reasonable efforts" to find employment? A 1986 case revealed the policy on this issue that has been operative in Ontario's Simcoe County. In addition to being registered at the local Canada Employment Centre, employable welfare recipients "should spend at least six hours per day, five days per week, Monday through Friday, making *personal* contact with prospective employers." While the Divisional Court of the Ontario Supreme Court categorized this policy as "arbitrary", we have to be concerned about the extent to which bureaucrats in this area attempt to regiment their vulnerable clients. And we must be concerned also about the texture of the whole cloth from which these dubious policies are fashioned.

In many Canadian jurisdictions, welfare assistance will not be paid to a person who is not working because of a labour strike. Some administrators have argued that such people are not experiencing "unemployment" because, according to the relevant labour legislation, they are still regarded as "employees". But the labour laws preserve the status of "employee" as a *protection* for strikers. Among other things, for example, this enables the striker to retain voting rights in subsequent decisions concerning which union, if any, may represent the employees of the strike-bound employer. Is it not permissible to say, therefore, that, while persons may be "employed" for the purpose of labour legislation, they are nevertheless "unemployed" for the purpose of welfare legislation? Isn't the crux of the word "employment" within the welfare context the receipt of money for the performance of service?

The Ontario Social Assistance Review Board, however, has ruled strikers ineligible for welfare assistance on other grounds. It has decided that their unemployment cannot be attributed to circumstances beyond their control, but rather is a "result of [their] own voluntary act". In the opinion of the board, "by joining a union or taking a union job, [a person] has ceded to the union the right...ultimately to withdraw his services."

Such generalizations hardly seem warranted. Suppose that certain persons *refused* to take available union jobs? This could confine them to inferior jobs or even to unemployment. In the latter case, they might very well be ineligible for welfare. Under such circumstances, how could their acceptance of union jobs be described as a "voluntary act"?

Moreover, why should mere membership in a union give rise to a conclusive inference of consent to union decisions? Although most union members gladly abide by such decisions, they are under no legal compulsion to do so. Indeed, some union members have been known to report for work during strike situations. During certain strikes, the inability of some union members to work is attributable less to a decision of theirs than to a decision of management's to suspend operations. Couldn't the resulting unemployment for those workers fairly be described as "due to circumstances beyond their control"? Of course, there would be intense controversy if welfare tribunals undertook to conduct inquiries into the extent of support for any given strike. But what must be realized is the hollowness of the generalization that all strikers and union members necessarily consent to such union decisions.

If the legislatures of this country believe that, as a matter of public policy, strikers should be ineligible for welfare assistance, it would be better for them to say so in specific terms. In such event, the legislatures should also consider how far strike-bound employers deserve to enjoy the benefits *they* get from the government. Then the matter could be discussed and debated as a public, political issue. What is inappropriate, however, is the resolution of such matters through contorted interpretations of the existing legal criteria.

Democrats are disquieted by such state intervention not only in the choice of work but also in the patterns of consumption. Inherent in the very concept of democracy is the right of all citizens, as far as possible, to choose for themselves where to live, what to eat, drink, watch, wear, read, and hear. The payment of welfare assistance, however, appears to carry with it some special attempts to restrict this range of personal choice.

Some welfare laws, for example, provide for trusteeship arrangements where, in the opinion of the relevant administrator, "the recipient is using or is likely to use his assistance otherwise than for his own benefit". In such circumstances, the assistance will be paid to a trustee on behalf of the recipient. It would be hard to quarrel with such arrangements for substitute decision-making under some circumstances. But, in view of the substantial loss of freedom involved, why should incompetence *on* welfare be treated so differently from incompetence *off* welfare? In the mental health context, more stringent safeguards are usually available before substitute decision-makers can be imposed upon people. While there may be an argument for a somewhat more expeditious procedure in the welfare law than in the mental health law, the breadth of the gap is disquieting.

One of the freedoms most prized by the citizens of a democracy is the freedom to be left alone. Most people object to being investigated. The more frequent the investigation, the greater the objection to it. But those who wish something from government must be willing to cooperate with those in authority.

The question is *how much* they must cooperate. From time to time, recipients are asked to come to the welfare office in order to be questioned about their circumstances. Such command appearances have covered a wide range of matters: answering general questions, signing forms, seeking support from husbands, outlining relationships with men, discussing job possibilities, bringing lists of places where employment has been sought, and so on. These periodic pilgrimages to the welfare office and their accompanying interrogations may represent a small price to pay for the receipt of subsistence income but, if they are frequent and are accompanied by additional unpleasantness, the issue cannot so readily be dismissed.

Over the years, many recipients have reported a variety of hardships associated with these office visits: cramped space, hot and humid conditions, lengthy line-ups requiring waits of more than an hour and sometimes more than two or three hours. A shortage of money for babysitting services has obliged many women to bring their children with them to these appointments. It will be appreciated how the presence of restless infants and children can exacerbate the unpleasant circumstances. The length of the waits and the fear of neglect have produced stories of special hardships such as breast feeding infants in the washroom and missing meals.

In view of the fact that people's circumstances are subject to change, it is difficult to deny to the welfare departments the opportunity of conducting some periodic review. But how often is it necessary to do it by requiring these attendances at the welfare office? Moreover, might there not be some way of reducing the unpleasantness? Is it not possible at least in some cases to interview by telephone? Could there not be more assistance for babysitting and transportation? Is it impossible to arrange more definite appointment times in order to eliminate the oppressive delays? Finally, does the recipients' continuing onus to demonstrate eligibility mean that they must attend virtually whenever and wherever they are called?

The Fairness of Welfare Procedures

Civil libertarians are concerned not only with what encroachments the individual sustains or avoids, but also with how such issues are determined. Since the days of Magna Carta, the common law has been preoccupied with the quest for procedural fairness.

One of the requirements of procedural fairness is that relief must be real, not illusory. In light of such ideals, what are we to make of the rule in some places that, in order to obtain assistance, applicants must indicate their residence? In a number of situations, this requirement has created some vicious circles because many applicants need welfare assistance in order to obtain a residence. Without some help, they cannot afford to pay rent. While interim assistance is often provided in such circumstances, this has not always been done. Numbers of people have been flatly turned down on the grounds that they had no residence. Rules and regulations are supposed to effectuate, not emasculate, the intentions of the legislature.

One of the key components of procedural fairness is accessibility. The most generous benefits in the world are of little value unless the intended beneficiary has ready access to them. In the case of the welfare systems, this means access to the welfare workers. Usually they are the ones who transmit the system's benefits. Welfare recipients encounter a host of difficulties in this regard. In many places, it is virtually impossible to make an appointment; the recipient is obliged to go to the office and get in line.

In a late 1986 brief to a special Ontario government committee, Local 79 of the Canadian Union of Public Employees described the particularly frustrating situation in some of the Toronto welfare offices: "In the recent past, when numbers were given out but names were not taken, some would tell the clerks and counsellors that they had bought their numbers for five dollars from the street [*sic*] in order to make sure that they would be seen that day." Despite the apparent adoption of certain remedial measures, the union noted that "only those who line up at the office long before it opens can hope to see a worker that day."

A central feature of procedural fairness is an adequate knowledge of one's legal rights. Regrettably, ignorance of the relevant law is widespread in the welfare constituency. Significant numbers are unaware of some of the most basic components of the welfare system: the right to work while on welfare; the availability of special discretionary benefits such as drugs, dentures, clothing, transportation; the right of appeal. In fairness, many welfare departments make efforts to inform their clients of their rights, but these efforts are uneven.

A central concomitant of what the common law calls "natural justice" is the right to a hearing—that is, some opportunity to challenge an adverse decision before it is made. Subsequent recourse to appeal is not adequate. Even if the appeal tribunal ultimately were to find in favour of the recipient and award back payment, there would be no guarantee of assistance in the meantime. In short, retroactive payment cannot provide retroactive sustenance. It is important, therefore, that before applicants or recipients sustain a decision against their interests, the departments grant them some opportunity to persuade the decision-makers.

Unfortunately, our welfare legislation does not uniformly provide such safeguards. Even in Ontario, with the influence of the McRuer Report on Civil Rights, there is less than adequate provision for this vital component of due process. At the time of writing, the General Welfare Assistance Act requires advance notice of cancellations and suspensions of assistance only "where practicable". Legal-aid clinics report that, in fact, such notice is rarely provided. According to one lawyer, "In over five years of practice in the social assistance field in Toronto, not once did I ever have a client where [*sic*] the administrator apparently thought that it was 'practicable' to inform the client prior to...cancellation."

By contrast, the Family Benefits Act in Ontario, under which longer-term assistance is provided, does require such advance notice to those who are about to be denied assistance. As a matter of practice, however, such notice is often of little value. The following is a not untypical letter advising an applicant of an impending adverse decision:

> Your application for an allowance under the Family Benefits Act has been carefully considered. We wish to inform you that we intend to consider you not eligible as our Medical Advisory Board has reviewed the medical evidence submitted in support of your application and have [*sic*] reported to me that you are not considered to be a disabled or a permanently unemployable person.
>
> If you disagree with our decision or if you have additional information to submit, you may appeal directly to my office by writing within ten days of receiving this letter. Please use the enclosed envelope and refer to the file number above so that we may be able to reply to your letter promptly.
>
> If we do not hear from you, we will confirm our decision at a later date.

How is a person supposed to reply to a letter like that? The letter fails to provide the slightest indication as to why the Medical Advisory Board made the judgment it did. Unless you know the case you have to meet, advance notice is useless. To the extent that the province of Ontario relies on letters of this kind, its commitment to the canons of due process must be regarded as something of a sham.

Unfortunately, the state of due process also leaves a lot to be desired in Ontario's appellate tribunal, the Social Assistance Review Board. In the early to mid-1980s, four separate court cases had occasion to impugn the practices of the board. Mr. Justice Robert Sutherland of the Ontario Supreme Court complained that "too many similar cases involving a decision by the Director to cancel benefits upon inadequate evidence are upheld by the Board and find their way to the court." In another case, his colleague Mr. Justice Robert Reid talked about "the disturbing frequency with which claims appear to be rejected on nothing more than 'mere suspicion'...." In yet another case, Mr. Justice Edward Saunders of the same court declared that "the Board must act on more than mere suspicion to take away an allowance." And in a fourth case, Mr. Justice David Henry said that "although the Board had the right to reject the affidavit evidence, the manner in which it rejected this important and relevant evidence was arbitrary."

Legislative amendments are called for. Welfare administrators should be required to ensure that, before short-term assistance is cut off and before long-term assistance is denied or cut off, there is written notice containing at least an outline of the relevant evidence. The notice should also include information about the right to legal aid and the location of clinics where it might be obtained. In that way, there would be at least some substance to the right to make representations against an impending loss of eligibility. And the appeal tribunals should be required to furnish written reasons for rejecting the evidence or impugning the credibility of the witnesses who testify at their hearings. It is more difficult for adjudication to be arbitrary and inadequate when written reasons must accompany the exercise.

Nevertheless, legislative amendment, while necessary, would be insufficient. No matter how comprehensively the law purported to grant the right to a hearing, for example, there is little assurance that some of the administrators and appeal tribunals would not grotesquely misconstrue it. And, as we have seen, many of the welfare issues are not readily amenable to improvement by amendment. So many of these issues require efforts at sensitive adjustment. How, for example, could legislation delineate between acceptable and unacceptable demands for recipients to come to the welfare office, and how could legislation ensure the reasonable accessibility of welfare workers?

In many of the foregoing situations, what finally saved the day for hapless welfare claimants was the availability of a special advocacy service to press their cases. Such interventions appear to have secured benefits otherwise denied, and eased restrictions otherwise imposed. There have been cases, for example, in which welfare departments have declined to provide assistance because they have relied upon an employer's version of how the claimants left their jobs. Special advocates have managed to reverse departmental refusals under such circumstances. In one case, an advocate broke the impasse by filing a sworn affidavit in support of the claimant's position. In another case, an advocate investigated the details of a person's impugned employment record and subsequently advised the department that the employer's representations had been incorrect. There have also been situations in which advocates advised people of possibilities for assistance which welfare departments simply never mentioned.

During an eighteen-month period in the early 1970s, the Canadian Civil Liberties Association operated such an advocacy service in a few downtown Toronto welfare offices. In all, the service handled some 613 cases. In 298 of them, the advocates provided only general assistance and information: how to apply, how to fill out various forms, amounts of entitlement, special assistance items, and so on. In 100 cases, the results are inconclusive—for example, the advocate may have advised the recipient, discussed the matter with a worker, or even filed an appeal, but the decision is not known. Since many recipients are transients, they frequently leave the jurisdiction before their cases are completed. The remaining three categories of experience are most significant. In 40 of the cases, the advocates failed to help the recipients. In 138 cases the advocate's intervention was followed by success in obtaining a material benefit—many times in situations where the benefit had previously been denied. In another 35 cases, the advocates obtained and imparted to the recipient some rather crucial information which the welfare workers had previously withheld or overlooked.

What made the difference was the physical presence in the welfare office of advocates for welfare claimants. They were on the spot when the problems arose. Having been trained in the intricacies of welfare law and having an organization prepared to back them up, these advocates demonstrated both skill and clout in producing results. In the case of the CCLA, most of the advocates were lay people in the field of law: homemakers, businessmen, dentists, students, and in some cases even welfare recipients.

Since the early 1970s when the Canadian Civil Liberties Association provided this service for people seeking welfare, the country has experienced a substantial growth in legal clinics to serve the interests of the poor. There is little question that these clinics are performing an invaluable service. Because of their physical location in the neighbourhoods of their constituencies, the clinics are accessible to those who need them. These are not intimidating offices in plush downtown buildings. They are modest, storefront operations on neighbourhood street corners. Both the lawyers and the paralegals have been providing a dedicated and competent level of professional service.

In 1984–85 in Ontario more than 25 per cent of those who had legal representation won their appeals, as compared with fewer than 16 per cent of those who had no such representation. The dichotomy has continued to grow. In 1985–86 more than 37 per cent of represented clients won their appeals as compared with 15.5 per cent of the unrepresented ones. In 1986–87 the success rate for represented people climbed to more than 50 per cent, compared with fewer than 25 per cent for the unrepresented appellants.

Yet precious few of these appellants are actually getting legal assistance. As late as 1984–85, lawyers or legal-aid clinics were involved in fewer than 9 per cent of the appeals before the Ontario Social Assistance Review Board. In 1986–87 the number of such represented appellants was only 14 per cent. A six-month project conducted between the fall of 1984 and the spring of 1985 found that 76 per cent of Toronto appellants at the Ontario Social Assistance Review Board had received no legal advice of any kind prior to the hearing. And 73 per cent of those said they were not aware that free legal advice was available to them.

These legal services must be made more accessible. Indeed, there is a good case for posting clinic advocates right in the welfare offices where they could be available as problems arise. Such a measure would substantially increase the prospect for satisfactory settlements—an outcome far preferable for most people than involvement in the appeal process. This is not to suggest that the adoption of my proposals would usher in a state of justice in the welfare arena. But it is to say that the incidence of the current injustice could be significantly reduced.

Chapter Nine

INVOLUNTARY

CIVIL COMMITMENT

The Demands of Therapy
versus the Desire for Liberty

There is hardly a family in North America that has managed to avoid the scourge of what is generally called mental illness. It might take the form of an old auntie who embarrasses her relatives by acting out the delusion that she is the Queen of England. Or a grandfather who stands on a street corner giving away large sums of money so as to leave himself (or perhaps more important, his heirs) bereft of his fortune. Or a hitherto productive husband who has become so depressed that he stops working and repairs to his attic, where he sits all day and night brooding about what a terrible person he is.

As long as the auntie, grandfather, and husband bow willingly to family pressures that they seek psychiatric treatment, no civil liberties issue will be involved. But suppose they resist? Suppose the auntie insists that she likes being the Queen of England, the grandfather tells you that he is acting under the direct orders of God, and the husband refuses treatment because he feels unworthy of help. Psychiatrists might well advise you that, if they could force hospitalization and drug therapy on your relatives, within a few weeks these disturbing symptoms would likely start to disappear.

Compulsory hospitalization and treatment raise serious civil liberties issues. They threaten what the late great justice of the U.S. Supreme Court, Louis Brandeis, described as the value most prized by civilized people—the right to be left alone. This right, of course, is the very essence of what we mean by freedom. And there are not many more intrusive encroachments a democratic society can impose upon people than to lock them up against their will and to force upon them behaviour-altering drugs. And, even if the motive is their welfare and not anyone else's pleasure, the exercise does not constitute any less of an encroachment. For the person who does not want to be locked up, it hurts no less if it is done by a psychiatrist who smiles than by a constable who growls.

Since there are no absolutes, this precious freedom to be left alone must sometimes give way to other values and interests. In order to preserve social peace, for example, we have enacted criminal laws. In order to promote greater economic security, we have enacted a host of regulatory laws. All of these laws interfere, in one way or another, with our desire to be left alone. Indeed, if we violate certain of these laws, we become susceptible to an even greater intrusion on our freedom: imprisonment.

Mental illness, so the argument goes, justifies another intrusion on personal freedom. According to the proponents of this view, some mental diseases are so debilitating that the persons suffering them have effectively lost their freedom in any event. I have little doubt that many people would express just such an opinion about the auntie, grandfather, and husband in our earlier examples. We would be told that, in the case of such deluded people, it is not meaningful to regard hospitalization as an invasion of their freedom. We would be told that the only way our relatives will ever acquire real freedom is to be cured of their mental afflictions. Indeed, these afflictions are often seen as the reason such people refuse the benefits of psychiatric treatment.

But, even if we wish to impose hospitalization and treatment on the auntie, grandfather, and husband, what criteria shall we enact into law in order to make it possible? The problem is that we are unlikely to find language precise enough to apply to these people without simultaneously imperilling a lot of others. In short, there is a great risk of casting too wide a net.

The diagnosis of "mental illness" is laden with value judgments. Consider, for example, *DSM III*, the most recent manual of mental illnesses published by the American Psychiatric Association. In defining the components of schizophrenia, the most common of the psychotic illnesses, the manual includes the following words: "markedly peculiar behaviour", "inappropriate affect", "metaphorical speech", "odd or bizarre ideation", "unusual perceptual experiences". In a democratic society, we are supposed to tolerate—to some extent even to encourage—diversity. Unless a person is violating a law which was enacted to serve an overriding public interest, we are supposed to protect the right to "markedly peculiar behaviour", "metaphorical speech", and "odd or bizarre ideation".

In their day, Moses and Jesus were certainly subject to "odd and bizarre ideations". In our day, leading writers and poets frequently use "metaphorical speech" and have "unusual perceptual experiences". Indeed, these people have been enabled to make the enormous contributions they have made precisely because of the character traits that set them so far apart from the rest of the community.

Ah, you say, but some peculiarities are more peculiar than others. Perhaps so, but then how does one formulate criteria that will adequately make this distinction? Clearly, if you use the kind of language contained in *DSM III*, you will create a power to impose upon people just for being different. If there is other language precise enough to make these distinctions, I have never seen it.

In the mid-1980s, an attempt was made to provide, in Canadian mental health statutes, a power to confine involuntarily those persons whose mental disorders were such that they were causing serious emotional harm to other people. Presumably this terminology would be wide enough to authorize the compulsory hospitalization of the auntie, grandfather, and husband in our earlier examples. Unfortunately, however, it would likely be wide enough to catch a lot of other people as well.

Here again it would be useful to invoke the case of Jesus. He suffered from what many thought was a delusion that he was the son of God. Biblical accounts of the period suggest that Jesus' beliefs about his origins caused severe emotional upset to the occupying authorities of Palestine. Had "serious emotional harm" permitted involuntary confinement in the mental health laws of that period, Jesus might have been locked up at such an early stage of his career that he never would have been able to make the contribution he did to the welfare of the human race.

Consider what would happen in our time to those who decided to leave their families in order to write the great Canadian novel. Many people would believe, and perhaps rightly, that this decision revealed a mental delusion about personal greatness. Moreover, it's not hard to imagine the serious emotional harm that would be suffered by the abandoned spouses and children. To what extent, therefore, would the terminology in question permit society to incarcerate our would-be authors? What judgment do we make about the person who wants to chuck his family for the priesthood? Is this admirable dedication or unacceptable craziness?

What we have in these situations are conflicts of emotional harm. If the persons who wish to leave are required to stay, they will suffer. If they are allowed to leave, their families will suffer. Inevitably this will lead to an attempt to determine which of the parties *ought* to have the higher tolerance level. To a great extent, such determinations depend less upon psychological evaluation than upon philosophical orientation. This is just the kind of situation that a democratic society should seek to avoid. One person's freedom should not be so dependent upon another person's value preferences. To allow people to be locked up on such a basis is to incur a substantial risk of creating a form of tyranny.

One of the more recent attempts to articulate these distinctions has involved the concept of competence. In addition to the kind of definitions of schizophrenia found in *DSM III*, it has been suggested that there be a test of competence. Is the mental disease so severe as to impair the person's ability to understand the nature and consequences of the condition and the potential risks and benefits of treatment? If so, the person might be judged incompetent and, in addition to the other criteria, such a finding would render the person subject to involuntary commitment and treatment in a mental hospital. In support of such a competence test, we are reminded that the law already sanctions its use in a number of other situations—for example, the imposition of a special trustee to manage the financial assets of an incompetent person.

Admittedly, the addition of a competence test would represent an improvement over not having one. Nevertheless, the concept is fraught with danger. People might appear incompetent because they lack the facility to communicate in terminology that is meaningful to the therapist. If therapist and prospective patient belong to different classes or cultures, there would be an increased risk that a judgment of incompetence would be made.

In the early 1980s, for example, a man of Serbo-Croatian descent spent a year in a maximum security mental hospital after an Ontario court declared him unfit to stand trial. Initially he had been charged with assault for an alleged attack on his wife. When he appeared in court, he was highly agitated and seemed to be talking gibberish. A psychiatric assessment was ordered and, in the result, he was found unfit and committed to hospital. On the occasion of his appearance before a review panel, he had the benefit of an interpreter who spoke his dialect. When he could communicate through the interpreter, he no longer appeared incoherent. On the contrary, the accounting he gave of himself and his previous conduct impressed his listeners as sufficiently rational that they returned him to court with instructions that an interpreter be provided. Apparently his inadequate grasp of the English language had rendered him susceptible to an assessment of unfitness and incompetence.

In highlighting these dangers, I do not propose the complete withdrawal of the competence test from all the areas where the law now sanctions it. Where control of financial matters is concerned, for example, there is an arguable case for it. There is even a case for allowing incompetence to trigger a range of limited guardianships. But the more that physical freedom is the issue, the less we should be willing to allow a finding of incompetence to redeem vague definitions of schizophrenia.

Those who agree about the risks of such a commitment power and advocate it nevertheless are willing to repose an awesome trust in the decision-makers. Usually, this means the psychiatrists.

Let us argue by analogy. Suppose the police, frustrated by the problems of law enforcement, were to ask that the Criminal Code be repealed and replaced simply with a power in the police to incarcerate anyone for being a threat to public peace and security. I have little doubt that such a proposal would be universally condemned. Yet, if psychiatrists are considered the experts on mental health, why aren't the police similarly esteemed with respect to public peace and security? Most police officers, like most psychiatrists, are decent, moral people. What is at issue, however, is not their integrity but their omnipotence.

Freedom is too crucial to leave to the value judgments of any elite. An expertise with respect to public safety or mental disease does not create a concomitant expertise as to what level of threat or disease *should* trigger imprisonment or forced hospitalization. That determination does not call simply for investigative or clinical judgment; it is essentially a matter of value judgment. And, in this area, no elite is more expert than anyone else.

In short, psychiatrists are no more able than the rest of the community to distinguish between tolerable and intolerable behaviour. That demarcation is a political exercise for the entire community to make. Because of the importance of personal freedom in our panoply of social values, no persons should be deprived of it unless their behaviour falls within the most precise and objective set of standards that the community can articulate. This is the reason, of course, that our criminal law is drafted in such objective language and detail. In view of their comparable impact on human freedom, our mental commitment laws should be allowed nothing less.

The Issue of Psychiatric Reliability

On the basis of many studies, it is impossible to acquire an acceptable level of confidence in the diagnostic skills of the psychiatric profession. Consider, for example, a classic study performed in 1970. Five psychiatrists, carefully selected on the basis of at least ten years' experience and peer acknowledgement of expertise, took turns in diagnosing 256 patients who were being admitted to a private American psychiatric hospital. Each patient underwent two diagnoses—on admission, by one of the five psychiatrists, and twenty-four hours later by another one. Throughout the study, the group of five was constantly being rotated so that each would be paired with a different psychiatrist as much as possible. In the result, there was no more than a 54.8 per cent rate of agreement on the diagnosis of functional psychosis. Yet it is in the area of psychotic disturbances that many psychiatrists are seeking a greater power of commitment.

In a 1969 study, 43 psychiatrists looked at a filmed interview with a mental patient; 17 diagnosed the subject as psychotic, 26 disagreed. Depression has long been considered one of the mental diseases most amenable to treatment. In a 1959 study, 2 skilled psychiatrists attempted to diagnose for depression a selected sample of 20 hospital patients. Both agreed that 6 patients were suffering from depression. But they *disagreed* as to which 6. In another American study, mental health professionals viewed as more disturbed a patient who expressed radical political views than one who expressed more conventional opinions, despite the fact that otherwise they both exhibited the same psychiatric symptoms. Moreover, both radical and moderate had their insanity rating increased when they criticized the mental health professions and decreased when they complimented them. Significantly, no less an authority than Dr. Robert L. Spitzer, the chairman of the American Psychiatric Association committee that prepared *DSM III*, has pointed out that many of these studies actually *over-rated* the reliability of psychiatric diagnosis because they failed to account adequately for chance agreements.

There are also serious questions about the validity of psychiatric predictions. In this regard, consider an American study done in the early 1960s, which examined what happened to a group of mental patients who won their liberty from hospital despite the objections of psychiatrists. One year later, more than 40 per cent of these people had made a satisfactory adjustment to the community in the sense that they had not had serious trouble with the law, had not been rehospitalized, and were caring for themselves. Significantly, these results compared favourably with the adjustment record of patients who had been released on the recommendation of psychiatrists. In the words of J. Zisken, a psychologist and former president of the American Psychology-Law Society, "...in every study I have been able to find where it has been possible to test the psychiatrists' conclusions against objectively determinable hard data, they have consistently been wrong more often than right at degrees varying from 53% to 100% wrong [*sic*]."

None of this is to question the benevolence or even the competence of our mental health professionals. It is, however, to appreciate the special difficulties of their discipline. When well-intentioned and skilled practitioners so often reach such different conclusions, the most plausible explanation is that it is not they but their discipline that is lacking. The defect is what I suggested above: the concept of mental illness entails no less concern with value judgments than with clinical ones. And psychiatrists have as many differences in philosophical orientation as the rest of us.

It is fair, therefore, to confront those sectors of the psychiatric profession who are seeking greater commitment powers. How many false positives are they entitled to when they are involved in depriving people of one of their most precious possessions—their freedom? So cautious is our society about this matter that, where the criminal law is concerned, we have attempted to live by the adage "It is better for nine guilty persons to go free than for one innocent person to be convicted." For criminal law purposes, this represents a false positive rate of 10 per cent. According to the psychiatric literature, the false positive rate for psychotic diagnosis is substantially higher.

Moreover, it is not even clear that psychiatric treatment (including the much vaunted drug therapies) can be relied upon to produce significant benefits. Indeed, there are indications that on some occasions hospitalization and treatment have produced some negative results. In a 1968 study, people who were found to require hospitalization were randomly divided into two groups. One group was treated in the hospital and the other outside. After a substantial period, only a few of the community patients failed to get along and had to undergo hospitalization. In fact, on the whole, they recovered more quickly than the hospitalized patients.

By now there have been a number of studies concerning the effects of the anti-psychotic drug chlorpromazine. This drug is widely used in the treatment of the most prevalent psychotic disorder, schizophrenia. In a mid-1960s study of how this drug affected job performance, researchers considered a number of factors such as the amount of time worked and the number of days missed. A group on chlorpromazine was compared with a group that was taking a placebo (a substance with no curative properties). The results were mixed. The genuine drug-takers with a poor work history improved their job performance. But the drug-takers with a good work history were found to regress.

More mixed results emerged in an unpublished study of general social functioning which was conducted in the mid-1970s. Those on the drugs appeared to improve between their hospital admission and discharge, but not between their discharge and their follow-up examination, thirty-six months later. At that point, 57 per cent of the chlorpromazine consumers showed improvement. By contrast, such improvement was found in as many as 79 per cent of those on the placebo substance. And, while only 8 per cent of those on the placebo were rehospitalized, this happened to 59 per cent of the people taking the genuine drug. Moreover, a number of studies have reached the conclusion that institutional dependence is one of the great risks of the treatment programs.

In addition to whatever benefits are claimed for these anti-psychotic drugs, there are also some disturbing side effects. Among the more common are the development of skin and eye defects. The skin may become quite sensitive to sunlight and turn grey, blue, or purple on exposure to the sun. In the eye, fine particles may appear in the lens and cornea and grow to areas of opacity. These opacities have been known to persist for as long as six months after drug therapy stopped. Such problems appear in from 1 to 30 per cent of all patients who take anti-psychotic drugs; their incidence apparently increases with high dosage and long therapy.

Another of the more prevalent of the negative side effects is tardive dyskinesia. The following is a medical description of this condition:

> It is characterized by…sucking and smacking movements of the lips, inconsistent lateral jaw movements, as well as the rhythmical forward and backward (sometimes lateral) movement of the tongue ("fly-catcher movement"). Other parts of the body are usually only mildly affected. Choreiform-like movements can occur, with jerky sometimes athetoid movements of the extremities, particularly of the fingers, ankles, and toes. Tonic contractions of the neck and back muscles are sometimes seen. Swallowing may become a problem with consequent weight loss. There may be disturbances in respiratory rate, rhythm, and amplitude.

This condition may persist for years even when the patient stops taking the drug. Indeed, cessation of the drug has been known also to precipitate it. Unfortunately, there does not appear to be any effective treatment for tardive dyskinesia.

Although less frequent (occurring in one of every three thousand patients on chlorpromazine), agranulocytosis is the most serious side effect. It involves an erosion of white blood cells, and a resulting increased susceptibility to infection. Worse still, this condition is likely to be fatal in at least 30 per cent of the cases.

In fairness, it must be acknowledged that, in many of the studies, the patients on anti-psychotic drugs experienced a substantial reduction of the symptoms associated with their particular disorder. To put it in plain English, many of the drug-takers wound up much less crazy. No doubt, numbers of them preferred the risks and even the experience of the side effects to the debilitations of their psychosis.

I mention these negative results and disturbing side effects not to condemn all or even most hospitalization and drug therapy, but rather to indicate that what we are dealing with is a long way from an unqualified benefit. I am simply questioning whether the benefits are sufficiently great and the costs sufficiently slight to sustain a power of *coercion* in these matters. My hope is to introduce a note of caution among the proponents of forced hospitalization. Even if they cannot completely accept the principles of civil liberties, they might be dissuaded by the mixed results of modern medicine's performance.

Towards a Better (or Less Bad) Basis for Involuntary Commitment

There are some circumstances in which a power of involuntary civil commitment might arguably be permissible. But, in view of the centrality of liberty in our society, such circumstances should involve the most overwhelming threats of injury to our most vital values. In my view, the anticipated injury should require, at the very least, a combination of three characteristics: severity, high probability, and immediacy.

The need for severity is designed to restrict these intrusions on freedom to the most serious of possible injuries. Involuntary confinement should not be available in order to deal simply with weird behaviour or unhappy situations. The need for high probability is designed to require substantial evidence that, unless some action is taken, the apprehended injury will, in fact, occur. Since commitment means the certainty of liberty being curtailed, there should be much more than a mere possibility of injury being sustained. The need for immediacy is designed to restrict these intrusions to those situations where nothing less than confinement is likely to prevent the apprehended injury. If there is enough time and chance for something less drastic to work, confinement should be avoided.

From this, it follows that no persons should be subject to involuntary civil commitment unless, at a minimum, they suffer from a mental disorder of such a nature that there is a high probability they will imminently cause themselves or someone else serious physical injury. On this basis, it would still be possible to commit dangerous and suicidal people. For such purposes, I would even include those who are deteriorating from an inability to handle their most elementary bodily needs and functions.

By now a minority of Canadian provinces provide that involuntary hospitalization cannot occur unless the targeted persons suffer from a mental disorder that will likely result in serious bodily harm to themselves or others, or in imminent and serious physical impairment of themselves. In 1987 a committee, appointed by the various provincial governments and territories, proposed similar criteria for universal adoption. While this recommendation would certainly improve upon the vague and broad criteria that currently exist in most provinces, it does not go far enough. Where serious physical impairment is concerned, there is a requirement that it is likely to be imminent. But there is no such requirement in the case of serious bodily harm. In my view, there is simply no basis for such distinctions.

Sometimes an outlandish example helps to make the point. Suppose a mentally disordered bachelor threatened to kill himself if the Pope did not marry by the year 2000. On the basis of the foregoing criteria, it appears that this person could be involuntarily confined *today*. In consequence, I believe that mental commitments should require a strong element of urgency: that there be no time for anything other than confinement to prevent the apprehended injury.

On the other hand, how will I now answer the libertarian purists who will regard *any* civil commitment power as a betrayal of all the arguments I advanced earlier? Since I am willing to allow compulsory confinement where no criminal offence is necessarily suspected, am I not prepared to run the kind of risks of subjectivity that I have just condemned? The answer obviously must be "yes".

But the distinctions must be appreciated. I am prepared to incur such risks only on the basis of criteria narrowly addressed to overwhelming emergency circumstances. In my view, the greater and more imminent the peril, the more the normal safeguards can be relaxed. Mr. Justice Oliver Wendell Holmes of the U.S. Supreme Court enunciated a similar test when he said that, despite the general centrality of freedom of speech, it can be restricted in a situation of "clear and present danger". Such tests do not and cannot eliminate the risk that some person's freedom will suffer an unjust encroachment. But, by insisting on such narrow, emergency-oriented criteria, I would expect this risk to be substantially reduced. Moreover, it would be intolerable for a civilized society to watch helplessly the development of a terrible emergency. To insist on waiting for a completed criminal or self-destructive act is to run a great risk of being unable to avert the damage. This leads us back to the question as to which risk is the less bad.

But what about all those poor, tortured souls who are likely never to be helped because my proposed criteria are still too stringent for them? I see no reason to give up trying to help these people. With an ever more ingenious combination of medical, family, social, and economic pressures, it might be possible to persuade more of them to seek the help that psychiatry can offer. I have less difficulty with the attempt to persuade than with the power to compel.

Nevertheless, it will be asked, what will we do about the terrible suffering of those who continue to resist our efforts to help them? And what will we do about the agony experienced by their families and loved ones? I acknowledge that there are no satisfactory answers to these questions. If the unproductive husband is too much of a burden, there is always separation and divorce. If the old auntie is too embarrassing, she can be denied entry to the premises. If the grandfather has become too crazy with his money, perhaps there can be recourse to a court-appointed trustee. If the husband, auntie, and grandfather "carry on" unacceptably in public, they might, at some stage, violate one of our laws dealing with public nuisance. For this, of course, they could be subject, like anyone else, to the restraints of the general law.

I understand that many people will be emotionally unable to divorce the unproductive husband, evict the nattering old auntie, or seize the grandfather's money. Indeed, even the authorities might shrink from invoking the weapons of prosecution available to them. Moreover, such actions would protect only certain limited interests of the other family members and society at large. Obviously, these actions would provide no help at all to the persons who are suffering the emotional disabilities. As unsatisfying as all these solutions might be, what is the alternative? A broader commitment law with its inevitable risks to the freedom of a wide variety of non-conformists and dissenters *beyond* the kind of people we have been discussing. I don't claim that my position will lead to happy results. My point is simply that, in view of the alternatives available, what I advocate is likely to produce a *less* unhappy outcome.

Towards Better (or Less Bad) Commitment Procedures

No less important than the criteria upon which commitment is based are the procedures by which decisions are made. The psychiatric profession should be divested of a major adjudicative role in these matters. The interpretation and application of statutory criteria are not really the psychiatrists' domain. A rather significant situation developed a few years ago when the Ontario Mental Health Act was amended. Where it had earlier permitted involuntary commitment to serve the "safety interests" of the prospective patient or others, it was then changed to require an apprehension of "serious bodily harm" or "serious physical impairment". Organized psychiatry denounced the amendment as "frightening" and even "terrifying". A former president of the Ontario Psychiatric Association charged that the only freedom the amendment offered for the vast majority of mentally ill people was the "pseudo-freedom to lose their job, their family, their self-respect, and their marriage".

This was a most revealing reaction. Although it may require a certain amount of bravado to impute impaired judgment to a group of psychiatrists, I cannot avoid characterizing this response, at the very least, as confused. In view of the fact that the Mental Health Act in its earlier form limited involuntary commitment to considerations of "safety", why hadn't those psychiatrists complained earlier? By what feats of verbal gymnastics could anyone suggest that the criterion "safety" was able to authorize compulsory hospitalization to protect a job, a marriage, or a family? While the former provision of the Mental Health Act was admittedly vague, there were nevertheless limits to how far it could be stretched. Indeed, it is much more reasonable to regard the amendment as a clarification, rather than a modification, of the "safety" requirement. To the extent, therefore, that these psychiatrists complained in this way about "new" intrusions on their commitment practices, they may have been implicitly acknowledging past violations of their statutory authority.

Corroboration for this view appears in a master's thesis written by Burton P. Perrin for the psychology department of York University in the mid-1970s. This thesis analysed 200 certificates on the basis of which doctors (mostly psychiatrists) had actually committed people to various periods of involuntary confinement in an Ontario psychiatric facility. With Mr. Perrin's cooperation, the Canadian Civil Liberties Association arranged to have two senior counsel provide legal opinions as to the adequacy of the certificates concerned. In the result, both counsel agreed that at least 142, or 71 per cent, of the certificates failed to satisfy the requirements of the Mental Health Act, as they then stood.

At the time, a certificate of committal signed by one physician constituted authority to hold persons against their will in a mental institution for up to one month. As a safeguard against excess or abuse, the statute required the committing doctor to provide the following written information:

1. Facts indicating mental disorder observed by the doctor (e.g. appearance, conduct, conversation);

2. Other facts, if any, indicating mental disorder communicated to the doctor by others (state from whom the information was received);

3. State reasons why no measure short of hospitalization would be appropriate in the case of the above-mentioned person;

4. State reasons why the above named is not suitable for admission as an informal (voluntary) patient.

Verbatim texts of a few of these certificates will help to illustrate why the lawyers impugned them.

005
1.Crying on phone. Was admitted [to hospital]...discharged self.
Was in emergency [another hospital]...discharged self.
2. Unable to stop drinking.
3. Leaves hospital.
4. Leaves hospital.
024
1. Shouting obscenities—very disturbed.
2. Discharged from [hospital]....
3. Unpredictable—disturbed.
4. Unpredictable.
084
1. Patient very paranoid, no insight. Will not cooperate.
2. Wife reports she doesn't want him back.
3. Dangerous to himself, will not follow his diet.
4. Will not cooperate.
159
1. Extremely agitated and vociferous.
2. Speech incoherent and suspicious—almost paranoid.
3. Two previous admissions to Ontario Hospital.
4. Previous experience.

In addition to the absence of the required information, these certificates were virtually devoid of any suggestion that "safety" was a factor in the commitment decision. Without a lot more detail, allegations like "shouting obscenities", "will not cooperate", "leaves hospital", and "unpredictable" were hardly a proper, let alone a legal, basis for encroachments on liberty.

The publication of the survey was greeted with the criticism that all it had succeeded in uncovering was that the psychiatrists were bad form-fillers. There was no evidence that they had actually confined people without the requisite legal grounds. There was, of course, some validity to this criticism. But while it is possible that despite an inadequate certificate there may still be grounds for commitment, it is also possible that in such circumstances the grounds may *not* exist. The psychiatrists who pooh-poohed the survey exhibited a disquieting insensitivity to the fact that a properly completed certificate was the primary safeguard against an unlawful confinement.

To argue by analogy, there may be grounds for the conviction and imprisonment of a criminal accused. But unless such grounds are based upon proper evidence in court, the judge is required to dismiss the charge and to acquit the accused. The incarceration of the criminal offender requires at least a record of cogent evidence. There is no reason why the incarceration of the mentally disordered should be allowed to take place on the basis of anything less.

The decision to commit is not a medical decision, it is a legal one. It should not be made, therefore, by doctors. The judgment of whether the evidence in a particular case satisfies the requisite statutory criteria is exactly the kind of judgment that courts make all the time. To whatever extent the judges may lack the expertise to appreciate some of the evidence, expert witnesses can be called to testify. There is no reason why such witnesses could not include psychiatrists. It is one thing for a psychiatrist to advise a court about a person's emotional and mental condition; it is another thing entirely for the psychiatrist to make the effective decision in the case.

I have no objection to allowing a psychiatrist the power to commit in an emergency situation. But commitments of this sort should expire automatically after a very short period—say, a maximum of three days. Involuntary confinement beyond such a period should require the adjudication of the courts or some other independent legal tribunals. According to the procedure I envision, those hospital authorities seeking to extend a commitment would be required within the three-day period to serve upon the patients, their counsel, and the tribunal an application to commit, along with all of the relevant documentation. Either the hospital authorities or the patient would then be entitled to make additional representations, either orally or in writing. In the absence of any desire for oral submissions, the tribunal would dispose of the commitment application solely on the basis of the written documentation. At the option of the patient, there could be a full-scale hearing, in public or private, with the right to call and challenge witnesses.

In order to ensure that these procedures work properly, a copy of the emergency commitment certificate should be given to the patients or their representatives as soon as practicable after the initial emergency commitment begins. The law should also oblige the psychiatric facility to take all reasonable steps as quickly as practicable to ensure that the committed persons have speedy access to legal counsel. And public funds should be available, at least in needy cases, to subsidize competent advocacy.

At the time of writing, the province of Ontario has finally reduced the emergency commitment power which a physician may impose from five days, as it was earlier, to three days. But it provides that other physicians employed in the hospital can extend the commitment period for up to six months thereafter. The problem is that in any conflict between patients who seek to get out and a hospital that seeks to keep them in, a physician employed there would not look adequately impartial. Despite the good intentions of both hospital and physicians, the demands of procedural fairness would be better served by having a court or other independent tribunal empowered to make the subsequent decisions.

While the Ontario system currently provides for earlier and periodic recourse to independent review, that's not good enough. In fact, such review occurs in less than 15 per cent of the cases. The problem is that, until people have endured six months of forced confinement, the review process depends on *their* initiative. We know from experience that many mental patients are intimidated about taking action. In view of the basic freedoms involved, I believe that independent adjudication should be mandatory in every case and it should occur near the inception of the confinement.

In my scheme, the onus would devolve throughout on those who are seeking to extend the commitment. Thus, defective documentation, untimely notice, and/or inadequate evidence could precipitate the discharge of a patient committed involuntarily. But, even if a certificate were validated through this process, the commitment nevertheless should be of a short duration—say, one month—and it should continue to be susceptible to other existing safeguards such as habeas corpus and whatever review process may exist.

A Word about Compulsory Treatment

In a number of Canadian jurisdictions, involuntarily committed mental patients are susceptible to certain forms of compulsory treatment. I have no serious quarrel with temporary and minor restraints that are designed to avert an imminent peril. They may be necessary, for example, to restrain or sedate an inmate who is bent on suicide.

The problem becomes more serious when the authorities seek to impose not a short-term restraint but a long-term cure. In most jurisdictions, there is a power to impose treatment including even electro-convulsive therapy ("shock treatment") against the expressed wishes of involuntary patients—both competent and incompetent. No justification exists for such compulsion in the case of competent persons. Competent patients with physical disorders are not required, for example, to take medicine for pneumonia, radiation for cancer, diet for strokes, or even rest for heart disease. No matter how much medical experts or even the patients themselves may agree that such treatments would be helpful, compulsion cannot be exercised. Why should competent patients with *mental* disorders be treated any differently, even if they have been involuntarily committed?

Frequently psychiatrists have argued that, unless they are permitted to force treatment on involuntary patients, the hospital is effectively transformed into nothing more than a prison. Perhaps so. But the only justification for involuntary commitments, in my view, is to avert imminent perils, not to restructure personalities. Once that peril abates, the commitment has served its purpose. To encroach upon patients beyond that point is to transform the hospital, not into a prison, but into a torture chamber. It may be wise for patients to take treatment. But so long as they are competent, why shouldn't *they* decide which of the unpalatable alternatives they prefer to face?

Hospitals are for treatment, not for warehousing, is the reply of some psychiatrists. In their view, patients who must be held and won't be treated should be sent to jail, not to hospital. But, if we really believe that treatment is in the best interests of those patients, shouldn't we keep them in the setting that is most conducive to voluntary persuasion? I would think that such persuasion would be more likely in the caring atmosphere of a properly run hospital than in the alienating environment of a hostile prison.

The only arguable justification for such compulsion is in the case of the incompetent patient. But even here we should improve upon the procedures for determining incompetence. So long as such judgments are made essentially by hospital staff, there is a violation of our society's concept of procedural fair play. Since physicians and their colleagues are concerned primarily with treating what they consider to be disease, they are likely to lack the appearance of impartiality. While their desire to cure disease is certainly laudable, it renders them vulnerable to the perception that they will find incompetence whenever a patient refuses medical advice. In all cases where patients object to treatment, decisions of incompetence should be reviewed by a tribunal independent of both the health-care providers who seek to treat and the patients whom they seek to treat.

Moreover, the treatment to be imposed on anyone found incompetent should be limited as much as possible to what is reasonably necessary to restore competence. The goal should be to enable the patients to decide for themselves what encroachments they wish to sustain. Since incompetence is what made compulsion permissible, the promotion of competence, wherever possible, should be its sole purpose.

Chapter Ten

THE CONSTITUTIONAL
ENTRENCHMENT OF OUR
FUNDAMENTAL FREEDOMS

Minority Rights versus Majority Rule

Democracy is characterized by a continuing tension between majority rule and minority rights. Majority rule is democracy's safeguard against minority dictatorship. And the fundamental rights such as freedom of speech, freedom of assembly, and due process of law are democracy's safeguards against majority rule itself becoming a dictatorship.

But what happens when a majority uses its legislative power to curtail fundamental rights? Such an action could effectively vitiate the democratic processes. It could deprive minorities of the one vehicle by which they could peacefully influence, or become, the majority. The answer to this dilemma, in some countries, is a written constitution in which the fundamental rights and freedoms are entrenched—that is, they are immune from encroachment by the government of the day. In countries such as India, Ireland, and the United States, even legislative majorities may not generally interfere with the fundamental rights and freedoms of the democratic system. This was the philosophy that gave rise, albeit in modified form, to Canada's new Charter of Rights and Freedoms.

As appealing as entrenched rights may initially sound, I remain a skeptic. Like everything else in human society, constitutional rights do not enforce themselves. Someone must be entrusted with the job. This means that someone has to be given the power to overrule even the government. In those Western democracies that have written constitutions, this job falls upon the judges of the law courts.

I am not particularly troubled by the prospect of a court using a constitutional principle to restrain the *administrative* branches of government: police forces, welfare departments, immigration authorities, and so on. But I am disquieted when I see those same courts purporting to overrule the *legislative* branches of government: the federal Parliament and the provincial legislatures. After all, the legislative branches of government are occupied by elected politicians who are accountable to the people. The courts, on the other hand, are occupied by appointed judges who owe no such accountability to the people.

Inevitably, constitutional principles are expressed in exceptionally broad and vague language. This is because constitutions, unlike ordinary statutes, are designed to endure for centuries. Ordinary statutes can be amended, repealed, and even replaced by a simple majority in the appropriate legislative assembly. But constitutional changes usually require a much more complicated set of procedures.

As a practical matter, this gives enormous power to the judges. The very breadth and vagueness of the constitutional language mean that the critical factor is the interpretation of that language. And, as we have seen, none of the constitutional principles can claim the status of an absolute. Every one of them is subject to some exceptions under some circumstances. So the paramount questions become who shall determine the permissibility of any given exception, and by what criteria shall that determination be made?

As indicated, the persons who make the determinations are the judges, and the criteria are largely created by them. Apart from such unhelpful terms as "reasonable limits", the constitutional document is unlikely to contain anything resembling a guideline. The language is simply too broad for such purposes. Thus, the scope of the constitutional principles and the permissible exceptions to them will become essentially what the judges say they should be. In short, the value judgments and policy preferences of the appointed judges could well become the ultimate authority in the entire society.

This is a potentially undemocratic situation. To the extent that the value preferences of appointed judges prevail over those of elected politicians, democracy becomes replaced by a form of oligarchy. After all, isn't popular accountability the very essence of the democratic system? When judges are called upon to apply ordinary statutes, there need not be the same concern about judicial power. In that context, the role of the judge is to discern and give effect to the will of the legislature. But when judges are called upon to apply constitutional principles to ordinary statutes, it's a different ball game. The judges then rule on the propriety of the legislative will itself.

In any collision between the policy preferences of elected politicians and those of appointed judges, I have little difficulty opting for the former. My choice is based upon the principle of democratic accountability. We can get rid of our politicians. We can vote them and their parties out of office. Our judges, on the other hand, are not so vulnerable to our will. Their tenure of office is dependent essentially on chronology and mortality.

Nevertheless, the pro-entrenchment advocates argue, it is the very invulnerability of our judges to the popular will that makes them so well suited to the role of protecting the more fundamental values of our society. But how is this different, in principle, from rule by feudal aristocracy, clerical theocracy, or Lenin's revolutionary vanguard? What these systems have in common is a fundamental distrust of the ordinary people to do the right thing. The underlying theory is that someone has to be entrusted to interpret the true interests of the people for them.

By now, hasn't history produced enough examples of how *untrustworthy* special elites can be? Why should they become more acceptable just because they are supposed to be upholding the broad and idealistic generalities of a democratic constitution rather than the broad and idealistic generalities of *The Communist Manifesto* or the Ten Commandments? Admittedly, democratic majorities can be tyrannical, but so can undemocratic minorities. Why should we assume that a few years of law practice can better qualify a person to tell us what's good for us than can a few years of feudal exploitation, revolutionary agitation, or church-sponsored bingos?

In making these observations, I am not unmindful of the possibility that a legislative majority could move so quickly and completely against our fundamental rights and freedoms that there would be little opportunity for redress within the political system. If, for example, a legislative majority simply outlawed all other political parties together with democratic elections and freedom of speech, there would be no way, short of violent revolution, to turf the culprits out of office.

The prospects of such a disaster give redress to the courts an alluring appeal. But the hope for judicial rectification in such a situation would be more academic than real. If we ever faced so overwhelming an assault on the democratic processes, I can't imagine that the courts would be able to do anything about it. Indeed, it is likely that they would be abolished along with the other components of the democratic system. My argument against giving the courts such constitutional power presupposes the general operation of political democracy. If such were not the case, the courts would not likely be helpful in any event.

How well, in *fact*, have the courts of the Western democracies performed as the custodians of our constitutional principles? The most extensive experience has been in the United States. Its record is not impressive. Rarely, for example, has the U.S. Supreme Court struck down federal legislation that suppressed civil liberties. While the pronouncements of certain judges like Oliver Wendell Holmes and Louis Brandeis have become the poetry of American democracy, their declarations usually appeared in *dissenting* judgments.

There have been times, of course, when the U.S. Supreme Court produced some marvellous decisions protective of civil liberties. Such was the case, for example, during the fifteen years or so when Earl Warren was chief justice. But even for so young a country this represents a mere interlude in its history.

Pro-entrenchers also argue that judicial involvement is particularly needed in an emergency situation. When a country is threatened by war or some other great peril, popularly elected governments are unlikely to be conscientious about civil liberties. They will be far too susceptible to mass passion and prejudice. Thus, the courts are seen as necessary to preserve a sense of balance. Yet the U.S. Supreme Court has hardly been a reliable protector of civil liberties during the great crises of American life. Perhaps the most scandalous example occurred during the Second World War, when the court upheld the constitutionality of the forced relocation perpetrated against the Japanese Americans. Significantly, the majority judgment was written by the most liberal justice of that era, Hugo Black.

During the early years of the American–Soviet Cold War, the U.S. Supreme Court failed again to rise to the challenge. It upheld the constitutionality of the Smith Act under which it became an offence to conspire to organize a group that teaches the violent overthrow of the government. It required a particularly fertile imagination to conceive how conspiring to organize to teach could be regarded as a "clear and present danger" to the national security of the United States. But that is what the U.S. Supreme Court effectively held. On the basis of historical experience, it is fair to conclude that the emergency situation is probably the least likely to attract judicial intervention.

One of the strongest claims that has been made on behalf of entrenchment is how well American blacks have been served by it. Pro-entrenchers insist that, without the Supreme Court, it would have been impossible to challenge racial segregation in the southern American school systems. They point to the court's ground-breaking decision of 1954 which finally ordered the schools to desegregate. This argument reveals an inadequate grasp of American history. While it is true that in recent years the court has chipped away at racial segregation, this has not always been the case. Indeed, the court's 1954 decision was made necessary by a terrible decision which it had rendered some sixty years earlier. In the infamous case of *Plessy v. Ferguson* in 1896, the court interpreted the American constitution as permitting "separate but equal" facilities for black people.

Not only did the court fail to help the cause of racial integration throughout much of American history, but at several key points it was downright harmful. In the early part of the nineteenth century, the court struck down the Missouri Compromise, an attempt by Congress to limit slavery in the new territories. This decision has been widely regarded as one of the primary causes of the Civil War. Towards the latter part of the nineteenth century, the Supreme Court frustrated another congressional attempt to promote racial equality. The justices struck down a federal statute purporting to prohibit racial discrimination in certain public places.

During a significant period of American history, however, the court did consistently champion the cause of another minority: the rich. And, remarkably, it used the Bill of Rights to do it. From the latter part of the 1800s until the latter part of the 1930s, the Supreme Court struck down one statute after another that had been enacted especially to protect the under-privileged from the over-privileged. Among the casualties of such court action were laws to limit the hours of work, provide minimum wages, protect child labour, and prohibit discrimination against unions. In most of these cases, the court invoked the section of the Bill of Rights that requires the legislative branch of government to observe "due process of law" when encroaching on "life, liberty, or property".

These judicial interpretations were simply Neanderthal. In striking down a New York State statute that prohibited employment in bakeries for more than sixty hours in a week or ten hours in a day, the court said, "the general right to make a contract in relation to his business is part of the liberty of the individual protected by the fourteenth amendment of the federal Constitution". In the course of over-turning a Kansas statute prohibiting discrimination against unions, the court declared that "included in the right of personal liberty...is the right to make contracts". In doing likewise to a federal law that prohibited discrimination against unions, the court added a remarkable ingredient to the sacred right of contract: "...the employer and the employee have equality of right, and any legislation that disturbs that equality is an arbitrary interference with the liberty of contract". No doubt the object of Congress in passing this statute was to reduce what it saw as the stark *inequalities* which the marketplace had inflicted upon employees in favour of their employers. In another case, the court condemned as "arbitrary and oppressive" a law which prohibited employment agencies from requiring that workers pay them fees. Despite the widespread denunciations of these employment agencies as parasitic, the court considered them a "useful business".

The examples go on and on. At the very least, they should demonstrate that entrenched rights do not always protect disadvantaged individuals against a malevolent government. Often they have a contrary effect. In these cases, it was the legislature that was attempting to help the disadvantaged people and the court that was frustrating the effort.

Pro-entrenchers are fond of pointing out that this regressive line of cases came to a halt at the end of the 1930s. Since then, the American court has explicitly reversed its earlier judgments in the course of upholding a host of comparable welfare-state measures. While this is largely true, there have been flashbacks to the old jurisprudence. In one recent case, the United States Supreme Court held that warrants were required before government inspectors could insist on entering factory premises to check for compliance with occupational health and safety requirements. By contrast, the court held that warrants were not needed for welfare administrators in order to require access to a welfare recipient's home as a condition of granting assistance.

In the early 1980s, an appellate court in California used the "due process" clause again to strike down municipal ordinances which required the owners of mobile-home parks to give their tenants priority in the event that the land was to be sold. The idea was to provide the tenants with some semblance of residential stability. Despite the fact that there was no compulsion to sell the land or to give the tenants a better price than any other potential purchasers, the court held that the ordinances represented an unconstitutional "taking" of the owners' land.

But even if these judicial relapses had not occurred, the pro-entrenchers could derive little sustenance from the post-1930s jurisprudence of the American courts. No matter how progressive a subsequent line of cases may be, there is nothing to ensure that there won't be further reversions. The courts are governed neither by the laws of nature nor by the laws of logic. Indeed, not infrequently, the courts contravene even the canons of consistency. Much depends upon the cosmic coincidence of which judges are sitting on which cases at any given time. The judges have done an about-face before, and they can do it again.

Canadian partisans of entrenchment often express a deep confidence that the Canadian courts will not be influenced by the earlier line of American cases. Perhaps not. But how can they be so sure? As late as 1980, an Irish court struck down rent control legislation as being unconstitutional. The court's reasoning sounded like a rerun of the old American cases:

> ...but I am of opinion that both parts of the Act are repugnant to the provisions of the Constitution in that a group of citizens arbitrarily selected has been deprived of property for the benefit of another group of citizens, without any compensation, with no limitation of the period of deprivation and with no indication of any occasion which necessitates their selection for this purpose from amongst the general body of citizens.

In short, the Irish Constitution was read as embodying the principles of *laissez-faire* economics.

If this can happen in 1980 Ireland, why not in contemporary Canada? Some pro-entrenchers argue that both the American and Irish constitutions are more susceptible to such interpretations than the Canadian Charter because they, unlike the Canadian document, have entrenched property rights. This argument overlooks the fact that some of those reactionary American judgments were not based entirely on the property protection of the Bill of Rights. Some of them relied on the word "liberty", holding that it included liberty of contract.

Section 7 of our Charter reads: "Everyone has the right to life, liberty and security of the person and the right not to be deprived thereof except in accordance with the principles of fundamental justice." What is there to prevent the Canadian courts from construing the word "liberty" to include liberty of contract? And what is there to prevent "the principles of fundamental justice" from receiving a substantive rather than simply a procedural interpretation? A substantive construction means that the judges would consider the *merits* of the legislation at issue, as the U.S. Supreme Court did when it used the counterpart "due process" provision in the American Bill of Rights to nullify all those social and economic welfare statutes.

The drafters of the Canadian Charter have pointed out that much of the language they chose was designed precisely to avoid such problems. The Supreme Court of Canada has already declared, however, that those concluding words of Section 7 are capable of a substantive interpretation. Whether this reasoning will lead the Canadian courts on the same dubious path as the one adopted earlier by the Americans we do not yet know. But judgments such as this serve to remind us that the broader and vaguer the language of a constitutional document, the greater and more frequent the opportunity for judges to act as legislators.

In this connection, consider the 1983 case involving the Ontario government's wage restraint program for civil servants. There the Divisional Court of the Ontario Supreme Court invoked the Charter's protection for "freedom of association". According to the court, freedom of association for workers in unions would be rendered hollow unless it included the freedom to engage in collective bargaining and the freedom to conduct a strike if the bargaining broke down. Despite the fact that the court held some of the Ontario restrictions were "reasonable limits" and "demonstrably justified", the case nevertheless asserts the proposition that, presumptively at least, wage controls violate union members' freedom of association. On the basis of similar reasoning, the Saskatchewan Court of Appeal impugned a law banning certain strikes in that province.

Despite my sympathy with the judicial willingness to protect these components of trade union strategy, I worry about the implications of the analysis. On the basis of this reasoning, could it not be just as validly held that anti-combines legislation, presumptively at least, violates freedom of association for those involved in combines? Isn't the freedom to set prices just as vital to the members of a combine as collective bargaining is to the members of a union? To what extent, therefore, could "freedom of association" perform some of the mischief for us that the "due process" clause did in the United States?

These anxieties are only partly allayed by a subsequent Supreme Court of Canada judgment that effectively overruled the Ontario and Saskatchewan decisions. There is no inherent reason why the situation could not have been reversed. Indeed, a slight change in the composition of any of those courts might well have changed the results in all of them. Terminology as vague as "freedom of association" invites a wide variety of interpretations and approaches. In a 1986 case, for example, there was an attempt to use it *against* union interests. A chartered bank invoked freedom of association to stop a labour arbitrator from reinstating a discharged union member. While the attempt failed, the union was put to the expense of fighting it. We have only begun to see the enormous potential of this provision.

In connection with these flexible uses of language, consider also how a provincial court judge in Ontario used "freedom of expression" to strike down the federal government's compulsory metrification program. In the opinion of this judge, the prohibition against selling and advertising in imperial measure constitutes a violation of a merchant's freedom of speech. Although this judgment was reversed on appeal, the case shows how even our fundamental freedoms can be used to upset the initiatives by government to regulate the market.

For these reasons, the philosophy of our various judges is likely to be a more reliable gauge than the language of our Charter. Historically at least, Canadian judges have shown something less than enthusiasm for the principles of civil liberties. Since 1960 there has been a statutory Bill of Rights operating at least at the federal level. The language of the bill could have sustained some far-reaching protections for human rights and civil liberties. Regrettably, that same language could also support a more feeble construction. With few exceptions, the senior Canadian courts chose the latter approach.

Perhaps the most devastating blow which the Supreme Court of Canada inflicted on the 1960 Bill of Rights was its promulgation of the "frozen concepts" theory. Many of the court's judgments restricted the ability of the Bill of Rights to affect any practices that pre-dated it. On the basis of this theory, only *post*-1960 violations would be subject to judicial remedy. Unfortunately, this did not leave much room for the Bill of Rights to operate. Injustice in Canada is singularly devoid of originality.

Other court decisions reduced the Bill of Rights' impact even further. In the early 1970s, for example, the Supreme Court of Canada held that, despite the police violation of an arrested person's "right to retain and instruct counsel without delay", evidence obtained under the circumstances was nevertheless admissible when the arrested person came to trial. Thanks to the judiciary, this safeguard in the Bill of Rights was effectively denuded of its most practical sanction.

In yet another case, the Alberta Court of Appeal came up with a stunning example of the lengths to which language can be stretched. A sixteen-year-old boy was convicted for contributing to juvenile delinquency because he had had sexual intercourse with a sixteen-year-old girl. Under the Juvenile Delinquency Act, girls under eighteen in the province of Alberta were designated as "children", but boys of that age received no comparable status. The Alberta Court of Appeal held that this distinction did not constitute sexual "discrimination" against boys within the meaning of the Bill of Rights. Instead, it was held to be a benefit conferred upon girls. Consider the implications of this judgment. An increase in family allowances for Christians is not discrimination against Jews—it's a benefit for Christians.

These exercises in linguistic contortion influenced the drafters of the new Charter of Rights and Freedoms. Much of the language chosen was designed to forestall the damage that had been done to the older Bill of Rights. For reasons already indicated, we simply cannot be so confident that linguistic change will adequately influence judicial interpretation. But, even if the new language does help, this would address, at best, only a few sections of the Charter. We can only speculate on the infinite varieties of interpretation that might be given to all the other sections of the Charter in light of the infinite number of problems they will be invoked to resolve.

In fairness, I have to acknowledge that our superior courts have produced some encouraging interpretations of the Charter. They have struck down, as a violation of the presumption of innocence, the section of the Narcotic Control Act which effectively required those in possession of illicit drugs to prove that their purpose was not trafficking. The same fate was suffered by another section of the Narcotic Control Act which empowered the police, without warrant, forcibly to enter and search places other than dwelling houses in a rather wide variety of circumstances. This was held to violate the Charter's protection against "unreasonable search and seizure". Quebec's French-only sign law was overturned as a contravention of the Charter guarantee for "freedom of expression", as was the criminal offence of scandalizing the courts.

One of the most noteworthy judgments occurred in the Morgentaler case, where the Supreme Court of Canada struck down the federal abortion law as an infringement on the right of women to "security of the person and the right not to be deprived thereof except in accordance with the principles of fundamental justice". The significance of this case lies in the willingness of the court to look behind the words of the statute and assess what is really happening in the community. The court received and acted on evidence that, in many areas of the country, women had insufficient access to therapeutic abortion committees.

On the other hand, the Divisional Court of the Ontario Supreme Court in two separate cases upheld the use of the Lord's Prayer and formal religious instruction in the public schools of that province. Despite the Christian nature of the prayer and the instruction, the court refused to find that they constituted unwarranted discrimination or an unjustified encroachment on freedom of religion. In a remarkable manifestation of insensitivity to minority experience, the judges expressed their satisfaction with the existence of the right of exemption. The court simply attached little significance to the argument that many minority parents would be reluctant to exercise exemption because withdrawal from the classroom on religious grounds could expose their youngsters to the disapproval of their classmates. Despite the undue breadth and vagueness of the anti-hate and false news laws, superior courts in Alberta and Ontario found that they did not violate the free speech protections of the Charter. The federal court upheld an order-in-council requiring ministerial permission for a person to come within a certain distance of the annual East Coast seal hunt. Despite this apparently blatant attempt by government to interfere with the "animal rights" protest, the court thought that the circumstances justified such limits on free speech.

On the question of economic and social legislation there is very little experience at the time of writing. Workers' compensation laws have met a mixed response. The constitutionality of the Ontario law was upheld at trial. But the Newfoundland law was struck down at trial and sustained on appeal. In Alberta the counterpart legislation was upheld at trial and struck down on retrial. Mandatory retirement has been sustained in some places and upset elsewhere. The same with the right of unions to spend conscripted dues for political purposes. At the moment, the Ontario Medical Association is waiting for a court date to challenge the constitutionality of Ontario's ban on extra billing by doctors.

Despite the ultimate result in these cases and many others that have not yet even been launched, the process is disconcerting. For supporters of the welfare state, it is enough that vital legislation is attacked. Regardless of the outcome, precious resources have to be diverted from the strengthening of the statutory protections involved. The situation is exacerbated when non-government bodies, like unions, are forced to divert their resources for such purposes. For supporters of the welfare state, a successful constitutional defence means that a lot of valuable time, money, and energy has been used simply to mark time.

In the final analysis, however, the issue is not whether our society is to be governed by conservative, liberal, or radical value judgments. The issue is whether the key decisions will be made by elected representatives of the people or by an unelected elite. While the judicial influence has usually been conservative, my position ultimately is based, not on the philosophy of the result, but on the integrity of the process. In short, I believe that democracy means the people and their representatives must prevail, even if they do the wrong thing. The risk of error cannot be avoided. The only question is who shall have the right to make the last mistake—those who are elected or those who are appointed.

For entirely the wrong reasons, Canada has devised a rather ingenious compromise between constitutional entrenchment and parliamentary sovereignty. During the eleventh hour constitutional negotiations between the federal and provincial governments, all parties agreed to include in the Charter a section allowing the federal Parliament and provincial legislatures to immunize any of their otherwise competent enactments against the application of key Charter provisions. No need to resort to the cumbersome processes of constitutional amendment. All they have to do is pass, by ordinary legislative process, a special provision declaring that the enactment in question will be valid, "notwithstanding the Charter of Rights and Freedoms". And this ouster of Charter jurisdiction will remain in effect for five years, at which point it will automatically lapse unless explicitly re-enacted.

Legally, therefore, it would be easy for our elected legislatures to prevail, in key Charter areas, over our appointed judiciary. Politically, however, the process could be a veritable minefield. The mere introduction of a bill to oust the application of the Charter would likely spark an enormous controversy. After all the homage which has been paid to the Charter, how could it be otherwise? Without solid support in the legislature and the community, a government would be very reluctant to take the heat that such action would invariably generate. And the prospect of having to endure such flak every five years thereafter can only increase the reluctance to embark on such a course in the first place.

Despite the existence of such "notwithstanding" clauses in the Alberta and Saskatchewan Bills of Rights, they have not so far been invoked. The comparable clause in the Canadian Bill of Rights was used only once—to protect emergency legislation during the 1970 FLQ crisis. A similar provision in the Quebec Charter of Rights has been invoked on only one controversial occasion: to protect Quebec's 1983 statute curbing pay raises in the public sector. Of course, Quebec also invoked the "notwithstanding" clause of the Canadian Charter in this case and it enacted a bill to immunize *all* of its legislation from key Charter review. But since Quebec dissented from the constitutional accord until Meech Lake, the Canadian Charter did not then enjoy the prestige in that province that it did everywhere else. The only other province that has used the Charter's "notwithstanding" clause is Saskatchewan. There it was used to protect special legislation aimed at preventing a series of civil service work stoppages which were seen as particularly disruptive.

Thus, we have arrived at a most interesting situation in this country. While the appointed judges can restrain, they have little power of veto. While the elected legislators have a substantial power to override, they would likely be cautious about doing so. Legislative supremacy is largely restored. But, in certain areas of fundamental significance, legislative intrusion would likely require a substantial consensus.

Self-congratulations are unwarranted. This arrangement was the product not of transcendent statesmanship but of parochial wrangling. It represented an attempt to appease eight provinces, most of which had refused, for reasons of self-interest, to accept the federal government's plans for constitutional repatriation. Motivation, however, is usually irrelevant in public affairs. In this case, as in so many others, questionable motives may well have produced a sensible result.

In any event, Charter or no Charter, the most effective way to protect civil liberties is through the *ad hoc* enactment of specific statutes addressed to specific situations. Whether the issue be involuntary civil commitment, the rights of arrested persons, or search and seizure, the relevant legislation should be amended in order to spell out as precisely as possible the rights of those affected, the duties of the authorities, and the consequences which would flow from any violation of such rights and duties.

Faced with that kind of particularity, the courts could be reasonably relied upon to implement the legislative will. By contrast, the generalities of the Charter give the courts an abundance of power without the requisite guidelines. As a practical matter, of course, civil libertarians should press for the best Charter judgments they can get. But they should recognize that the Charter is no substitute for specific legislation addressed to specific problems. And they should also be grateful for whatever potential there is in the "notwithstanding" clause to rescue the sovereignty of the people from possible usurpations by the judiciary.

POSTSCRIPT

Since the Charter has given the courts such unprecedented power, it is worthwhile to say a word about the proper scope of judicial review. In this connection, consider again the pending challenge by the medical profession of Ontario's ban on billing patients beyond the amounts covered by the Ontario Health Insurance Plan. To whatever extent the doctors were to succeed in persuading the courts that this was a Charter issue, our entire panoply of social and economic legislation could be imperilled. For such purposes, it would not suffice even if the courts upheld the impugned legislation under the "reasonable limits" exception in Section 1 of the Charter. To sustain the legislation on this basis is to enable the courts to second guess virtually all of the policy choices made by the politicians.

While I have to acknowledge that the adoption of the Charter entails a substantial power of judicial review, *this* amount would be unacceptably undemocratic. Moreover, it would be tantamount to saying that free enterprise capitalism was entitled at least to presumptive Charter protection. Such a result could not plausibly be attributed to the drafters of the Charter. Most of our economic and social policy questions involve conflicts between a free enterprise approach, more or less, and a social democratic approach, more or less. If it had been intended for the Charter to favour one side in these conflicts over the other, you'd think that more of the key players would have said so during the debates. If anything, the deliberate refusal to entrench property rights can be seen as expressing an intent to limit the courts' role in such matters.

But, given that the adoption of the Charter means *some* additional review power for the courts, how far should it extend? In my view, the Charter should be seen as a special protection for the norms of political and legal democracy but not for the norms of free enterprise capitalism. The norms of political and legal democracy are essentially fourfold. They embody the components of political autonomy, personal integrity, ethical equality, and procedural propriety.

Political autonomy refers to the essence of democratic government—that the powers of those who govern derive from the freely given consent of those who are governed. In order to have free consent, there must also be free dissent. This explains the role of such key rights as freedom of expression, freedom of the press and other media, freedom of assembly, and freedom of association. It also explains the limited terms of elected office and the necessity for secret-ballot elections. In some ways, the freedoms that comprise political autonomy are strategic in nature. Their exercise helps to ensure that all our other rights and freedoms will be duly respected. The assumption is that governmental improprieties are less likely to endure in an atmosphere of free public debate which can culminate in secret-ballot elections.

Personal integrity requires respect for the physical body, spiritual conscience, and social privacy of an individual. Thus, democratic societies are loath to kill or maim even their criminals or wrongdoers. While some such societies retain certain forms of capital punishment, the issue invariably provokes deep crises of conscience. Even imprisonment is seen as something that, while arguably necessary, should be reduced as much as possible. At the very least, of course, no such encroachments should be permitted without the most exacting procedures. The requirements of spiritual conscience are protected in the guarantee for freedom of religion and in those parts of the right to freedom of expression which refer to inquiries of a philosophical and scientific nature and creativity of an artistic, literary, and cultural nature. Social privacy addresses the right to withdraw from unwanted scrutiny. All of us seek a retreat where we can indulge our desire for intimacy. Thus, our homes, papers, and conversations should enjoy presumptive protection.

But, it will be asked, don't the components of personal integrity also include freedom of contract—the right to make money? In all of the above cases involving personal integrity—physical body, spiritual conscience, and social privacy—the freedom claimed concerns our right to protect or express some of the most basic and intimate components of our very being. But, generally speaking, where contract is concerned the freedom claimed concerns essentially public market transactions, characterized by a posture of arm's length relationships and conflicts of interest—the kind of matters that are traditional subjects for the refereeing role of the law. These are some of the reasons why freedom of contract cannot make the same claim to being a constituent part of personal integrity.

Ethical equality means equality of concern. Despite the fact that people differ in race, creed, colour, sex, wealth, talent, and ability, the democratic system deems them to be equal in *dignity*. No one is deemed to be more or less important than anyone else. Thus, while it is impossible to avoid legislation that may benefit some and burden others, democratic societies believe in the principle of equal consideration. Even if people are often subject to differential treatment, they must receive equal consideration.

Most families operate on a similar basis. Parents might permit their older children greater privileges than their younger children. They might bestow greater protection upon their sick children than upon their healthy ones. Notwithstanding the different ways that parents may treat their offspring, they nevertheless can *love* them equally. Similarly, notwithstanding the different ways that a democratic society may treat its citizens, it must nevertheless *regard* them equally.

Procedural propriety refers to the way decisions which affect us are made. Before we can be burdened by a decision adverse to our interests, certain procedures must generally be followed. They would usually include advance notice of what is to be claimed against us, the opportunity to confront and cross-examine those who are testifying against us, and an opportunity to tell our side of the story. Most important, the decisions must be made by people who have no interest in the outcome of the dispute: independent judges or juries of our peers. The complexities of modern society require also the right to the assistance of trained legal counsel. And, as a further protection against unfairness, hearings generally should be held in public and the subsequent judgments should be published for all to inspect.

The foregoing is addressed, not to the precise terms of the Charter, but rather to the philosophy of the democratic system. My argument is that it would be wise to interpret the Charter, so far as possible, according to the democratic philosophy. The rights and liberties set out in that document should be seen as devices to promote political autonomy, personal integrity, ethical equality, and procedural propriety. Of course, none of these rights or liberties is absolute; they are all subject to "reasonable limits". But any claims which go beyond these rights and liberties (such as the norms of free enterprise) should not even be accorded the threshold recognition of a presumptive Charter protection.

I will leave to other contexts the difficult task of attempting to resolve problems such as commercial speech which may involve *both* the norms of political democracy *and* those of free enterprise capitalism. The effective autonomy of the individual might require a free flow of information regarding the goods and services available for consumption. At the same time, however, the individual might require protection against the injuries that can be perpetrated by powerful corporate interests. In any event, the application of the Charter should depend upon how far the norms of political democracy or free enterprise capitalism are at issue.

The Charter was designed to protect the enduring values of the politically democratic system. For these purposes, we have additional recourse through the expanding role of the courts. But our ordinary statutes must continue to resolve how much free enterprise and social democracy we are to have at any given time. For that, we should look, as we always have, to our elected legislatures. While it won't always be easy to make such distinctions, the quality of our democracy requires that the effort be made.

Chapter Eleven

RACIAL INEQUITY

AND LEGAL REDRESS

Free Choice versus a Fair Chance

In the winter of 1982, I participated in a radio exchange with Toronto *Sun* columnist Barbara Amiel on the national CBC show "Morningside". The topic was racism and the law. The following are some key excerpts reproduced from the transcript.

> *Borovoy*: ...I think that there are serious racial problems in this country...that...can effectively be reduced...by the wise use of intelligent legislation such as our various human rights statutes. I'm saying that partly because it's true, of course, and partly because I know it will goad Barbara no end.
>
> *Amiel*: ...I assume what Alan means, for example, is that there should be no discrimination in private employment; that if an employer is stupid enough to say, "I won't hire black or yellow people," that should be made illegal. Is that the sort of thing you're getting at, Alan?
>
> *Borovoy*: Yes....
>
> *Amiel*: ...while I have no sympathy with those employers and I think they are stupid...private employment...is an area that the state should stay right out of.
>
> *Borovoy*: ...It's a matter of private employment on the public market. These people are selling their services and their products on the public market, and I, therefore, see no problem with requiring that they comply with public standards of fair play, namely...they do not inflict the indignity of discrimination on people....

217

Amiel: Alan, once you go beyond legislating the safety of a person or a property, then the state will invade every area of our life. State legislation will permeate everything...once you go into private businesses, I absolutely draw the line. You should know that...the real racists...will find another way to get around it. You won't change racism that way, and what you will do is polarize those people who suddenly find government inspectors in there saying, "You don't have the right quota. This person didn't get in here because of their skin colour," and you will undermine the whole system in this country.

Borovoy: You're addressing yourself to the wrong problem. I am not suggesting for a moment that the legislation aims to improve the attitudes of those people or to make non-racists out of employers. What I am suggesting...is it improves their *behaviour*.

Amiel: ...I'm talking about a situation in which you are actually making racists out of people who have no attitude towards it at all by invading their private businesses and their private lives and telling them that—a person who's from Russia, for example, may not like employing people of a certain background. A person may not like employing Germans.... Why are you going to force people into this situation?

Borovoy: I suggest to you that you are somewhat begging the question between us when you define the area as "their privacy". I am suggesting to you that, when they are selling their products or their services on the public market, there is a large measure of that privacy that they have already surrendered....

Amiel: ...I may want to get married again one day, and I may like someone very much, I may think they have a terrific personality, they may suit me in every possible way, but I don't like the pigment of their skin. Are you going to move into that too?

Borovoy: I promise you, Barbara, that, as far as the selection of your marital mates is concerned...I will go to the barricades to defend your right to be as prejudiced and bigoted as you want to be. But when you are talking about employment on the public market...a...different standard [applies].

This short exchange managed to touch on some of the most important differences in the philosophies of those who favour and those who oppose our human rights laws. At the heart of many of these differences is the fundamental distinction between universal love and fair play. In my view, the legitimate goal of our efforts is the latter, not the former. I don't ask employers, for example, to *like* blacks or Jews or native people; I ask employers to *hire* the qualified members of these groups whether they like them or not. My concern is not with what people like; it's with what they *do*. It's not with how they feel; it's with how they behave.

Of course, I would not want anyone to get the idea that I am opposed to universal love. But I am simply not prepared to wait for the millennium—if it ever comes—before I insist that people play fair with one another in the here and now. As that great economist John Maynard Keynes once observed, "In the long run, we are all dead."

People can be fair in their behaviour without being lofty in their attitudes. Montgomery, Alabama racially integrated its bus service in the 1950s, not out of love for its black citizens, but in response to a black boycott. The history of the struggle against racial injustice overflows with similar examples. Sit-ins, wade-ins, pray-ins, freedom rides, court judgments, civil rights statutes—in the wake of these developments, the American South became legally desegregated. Love was beside the point. As that legendary American radical Saul Alinsky once declared, in the real world, most people who do the right thing do so for the wrong reasons. Since I am concerned more with the improvement of behaviour than with the purification of souls, that's good enough for me.

Conversely, the quest for love and bliss has often proved obstructive. Throughout the years, many politicians and commentators opposed the enactment of human rights statutes on the basis of the kind of reasoning Barbara Amiel employed: that resentment of state coercion would make employers more racist than they otherwise would have been. The problem with this approach is its misconceived focus. In my view, we should be more concerned with the welfare of those who suffer discrimination than with the psyches of those who practise it.

During the debates surrounding the 1981 Human Rights Code in Ontario, a number of critics echoed Barbara Amiel's concern for keeping government out of the market decisions of private parties. According to this view, the coercive power of the state has no business intruding upon people's freedom of choice. Whether these choices are good, bad, helpful, or harmful, they should not be subject to governmental encroachment.

I can understand this exaltation of freedom of choice so long as it deals with the more private and intimate sphere of human relationships. To whatever extent, therefore, blacks and whites, Jews and Gentiles, natives and immigrants seek to avoid dating, sleeping, or marrying together, I would agree that the law should not intrude. But our human rights statutes are addressed primarily to the public, not the private, arena. The discrimination they prohibit arises on the public market— in the selection and treatment of employees by employers, tenants by landlords, purchasers by vendors, customers by proprietors, clients by professionals, licensees by licensors, and workers by trade unions. The people whose conduct is being regulated put their goods, services, and facilities on the public market in the hope of making a profit or deriving some other benefit. As a condition of this right to participate on the public market, the law requires compliance with certain standards of fair play in the interests of the public at large. At the very least, this means no racial or ethnic discrimination in the transactions at issue.

Why, then, should there be such vociferous objections to our human rights legislation? During this century, the Western world has enacted a host of legal restrictions on the choices property-owners may make— anti-trust statutes, minimum wage and maximum hours laws, child labour acts, zoning by-laws, and so on. In view of all these precedents, why should our anti-discrimination laws be regarded with such special contempt?

I recognize that some Human Rights Code opponents do not feel bound by these precedents. If they had their way, they would dismantle all or most of the welfare state. In response to their fantasizing, I return to a central theme. In the real world, there are no absolutes— not freedom of choice or anything else. Our most precious values inevitably collide. Every problem, every situation must be analysed, therefore, on its own merits, to determine which of the alternative solutions is likely to produce the least bad results.

On this basis, I believe it is appropriate to restrict freedom of choice in public life to the extent that its exercise would be likely to inflict corrosive indignity and deny equal opportunity. This is what the experience of racism is all about. The history of the last fifty years should suffice to dramatize the depths to which racism is capable of propelling an entire society. The experiences of Nazi Germany, South Africa, and even the American South have for ever seared the consciousness of humanity. In the light of this history, it is not hard to appreciate the depths of the indignity our minorities suffer when they encounter even the milder forms of racial and ethnic discrimination which exist on the public market of this country. When such discrimination produces a denial of jobs, housing, or some other benefit of the public market, the indignity is compounded by a serious loss of economic opportunity.

While racial discrimination causes a great deal of harm to values cherished by democrats, the intrusions of human rights legislation on the liberty of property are minimal. Employers, proprietors, and landlords do not lose all or even most of their powers of selection. They lose them only to the extent of those limited interests specifically protected in our human rights statutes. Beyond those few specified categories (race, creed, ethnicity, and so forth), our property owners remain free to choose as they wish.

Moreover, as I argued in an earlier chapter, the issue of freedom is not all on the side of those who control property. It also affects those who deal with them. If blacks, Jews, or native people cannot obtain jobs, services, or housing in certain places, *their* ability to make choices is obviously curtailed. Once more, therefore, we face a conflict of freedoms. And so we must decide which freedom and whose freedom should prevail in which situations. These factors taken together—the infliction of corrosive indignity, the denial of equal opportunity, and the inhibitions on freedom itself—make a stronger case for having than for not having human rights legislation.

Unfortunately, the opponents of this legislation often take yet another tack. They argue not simply the impropriety of outlawing discrimination, but also its futility. How often have we heard the cry, "You can't legislate morality"? If this means that you can't legislate people's moral *feelings*, I have very little quarrel with the statement. But the legitimate focus of the law is not feelings at all, it is *behaviour*. Since when has it become impossible to legislate moral behaviour? What, indeed, is our criminal law all about, with its prohibitions against murder, robbery, theft, fraud, and assault? The inability of the law to deal with moral feelings has never produced a reluctance to legislate against the moral misconduct found in the Criminal Code. Why then should there be so many misgivings about curbing the moral misconduct found in the Human Rights Code?

Methods of Enforcement

In contrast to the criminal law, the key to the enforcement of our human rights law is the procedure of conciliation. Upon receiving a complaint that a person has been denied employment, services, or housing because of race, creed, or ethnicity, our federal and provincial human rights commissions will not only investigate, they will also attempt to conciliate. Once they are satisfied that there is a plausible case against the alleged offenders, the commissions will attempt to persuade them to rectify the situation. This could mean giving the minority group member what has been denied, paying that person compensation, and/or providing binding assurances of future compliance with the law. If the alleged offenders are prepared to make such concessions, the case is considered settled; no further action is taken against them.

If, however, the alleged offenders refuse to settle—if they are adamant in their resistance to the law—a board of inquiry can be established to hold a public hearing into the complaint. To those who are accused, this means the inconvenience of being away from their businesses for at least the better part of a day. It means witness fees, legal fees, disbursements, and the embarrassing publicity that invariably accompanies such public proceedings. And, if the board of inquiry is satisfied that a violation of the law has occurred, it can order the offender, in the words of the Ontario statute, "to do anything...to achieve compliance...both in respect of the complaint and in respect of future practices, and...to make restitution...." Such orders are enforceable in the same manner as judgments of a superior court: the failure to comply could precipitate punishment for contempt of court.

The simple psychology behind this legislation is that only a minuscule number of Canadians are so hopelessly bigoted that they would put themselves through all that trouble and inconvenience simply to bar a few minority groups from their places of business. The willingness to comply has nothing to do with universal love. It has everything to do with self-interest. Our law is aimed at making the practice of racial discrimination more inconvenient than the avoidance of the practice. This is a message which people in the real world can understand and absorb.

Not surprisingly, the number of settled complaints substantially exceeds the number referred to boards of inquiry. (In Ontario 690 cases were settled in 1983–84 while only 33 boards were appointed to inquire into 60 complaints.) It doesn't take a very vivid imagination to anticipate the unpleasant experience that is likely to accompany a board of inquiry hearing. For the vast majority of alleged offenders or respondents, conciliation in a private office is far preferable to confrontation at a public hearing. On some occasions, settlements have been reached just as hearings were about to begin. A mere glimpse of the setting—lawyers, witnesses, reporters, spectators—was enough to undermine the resolve of many otherwise resistant respondents.

I can even remember one case that was settled right in the middle of a hearing. A marina owner who had refused to rent fishing boats to blacks was being pummelled with questions by counsel for the black complainants. In the middle of the cross-examination, he cried out that he was willing to change his policy. An adjournment was hastily called while the parties and their counsel repaired to private chambers at the back of the hearing room. On the spot, the black complainants and a number of their friends came forward, paid deposit money, and reserved boats from that day until the end of the season. Those who didn't like fishing were politely admonished by their comrades that, in the interests of the cause, they had to go fishing. In the result, the marina underwent instant racial integration.

Experience demonstrates that the law has been and can be a most effective weapon for promoting racial fair play—as long as it is enforced with vigour, intelligence, firmness, imagination, and, above all, some flair.

Yet in recent years a number of activists have begun to clamour for a different approach to human rights enforcement. They argue that the conciliation method is too soft and that those who violate the Human Rights Code are often treated too leniently. They prefer that racial discriminators be prosecuted or sued without having any opportunity to make amends.

These arguments are profoundly mistaken. It is more important that a qualified complainant be hired or housed than that a delinquent respondent be sued or jailed. If the law secures employment, accommodations, or other desired benefits for minority group members, it will have achieved its essential purpose. Why should we even consider the question of criminal or civil litigation, unless the respondent refuses to play ball? If respondents knew they were going to be dragged through a hearing in any event, what would motivate them to cooperate? One of the chief virtues of the conciliation process is the incentive it provides for respondents to accommodate complainants. Litigation without conciliation would be likely, therefore, to reduce the benefits to the victims of discrimination.

What about the argument that more litigation will deter tomorrow's potential discriminators, that even though today's complainants may not secure the benefits they sought, the overall rate of discrimination would be reduced and the opportunities for our minorities would be increased? Even apart from the speculative nature of this hypothesis, I question the priorities of those who are willing to neglect the interests of the present in order to build a more glorious future. My pragmatism impels me to put more emphasis on the here and now. As much as possible, the goal of the law should be to secure concrete benefits for those with valid complaints.

Some critics have suggested that complainants should be able to choose litigation, in some cases instead of conciliation and in other cases if they are unhappy with the commission's handling of conciliation. While I am not prepared, at this point, irrevocably to rule out any and all separate court actions by complainants, I urge a policy of caution. There are potential risks as well as benefits to any approach that divests the commissions of their control over human rights enforcement. One of the defects in this approach is that it would multiply the current involvement of the courts in the business of human rights. The experience with the judiciary should deter human rights activists from making such proposals. So often when the courts have been drawn into these matters, they have wound up rendering unduly conservative decisions. There is a risk that more of these decisions will become precedents which could encumber human rights work. Human rights commissions are more likely than courts to develop the flexibility and imagination to advance the cause. This is not to say that the commissions *will* perform in an acceptable manner; it is to say that the courts are *less* likely to do so.

It may very well be, however, that our human rights commissions have not been taking tough enough positions in the conciliation process. In numbers of situations they might be more demanding in extracting concessions from respondents, and more imaginative about the terms for future compliance. But these considerations address the methods by which conciliation is waged; they do not address the principle as to whether conciliation ought to be undertaken at all.

Indeed, there is a strong argument for reducing even further the possible resort to prosecution which many human rights statutes have retained. Since the orders of many boards of inquiry may now be directly enforced as orders of the court, it is difficult to appreciate what further purpose is served by prosecution and conviction. Unlike the boards of inquiry, the criminal courts can do virtually nothing more than impose fines. But even an increase in their punishment powers could not compete with the substantial rectification powers currently reposed in many boards of inquiry.

What purpose, then, is served by providing this second proceeding to adjudicate identical issues? Indeed, its very existence might be a distorting factor. To what extent, for example, might respondents be able to argue that, where a prosecutorial remedy exists, the state is obliged to adopt such a route first? Without necessarily imputing merit to such a claim, it is enough to question the wisdom of risking such arguments. Apart from collateral matters such as obstructing complaint investigations, the criminal process can safely be eliminated from human rights matters.

There is, however, one further sanction that should be more available to punish unlawful discrimination. The human rights statutes should provide that certain violators may lose temporarily, or even permanently, their licences to operate the business within which the discrimination was committed. In many ways, this represents one of the most appropriate and effective sanctions possible. It incorporates into the law the equitable principle that the right to enjoy the opportunities of the public market should require compliance with the standards of that public market.

The Problem of Employment Agencies

Like everything else, racism has become more sophisticated. Employers who wish to avoid minority employees no longer have to do the dirty work themselves. Some employment agencies may do their screening for them. Minority applicants have no way of knowing the identity of the agency's employer-clients. Thus, if a client expresses a disinclination to receive applications from certain minorities, the agency can easily screen these people out. What an applicant doesn't know cannot become the basis for a complaint to the human rights commission. By using these agencies, employers can circumvent their obligations under the law.

From the mid-1970s on, there has been considerable indication of discrimination practised by employment agencies in this country. On the basis of telephone calls to randomly selected agencies, researchers from the Canadian Civil Liberties Association periodically posed as representatives for potential employers. They asked each agency whether it would be prepared to screen out non-whites. Of 15 agencies surveyed this way in Toronto during 1975, 11 expressed a willingness to accept discriminatory job orders. Of 15 agencies tested this way in Hamilton, Ottawa, and London during 1976, 11 indicated their willingness to fulfil discriminatory requests. Of 25 agencies surveyed during the fall of 1980 in Halifax, Toronto, Winnipeg, and Vancouver, only 3 clearly said "no"; 5 were somewhat vague in their responses and 17 expressed a willingness to abide by the "whites only" restriction.

At the end of 1982, the Ontario Ministry of Labour was sufficiently concerned about the problem that it circulated for discussion a position paper outlining a number of possible responses. In 1983 a comparable survey conducted by the Calgary Civil Liberties Association found 4 out of 6 randomly selected agencies in that city were willing to accept discriminatory job orders. In 1987 a student paper researched under the supervision of Toronto's Seneca College concluded that "by allowing employment agencies to operate with untrained recruiters who are likely to act in a biased fashion the E[mployment] A[gencies] A[ct] is, in essence, promoting potential employment discrimination." Shortly thereafter, the president of the Canadian Recruiters Guild found, in a survey of more than 40 agency recruiters, that more than 90 per cent have accepted discriminatory job orders.

Even if it is contended that the surveys of the Canadian Civil Liberties Association are outdated and the assessments of the Canadian Recruiters Guild are inflated, we have to acknowledge that racial discrimination is a significant phenomenon in the placement agency industry. This impression is fuelled by some of the actual remarks that agency representatives have made in the above surveys.

"I'm a businessman.... If you don't want a black, we don't send you a black. If you don't want any Indians, we don't send you any Indians.... My business is to make a placement and make some money. I'm going to send you what you want."

"White and bright, eh?"

"...it's not uncommon for clients to ask for this type of thing and it really doesn't bother me...that's an obvious screening point...you're the one making the choice of whom you want to sell your products.... I'm not."

"We have...several companies with the same position."

"Oh yeah, but I can't talk about it, okay?"

"Anyone we refer will not be a coloured person: 99 per cent of the other employers feel the same."

New strategies are required. Human rights commissions should be given adequate power to undertake, on their own initiative, an ongoing program of auditing this industry. Without waiting for complaints, the commissions should engage in periodic reviews of employment agency practices. Who are the agency's clients and applicants? Is the agency bringing together those who appear suitable? If not, why not? Such an approach would increase the probabilities that discrimination would be detected. Detection, of course, would increase the opportunities for discrimination to be corrected.

Invariably, there be those who will consider such an approach unduly intrusive. Yet similar measures have been in effect for some time in many other fields. Restaurateurs, for example, are required to provide government health inspectors with access to their kitchens; solicitors are required to provide law society auditors with access to their financial records. In exchange for the right to sell their goods and services on the public market, our community requires of many entrepreneurs a reasonable demonstration of their compliance with the standards of the public market. Only a minority of restaurateurs sell contaminated food and only a minority of lawyers misappropriate trust funds. Yet all are subject to audit. Why should racism in employment agencies be treated differently?

Indeed, in some ways there might be an even greater need to audit this sector of the economy. These agencies are subject to intense competition. This makes them especially vulnerable to discriminatory instructions. A refusal to comply could mean the loss of a client. The agencies face the perpetual hazard that, if they refuse such a request, any number of their competitors might be prepared to fill it. This, of course, is confirmed by our surveys. The agencies also know that traditional complaint enforcement is unlikely to discover such racist practices. But industry-wide auditing could finally provide the law-abiding agencies with the feeling of security they need. The knowledge that these improprieties are likely to be uncovered could reduce the competitive disadvantage of obeying the law. An agency would be able to refuse a discriminatory request with a greater conviction that the competitors who accept it do so at their peril.

Systemic Discrimination

In the late 1970s, the Canadian Civil Liberties Association conducted a number of surveys relating to the employment of non-whites in both the corporate and public sectors of Canadian society. Here are some of the findings.

-a 1975 survey of the Toronto Fire Department disclosed, that of more than 1,100 fire fighters, there were only 2 non-whites;

-a 1976 survey revealed that London, Ontario had only 1 non-white police officer; Hamilton and Kitchener-Waterloo did not have *any*;

-of 235 senior positions in the Ontario government, a 1976 survey found only 3 non-whites: 1 black and 2 of Japanese extraction; not a single native Indian or anyone of East Indian or Pakistani origin held such a position;

-a survey of the *Financial Post* for the year 1976 disclosed that, of 1,913 promotions and appointments in the corporate sector which were announced with photographs in the newspaper, no more than 6 were awarded to non-white people;

-despite a relatively high proportion of native people living in the areas around Kenora, Fort Frances, and Sault Ste Marie, a 1978 survey of more than 500 bank positions in those communities found that only 2 were occupied by native people and 1 of them was part-time.

Surveys conducted by others in the mid-1980s reveal too little change. Despite a growing native population in Winnipeg, a 1985 survey showed that of more than 1,000 police officers, only 3 were native. Of more than 1,100 police officers in Calgary, the same survey showed that only 1 was a native person. Despite its highly cosmopolitan population, of the more than 4,500 police officers in Montreal, only 5 were members of visible minorities. While the Ontario Provincial Police had 131 officers of native origin, its roster of more than 4,000 officers contained *no* other members of visible minorities.

In view of our growing non-white population, it is difficult to believe that deliberate discrimination was not a factor in at least some of these cases. Experience tells us, however, that deliberate discrimination is not the only cause of such inequities. Even in the absence of an intent to discriminate, certain systems create barriers to racial equity and mobility. Perhaps, for example, an outmoded recruitment or promotion practice has unwittingly retarded the advancement of non-whites.

For some people, however, it is wrong to focus on systemic factors. Consider, for example, the opinions of Barbara Amiel:

"Systemic discrimination"...is a term which means that no one is actually discriminating...the system itself just inadvertently is discriminatory. That's sort of like saying that a murderer never intended to murder, it happened involuntarily. I do not know of such a thing as unconscious, unintended murder. If you don't intend to murder, there is no murder committed.

To Barbara Amiel, the world is marvellously simple. Either there is conscious evil or there is no evil at all. If there is no evil, of course, no state action is warranted. But reality is more complex.

In the Toronto Fire Department years ago, for example, job openings were never publicly posted. The personnel officials relied exclusively on the applications which had been previously submitted. As uninvited applications came in, they were given priority based on date of receipt. Whenever there were openings in the department, that file was the sole source of employee recruitment. In view of the small turnover of fire fighters, this policy effectively foreclosed the hiring of immigrants. In the main, they could not have been here long enough to have established the requisite seniority in the file of applications.

Another example of a similar phenomenon is the practice, at one time in greater usage than now, whereby employers advertised for job candidates with "Canadian experience". Suspicions became particularly aroused when this stipulation was advertised by an employer who was seeking a dishwasher. While such a job requirement was not, by itself, unlawful, it could easily be used to bolster unlawful discrimination. Moreover, even in the absence of a discriminatory intent, such employment advertisements could well have a discriminatory effect. Large numbers of immigrants would simply be unable to qualify.

The height and weight requirements in some police departments have operated to reduce the number of Orientals who could qualify for constabulary positions. In other police departments, the regulations with respect to headgear effectively ruled out Sikhs who felt obliged to wear turbans.

I remember processing a case a number of years ago in which a young Jewish woman was discharged from her job because she refused to work on a particular Jewish holiday. At no point did the employer formulate a policy of excluding Jews. He simply insisted that all of his employees, including Jews, must work on the day in question. Such a policy had the effect of excluding Jews even if that was not its demonstrated intent.

As a result of reflexive custom rather than conscious intent, certain employers may have confined their employee recruitment to their network of "old boys" clubs. As a consequence of coincidence rather than discrimination, those clubs may never have had occasion to process a membership application from a non-white. But so long as employers continue to rely on them, they are unlikely to attract non-white employees.

The factor that makes all of these practices unacceptable is their unreasonableness. No valid job-related considerations require that employers search for recruits only in their old boys clubs. There was no good reason why the Toronto Fire Department could not publicly post job openings as they arose. For the overwhelming number of jobs on the Canadian market, "Canadian experience" is simply irrelevant. As for police jobs, a small size may well be accompanied by the requisite strength and ability, and wearing turbans does not impede performance. Most employers can easily accommodate the conscientious objections of some religious people to working on particular days of the year. If unreasonable practices produce discriminatory results, why shouldn't the law require that those practices be changed? For people whose sense of complexity goes beyond that of Barbara Amiel, the law quite properly concerns itself with systemic impediments to racial and ethnic equality.

Beyond these systemic practices, there is another factor that could influence the under-involvement of non-white minorities in key sectors of our economy. In many cases, non-whites themselves probably hesitate to apply for certain positions in the belief that they will encounter discrimination. Even in those cases where such beliefs are wrong, they may well be understandable. If, in certain places, there has been nothing but a sea of white faces for generations, it is quite reasonable to suspect discrimination.

Obviously, the traditional methods of complaint enforcement will not suffice to alter these structural inequities. Complaint enforcement depends upon the coincidence that an aggrieved person and an available job will be suited to one another. The number of such coincidences is not likely to be great enough to make a significant dent in these entrenched patterns. In any event, this approach does nothing about the people who never get to file complaints either because they never hear about the available jobs or because they are too intimidated to apply even if they do hear about them.

Affirmative Action

A key response to these systemic barriers is the concept of affirmative action—the development of initiatives designed to increase the participation of disadvantaged groups in various sectors of the economy. Under this approach, human rights commissions not only respond to the filing of complaints; they also initiate action in order to expand opportunity.

No racial issue in recent years has generated more bitter controversy than the issue of what constitutes appropriate affirmative action. Tragically, the issue has forged splits even within the human rights and civil liberties movements. The cause of the trouble is the idea of goals, quotas, or targets regarding the number of minority group members who must be hired or admitted within specific periods of time. Opponents of this approach have argued that it is tantamount to reverse discrimination. In their view, such discrimination remains evil even if the victims are white rather than non-white. To them, racial discrimination is invidious, no matter who practises it against whom. Proponents have counter-charged that, without such measures, disadvantaged minorities simply won't make significant progress. Because of yesterday's discrimination, not enough of them can compete on an equal footing with the majority groups.

At least as a starting point, a democratic society must question the validity of sanctifying racial targets, goals, or quotas in its public marketplace. No matter how strong an argument there may be for compensating victimized minorities, we are forced to question whether such employment schemes might not require essentially *innocent* people to pay the price. How often would the pressure to fill a non-white target, goal, or quota lead employers to reject more qualified whites? In such circumstances, could it not be said that the whites were victims of racial discrimination? True, such white people may enjoy certain advantages in society over non-whites because of the discrimination committed by their predecessors. But why should *they* suffer for the misconduct of other people?

And how are we supposed to determine the appropriate number for a target, goal, or quota? Most formulas have been based upon the percentage of non-white people in the available work force in the locale under consideration. This percentage then becomes the target for a particular enterprise. But why should this be so? People are attracted to and repelled from certain occupations on the basis of a wide variety of historical, cultural, and personal factors, not all of which are related to unfair discrimination.

Indeed, to what extent can the imposition of numbers produce outright absurdity? We know, for example, that there is a rather large number of Oriental people in jobs involving the natural sciences. If the number of blacks in such jobs were disproportionately small, to what extent would this make employers feel obliged to reject Oriental applicants in favour of black applicants, even if the former were more qualified? In short, how far will the fixation with numbers permit one victimized minority to profit at the expense of another?

At this stage of history, I believe it would be wise generally to avoid numerical targets, goals, and quotas. Politically the numbers approach provokes an overdose of hostility and feelings of injustice even among human rights activists. Ethically this approach creates a number of moral dilemmas that have not adequately been resolved. Moreover, I am not convinced that numerical targets, goals, and quotas represent the only way to promote an acceptable level of racial equality. Indeed, there are signs here of the either-or fallacy. Why must we choose between the excesses of affirmative action and the inadequacies of complaint enforcement?

There are untried measures by which greater equality could be "proactively" pursued. The essence of these measures is to broaden job recruitment practices. We have to make employers look where they may not have looked before: place ads in the non-white press; go to non-white organizations, well in advance of anticipated job openings, and ask them to recruit suitable candidates—indeed, pay such organizations a recruitment fee in the same way that an employment agency might be paid; visit native friendship centres and advise native people of impending job opportunities and urge them to apply. Imagine, for example, what kind of impact would be created on the long-suffering and neglected people of the White Dog Indian Reserve if the personnel manager of a nearby Kenora groceteria attended their band meeting to request that candidates come forward for jobs in the store.

Of course, we cannot rely on employers to undertake such initiatives on a voluntary basis. There have to be enforceable sanctions. Consider the following possibilities.

Every year governments in Canada award thousands of contracts which produce millions of dollars for the private sector. Legislation should be enacted requiring that, as a condition of obtaining such government contracts, private-sector employers would have to undertake the most appropriate of the above measures to broaden the participation of disadvantaged non-whites in their respective business operations. To whatever extent such employers failed to comply with whatever measures they had undertaken to perform, the human rights commissions should be empowered to seek a variety of remedies including damages, cancellation or performance of contracts, and future compliance.

Conceivably this approach may not be adequate to produce great enough change at a fast enough pace. Moreover, it would not touch those private-sector employers who are not seeking government contracts. For such purposes, the commissions might be empowered to order public hearings on an industry-by-industry basis. Such hearings would ask the industries themselves to indicate what initiatives would be workable and desirable for them. Other constituencies (minorities, labour, human rights groups, and so on) would also be invited to make representations. The hearings would recommend broader ethnic recruitment programs geared to the particular circumstances of the industries involved. At that point, the commissions could be empowered to negotiate with the industry representatives for enforceable agreements like those above. The incentive for the companies to sign such agreements would come from the publicity and pressures generated by the hearings.

In any event, employers would be hard put to resist. Remember, the contracts would essentially specify additional areas and methods of employee recruitment. Any employers who refused to agree to obviously reasonable steps would make themselves look unreasonable, and that could hurt business. Indeed, I believe that a significant number of employers would sign such agreements without any public hearings at all.

Another approach might involve a flat-out legislative requirement that employers make every "reasonable effort" to attract racial minorities. Such efforts could be defined to include some of the foregoing measures. Human rights commissions could also undertake special initiatives to enhance the impact of such a law. The commissions might conduct surveys among non-white groups and their organizations so as to make available to employers the names and addresses of people who could assist in the recruitment effort: leaders of organizations, editors of their newspapers, and even potential job applicants themselves.

Such a commission effort would make it virtually impossible for employers to be excused for any failure to take the kind of minimal steps indicated here. And it would also reduce the difficulty that boards of inquiry or other adjudicators might find in applying the "reasonable effort" test in the legislation. Sanctions might include the power to award damages and order rectification.

The measure of an employer's performance would be, not necessarily the number of targeted people hired, but the nature of recruitment efforts made. As long as they made the requisite efforts, employers would not be required to prefer one group at the expense of another. But there is good reason to believe that a significantly increased hiring from the targeted groups would be likely to accompany an increased attempt to recruit them.

Once a greater number of disadvantaged non-whites began to apply for a greater number of available jobs, it would become increasingly difficult for the affected employers to discriminate against them. In the very process of attracting so many such candidates, the employers would be creating a pool of potential human rights complainants in the event that their hiring practices appeared unacceptable. Indeed, the mere knowledge that they were subject to this additional scrutiny would likely induce employers to behave more fairly.

The feasibility of these proposals is based upon the assumption that the greatest number of employers in Canada are neither bleeding hearts nor hardened bigots. Faced with the pressures of these programs, most employers would take the path of least resistance: cooperation.

Our commissions might also be empowered to initiate inquiries into employment patterns among racial and ethnic minorities in various industries. This could include the collection and retention of statistical information on the companies surveyed. Such probes might address practices relating to promotion as well as those relating to recruitment. A situation of no or slow progress as compared with employers in similar industries should trigger further and deeper inquiry by the human rights commissions. Does the company practise discrimination? Is there some systemic impediment to greater minority progress (for example, an irrelevant requirement of Canadian experience or an unnecessary height and weight restriction)? To whatever extent such improprieties or inadequacies were found to exist, the commissions might be empowered to attack them in many of the ways indicated above. On the other hand, if no such inequities were uncovered, remedial action would not be warranted. By itself, statistical imbalances would not justify governmental redress.

This is not to say that the measures advocated here are free of defects. It is only to say that their defects are likely to be less bad than those of the alternatives. Nor is this necessarily to urge the adoption of all these approaches at once. It is simply to indicate the fact that there is a wide range of possible affirmative action which might be effective and which does not require numerical targets, goals, or quotas.

As I write these words, I am not aware of a single jurisdiction in Canada which has legislatively adopted the essence of the approach that I have outlined here—a mandatory requirement without numerical targets, goals, or quotas to recruit employees from the non-white sectors of the community. Because of both the ethical and the political difficulties raised by numerical targets, goals, and quotas, their use should not be encouraged at least until the alternatives have been subjected to a fair trial.

Institutional Rigidities

Another cause of racial inequity is the failure of our various institutions to adapt their policies and procedures to the needs of the various groups in the community. Consider, for example, how responsive (or unresponsive) our licensing bodies have been to the needs of recent immigrants. One case history will illustrate the problem. In mid-1975, the Canadian Civil Liberties Association took up the case of an East Indian who had graduated in veterinary science from the University of Kerala. Along with a number of his colleagues from India and Pakistan, this man could not obtain a licence to practise as a veterinarian in the province of Ontario. Indeed, he could not even get permission to write the qualifying examination for foreign graduates. The trouble was that the Canadian Veterinary Medical Association (CVMA) did not recognize the University of Kerala or, for that matter, any other school in almost the entire Third World. The CVMA recognition lists included all kinds of schools in the United States, the United Kingdom, continental Europe, South Africa, Australia, and New Zealand, but virtually no school in the non-white countries.

After prolonged attempts to determine what was missing in the basic education at the University of Kerala, it finally emerged that the CVMA did not recognize that school because it had never carried out an on-site inspection there. And why not? Because at one point in the

1970s, the CVMA decided that the cost of inspecting foreign schools was prohibitive. In future, therefore, no such foreign inspections would be made unless the foreign schools themselves requested it and paid for it. This, of course, was tantamount to saying that graduates of schools in the Third World could never hope to qualify in Canada unless they went back to school here or in one of the countries recognized by our licensing agency. Why would Third World schools be willing to pay for such an inspection of their facilities? It would hardly serve their interests.

Somehow the Canadian authorities had managed to initiate and subsidize the inspection of foreign schools throughout the white Western world. Somehow that generosity abated when this country began to receive a heavy influx of immigrants from the non-white Third World. At the very least, therefore, there were reasonable grounds to suspect discrimination. But, even if discrimination was not the intent, it was certainly the result.

At best, the CVMA was guilty of unwarranted rigidity. It simply refused to accommodate the needs of our changing population. There are a number of steps it could readily have taken. It might have requested financial help from the senior levels of government in order to carry out further inspections of foreign schools. A few years earlier, the federal minister of immigration had offered such help to the medical licensing authorities. The veterinary body could also have followed the lead of the United Kingdom and the United States: it could have developed its own examinations of foreign graduates and instituted supervised internship programs. Fortunately, some of these reforms finally were made. But it took several years of badgering by the Canadian Civil Liberties Association and ultimately an effort from the Ontario Human Rights Commission.

Institutional rigidity has hurt not only those who have been here the least amount of time (the immigrants) but also those who have been here the longest (the native people). A few years ago, an Indian man was intentionally pushed from a moving train. He suffered brain damage, a semi-paralysed arm, and an amputated leg. Yet he received no legal assistance for more than seven months. In the following year, a field worker employed by the Canadian Civil Liberties Association discovered this man vegetating in a north-west Ontario hospital. It didn't take very long for our staff representative to swing into action. He promptly informed the man and his family about the Criminal Injuries Compensation Board of Ontario and assisted them in preparing and filing an application for assistance. Shortly thereafter, he appeared on the man's behalf before a hearing of the board. In the result, the aggrieved Indian was awarded monthly compensation for the rest of his life.

Why was nothing done about this case for as long as seven months? Neither the hospital authorities, nor the Department of Indian Affairs, nor the Ontario Legal Aid Plan, nor anyone else (as far as we know) did anything to inform this man that he might have an enforceable legal claim. Nothing was done until the coincidental visit of the Canadian Civil Liberties Association, an organization utterly devoid of government money. If it had not been for that coincidence, might that man still be languishing without compensation?

Apparently, the new legal-aid clinics have had similar experiences. In 1981, for example, a clinic in northern Ontario investigated the case of an eighty-year-old native woman whose health was impaired by failing eyesight and mobility problems. The daughter with whom she lived had a severe case of arthritis. Since neither was able to work, their financial situation was desperate. Upon investigation, the clinic discovered that the old woman had been eligible for a veterans affairs pension since the early 1970s. During all that time, she was apparently unaware of her legal claim. When the matter was raised with the department, regular pension cheques were soon forthcoming. In addition, the woman received a retroactive payment of more than four thousand dollars.

Recently another clinic discovered that numbers of native people had not been filing their income tax returns. Since many of these people did not earn enough money to have a taxable income, they were missing out on money in the form of tax credits from the federal government. Until the advent of the clinic, so many of these native people simply did not know of the existence of such entitlements. In one of these cases, for example, the clinic was able to obtain more than nine hundred dollars for a native person who had not filed a return.

On almost every occasion when CCLA staff representatives have gone into a northern native community, they have found a significant number of native people who had unfulfilled but valid legal claims. Time and time again, follow-up action has produced hundreds of dollars paid to native people in unemployment insurance, workers' compensation, minimum wages, vacation pay, and so on.

Somehow the government institutions have simply failed to help. Of course, if the native people on their own had applied for legal aid or had filed claims under the relevant statutes, they might well have obtained the benefits. But to apply for such assistance is first to recognize that you may be entitled to it. Unfortunately, significant numbers of native people in the northern regions are not aware of their rights and remedies. They are not familiar or comfortable with our customs and institutions. They lack fluency in the English language and share a widespread attitude of resignation to the mistreatment they suffer.

Sheer physical distance further frustrates the realization of Indian legal rights. Many of these people live far away from the places where service can be obtained. Even if they are entitled to medical or legal assistance, how are they supposed to obtain it when they may live forty, fifty, sixty miles or more from a doctor, hospital, or lawyer? In many of these regions, there is no low-cost public transportation. The only alternative is to hire a taxi at a rather substantial cost. Even long distance telephone calls to acquire information are prohibitively expensive.

It is not enough for a society like ours simply to enact a number of statutory benefits for disadvantaged people. There must be considerable attention to the question of *delivering* the benefits. Where remote-based native people are concerned, how do we go about informing them of their entitlements? What combination of oral and written material is needed and in what languages? How do we encourage them to take advantage of what the law has provided for them? And how can we help them overcome the hardships of distance? To what extent should we institute travel vouchers, low cost transportation, toll free telephones, and other measures?

In fairness, it must be recognized that some such reforms have been adopted. But not nearly enough to provide remote-based native people a semblance of equity with their white counterparts in the urban centres or to provide new Canadians with some of the opportunities enjoyed by longtime residents. Unfortunately, the institutions of our society have revealed too little of the flexibility that is required for a pluralistic population.

Racism beyond Human Rights Law

No matter how comprehensive or sophisticated our legal weapons may be, democratic societies will always leave a certain amount of racial and ethnic discrimination untouched by the law. From time to time, for example, we hear about a private golf club or college fraternity that bars blacks, Jews, and Orientals from membership. In no way could this be considered the kind of public market transaction that should be the subject of our human rights legislation. But the reluctance to legislate in the private arena should not be taken for a lack of concern about the racism that occurs there. The issue is what to do about it. There are some who favour an aggressive approach—perhaps a test case to focus public attention on the barriers in the private arena. Others argue that no response is appropriate because private organizations have a perfect right to choose their members in any way they please.

In my view, both approaches are incorrect. Granted, the private club enjoys and should enjoy the legal right to discriminate in its membership policies. But we must not confuse legal permissibility with moral propriety. Even though there is a right to choose members on the basis of ethnicity, it is not right to do so.

Yet the aggressive approach is also incorrect. We use the aggressive test case in public places because we deny to the public place the legal right to discriminate. Thus we can force open their doors in the conviction that there should be no right to keep them closed. But, as indicated, private clubs should continue to enjoy legal immunity.

Our response should be commensurate with the nature of the provocation. In private clubs, people exercise the right to choose their associates in any way they please. But the rest of us are also free to choose our own associates in any way we please. If others choose their associates in a manner which is repugnant to our moral standards, we should choose not to associate with them.

A number of years ago, for example, the B'nai B'rith organization took just such a position with respect to a dance that an international agency had scheduled at a restricted social club. B'nai B'rith advised the agency that, in view of the club's anti-Jewish and anti-black membership policy, B'nai B'rith would not attend any such functions on those premises.

A few years ago, the United Auto Workers (now the Canadian Auto Workers) signed a contract with a private golf club which was reported to have a racially restricted membership. In consideration for the UAW agreeing to rent the club's premises for the union's golf league, the club committed itself to refrain from practising discrimination in its entire membership policy. The rationale behind this approach is that, although a private club has the right to choose its members in any way it pleases, the UAW also has the right to choose the site for its golf league in any way it pleases. The UAW made its association with the club contingent upon the club's abandoning any possible membership policy of discrimination—an enlightened *quid pro quo.*

There are some purely ethnic and religious organizations whose restrictive policies should not offend our moral sensibilities. Very simply, we should not condemn ethnic restrictions within the framework of organizations whose purposes and programs reflect a commitment to religious and cultural self-perpetuation. There could be no valid objection, for example, to religious membership restrictions in the Knights of Columbus organization—which exists to further Roman Catholicism—or in the B'nai B'rith—which is committed to Judaism. A democratic community is comfortable with a multitude of diverse cultures flourishing within its boundaries. Where the pattern of membership in an organization reflects such commitments, no ethical objection can arise.

An objection does arise in those situations where ethnic and religious restrictions bear no relationship to the goals and program of the group. For example, golfing, boating, skiing, and curling have no religious or ethnic content. Thus, any club which exists primarily to further such activities commits an impropriety when it restricts membership on a religious or ethnic basis.

There is no reason why our opposition to racial and ethnic discrimination should be circumscribed by the parameters of the law. On the contrary, the law should be regarded as only one of the appropriate responses. Even in those areas where legal involvement would be inappropriate, committed democrats should still feel obliged to rebuff the evils of racism. There can be legitimate concerns about what tactics to employ but not what values to apply. The only issue is how—not whether—to express our revulsion.

Human Rights Law beyond Racism

During the last twenty-five years, our human rights laws have extended their focus well beyond their original concerns with race, religion, and ethnicity. In many respects, this expansion was both inevitable and desirable. In view of the structural mistreatment and pervasive undervaluing of women (50 per cent of our society), it became important to enact strong prohibitions against discrimination on the basis of sex. In view of the inability of many disabled people to obtain jobs for which they were eminently qualified, fundamental justice demanded legal redress for them too. Similar considerations also apply in a number of other areas. Unfortunately, however, the rapid increase in jurisdiction was not accompanied by a sufficient increase in resources. Thus, expectations rose out of proportion to the ability to satisfy them. In the result, many people became resentful of our human rights codes and commissions.

While several of the new prohibited grounds of discrimination could be seen as needed additions to the law, there is some question whether other situations should be handled by the law at all. Moreover, even in some of the areas where legislation is clearly appropriate, there is a question as to whether it should appear in the form that it does.

A British Columbia case in the mid-1970s can serve as a paradigm for some of the problems that have been caused. A board of inquiry convened under that province's Human Rights Code held that it was unlawful discrimination for a pub to refuse to serve two potential customers because of their long hair. This decision was made possible by a provision in the province's code against cunreasonable" discrimination.

Without question, the behaviour of the pub was indeed unreasonable. It was also offensive. The more difficult question, however, is whether the circumstances justify the invocation of state coercion. Just imagine—this ban on long hair wound up involving a full-scale hearing and ultimately an order that could have been enforced with the possible sanction of prison. One would think that such concomitants of state coercion would be saved for something more serious than what was involved here. It's hard to fathom that the very law that was conceived to attack racism in jobs was now being used to defend hairiness in pubs.

If this wasn't enough to trivialize British Columbia's human rights statutes, the board went even further. In the course of tracing the history of these provisions, the board attempted to extol their virtues. The judgment correctly pointed out that the original impetus for the human rights legislation was the "notorious examples of...racial prejudice which have attracted increasing tension and concern in the last half century...." But then the judgment went on to declare that there were other types of "prejudicial conduct" in our society that were often "as devastating in their consequences" as racism. Remember the context: because of their long hair, two people were unable to buy drinks in a pub. When an official adjudicator acting pursuant to statutory power describes such situations as being on a par with racism, the law is bound to undergo a significant loss of prestige. Our human rights legislation cannot hope to enjoy public respect in a situation where minor disparities are treated like major inequities.

Nevertheless, other forms of discrimination against the hirsute might well merit legal redress. A number of years ago, for example, I appeared before the board of education in a small community to protest the action of a high school principal who had suspended a student for refusing to shave his beard. Arguing that there was no correlation "between hair length and brain growth", I succeeded in persuading the board to reinstate the student with his beard and warts intact. It is one thing when an alleged excess of hair results in the denial of a drink in a pub. It is another thing entirely when it deprives a person of a public education.

In view of the differences in many of the problems which our human rights laws attempt to address, it might help also to develop a variety of legislative responses. This could even include a variety of administrative agencies. In my view, for example, the activists against "adult only" apartment buildings make a compelling case for legal redress. Query, however, whether this form of discrimination is properly included within our human rights legislation. Our human rights laws protect blacks from discrimination in part because no negative conduct can validly be attributed to blacks as a group. Despite our love for children, however, no such statement can be made about *them*. At the very least, children, as a group, are more likely than adults, as a group, to behave in certain ways. Babies, for example, have a tendency to cry at inconvenient hours of the night. This is not necessarily to say that "adult only" apartments are desirable or acceptable. It is simply to say that they are not the moral equivalent of "whites only" apartments.

Thus, it might be better to avoid a generalized prohibition like those found in our human rights laws. The problem is a shortage of affordable housing for families with children. Why not consider a mix of carrots and sticks? We might offer subsidies or tax relief to builders and landlords who are prepared to make affordable housing available to families with children. And we might require that, in order to obtain a permit to build in certain areas, there must be an undertaking to supply the requisite accommodations. The point is that we don't have to choose between providing or avoiding a legal remedy. We might consider altering the nature of the remedy in order to better suit the circumstances.

This is not the place for an exhaustive delineation of how to treat the problems that arise in the human rights field. The purpose of the foregoing is simply to provide an indication of how different solutions might be devised for different problems. For some forms of discrimination, the most effective response is our human rights legislation. For other forms of discrimination, it would be better to enact a number of different statutory remedies. For still other forms of discrimination, our response should be non-statutory, varying in vigour with the seriousness of the provocation. For too long there has been a tendency simply to expand our human rights codes any time some unwarranted discrimination was identified. In the result, we may have bequeathed ourselves a cumbersome, under-funded instrument which is ill-suited to the variety of problems it must address. In future we would be wise to respond less automatically and more creatively than we have in the past.

Chapter Twelve

SOME FUNDAMENTAL
MISCONCEPTIONS ABOUT
OUR FUNDAMENTAL
FREEDOMS

Few people express their desires in terms of their naked self-interest. They realize that such an approach would not likely cut much ice. Instead they wrap their claims in the packaging of objective morality. Thus, for example, certain capitalists who resent government intrusion will talk, not about their desire to make money, but about the integrity of the free enterprise system. If pushed, they might even use words like "authoritarian" or "Communist" to describe the government policies they dislike.

Because of the standing which the principles of civil liberties enjoy in the folklore of our nation, they are often invoked in this rather questionable way. Self-interested claims and even outright selfish ones are packaged in the universal rhetoric of our fundamental freedoms. In fairness, we cannot simply accuse those we suspect of such semantic charlatanism. We are obliged to answer argument with argument rather than with an *ad hominem* assessment of motivation. And, to be even more fair, not everyone who commits this packaging fallacy is guilty of deliberate semantic fraud. A good many people are legitimately confused and a number of others are simply misinformed. To all of them, this chapter is dedicated. It is an attempt to dissect some of the striking and recurring manifestations of questionable thinking about civil liberties violations.

The Right against Intrusions on Property

In general, government agents require judicial warrants in order to compel entry to people's property. Such warrants usually require reasonable and probable grounds to believe that the property in question contains evidence of an offence against the law. Ironically, these safeguards became the subject of a public controversy as a result of a revised Human Rights Code that the government of Ontario introduced in the early 1980s. In common with its predecessor, the revised code purported to give human rights investigators certain powers of warrantless access to the premises and papers of alleged violators.

These sections provoked a storm of protest. From the editorial pages of the right-wing *Toronto Sun* to the Queen's Park legislative benches of the left-wing New Democratic Party, the invective poured forth. The epithets of denunciation included "fascism", "totalitarian", and "storm-troopers". To what extent were the complaints justified? To what extent did the powers at issue violate the principles of due process? A competent response requires a willingness and ability to penetrate the rhetorical fog that has engulfed the issue. In short, it requires something that was largely missing from the debate at the time: a careful look at precisely what was involved.

Under the terms of the government bill, human rights investigators were to be empowered to enter, without warrant, any place other than a dwelling, and, once inside, they could require the production of materials that appeared relevant to a complaint, remove temporarily such materials for copying, question anyone with relevant information, and exclude other persons from such questioning. In response to some of the controversy, Labour Minister Robert Elgie promised further amendments to ensure that warrantless *searches* would not be permitted and that, during questioning, lawyers or other representatives would be permitted.

Contrary to a number of widespread misimpressions, human rights investigators were not to be given a warrantless power to ransack the places they entered. If the property owners did not provide the material at issue, the investigators would be obliged to seek some form of adjudicative assistance—a warrant, a board of inquiry, or perhaps even a prosecution. Moreover, the power to question would not be accompanied by a duty to answer. And, unlike many jailhouse interrogations by the police, human rights investigators would not have been able to exert the pressures of an arrest. The people they wished to question would remain free to leave at any time.

Nor would the Human Rights Code have permitted these warrantless intrusions in the place where our privacy interests are unquestionably strong—in our homes. In order to invade our parlours and our bedrooms, human rights investigators, like police officers, would generally have needed a judicial warrant.

What was at issue was a limited power of intrusion on business places and records. While even this kind of property attracts a legitimate privacy interest, its magnitude is much less. Business establishments and documents have long been amenable to a wide level of warrantless outside scrutiny. Indeed, a host of statutes in this country has long contained powers of striking similarity to those which caused the furor here—the Employment Standards Act, the Labour Relations Act, and the Unemployment Insurance Act, to name only a few.

In view of the volume of comparable powers in so many situations, it is fair to say that government audits of business activity have become, to a great extent, a condition of doing business in our society. Why, then, should the Human Rights Code attract so much venom?

We should not be cavalier, of course, even about the limited powers involved here. They cannot be justified merely because they have numerous counterparts. The issue must also involve an assessment of whether the proposed intrusions are needed to serve an overriding interest. The Human Rights Code is concerned with the protection of human dignity against various forms of discrimination—racial, religious, sexual, and so on. When such discrimination also produces a denial of economic opportunity, the affront to dignity is seriously exacerbated. On balance, therefore, the privacy interests to be breached are quite minimal by comparison with the dignity interests to be served.

But I do not wish to rely even on such overriding interests. There is also a strong argument that, if warrants were required to exercise the kind of powers involved, the Human Rights Code could well become virtually unenforceable. As indicated, warrants generally require a demonstration of reasonable and probable grounds that the proposed intrusion will yield evidence of an illegal act. But complaints of discrimination, by their very nature, rarely generate this kind of evidence.

Unlike most other illegal acts—assaults, thefts, robberies—most acts of discrimination are inherently incapable of being witnessed. Suppose, for example, a black, a woman, or a native person has been denied a job. That part of the transaction, of course, can be witnessed. But the essence of discrimination is the *reason* for the denial. Unfortunately, only the person who did it really knows the reason for it. In the absence of a willingness to disclose the reasons, there would rarely be enough evidence to satisfy a "reasonable and probable grounds" test. And how many discriminators can be counted upon to make such disclosures?

Apart from the discriminator's psyche, there is usually only one place where some evidence of the reasons might be found—the place of business. Either records or employees might be able to indicate something about the identity and qualifications of other candidates for the same job. When did such persons apply and how do their qualifications compare with those of the complainant? These same sources might also be able to disclose possible disparities in wage rates between various categories of employees—men and women, whites and non-whites. Without information from these sources there would rarely be anything close to "reasonable and probable" evidence of discrimination.

Thus, if warrants were required in the usual way, we might well have a "catch-22" situation. The only way to get the reasonable and probable grounds necessary for a warrant would be to inspect the materials at issue; the only way to get access to such materials would be to have the reasonable and probable grounds necessary for a warrant.

It is well to remember also that, unlike the criminal investigation, the human rights investigation is not aimed primarily at the prosecution of offenders. It is much more interested in changing their practices. Thus, the focus of the process is conciliation. If an implicated employer agrees to hire a qualified complainant and/or provide assurances of future compliance, the matter can usually be settled without further complication. Significantly, the code requires such an effort as a prerequisite to any further action. This is not to discount, of course, the unpleasantness in even the comparatively mild pressures of attempts at conciliation. It is simply to put these situations in perspective. The privacy interests to be breached are minimal; the dignity interests to be served are substantial; the powers to be used are crucial and every effort must be made to avoid penal sanctions. Hardly the stuff of a police state.

The Right against Intrusions on the Person

Earlier in this book, I mentioned the unacceptable powers of search and seizure under the Narcotic Control Act. In this connection, I referred to the very real probability that the notorious Fort Erie search-and-strip drug raid was essentially lawful. It was noted also that such dragnet search powers are a rarity in our legal system and, in any event, they might well now be challenged under the Charter of Rights and Freedoms.

During the summer of 1984, an incident in the city of Toronto threatened to revive the images of the Fort Erie fiasco. At the Argonaut football games, Canadian National Exhibition stadium attendants in the company of Toronto police officers began to demand that patrons reveal the contents of any parcels or bags they were carrying. The object of the exercise was to curtail the illegal consumption of alcohol at the games in question. Apparently, in the stands and in the cars outside, there had been a number of incidents that were alcohol-related.

The stadium crackdown triggered a wave of angry denunciations. Some patrons even threatened to boycott the games. There are respectable arguments on both sides of the question. What I found unacceptable, however, was the emergence of a widespread argument that the crackdown represented a violation of civil liberties. "Unreasonable search and seizure", thundered many of the critics.

Apart from the absence of intrusions into body orifices, there was another key distinction between Toronto, 1984 and Fort Erie, 1974. At Fort Erie the patrons in the hotel *had* to submit to the search of their persons. In Toronto there was no such compulsion. Submission to the search simply became a condition of entry to the game. If you objected to the search at Fort Erie, you were searched anyway. If you objected in Toronto, you could simply leave the stadium.

Clearly, therefore, the Charter had no place in the controversy. While I appreciate how important the games are to dedicated sports fans, it would be difficult to argue that the authorities were threatening to withdraw the necessities of life. The situation was hardly analogous to telling welfare recipients that their entitlement to food and rent depends upon their submission to any number of indignities.

Indeed, the situation more closely resembled the practice which emerged a number of years ago at our airports. In order to get on a plane, you have to submit to some level of inspection and search. For some people at least, the right to travel by air comes closer to being a necessity of life than the right to attend a ball game. No doubt some of the sports fans might argue that the liquor-related offences in and around the stadium could not match the severity of an airplane hijacking. Perhaps not, but some alcohol influenced conduct does endanger life and limb. However the situation may be conceptualized, the fundamental liberties of the citizen were not at issue.

In December 1981, a new law was enacted in Ontario empowering the police to stop cars at will and if they reasonably suspect the drivers of drinking, to require them to blow into a machine in order to test their blood alcohol level. Moreover, if the alcohol level exceeds a certain amount (below what constitutes impaired driving), the police are empowered to suspend a driver's licence for a period of twelve hours. Again, there were vigorous denunciations of this new law and they were based on the principles of civil liberties.

In the first place, this law was seen as a violation of the citizen's presumptive right to be left alone. The citizen is generally not supposed to be susceptible to interception by the police unless, at the very least, there are reasonable and probable grounds to believe that a violation of the law is involved. A police power to stop people at will was seen as an obvious violation of this principle. In the second place, by empowering police officers not only to stop drivers at will but also to suspend their licences under certain conditions, the new law was seen as a dangerous expansion of the role of the police. In addition to performing their regular functions as police, they acquired, all at once, the powers of prosecutors, judges, and juries.

"The Court by the Curb" was the heading under which the *Globe and Mail* newspaper editorialized its condemnation of this alleged breach of democratic practice. Much other media commentary echoed the sentiment. The Liberal opposition in the Ontario legislature denounced the new law as a provincial usurpation of the federal criminal law. Under the federal code, drivers reasonably suspected of drinking could be stopped and required to blow into the machine. If they refused to blow, they were guilty of a criminal offence. If their blood alcohol level measured beyond a certain point, they were guilty of another offence. In both cases, however, the judgment of guilt could only be made by a duly constituted court of law. In the opinion of these opposition members of the legislature, it was wrong in principle for the provincial jurisdiction to by-pass all of these safeguards of the federal criminal law.

There was more ritual than reasoning in much of what the critics had to say. I don't see why it is necessary to have reasonable and probable grounds of an offence in order to stop a car. An automobile is potentially a dangerous weapon; it has the power to maim and to kill. For this reason, we do not recognize a universal right to drive cars. It is a privilege we confer on those who demonstrate, initially by means of a driving test, that they are fit for such purposes. In view of the enormity of the potential dangers involved, I see nothing wrong with society requiring the drivers of cars periodically to undergo additional reasonable inspections of their fitness and ability to exercise this privilege.

Our society permits such inspections to be carried out in other areas of possible risk to public safety, such as food contamination, occupational health and safety perils, and so forth. To a great extent, neither a warrant nor special evidence is required to justify the intrusion of an inspector on private property for such purposes. The same rationale applies to driving.

I found it hard also to appreciate the argument that this legislation was usurping the federal criminal law. Why can't a province set a higher standard for the privilege of driving a car than the country sets for the right to stay out of jail? This provincial legislation did not purport to create a crime punishable by a term of imprisonment. It purported only to set a standard of sobriety for the right to drive a car.

At some point, for example, if lawyers abused the trust funds they administer, their conduct would run afoul of the federal criminal law. Nevertheless, the provincial licensing bodies frequently condition the right of lawyers to practise law on their compliance with certain rules that make their books available for periodic audits. The provincial authorities hope that such audits will both deter and detect impropriety before much damage can be done. In short, the province exacts a higher standard for the right to practise law than the country exacts for the right to stay out of jail.

The "court by the curb" argument is equally unpersuasive. What should the police do if they find a blood alcohol level in excess of the required minimum? Of course, the law could have provided that there be a subsequent trial as to the fitness of the drivers to keep their licences. It seems absurd, however, to go through the process of such a trial without providing a penalty significantly in excess of a twelve-hour licence suspension. What, then, should it be? One month, two months, three months, or longer? In any event, society cannot allow drivers to continue driving on those occasions that they are found with too much alcohol in their blood. So their right to drive would have to be suspended at least for a while at the time in question.

It's hard to fathom why a short suspension at the scene followed by a trial and a longer suspension thereafter would more adequately satisfy our libertarian purists. The virtue of the Ontario law lies in the balance it strikes among all of the competing interests. The advantage for society is the efficient and inexpensive removal of potentially dangerous drivers. The advantage for the drivers is that their licence suspensions will rarely be long enough to cause more than temporary inconvenience. Why should a devotion to the ritual of civil liberties deprive everyone of the benefits of common sense? If these critics had paid more attention to the reality than to the ritual of civil liberties, they might have discerned the true defects in this law. At least two changes are needed in order to ensure an adequate level of fair play.

In the first place, the police should not have the power to stop cars at will. While they should not necessarily require special evidence of wrongdoing, they should not be able to act in a completely arbitrary manner. The law should require the police to employ some kind of rotational system for stopping the cars whose drivers they inspect. Perhaps, for example, they should be allowed to stop only every fifth or every twelfth car. The idea is to ensure that blacks and whites, men and women, straights and gays, and Fords and Cadillacs have the same chance to avoid the police net.

In the second place, there is an aspect of "roadside justice" that could sustain unacceptable police behaviour. Suppose, for example, a police officer wilfully, negligently, or incompetently misread the breathalyzer. Democrats have to be offended at the prospect that such police error could inflict an upsetting inconvenience on an innocent citizen. There are also other possibilities. Suppose, for example, the driver's alcohol reading exceeded the minimum but there was a passenger who was quite able and fit to take over control of the car? Suppose, in such circumstances, an officer unreasonably refused the passenger this access? If a situation of this kind occurred in the middle of the night on a dark country road, it's not hard to imagine the impact on the affected people. At the very least, they might incur expensive taxi fares and perhaps also substantial towing and storage fees for the abandoned car.

As a special precaution against such possibilities, the law should provide that, at the option of the suspended driver, the matter could subsequently be heard in court, perhaps even traffic court. At such a hearing, the police would be required to make the case much as they do in other situations. The onus would be on them to show first that they had reasonable and probable grounds to stop the car, or that the car fell within a certain rotational system that was being employed. Secondly, they would have to show that the breathalyzer revealed a blood alcohol level in excess of the acceptable minimum. Thirdly, the police would also be required to demonstrate that their behaviour was reasonable in the circumstances. To whatever extent the police case failed on any of these counts, the drivers would be entitled to a court order that the state reimburse them for all reasonably incurred out-of-pocket expenses.

The proposed measures would operate as a deterrent to police misconduct and would make available a reasonable level of compensation if the misconduct materialized. There is no reason to believe that more than a small minority of the cases would ultimately come to court, thus making the likely cost of such safeguards quite manageable. Unfortunately, the government of Ontario refused to adopt these safeguards after I proposed them to a committee of the legislature. In the result, the debate was largely dominated by a government unreasonably resisting libertarian improvements and an opposition unreasonably alleging libertarian infringements. The antagonists richly deserved each other.

The Right against Self-Incrimination

There was some irony in the allegation that this "stop and check" provincial law threatened to usurp the federal law on the same subject. The federal law itself had been condemned in a number of quarters as a violation of civil liberties. Among other things, the requirement that drivers blow into the machine was seen as a violation of the revered right against self-incrimination.

Since the ordeals of the seventeenth-century Star Chamber, civil libertarians have attached a special importance to the right of accused people to remain silent. This right has been seen as an indispensable component of the presumption of innocence. The prosecution, rather than the accused, has the onus of making the case. If the prosecution fails to meet this onus, the accused is entitled to go free. To whatever extent an accused was forced to talk, the prosecution would be relieved of the burden it must carry. On the basis of a series of syllogisms deduced from this principle, critics condemned the compulsory breathalyzer test because it meant forcing accused people to provide evidence to incriminate themselves. In the critics' view, this practice was an affront to one of the most fundamental safeguards of our criminal law.

This criticism is yet another example of extravagant muddle-headedness. The right against self-incrimination was never designed to serve as an all-purpose immunity for the bodies and possessions of accused people. It was designed more narrowly to spare them the indignity of compulsory encroachments on their *psyches*.

As for innocent accused, a requirement to speak could expose them to pervasive intrusions on their private lives. The experience would be exacerbated by the fear and anxiety of knowing that the police suspected them of criminal conduct. Being forced to provide a breath sample or a personal possession is not the same as being forced to *tell* about yourself. By itself, the breath sample or personal possession represents a one-shot transaction which either discloses or fails to disclose what is being sought. Testimony, however, is a more drawn-out experience which is necessarily subject to the possible ordeal of cross-examination.

If there were a requirement to talk, many innocent people might be tempted to lie in order to conceal behaviour that was personally embarrassing, even if not legally implicating. If such lies were ultimately exposed, there would be an additional risk of convicting innocent people. Indeed, there might well be situations in which certain persons preferred to plead guilty to offences that they did not commit in order to spare themselves the prospect of embarrassing interrogations.

The right of silence protects innocent accused who would be poor witnesses. If such persons were required to speak they might run the risk of being convicted, not because of the deeds they committed in society, but because of the impression they created at the hearing. Of course, accused people may speak if they wish. But, in view of the terrifying consequences they face, the choice must lie with them, not with the prosecution.

The existence of a compulsion to speak might also render innocent people more susceptible than they are now to unfair prosecutions. Even if the police had insufficient evidence, they might lay charges against some people in the hope that the testimony of the suspects would supply the missing links in the case. Democratic societies should seek, however, to protect innocent people not only against improper convictions, but also against improper prosecutions. Since the accused cannot be compelled to speak, the police are less likely to prosecute without *first* having a substantial case.

The right of silence performs an important role even for guilty accused. A requirement to speak would pressure them to engage in the conscious articulation of their own undoing. In the circumstances, their only alternative would be to lie. The compulsion to face such a dilemma is seen, quite simply, as an unacceptable indignity.

From the standpoint of a proper definition and its proper functions, the right against self-incrimination must be seen to involve the concept of *testimony*, either oral or written. Blowing into a machine and emptying pockets do not involve testimony. There is no decision to lie or to tell the truth. There is no revelation of or encroachment on the psyche. The same analysis applies to another recent controversy: the compulsory extraction of blood samples from unconscious drivers who are suspected of alcoholic impairment. This is not necessarily to endorse compulsory blood or breathalyzer tests. It is simply to make the point that, whatever else these practices may be, they do not involve a violation of the right against self-incrimination.

One of the recurring grievances of police officers is that they are denied the right against self-incrimination. Usually this criticism is focused on the obligation many jurisdictions impose upon police officers to answer the questions of their superiors. Even if the questions relate to accusations of misconduct, the officers are often required to respond. Within the past few years, many working constables have been campaigning for the right not to answer such questions. In Toronto, for example, they have managed to secure a situation where they must answer but, in the context of civilian complaints, their answers may be excluded from disciplinary hearings.

Again, this invocation of the right against self-incrimination is largely overblown. Police officers are endowed with extraordinary powers for the protection of the public. Their jobs require a delicate public trust. Why can't society require that, as a condition of enjoying such public trust, police officers must provide a reasonable accounting of their behaviour? In short, cops who won't talk won't remain cops. It's one thing to jail police officers for refusing to talk. It's another thing entirely to fire them. The former would breach the right against self-incrimination. The latter would be a condition of employment.

Nor do I think there is any libertarian virtue in rendering the mandatory responses of police officers excludable as evidence at disciplinary hearings. We know of numbers of situations in which industrial employees such as auto workers and steel workers have been required, under threat of employment discipline, to reply to their superiors' questions concerning possible job-related misconduct. There is nothing in the law that would prevent such statements from being tendered in evidence at subsequent arbitration board hearings concerned with the workers' discipline or discharge. Why should police officers receive special solicitude in this respect? On the contrary, there might be an argument that, in view of the special public trust involved in their activities, police officers should be more susceptible than industrial workers to the use of their statements against them.

There is one situation, however, where police officers should be provided special protection. In view of their particular vulnerability to allegations of a criminal nature, there is some basis to keep out of evidence any such coerced statements in the context of a criminal trial where the police officer is an accused.

The Rights of the Unborn

How often have the opponents of abortion packaged their arguments in civil liberties terms! Understandably they see their role as one of championing the rights of the unborn. By attributing personhood to the fetus, they argue the issue in terms of life, murder, and fundamental rights.

To many of these people, the essence of the controversy is that life begins at conception. Abortion is seen, therefore, as the destruction of human life. During debates anti-abortionists have often produced photographs of aborted fetuses. Without question, many of the fetuses look human—well-formed heads, arms, legs, and bodies. Fetal heartbeats have been detected in early stages of pregnancy. All this evidence is assembled to corroborate the claim that abortion involves murder.

Yet this argument is contaminated by a fundamental *non sequitur*. Even if it is conceded that life indeed begins at conception, it does not follow that such life should have a right of sanctuary in the body of a person who doesn't want it there. The mother is also a person whose welfare is worthy of protection. The issue remains what to do when these interests collide.

As is often the case, inquiry might be helped by examining an actual situation. For these purposes, consider the saga of Dr. Henry Morgentaler. After twenty years of arrests, charges, trials, and even a jail term, the Montreal abortionist was finally cleared in 1988 by the Supreme Court of Canada. According to the court, the abortion law violated the procedural protections of the Charter. In some ways, however, the opinion of the judges is not nearly as significant as that of the many jurors who assessed Dr. Morgentaler's conduct in four different trials.

Each time he was tried for violating Canada's abortion laws, Dr. Morgentaler was acquitted by juries of his peers. Indeed, no jury has *ever* convicted him of this offence. In view of the divisions that exist around this issue, it is likely that most of the juries included people who were personally opposed to abortion. On all four occasions, the evidence, including Dr. Morgentaler's own admissions, was overwhelmingly against him and, at those points, he had no acceptable legal defence. Moreover, the juries were not even divided over their verdicts. They were, of course, unanimous.

How is it that, in the teeth of both the facts and the law, so many jurors simply refused to find Dr. Morgentaler guilty? What explains their unwillingness to convict a self-confessed abortionist? The most plausible explanation is that those jurors acted out of a visceral sense of the appropriate limits of state coercion. Even if they had been brought up to oppose abortion and respect the law, they had also been exposed to the norms of the democratic system, which accords a high priority to the autonomy of people over their own bodies. In short, the Morgentaler juries were caught up in a *conflict* of values. No matter how much they may have been opposed to what Dr. Morgentaler had done, they shrank from invoking the coercive power of the state as the remedy. The application of the law in the Morgentaler case meant intruding state power on the right of women to control their own bodies. That was something those juries were not prepared to do.

No matter what kind of abortion law our parliamentarians favour, they cannot afford to ignore the remarkable experience of the Morgentaler case. If they enact a law that juries find repugnant to enforce, our parliamentarians risk bringing the administration of justice into disrepute. This, in turn, could undermine public respect for the rule of law itself. Thus, even those opposed to abortion would be wise to provide for permissible exceptions. Historically, Western democracies have tended to permit abortions at least when a pregnancy was seen as endangering the mother's life or health. In light of the Morgentaler experience, it is hard to conceive how a law would be workable if it restricted the woman's choice any further than this.

Most anti-abortionists would readily grant the woman a right to have an abortion in order to save her life. But a number of them have great difficulty in acknowledging that any other circumstances could justify removing the fetus. Indeed, some of them opposed the provision in our former law that allowed abortions in order to preserve the woman's health. Understandably, those anti-abortionists lost that battle. The centrality of health in our society is such that there has been a great reluctance to inflict illness on women for the sake of their fetuses.

This part of the issue is central. Suppose a woman faced blindness if she carried to term? Even if the situation were not immediately life-threatening, it would take an enormous amount of sanctimony to coerce another person into accepting such a disability. To what extent, however, should our solicitude apply to *mental* illnesses? The physical diseases are more susceptible than are their mental counterparts to precise diagnosis. But the intensity and duration of the suffering could be just as great, if not greater, in the case of certain mental disorders. Indeed, isn't that the rationale behind the use of health as a criterion? It seeks to avoid imposing certain levels of suffering on people.

Once we adequately appreciate this rationale, we should be prepared to dispense with any requirement that women seek permission in order to have abortions. Where suffering is concerned, this is a decision that cannot appropriately be made by outsiders. There is something artificial, for example, in requiring a person called a doctor to label a woman's suffering as anxiety or depression. What this simply means is that the doctor, rather than the woman, is deciding that she will or won't suffer unduly. This is not so much a clinical assessment as it is a value judgment. And no one is more competent to assess the tolerable limits of a woman's pain than she is.

Granted, any situation that left the woman in control might be subject to abuse. Women might request abortions in situations that are less serious than those that we think could justify such action. But a requirement to have other people make the judgment is also subject to abuse. Outsiders might rule against abortions because they lack the sensitivity to discern the extent of the suffering caused by the pregnancies. On balance, it must be less bad to risk allowing abortions when the woman's pain is tolerable, than to risk denials when her pain is intolerable. The inherent indignity involved in having other people make such judgments constitutes a further basis for letting women decide for themselves the limits of what their bodies must endure.

This approach harmonizes with other aspects of our legal system. Except in very narrow circumstances, our law does not compel people to be Good Samaritans. We don't have to rescue those in distress; we are not required to give anyone our organs, bone marrow, or blood. Indeed, much of this even applies to the relationship between parent and child. While parents must provide certain care for their offspring, they have no comparable legal duty to donate parts of their bodies to their needy children. This is not to say that the behaviour of parents in such circumstances would be either personally admirable or morally acceptable. It is simply to recognize that the parents' conduct would be legally permissible. Similarly, we don't have to embrace the moral merits of an abortion in order to rule out state coercion as an appropriate remedy. By all means, the opponents of abortion should feel free to pursue the ethics of their position. As long as they have the convictions they do, they should argue, debate, implore, picket, demonstrate, march, advocate, educate, and pressure. But persuasion is one thing. Coercion is another.

The fact that women may be allowed to have abortions does not mean that doctors, nurses, or other health providers must be obliged to perform them. Subject to emergencies or other special circumstances, health providers should be no less entitled to have *their* conscientious choices respected. Opposition to all or some abortions, on either ethical or prudential grounds, should not generally render medical personnel any more subject than pregnant women to coercion.

This is not necessarily to deny all of the claims concerning the unborn. Perhaps there are many rights they should have. Once removed from their mothers, for example, there might be an argument for saving the fetuses, if that is possible. Once born, they might even acquire a right to sue for wilful or negligent injuries sustained during gestation. To be sure, such matters are difficult and complex. For my purposes here, I need not resolve these issues. It is enough for now simply to determine that, whatever rights fetuses should have, they do not include commandeering the power of the state to keep them in the bodies of their non-consenting mothers.

The Right of Freedom of Association

A favourite argument of certain free marketeers is that the union shop violates the principle of freedom of association. What creates particular glee for these free marketeers is the irony they see in the situation. After all, freedom of association has so often been invoked as a protection for the right to join unions. That's why free marketeers find it so much fun to argue that the same principle should equally protect the right not to join unions.

The union shop was designed as a protection for the unions themselves. Essentially it requires that, as a condition of employment, all employees in a particular unit must belong to the union. It is usually accompanied by the compulsory check-off, according to which the employer deducts from each employee's pay cheque whatever union dues are payable and then remits them directly to the union. In a number of situations, there exists the compromise known as the "dues shop" in which the employees' dues are compulsorily checked off and paid to the union even though the employees themselves are free not to join.

The ironies are not limited to the unions. They also involve the free marketeers who inveigh against the union shop. Whatever became of the old free-market argument? If employees don't like the union that has been voted into their place of employment, why can't they simply leave and seek work elsewhere? Isn't this the identical argument that free marketeers have used against such welfare-state measures as maximum hours and minimum wages? How is it that these ideologues are able to discern economic compulsion so much more readily when unions, rather than employers, are exercising it?

As delightful as it is to bait these free marketeers, I must acknowledge an element of *ad hominem* in the exercise. Even if these free marketeers may be inconsistent as between their treatment of employers and unions, that doesn't make them wrong on both counts. In any event, since I fully recognize the nature of the economic compulsion exerted by employers, I will not belittle it when it is exercised by unions. The issue, therefore, remains: to what extent, if at all, is the union shop an unwarranted encroachment on freedom of association?

Without question, compulsory union membership represents a restriction on the freedom of those affected. The problem, however, is that, for the greatest number of industrial workers, the lack of a trade-union presence will also restrict their freedom. With few exceptions, modern industrial workers lack the skills that would enable them to bargain effectively, on an individual basis, with their employers. As individuals, they are almost infinitely replaceable. Without unions, their employers would be in a position to dictate unilaterally their terms of employment. Obviously, such a situation would represent a severe restriction on employee freedom.

By bargaining collectively through unions, these same employees acquire a level of power they cannot individually exert. When they decide as a group to go out on strike, the employer will find it difficult to replace them. By increasing the employees' bargaining power in this way, the union presence contributes immeasurably to their *effective* freedom. It gives to the industrial workers a substantially increased measure of control over the conditions under which they work.

Despite all these possibilities, there might be some question whether the state would be justified in legislating compulsory union membership for all such industrial workers, regardless of their own wishes. Our respect for the dignity of these people requires essentially that *they*, rather than someone else, be empowered to make this choice. But the problem arises when the workers in any given place are divided as between wanting and opposing union representation. The situation becomes contentious at the point where a majority of the affected workers wants the union and a minority is opposed. In virtually every Canadian jurisdiction, this will suffice to give the union exclusive bargaining rights on behalf of *all* the affected and eligible workers. Increasingly, there has been pressure for the law to require the minority of workers in these situations to pay dues to the union. This development has resulted from a number of bitter strikes because of refusals by employers to agree to union or dues shop provisions. Almost invariably, the employer and the minority of workers invoked the slogan "freedom of association".

While a legislative or even contractual requirement of union membership does violate freedom of association for the minority, what does the absence of such a requirement do to the majority? To whatever extent members of the minority could deprive the union of their support, the members of the majority would be left with commensurately less bargaining power with which to negotiate the terms of their employment. Of necessity, then, *their* effective freedom would be diminished.

Suppose, for example, in the event of a strike, the majority went out and the minority remained? In many situations, this would enable the employer to maintain some level of normal operations which might well be enough to force the capitulation of the majority. Consider also the situation in which the majority pays for the service the union is providing but the minority does not. It is not hard to imagine the discontent such a situation would create and how such discontent could be exploited by an employer in order to acquire increased bargaining power over the union-supporting majority of employees.

This is not to argue for any kind of *carte blanche* for unions in their various relationships with employers. To be sure, no party to labour-management conflict has a monopoly on virtue or good sense. Nor is this the place to explore the economic merits or demerits of the union shop. All I am hoping to demonstrate here is that, as far as *freedom* is concerned, the argument generally favours, not the opponents, but the supporters of the union shop.

The issue is rarely freedom versus restriction. It is more often freedom versus freedom. To the extent that we were to favour the freedom of association of the minority, we would diminish the effective freedom of choice of the majority. In my view, there is no reason why the majority freedom should not prevail.

Not only are the interests of liberty served by the union shop, but so are the interests of equity. In all Canadian jurisdictions, a union granted certification by a labour relations board is obliged by law to bargain for *all* of the employees in the bargaining unit. It is not fair, therefore, that a minority should benefit from a service they don't pay for. Undoubtedly, such considerations of equity have influenced the compromise known as the dues shops, in which all of the affected employees pay but they don't all have to join the union.

In recognition of the proposition that union officials have no monopoly on fairness and virtue, there is an argument for providing some legislative safeguard against certain types of arbitrary treatment union members might experience at the hands of their leadership. To the extent that expulsion from a union could mean a loss of employment, there is an argument for some recourse to independent adjudication. Just as employees under collective agreement can appeal to independent arbitration when their employers suspend or discharge them, perhaps they should have similar recourse when their fellow employees exercise such power over them. Similarly, it might be appropriate for the law to require at least the minimum concomitants of internal democracy for any union that enjoyed a legislated union or dues shop benefit.

From time to time, certain employees seek an immunity from the requirement that they pay union dues. In response, most jurisdictions have provided an exemption for conscientious objection. Usually, a religiously motivated objection to trade unionism in general or some union in particular will entitle employees to withhold from the union the dues they would otherwise be obliged to pay. Most jurisdictions resolve the equity problem by requiring conscientious objectors to pay the requisite money to an agreed upon charity rather than to the union.

Often these claims are accompanied by considerable controversy. Arguments will develop over whether the objector's motivation deserves to be called "religious". To what extent, for example, does this mean that the objection must come from God? Why should ethical conscientiousness devoid of divine pretensions be treated in a less accommodating manner? Moreover, must the religious faith be a relatively conventional one or will an idiosyncratic belief suffice?

I have serious reservations about accommodating conscientious objection in these situations. Since the union is required to perform its bargaining service for all the members of the bargaining unit, what's wrong with requiring that they all pay for it? For these purposes, it may not be necessary to require that they all belong to the union, but it's hard to appreciate the impropriety in making them all contribute financially.

The most democratic of governments have had no difficulty in requiring all of their residents to pay taxes. Conscientious objection to governments in general, to the particular government in power, or to certain policies does not usually create a legal immunity from the payment of taxes. For such purposes, it does not normally matter whether the objection is based on conventional religious, idiosyncratic religious, or even irreligious grounds. In simple equity, the argument has always been that, whatever other freedoms people must have a right to enjoy, they must all pay their fair share for what the government provides. I see no valid reason for treating the relationship between unions and employees any differently.

But some dissidents have made the argument that many unions engage in activities beyond collective bargaining. These people point out that unions have taken stands on such diverse issues as abortion, medicare, housing, human rights, and international relations. They have even supported political parties and candidates for government. The dissidents believe that they should be entitled to withhold at least whatever portion of their dues money is spent for non-collective bargaining purposes.

With the backing of a right-wing pressure group, the National Citizens Coalition (NCC), community college teacher Mervyn Lavigne sought a court order restricting how the Ontario Public Service Employees Union (OPSEU) might spend his conscripted dues money. Among other things, the NCC complained that OPSEU and the central labour bodies to which it is affiliated have supported a number of political causes with which Lavigne does not agree. For example,

OPSEU has contributed financially to the New Democratic Party, and a recent convention of the Ontario Federation of Labour (OFL) passed a resolution calling for recognition, under certain circumstances, of the Palestine Liberation Organization (PLO). Since Lavigne's money has been used in this way against his will, the NCC argued, he has suffered a violation of his Charter right to "freedom of association".

In 1986 the Ontario Supreme Court held that Lavigne could deduct proportionately from his dues what the union spends for purposes other than collective bargaining. Unless this judgment is reversed on appeal, it will produce a situation of unwarranted discrimination against unions. It will mean that, of all the institutions in our society, unions will be prevented from treating, as their own, the money they receive for services performed. In a case such as Lavigne's, OPSEU is obliged by law to give him collective bargaining representation. In exchange for this service, Lavigne has become obliged to pay the union a stipulated amount of money. Why shouldn't the union feel free to regard Lavigne's dues money as its own?

In varying degrees, many institutions effectively coerce money from us. Ontario law currently requires car drivers to purchase automobile insurance. For some people, the right to drive is as much of a necessity as is the right to work at certain jobs for other people. Yet the auto insurance companies are also free to get involved in political and social causes. While we are free to choose our insurance companies, many people might never be able to find one with compatible politics or even charitable activities.

For an obvious case, consider Bell Canada. Many people cannot function without telephones. Since Bell is a monopoly, these people are effectively forced to enrich it. Yet Bell remains free, by itself or through its parent operation, to get involved in political and other causes. The examples go on and on.

So long as the insurance companies and monopoly utilities perform the service they have undertaken to perform, the money we pay them is considered essentially theirs to spend on all their valid interests. So long as unions perform *their* required functions, why shouldn't *they* have comparable rights over the money they receive? Significantly, unions have never been solely devoted to collective bargaining. Throughout their history, they have attempted, in a variety of other ways as well, to advance the interests of working people—through mutual welfare schemes, educational programs, and political action. Why shouldn't a union be as free as these other institutions to spend what it receives for all of its legitimate purposes? Indeed, why should its non-profit character endow a union with fewer rights, in this respect, than a profit-making operation?

Moreover, union-dues payers generally have more "say" over such matters than do their counterparts in these other institutions. Bargaining unit employees are generally entitled to become members of the unions to which they must pay dues. As such, they may participate in the critical questions affecting their union—its policies, officers, causes, and contributions. Insurance policyholders and telephone ratepayers enjoy no comparable right to influence the behaviour of the institutions they patronize. In this sense at least, most unions should be less vulnerable to the NCC argument than most of these other institutions.

The NCC argument also makes an arbitrary distinction between politics and bargaining. But bargaining is often critically influenced by politics. Of how much value, for example, is a pay raise if the federal budget greatly increases inflation or unemployment? Corporations, of course, have long recognized the importance of legislative and political action to their corporate objectives. In all equity, unions should be entitled to no less.

But some of the contested political action, according to the NCC, has no such demonstrable connection with collective bargaining. Consider, for example, the PLO resolution. Rightly or wrongly, however, resolutions on international affairs are often seen by union convention delegates as advancing the interests of working people. Surely freedom of association requires that the members of such organizations be free to make their *own* judgments as to what is in their best interests. If such judgments are to be impugned, the impetus should come from their own organization and not from the courts. (In this case, the Canadian Labour Congress actually repudiated the PLO resolution.)

This is not necessarily to foreclose on the possibility of legal action to ensure that unions discharge their contractual obligations and observe their constitutional limitations. It is simply to question whether, in general, unions should be less free than others to spend what they receive for political goals. Until and unless there is a radical restructuring of our social and economic institutions, it is unfair to single out unions for such special burdens.

The Right of Appeal to the Courts

In a 1981 article dedicated entirely to an attack on me, former *Toronto Sun* columnist Claire Hoy made the following statement: "Although I heard it myself, I can barely believe that Borovoy, a legend in civil libertarian circles, could advocate...believe it or not, denying the right to appeal a human rights board of inquiry." To Claire Hoy my desire to shelter human rights adjudication from the courts represented some kind of treason to the principles of civil liberties. Unfortunately, Mr. Hoy's attitudes are not unique. They are deeply ingrained in the legal traditions of our community. The influential McRuer report on civil rights in Ontario recommended bolstering the power of the courts to review the decisions of administrative tribunals. Writing in the late nineteenth century, the eminent English scholar A.V. Dicey declared that one of the central components of the rule of law is that "no man is punishable or can be lawfully made to suffer in body or goods except for a distinct breach of law established in the *ordinary legal manner* before the *ordinary courts* of the land [emphasis added]."

What is so sacrosanct about the "ordinary legal manner"? Our society has often found it necessary to enact special statutes in order to change some of the rigid and technical rules of evidence and other procedures that evolved in the "ordinary" common-law courts. Moreover, even if such rules and procedures are seen as meritorious in their settings, it does not follow that the legal resolution of *all* disputes should be handled in the same way. New problems frequently require new rules and procedures. In any event, nothing prevents the legislatures from requiring tribunals other than courts to use whatever old rules are seen as still fair and viable.

And why should the "ordinary courts" be the only ones trusted to dispense acceptable justice? The modern welfare state has produced a wide variety of additional tribunals which seem to be working fairly—labour relations, human rights, municipal zoning, securities, marketing, and so on. Why should the assumption persist that, despite the quality of decisions which these tribunals render, due process of law requires a right of recourse to the "ordinary courts"? Like the occupants of all the other tribunals, our "ordinary" judges are appointed by the government, not anointed by the Almighty.

This is not to say that I am necessarily opposed to any and all attempts at providing a right of recourse to the courts. Certainly, there are some situations in which the public interest is well served by the power of the judiciary to review and reverse the decisions of other tribunals. But I don't think that the existence of such a power is *inevitably* necessary or desirable. Beyond what has already been said, I can envision only four practical grounds for giving the courts the last word:

1. Two bites at the apple are preferable to one;
2. Courts centralize the administration of justice and help to ensure consistent interpretations of the law;
3. Courts are more independent than other tribunals;
4. Courts are more expert in the law than other tribunals.

Since we face these issues every time a new tribunal is established, it might help to examine both the arguments and the experience in a little more detail.

Even if it were conceded that two bites at the apple might be preferable to one, would it not also follow that three bites are preferable to two? By the same token, four might be preferable to three and five might be better than four. To what extent could this reasoning sustain an infinite number of appeals? Obviously, the appeals have to stop somewhere. The other factor to be weighed is time. The very nature of some problems demands that they be settled more quickly than others. On this basis, there may well be situations in which fewer bites at the apple are preferable because that is the only way to accommodate the need for speed.

In order to ensure consistent interpretations of statutes and contracts, there is an argument for some kind of judicial review as of right from the decisions of tribunals that are appointed on an *ad hoc* basis. This need might be seen to arise, for example, in the case of human rights boards of inquiry or labour arbitrations. Once those tribunals make their decisions, they go out of existence. Thus, recourse to the courts might be seen as a way of developing greater uniformity of interpretation. But there is no reason for adjudicative review to lie in the direction of the traditional courts. Some kind of administrative appeal system might be devised to suit the particular legislative scheme involved. While I am not necessarily conceding that there must be review even in the foregoing situations, I do suggest that, for reasons which will emerge, the felt need should often be accommodated outside of the courts.

It is true, of course, that the lifetime tenure for judges helps to ensure a large measure of independence. But judges are not the only adjudicators in our society who have relative security of tenure. While others may not be able to match the kind of conditions enjoyed by judges, many of them still have enough security to produce an adequate amount of independence. In some cases, such as with certain regulatory agencies, shorter terms of office make more likely a higher level of compatibility with the policy aims of the various statutes being administered. Indeed, sometimes even "one shot" or *ad hoc* appointments will be better than any alternatives.

Why should anyone assume a greater level of legal expertise from an adjudicator in a ceremonial kimono than from one in ordinary business clothes? The fact is that the appointments to many of the administrative tribunals are based upon the special familiarity the appointees have with the problems at issue. And the more experience they have with such problems, the more expert they are likely to become. On this basis, it might be expected that most judges would be discernibly less expert than the specialized adjudicators in the latter's area of involvement.

While the courts rarely have contributed greater expertise than the special adjudicators, they have frequently contributed more conservativism. Indeed, in many situations, judicial involvement has been unduly regressive, ritualistic, and even unwittingly subversive of legislative policy. A number of examples should help to illustrate the kind of impact the judiciary has often had.

Few areas of the law have been hurt as badly and as often by judicial interference as has the law of labour relations. In order to promote the development of a jurisprudence sensitive to the special needs involved, the legislatures in this country established a separate network of adjudicative arrangements. They created labour relations boards to deal with problems of status and recognition between companies and unions. And they provided for special boards of arbitration to resolve disputes bearing upon the interpretation of the consequent collective bargaining agreements. In the main, these tribunals have been composed of seasoned veterans in the labour relations area.

One of the first intrusions of the judiciary into the workings of these boards occurred soon after their inception. And it threatened to set back much of the progress that had been made. In the early 1950s, the Newspaper Guild Union applied to the Ontario Labour Relations Board for certification as the exclusive bargaining agent on behalf of a large unit of employees at Toronto's *Globe and Mail* newspaper. During the course of the hearing, the *Globe*'s lawyer attempted to cross-examine a union official in order to show that certain employees had resigned their union membership since the union application had been filed.

As a matter of policy, the board refused to allow the cross-examination. It felt that the union's membership records should be treated on a confidential basis. To do otherwise would unduly expose the employees to intimidation by management. Through a system of in camera inspections to authenticate the signatures on the union cards, the board hoped to serve the goal of cross-examination by a means which was less intimidating to the employees. Moreover, the board held that resignations at that point were not relevant for its purposes. "It is not the policy of the board to consider resignations," explained its counsel, "since it cannot take into consideration all employees who may change their minds." Presumably this policy could be expected to provide some protection for vulnerable employees against employer pressure during the course of union organizing drives. Accordingly, the Newspaper Guild was awarded certification as the bargaining agent for the employees involved.

The *Globe and Mail* took both the board and the union to court. After several years of litigation in three courts, the Supreme Court of Canada finally quashed the board's certification of the Newspaper Guild. In the opinion of the court, cross-examination was an indispensable component of natural justice and a fair hearing. Where the board had attempted to strike a sensitive balance between the competing interests of a fair hearing and freedom of association, the court bluntly invoked an absolutist dogma. The judges came off blissfully insensitive to the potentially intimidating consequences their dogmatizing would produce for the employees. Nor did the court majority even address the pivotal issue of whether the board was right as a matter of policy to disregard membership resignations after the application date.

In no sense could the court's decision be considered better law than that of the board. The governing statute did not expressly require one procedure over another. Indeed, the statute was silent on the issue. The court simply applied certain maxims of the common law that had been developed in an entirely different context. As a matter of law, there was no reason why the innovative and sensitive procedure adopted by the board should have been struck down.

Not the least of the problems caused by judicial intrusion is the amount of time involved. Labour relations are frequently characterized by great fluidity. The intimidating pressures are such that today's majority support for a union could be eroded by tomorrow. As a result, the delays occasioned by prolonged litigation, in themselves, could undermine the benefits that the legislature intended the parties to enjoy.

This may explain why the labour relations statute at issue also contained a section purporting to deny access to the courts. The Supreme Court of Canada brushed aside this "privative clause", holding that it could not exclude judicial involvement in those situations where an "inferior tribunal" like the board had exceeded its statutory jurisdiction. A breach of natural justice amounted to an excess of jurisdiction and therefore the court could interfere. This part of the court's judgment raises an intriguing question. How could an allegedly sovereign legislature *ever* keep the courts out of certain matters?

Fortunately, the common sense approach devised by the board was finally restored to labour relations in the province of Ontario. The benefactor was not a subsequent court; it was the provincial legislature. The Supreme Court judgment was so obviously destructive of the policy goals which the public and politicians had worked so hard and long to achieve that a consensus quickly emerged in favour of a statutory amendment. New legislation was soon introduced and enacted, ensuring that the board had the power to do what it had attempted in the *Globe and Mail* case.

There are those who would see in this situation a rather idyllic combination of board, court, and legislature. Believing as they do that it is preferable to permit those additional bites, they also maintain that the legislature can always cure any mistakes committed by the courts. Such reasoning is based upon a rather naïve perception of how the political processes work. We can't invariably count on quick legislative redress. We could well find ourselves in situations where, because of other pressing social problems, the matter at issue cannot command a sufficiently high priority to get action. It would make sense, therefore, to determine whether the kinds of issues involved are likely to be helped or hurt by board, court, and delay. Counting on the legislature can be very foolish.

Another case which will illustrate the dangers of judicial involvement arose in the mid-1960s and involved the Port Arthur Ship Building Company and the United Steelworkers Union. In that case, three employees were discharged for absenting themselves from their jobs in order to take temporary employment elsewhere for a few days. They deceitfully gave sickness as the reason for their absence. A board of arbitration under the collective agreement held that, in view of the employees' seniority (from fifteen to twenty-four years) and general good work record, management did not have "proper cause" for the dismissal as required by the agreement. The board substituted periods of suspension instead. Again the employer took the issue to court. And again the case reached the Supreme Court of Canada.

The court quashed the decision of the board. In the opinion of the judges, the board could not substitute a suspension for discharge. Speaking for a unanimous Supreme Court of Canada, Mr. Justice Judson expressed the rationale as follows:

> The sole issue in this case was whether the three employees left their jobs to work for someone else and whether this fact was a proper cause for discipline. Once the board had found that there were facts justifying discipline, the particular form chosen was not subject to review on arbitration.

But why should this be so? The board found that, in the circumstances, there was no proper cause for *discharge*. Having made such a decision, it went on to provide relief for the company against the inequity of having to pay all the back wages involved. The board's decision reflected its view of the equities—discharge was improper but suspension wasn't.

In the opinion of the court, however, such a decision amounted to the board substituting its own judgment for that of management. This it could not do without much more express authority in the collective agreement. In the opinion of the court, the board was confined to considering whether "an honest management, looking at the group of employees as a whole and at the interests of the company, [could] have reached the conclusion that they did."

I find it hard to believe that, when the company and union sat down to negotiate their agreement, they intended to restrict their boards of arbitration to such a narrow review function. After all, it would be very rare indeed that dishonesty would be a factor in a discharge. In the greatest number of cases, the issue would be the *reasonableness* of management's judgment. In the absence of express terminology to the contrary, I would have thought that it was more valid to interpret the agreement so as to give the board of arbitration something more than a ritual function. The terminology itself does not help. It simply provided that management had a right to suspend and discharge "for proper cause" and it went on to give aggrieved employees recourse to arbitration. The key issue then is what philosophy will guide the interpretation of such agreements.

The board chose broadly and the court chose narrowly. The approach of the board saw collective agreements as designed, among other things, to promote a new regime of job security for unionized employees. The court, on the other hand, believed that management retained all of its common law prerogatives subject only to what the agreement in express terms took away.

In addition to the difficulties I have already identified, the judicial view suffered from another fatal defect—a misconception of the collective bargaining realities. Unlike many other categories of contracts in our society, collective agreements are signed under great pressure, usually with a strike deadline facing the parties. Both management and the employees live in a state of interdependence almost unique among parties to contracts. Thus, the agreements they sign are usually put together in great haste and with comparatively little heed to dotting i's and crossing t's. If unions had to rely for the protection of vital interests on explicit terminology, it would become impossible to sign agreements before strike deadlines. In the result, our society would probably sustain a great many more strikes than it already does.

Putting it all together, I believe that the board's view was infinitely more sensible than that of the court. To whatever extent an agreement was silent on such issues, the board would assume that it was supposed to exercise a meaningful rather than an academic function. Instead of simply ritual pronouncements, it could sensitively adjust equities.

Once more the legislature stepped into the breach. The judgment of the Supreme Court of Canada was too disruptive of good labour relations. A legislative amendment was soon enacted giving to boards of arbitration the kind of powers the one at Port Arthur had purported to exercise in this case.

But, as I indicated earlier, not all of these problems get resolved by legislation. As an example of this phenomenon, consider the problem of compulsory retirement. In a number of cases, companies unilaterally instituted for their employees a policy of compulsory retirement when those employees reached the age of sixty-five. Some of those workers, anxious about both the loss of work and income, filed grievances, alleging, among other things, that the application of this policy to them amounted to a discharge without just cause. They argued that their work performance and health were exemplary and therefore they should not be forced to lose their jobs.

The boards of arbitration split on the issue. Some held that a unilaterally imposed compulsory retirement was indeed a discharge and would therefore require "just cause" as provided for by the collective agreement. Others held that retirement cannot be considered a discharge: it is an across-the-board policy and in no way reflects any dissatisfaction with the affected employees. On this basis, the discharge clause of the collective agreement was seen as having no application and aggrieved employees were bereft of a remedy. Finally, the Supreme Court of Canada pronounced on the issue. According to Mr. Justice Judson, "[d]ismissal, suspension and retirement on pension are three different and distinct concepts."

Once more I believe that the judicial intrusion caused a net loss to sound labour relations. The essence of a discharge is the unilaterally imposed termination of employment. How much difference would it make to those deprived of work and income if the employer behaved with warmth rather than with frost? One of the universally recognized purposes of the whole collective bargaining exercise is to secure for employees a measure of job security that eluded them under the common law of master-servant relations. On this basis, it is reasonable to interpret the discharge clause as the aggrieved employees did in the above cases. If there are to be exceptions in order to impose retirement at certain ages, it would be better for the agreement to say so in express terms.

Despite the torrent of justified criticism which was directed at the court's judgment, this time the relevant legislative authorities did not step in. If the job security of employees was to be protected against such unilaterally imposed company policies, collective agreements would have to provide something more directly on point. By itself, the discharge clause would not help.

On some occasions, when courts have upset decisions of administrative tribunals, they have revealed a disquieting insensitivity to the issues involved. In the early 1960s, for example, Chief Justice McRuer of the Ontario High Court of Justice quashed an order of the Ontario Labour Relations Board that denied certification to a trade union (an affiliate of the Christian Labour Association of Canada) because it discriminated on the basis of creed.

Among the reasons for the finding of the board that the union discriminated were clauses in the constitution requiring that members must uphold "Christian and social principles as taught in the Bible" and that meetings must be opened with prayer. In the opinion of the court, however, such requirements should not operate as a bar to a union's certification. There was no evidence that the union had, in fact, denied membership to anyone because of belief in a religious doctrine. The requirement to uphold Christian principles was held to refer to ethical conduct, not to theological doctrine. And, even though there was an obligation to open meetings with prayer, there was no obligation on every member to participate in it.

The judge's words are more revealing than any summation of them.

> This requirement of the constitution...sets a standard of social and ethical behaviour that could not be objected to by any law-abiding citizen no matter what his creed might be. I would be very loath to hold that the Legislature meant that a trade union that sought to maintain such standards of behaviour could not be certified, while one that permitted among its members anarchists, communists, and disciples of all sorts of violence could be certified.

In this quote, the learned judge attempted to compare incomparables. It's one thing for a union to *permit* membership to people of various predispositions. It's another thing entirely for the union to *require* certain kinds of behaviour from its members.

In any event, we should adopt a wider interpretation of discrimination than the one suggested in the court judgment. Discrimination involves more than an actual denial of membership. It includes also the adoption of programs and conditions that demean people on the basis of creed. To use a more extreme example, wouldn't a Protestant employer's religiously motivated harassment of Catholic employees amount to discrimination on the basis of creed? For such purposes, it would not matter that the employer had hired the people and declined to fire them. It would suffice to impose hardship on them. Might it not also be argued that non-Christians are demeaned to the extent that the ethical conduct they are required to uphold is described in exclusively Christian terms and the meetings they are obliged to attend must begin with essentially Christian prayers? There is more than one way to discriminate. As between the court and the board, the court revealed much less sensitivity to this dimension of reality.

In recent years, there has been an apparent decline in the number of dubious court intrusions on labour relations. Perhaps a growing number of judges are prepared to defer to the obviously superior expertise of the boards. Perhaps the boards are increasingly tailoring their decisions to the requirements of the courts. In a 1979 judgment, the Supreme Court of Canada put its stamp of approval on this development when it described as "straightforward and compelling" the rationale for protecting the decisions of our labour boards.

Despite this trend, judicial interference is far from obsolete. And, at times, the judges remain as insensitive as ever to the realities of the arena in which they are intruding. As recently as 1985, for example, the Divisional Court of the Ontario Supreme Court overturned a decision of the Ontario Labour Relations Board because, prior to writing their judgment, the panel members who had heard this case discussed the legal issues at length with members and staff of the board who had not heard the case. Apparently, the board has maintained the practice for some years whereby it convenes a full meeting of the board and staff to discuss policy implications of various issues in the cases that are being decided. No vote is taken at these meetings; no minutes or records are kept; no one but the panel members participate in the ultimate decision of the board.

At the time of this case, the Ontario Labour Relations Board consisted of seventeen impartial adjudicators (full- and part-time), ten full-time members representing labour and management, and twenty-two part-time members representing the parties. In view of the fact that the decisions of the board affect the well-being of the entire complex Ontario economy, it was thought advisable to take steps to promote coherence and consistency in the board's jurisprudential policies. Despite the board's safeguards and common sense, the Divisional Court invoked the common law dogma "he who hears must decide" and on that basis, it quashed the board's decision. While the Ontario Court of Appeal has since reversed this decision, there is no cause for joy. There could be another round in the Supreme Court of Canada and, in any event, the protracted litigation could create enormous costs and delays for all of the parties.

The labour field is not the only area where we have experienced these judicial misjudgments. They have occurred also in the field of human rights. In the early 1980s, a recent convert to the Seventh Day Adventist religion told her employer, a department store, that she could no longer work on Saturdays. As a consequence, she wound up doing part-time work at a loss in salary and fringe benefits.

Following her complaint to the Ontario Human Rights Commission, a board of inquiry found that the facts necessary to establish a breach of the Human Rights Code had not been proved. But, while the result of the board's judgment was in favour of the employer, some of its observations promised to act as an important precedent for people of minority religious points of view. In the opinion of the board, unlawful discrimination does not necessarily require an *intent* to discriminate. An employment policy, otherwise unreasonable, will suffice for these purposes if its *effect* is discriminatory. Unfortunately, the case wound up in the Ontario Court of Appeal, and the court expressly disagreed with this aspect of the board's decision. In the words of the court "an intention to discriminate…is essential to a contravention" of the code.

Once more the board exhibited a greater "feel" than the court for the realities of the situation. To whatever extent an intent to discriminate must be proved, the code will be rendered less effective. For one thing, such an onus is often very difficult, if not impossible, to meet. For another thing, such an interpretation will leave many obvious ethnic injustices without a remedy. As indicated earlier, the discriminatory impact of unreasonable employment policies is one of the important systemic impediments to inter-group equality.

Significantly, the Ontario legislature stepped into the breach and amended the Ontario Human Rights Code so as to make the board's position on this issue the law of the province. While the Supreme Court of Canada finally reversed the Ontario Court of Appeal on this point, those favouring a right to judicial review have little cause for consolation. It took a number of years and a pile of money to get from the courts the interpretation that the board of inquiry had right in the first place.

Even if the reader does not agree with every detail of the criticisms I have made in regard to these judgments, the foregoing should be enough to challenge the myth of judicial superiority. Once this myth is punctured, we can liberate ourselves from the stultifying dogma that recourse to the courts is a necessary prerequisite for civil liberties. We can also recognize the mischief that this dogma has caused. The right of judicial redress has been used by conservative elements to undermine progressive adjudication in labour relations, human rights, and other key fields. These elements have often exploited the process as much as the substance. Going to court usually creates greater costs and delays than does the process at other tribunals. Such costs and delays have best served the interests of those who could best afford it: the people with the most money.

Other civil liberties principles have been similarly misused: the right against intrusions on property, the right against intrusions on the person, the right against self-incrimination, the rights of the unborn, and the right of freedom of association. Sometimes these principles have been misused to upset common-sense measures; sometimes to frustrate progressive statutes; sometimes to thwart *genuine* principles of civil liberties. Thus, it is important that the propensity to invoke the principles of civil liberties be tempered by the intelligence to avoid their misapplication. Otherwise civil liberties become an obstruction to, rather than a vehicle for, the promotion of social justice.

Chapter Thirteen

OF DOVES, HAWKS, AND

THE MORALITY OF FORCE

At the heart of many civil liberties issues is the moral question of what circumstances justify the use of force against human beings. While civil libertarians acknowledge the appropriateness of using force on some occasions, they seek invariably to reduce the number of those occasions, and, even then, to reduce the amount of force that can be used.

Thus, there is a widespread expectation that, if you are a civil libertarian on domestic issues, you are likely to support the peace movement on international issues. Few uses of force could match what would be involved in an international war. Since civil libertarians are reluctant to use force against the freedom and autonomy of the individual, they are expected to be similarly reluctant to use force against the comparable interests of nations. Civil libertarians are expected, therefore, to oppose pre-emptive strikes and military interventions against the territory and affairs of other nations.

The restraints on force that apply in the case of conventional wars would be expected to apply many times over in the case of nuclear war. Since nuclear war could well mean the destruction of the human race, it is seen, at the very least, as an invasion of human rights. Indeed, the mere threat of nuclear weapons serves to make hostages of innocent civilians. What could be more repugnant to a civil libertarian than the infliction of such helplessness on millions of innocent people?

277

On the other hand, the willingness to threaten and use force in the international arena is seen as necessary to the survival of democracy itself. In a world in which totalitarians and terrorists are free to wreak their havoc, democracies are seen as being in mortal danger. Since there can be no reasonable guarantee of civil liberties without a democratic system of government, we are urged to support the stockpiling of nuclear weapons, periodic interventions against the territory of other nations, and so on. In short, we are admonished to behave internationally in ways that we repudiate in the domestic arena.

This is not the place to propose solutions for the complex issues of foreign policy. But it is the place to examine some of the moral issues raised by these questions. How far do the ethics of democracy entitle civil libertarians to support policies that could lead to killing or maiming? How far do such ethics permit distinctions to be drawn between international and domestic conflicts? Since many of these policy debates provoke recurring divisions between the proponents and opponents of using force, it would be useful to examine some of the underlying assumptions on both sides. For convenience, I divide our public into doves (those tending to oppose the use of force) and hawks (those tending to approve the use of force).

Dovish Innocence: An International Overview

In early June of 1981, Israeli war planes bombed into oblivion a $275 million nuclear reactor that was under construction in Iraq. While the bombing was described as a brilliantly executed surgical strike—the human casualties were minimal—the state of Israel was vigorously denounced by key sectors of public opinion throughout the Western world. It was to be expected, of course, that the Israelis would be condemned by the countries of the Soviet bloc and the Arab world. But particularly significant was the chorus of denunciations that reverberated throughout the democratic West. After all, Israel is a Western-oriented fellow democracy whose very right to exist has been called into question by so much of the undemocratic world.

In my view, this Western reaction to the Israeli raid reveals some serious impediments in the ability of the world's democracies to withstand the threats facing all of them. One of the most important of these impediments is dovish innocence. Consider, for example, the comments of Canadian newspapers. The liberal *Toronto Star* was fairly typical. While acknowledging as understandable the Israeli fear of nuclear bombs in the hands of its Arab neighbours, the *Star* editorial condemned the raid in the most unequivocal terms.

> But, under no circumstance—*none whatever*—can this fear justify the Sunday raid by Israeli planes.... In the simplest terms, what this raid represented was an attack by one state on a neighbour because it did not like what that neighbour was doing. If such an act were to be accepted, we would replace international law with international lawlessness, if we accepted the Israeli strike, we would have to accept the Soviet march into Afghanistan.... [emphasis added]

The *Star* made no distinction between an aggressive occupation that seeks to dominate and a one-shot pre-emptive strike whose purpose is defence.

Since the very inception of the state of Israel, its Arab neighbours have threatened it with annihilation. On at least four occasions, these threats have erupted into major military engagements. On many other occasions—too numerous to count—Israel has suffered various attacks of Arab terrorism. Throughout the tiny state's embattled life, Iraq has proclaimed its unremitting hostility. It has sent both money and troops to fight Israel.

What did the *Toronto Star* expect Israel to do? Should it have ignored Iraq's years, words, and deeds of hostility? How should it have responded to Iraq's impending acquisition of nuclear clout? Remember, it would not take many nuclear bombs to obliterate all of Israel. To whatever extent a pre-emptive strike is impermissible, the tiny state would be barred from using military force unless and until its own territory were under attack. This is tantamount to imposing upon Israel a special doctrine of *posthumous* self-defence.

In apparent anticipation of the kinds of questions I am asking here, the Halifax *Herald* delivered the following rebuke: "There are ways to express concern, and to bring world pressure upon countries suspected of planning attacks on another. Mr. Begin chose to by-pass them and to appoint himself the Middle East vigilante." Unfortunately, the Halifax newspaper was too immersed in its sermon to say precisely what other "ways" are open to a country like Israel in such a perilous situation. The use of the term "vigilante" suggests that Israel usurped the role of the police. Perhaps it did. But this implies that police assistance was available to Israel. Unfortunately, the Halifax *Herald* failed to tell us where the police were or even *who* they were.

Israel's other critics among the Canadian press were no more helpful than the *Star* and the *Herald*. Admitting that "nuclear power in Iraqi hands is a danger to the entire world", the Ottawa *Citizen* nevertheless warned that "wars are not prevented by acts of war. They are only delayed and made more probable." I don't know the source of this dogma, but I find it singularly unpersuasive. Indeed, there is good reason to believe that *some* acts of war have been quite effective in averting wider acts of war.

There is little doubt that the 1962 U.S. naval blockade of Cuba was an act of military confrontation, but it succeeded in securing the removal of Soviet offensive missiles from the entire island of Cuba. While it is impossible to prove what might have happened if the U.S. had not taken that action, the most likely outcome is that both the security of the United States and the peace of the world would have undergone even greater perils. Historians have advised us that if the Western allies had undertaken another act of militarily confrontation and intervened to stop Hitler's mid-1930s annexation of the Rhineland, the Nazi regime would likely have collapsed. A smaller conflict then might have prevented greater and more devastating conflicts later. The Ottawa *Citizen* needs to be reminded that the real world rarely affords us the choice between niceties and horrors. More often we are forced to choose between competing horrors.

The editorial in the *Edmonton Journal* reached particular heights of foolishness: "Israel cannot expect world acceptance of its struggle for existence to be elevated above that of mankind in general." Nor can the world expect Israel or any other country to commit suicide in order to accommodate the convenience of "mankind in general". Would the *Edmonton Journal* exact similar standards of suicidal altruism from other nations?

For my present purposes, it is not necessary to determine definitively the merits of Israel's action. My concern here is addressed not to the details of foreign policy, but to the mindset of those who debate foreign policy. At the core of the thinking in these editorials and among many other Western opinion-makers is the assumption that domestic concepts of law and order are adequately workable in the arena of international relations. For domestic purposes, pre-emptive assaults are generally impermissible. The accusation of Israeli lawlessness presupposes that if Israel avoided such exercises of force, it could rely on the rule of law to ensure its survival. But much of the international arena is a jungle where such standards will not be respected. These standards depend upon the existence of a police force that is able to apply sanctions in the event of violations. In the absence of such a police power, nations rely on concepts like law and order at their peril. In order to protect their vital interests, they must rely on whatever power they themselves and their allies can generate.

This is perfectly obvious to the enemies of democracy. The totalitarian Soviets and many of the authoritarian nations in this world, for example, have harboured a profound disdain for our notions of law and order. Thus, the only upshot of these editorial criticisms would be to tie the hands of the Western democracies. It stands to reason that if only one party to a conflict observes certain restraints, its adversaries will acquire a substantial advantage. When the conflict at issue concerns the very survival of democratic nations and their democratic institutions, the advantage so forfeited could produce disaster.

I hasten to point out that this is not to endorse a policy of extreme hawkishness. The Western democracies are not morally entitled to do anything at all to secure a power advantage. Morally there must still be some proportionality between the means to be used and the ends to be served. I had considerable doubt, for example, about whether the interests the Israelis were attempting to serve in the 1982 siege of Beirut could justify the consequent risks to the lives and limbs of so many thousands of innocent Lebanese. And I had similar misgivings about the extent of the American war in Vietnam. Even in the international arena, therefore, issues of morality are unavoidable. But the sensible resolution of such issues requires us to recognize that the setting for these conflicts is essentially that of a jungle.

If democracy is to survive in this dangerous world, it is necessary that the democratic nations acquire, maintain, and, where necessary, apply power. Unfortunately, many doves neglect these truths not only in the case of tiny democracies like Israel but also in the case of super-power democracies like the United States.

The Response to Super-Power Conflict

One way to reduce the discomfort of living in the jungle is to deny its dangers. Many people are likely to be consoled, therefore, by the kind of thesis that appeared in a *Toronto Star* column written by Gerald Caplan at the end of 1987. In that piece, Caplan, a former national secretary of the New Democratic Party, repudiated the central assumption of Western foreign policy—that the Soviet Union is "systematically bent on world conquest". It is important to note that Caplan did not base his position in any way on the changes in Soviet life and behaviour triggered by Gorbachev's policies of *glasnost* (openness) and *perestroika* (restructuring). Indeed, Caplan's piece did not even mention the growing ferment in Soviet society. Rather, he contended that the Kremlin has not behaved aggressively towards the West *for some forty years*. On the basis of Caplan's views, therefore, we don't have much to worry about from the Soviets even if Gorbachev's reforms fail.

What makes it especially important to reply to this column is the fact that it was written by a man of considerable ability and insight. Gerald Caplan has become a highly perceptive and respected commentator on Canadian political life. His views must command, therefore, our most serious consideration.

If Caplan were right, the world would be much safer than we have been led to believe. But *is* he right? One of his arguments was that "the Soviet Union has attempted no aggression or expansionism towards Western Europe or North America since the Greek civil war and the Berlin blockade of the late 1940s." Recognizing how the 1962 Soviet installation of missiles in Cuba seems to contradict his thesis, Caplan tried to explain it away as a matter of "bargaining chips against American missiles in Turkey". But the U.S. missiles had been in Turkey for years without incident. Suppose in 1986 the U.S. had suddenly threatened to tear down the Berlin Wall as a "bargaining chip" against the seven-year Soviet presence in Afghanistan. In international relations, you can't suddenly and unilaterally alter the power balance with impunity. Caplan did acknowledge that the Soviet missiles in Cuba were "fatally provocative", but he shrank from calling them "aggressive" and "expansionist". In view of the enormity of the provocation, the Soviets must have been up to something more significant than bargaining over a number of missiles in Turkey whose strategic value by then was in some doubt.

And what about Soviet sabre-rattling in the early 1960s over the status of West Berlin? By threatening to sign a separate peace treaty with East Germany, the Soviets renewed the pressures for the absorption of that beleaguered city into the Eastern bloc. Since the Second World War, West Berlin has existed as an enclave of democratic West Germany in the middle of Communist East Germany. The city's vibrancy has lured scores of East Germans into the West. A separate treaty would have imperilled West Germany's claim to West Berlin. The Soviets were ostensibly bound by a post-war agreement to respect the city's integrity; the East Germans had never been a party to any such agreement. The anticipated threat was that East Germany would attempt to choke off the supply lines and access routes in order to engulf West Berlin. Wasn't this Soviet policy, therefore, an "aggressive" and "expansionist" attempt against Western Europe *and* North America? Unfortunately, Caplan's article didn't mention it.

And why the selectivity about Western Europe and North America? Do we no longer count as expansionism the encroachments that are attempted in Asia, the Middle East, and Africa? Soviet arms promoted the Communist takeover of Southeast Asia, the Yom Kippur invasion of Israel, the coup in South Yemen, the consolidation of the dictatorship in Ethiopia, and Cuban militarism in Angola. Don't any of them qualify as manifestations of expansionism? Granted, they did not involve sending Soviet troops across the borders of other countries. But they did involve the use of Soviet resources and, in some cases, proxies to exert destabilizing pressure on other nations in order to create an international power balance favourable to Soviet interests. I hope these omissions do not mean that Mr. Caplan disputes the legitimacy of American and Western interests in those regions. He did refer to the Soviet invasion of Afghanistan as "loathsome" but, despite its proximity to the Persian Gulf, he did not include it as an issue of relevance to our defence efforts.

While conceding the likelihood that the Soviets have been deterred by Western nuclear power, Caplan dismissed ideology as a factor in the Kremlin's foreign policy. As his article acknowledged, this could be critical to the viability of his thesis. Certain components of the Leninist ideology appear to be a veritable mandate for aggressive behaviour. Within a few years after the Bolshevik Revolution in Russia, Lenin proclaimed that, "As long as capitalism and socialism exist, we cannot live in peace; in the end one or the other will triumph—a funeral dirge will be sung over the Soviet Republic or over world capitalism." Lenin also proclaimed that the Communist world had declared "a decisive war against the entire bourgeois world" including even what he called "the yellow Social Democratic parties".

Such statements can readily explain the litany of Soviet conquests throughout the years. If you really believe that your world and another will inevitably collide, it becomes "rational" to see yourself at war and to gobble up whatever you can. Not surprisingly, the Soviets began early to build an elaborate network of fifth columns and indigenous organizations designed to undermine non-Communist regimes all over the world. Since then, Moscow has been heavily involved in power politics on continents far from its own borders. This activity suggests that ideology has played an important role in the Kremlin's behaviour.

Significantly, Lenin's theories have never been repudiated by his successors. On the contrary, generations of Soviet Communists have been raised and nourished on his philosophy. To this day, his published works are regarded as the bible of the movement. Lenin's successors have tried to have it both ways. They periodically wooed the West with the rhetoric of coexistence and they simultaneously proclaimed their devotion to Leninism. They alternated between taking initiatives for peace and applying pressures of encroachment.

Notwithstanding his new arms treaty with the United States and the beginning of the Soviet pullout from Afghanistan, Gorbachev, as well, continues to credit Lenin as the ideological source for his policies. His response to the theoretical problems posed by the Leninist tradition has been simply to deny, despite the evidence, the expansionist mandate in Lenin's teachings. Of course, it is not in our interests to shackle any Soviet leader with the dogmas of Lenin. If Mr. Gorbachev wishes to break loose, we should give him every encouragement. But in order to assess what is happening, it would be helpful to see things in the context of the culture from which they spring. Soviet culture is such that Lenin's pronouncements could well continue to influence key sectors of the Soviet leadership, including Gorbachev himself. Radical changes in tactics have been an integral part of the Soviet repertoire. Certainly we cannot discount the possibility of irrevocable changes in their ideology, but it would be premature at best to formulate our policies on such a basis.

Of course, I do not *know* whether the Soviets are still guided by Lenin's original theories. But neither does Caplan. My point is a less ambitious one. If you don't know for sure, the reasonable course is to take precautions.

Moreover, even if we were to believe, as Caplan argued, that self-interest rather than ideology is the dominant factor propelling Soviet behaviour, it might not make enough of a difference. Their self-interest as well as their ideology could be a problem for us. Bureaucratic dictatorships naturally feel threatened by democratic societies because of the appeal that such societies have. Thus, we might still expect the Soviets to extend their hegemony and promote the establishment of Communist governments wherever they could safely and inexpensively exploit Western weaknesses. Since they have so often done this, it would be more difficult to expect drastic change now. This perspective does not see the Kremlin leaders as itching for war. Far from it. It simply sees them as prepared to take advantage of us to whatever extent we lower our guard.

Indeed, it would be hard to believe that *any* great power would decline to exploit whatever advantage it safely could. Apart from the fear of one another, the chief restraint operating on each of the great powers is fear of its own people. But such a restraint applies primarily in a democracy, where the existence of a free press gives the people some access to the facts and free elections give them some opportunity to change things. Such restraints could hardly apply to a totalitarian regime, whose monopoly control over the media of communication and the machinery of elections can keep its people relatively uninformed and powerless to act. Since the Second World War, the expansion of Soviet hegemony has meant the irrevocable totalitarianization of every country that has acquired a full-fledged Communist regime.

For democrats and civil libertarians, this has to be the crunch issue. We are living in a jungle with a powerful adversary that has fomented the destruction and obstructed the emergence of democratic institutions whenever it could expediently do so. The issue is not, I hasten to point out, the survival of economic capitalism; it is the survival of political democracy: the right of people to choose for themselves the economic system under which they live.

Yet Caplan treated the United States as though it, rather than the Soviet Union, was the greater enemy of democratic values. He lashed out against the "reactionary policies" which the U.S. has "actively supported around the globe". In his view, the United States deserves the epithets that the Canadian white paper on defence invoked against the Soviet Union: "A proven willingness to use force...to mould the world in its own image."

It is true that there have been abuses of American power on the world stage. But it is dangerously wrong to compare such abuses with those of the Soviet Union. Granted, American power has unwarrantedly sustained some dreadful autocracies. But it has also bolstered a number of liberal and social democracies. Soviet power, on the other hand, has been *systemically* opposed to democracy.

Within the American-led alliance, and indeed within the U.S. itself, it is possible to agitate openly and lawfully for changes in policy.

Within the Soviet-led alliance and within the Soviet Union itself, such activity has been virtually impossible. In saying such things, it is not necessarily my intention to puncture the hope that has been generated by the current Soviet policy of *glasnost*. But I simply cannot equate the controlled and selective liberalization that emanates from a self-perpetuating elite with the freedoms of speech, assembly, and association enjoyed by the general populations of the democracies. As recently as the spring of 1988, for example, a number of Soviet dissidents, influenced by the promise of *glasnost*, gathered in Moscow to announce the formation of a new political party. They were immediately arrested.

In today's world, only the United States and its allies have the power to prevent any further Soviet expansion. Since that expansion has posed a danger to the survival of democracy, it would be wise to ensure that Western power remains able and willing to counteract any resurgent abuses of Soviet power.

None of this precludes pressing America to adopt a variety of different policies. There is no reason advanced here why we cannot push the United States to do more about a number of situations it has tolerated for too long, such as apartheid in South Africa and dictatorship in Chile. Nor does any of this preclude the promotion of agreements between the superpowers. There is no reason why we should follow those hawks who are obsessed with military solutions and congenitally opposed to negotiation. By all means, test Gorbachev's good faith in the arena of diplomacy. But good sense requires us to recognize that the prerequisite for all our activities is the continued survival of free institutions. Whatever else we are for or against becomes academic unless we have a democracy within which we are free to pursue what we believe. And *that*, until and unless the facts clearly demonstrate otherwise, requires maintaining the power of the United States and the West to contain encroachments by the Soviet Union.

The Response to Nuclear Arms

If there is any area of foreign policy where the jungle character of international relations is particularly difficult for the dovish constituency to face, it is the issue of nuclear arms. In this area any departure from the domestic principles of law and civility could well produce the annihilation of the human race. The irreparability of such consequences creates an additional incentive for redemptive hope and wishful thinking. The U.S. has been admonished not to unduly anger its adversaries: don't deploy those cruise and Pershing missiles in Western Europe, even if they are a response to the Soviet nuclear build-up in the East. The assumption is that the adversaries of democracy will be most responsive to dovish reasonableness on the part of the United States.

In some quarters, this assumption has been spelled out in rather remarkable ways. Addressing the Canadian peace group Operation Dismantle, Dr. Helen Caldicott, former president of Physicians for Social Responsibility, made the following comments:

> Yes, it's inappropriate to negotiate from this macho position of strength. That's another thing that women can help the men with—conflict resolution...you never in a marriage negotiate from a position of strength because that almost always destroys the marriage. It doesn't work. We all know that. The only way to save a marriage is to move toward the other person, and capitulate...capitulate. That's what conflict resolution is.

There is no doubt that Dr. Caldicott's formula would resolve the conflicts between the Communist and democratic worlds. All we have to do is capitulate. I can't imagine that the Soviets would find this unacceptable. But should it be acceptable to *us*? The problem lies once more in this foolish analogizing between domestic and international relations. In the main, we choose the persons we marry. There is no comparable choice concerning the nations with which we must coexist. They are part of the environment we inherit. Presumably we love, or at least like, our chosen mates. But in the case of some of the world's regimes, we may despise them to the core. How then can we expect the two strategies of coexistence to be the same?

Dr. Caldicott has an answer for this too. In her view, "we must force our governments to grow up". She believes that "there is safety only in loving identification with others...and that means the Russians". She admonishes us "to learn to love those Russians". After all, "they have got sons and daughters just like you and me." You see how simple it is? All we have to do is love them and then her analogy to marriage becomes marvellously appropriate.

While the Russian people are indeed worthy of our affection, there is no reason to feel that way about their government. The Soviet government has been one of the most malevolent regimes in all of human history. During its seventy years of life, this regime has perpetrated unspeakable atrocities. It has killed, starved, and tortured countless numbers of people. It has engaged in the ruthless repression of the most elementary human rights. And to top that off, it has pursued a relentless drive to extend its sphere of influence and domination. It is not sensible, therefore, to love, or even like, the Communist government in Russia. On the contrary, we should have deep suspicion of its international activities.

This is not to discount the possibility that Mr. Gorbachev's policy of *glasnost* might make a difference. Perhaps it will. I certainly hope it does. But it is not reasonable to ignore several decades of Soviet repression because of a few months of relative relief. While current Soviet plans are full of promise, we know from bitter experience that there are often wide gulfs between promise and performance. Significantly, this is not the first liberal thaw in Soviet history. Khrushchev, for example, introduced a period of relative liberalism only to be succeeded by the conservative retrenchment of the Brezhnev era. Nor should we forget that Lenin was considerably less repressive than his successor Stalin. As welcome as Mr. Gorbachev's policies of relaxation are, it is premature to view them as the effective dismantling of the Soviet dictatorship. Until and unless such democratization occurs, it would be foolhardy to relate to the Soviets in the manner prescribed by Dr. Caldicott.

None of this is designed to discourage making deals with the Kremlin. On the contrary, I believe we should explore every avenue we can to promote international rapprochement. Mindless hawkishness is no more sensible than mushy dovishness. My point simply is that we should treat the Soviets cautiously and suspiciously, remembering that, at best, we are dealing with calculating adversaries rather than affectionate relatives. In any event, Dr. Caldicott's position is not enhanced by the fact that the remarks I have quoted here were made *before* Mr. Gorbachev enunciated his *glasnost* policy. Indeed, she made these statements before he had even assumed the top position in the Soviet hierarchy.

For a number of years, many leaders of North America's mainstream churches have been moving in a dovish direction on the issue of nuclear arms. They have pushed the West to adopt a nuclear freeze, a policy of no-first-use of nuclear weapons, and no testing or deployment of low-yield cruise missiles. Moreover, major church leaders have declared that, even if they knew Soviet missiles were on their way to strike North American cities, they would be opposed to pushing the retaliatory nuclear button against the Soviets. These positions express admirable compassion. They do not, however, make for wise strategy. On the basis of these positions, our top church leaders may have effectively ruled out *any* possible resort to nuclear weapons. If the West were to renounce first nuclear use, massive nuclear retaliation, and low-yield nuclear engagements, it is hard to imagine what would be left. In fact, these religious leaders have explicitly declared that they can conceive of "no circumstances under which the use of nuclear weapons could be justified" and that such weapons must also be "rejected" even as a "means of threat or deterrence".

Our mainstream church leaders do advocate a "planned multilateral process" but their policies and statements would hardly encourage Soviet participation. If our side cannot even rely on nuclear weapons for deterrence, what could possibly motivate the Soviets to play ball? If they knew that under no circumstances would we incur the risk of nuclear war, they could afford to be infinitely demanding and intransigent. It is an exercise they could not lose. They could have victory virtually without risk. If they could have it, is there any reason to believe that they would not have it? While the intent of the church statements is multilateral, their effect would likely be unilateral. You cannot unilaterally renounce nuclear strategy and expect to wind up with multilateral disarmament.

In view of the number and intensity of the conflicts between the United States and the Soviet Union since the Second World War, what accounts for the fact that we have endured so long without World War III? The most plausible explanation is the universal fear of nuclear annihilation. The feasibility of Western policy does not require a commitment actually to *use* nuclear weapons in specified circumstances. It means creating a situation in which there could be a *risk* of using them. A Soviet–American nuclear war is not likely to occur as the result of a cool, calculated decision to launch one. It is not highly believable that either Soviet or American planners would deliberately decide to extinguish all civilization including themselves. While a pre-emptive strike might be possible, it remains unlikely as long as the superpowers are seen as having enough retaliatory capacity both to survive a first strike and to inflict grievous punishment thereafter. If this world ever does face a nuclear war between the superpowers, it is much more likely to result from miscalculation and the out-of-control escalation of conventional hostilities.

The adoption of a policy based upon some level of willingness to incur such risks has operated both to keep the superpower peace and to reduce the encroachments on us by our adversaries. This is not necessarily to suggest we ought to be sanguine about the ability of nuclear arms to maintain this stability for ever. Of course, such reliance on nuclear deterrence makes for a bad situation. What I fear, however, is that the strategies advocated by our church leaders could make the situation even *worse*.

Of course, World War III might also be prevented through the avoidance of resistance. Against an adversary like the Soviet Union, this is always a tempting response. Generally, the Soviet strategy has been to nibble rather than to bite. Total invasions have been far less common than partial erosions. Rather than invade Western Europe in the late 1940s, for example, the Soviets blockaded West Berlin. The problem was that the cumulative impact of our failure to resist would have been victory for them on the instalment plan. In such a scenario, Soviet victory is not necessarily accompanied by invasion and occupation. It is a gradual process of what has been called "Finlandization", a growing and piecemeal acquiescence to Soviet hegemony.

By all means, the West should actively seek peaceful accommodations with the Soviet Union. I am simply suggesting, however, that this is best done while we retain, rather than unilaterally renounce, the nuclear deterrent. In the jungle, diplomacy works best when it is accompanied by a perceived willingness, if necessary, to risk the use of military force.

The Response to Questionable Alliances and Armed Interventions

A favourite target of the dovish constituency is the record of alliances and interventions which the United States has compiled in support of some of the most corrupt and authoritarian regimes in the world— Thieu in South Vietnam, Chiang Kai-shek in China, Pinochet in Chile, the shahs in Iran, the Somozas in Nicaragua. How, many doves have asked, can a self-respecting democracy come to the aid of such repugnant autocrats? In what sense can American policy towards these nations be regarded as harmonious with the interests of democracy?

Of course, not every criticism of American intervention in these nations emanates from the same sources. In some situations, certain critics have argued from a variety of practical perspectives—the costs outweighed the benefits, the insurrections were not really Communist-controlled, the Soviet influence was minimal, and so on. My comments here are addressed to those who oppose American interventions essentially *in principle*. Such people include certain members of the left-wing in the mainline parties of the U.S. and Canada, key segments of the peace movement, and some of the leadership in the mainstream churches of both countries. As far as these people are concerned, the critical issue is the intrusion on the self-determination of Third World peoples, and the primary threat is from the U.S.

At the outset, I should acknowledge that many of these criticisms are fully justified. The Americans have often demonstrated a remarkable capacity to be short-sighted, wrong-headed, and even unduly selfish. To be sure, the United States deserves contempt, not support, for backing many of the world's tin-pot dictators against the aspirations of their subjugated peoples.

At the same time, however, these attacks by the dovish constituency are often unwarrantedly indiscriminate—indeed, they are often downright doctrinaire. They neglect the fact that, in the circumstances of the jungle, policies must be measured, not against Platonic ideals, but in the light of their practical alternatives. What alternative was there in the 1940s, for example, to Western assistance for the totalitarian Soviet Union against the totalitarian Nazi Germany? Had the Western democracies adopted a purist posture of collaborating only with palatable regimes, they would have been obliged to spurn their alliance with the Soviet Union. In this regard, it is useful to remember that the Stalin regime at that time was particularly brutal. Nevertheless, the alliance with the Soviets was justified on the grounds that it was necessary to get all possible help to defeat an even greater and more imminent threat to the survival of democratic civilization: Hitler's Nazis.

Since the Second World War, the alternative to the corrupt and authoritarian regimes that the Americans have backed has frequently been a Communist-dominated insurrection that the Soviets have backed. Often these insurrections have succeeded in producing totalitarian regimes that have practised a comprehensive and severe form of repression. Remember, for example, the purge of the democratic opposition in Cuba, the Cultural Revolution in China, the re-education camps in North Vietnam, and the genocide in Cambodia.

While many dovish critics readily acknowledge the repressive practices of these Communist regimes, they insist nevertheless that some of the Western-supported right-wing autocracies have been no better. There is, of course, much truth to this contention. But the argument overlooks a critical factor: the staying power of the Communist

regimes. Many right-wing autocracies have been so thoroughly decadent that they were always likely to disintegrate or collapse. Even the
less decadent of these autocracies may give way because they have a
plurality of institutions (business, churches, professional groups, and
so on) that, in time, could challenge the government. But a Communist
regime, organized on the Soviet model, may be effectively irrevocable.

It is wise to remember that not once since the end of the Second World War has a full-scale Communist regime gone under. Small
wonder. Communist regimes seek not only political control but also
spiritual domination of their subject peoples. The stated goal is to transform the human psyche from capitalist to socialist. In consequence,
most sectors of those societies are subject to comprehensive control
and surveillance. In such a situation, it is extremely difficult, if not impossible, to spawn or nourish a basic transformation of society from
outside the governing elite. Alternatively, if something did erupt—as
happened in Hungary in 1956—there has been the likelihood of Soviet
intervention to restore a Communist regime. By contrast, many autocratic and outright fascist regimes have been replaced by democratic
successors: Portugal, Spain, Greece, Argentina, the Philippines.

Such comparisons are not likely to persuade enough of the dovish
constituency. Despite the evidence of Communist durability, many
doves challenge the propriety of our intruding in the affairs of other
countries. They challenge us to respect the revered principles of
self-determination.

While the self-determination of all peoples must enjoy a high priority among democrats, there is some doubt about its relevance to the
Communist conquest of many countries. On most occasions when the
Communists have come to power through armed invasion, insurrection, or *coup d'état*, the great majority of the affected people have
simply been helpless spectators. The mere fact that these people did
not militarily oppose the takeover does not mean that they politically
supported it. There is even less basis to attribute self-determination to
the subsequent events in Communist countries. One by one, genuinely
autonomous organizations and opposition political parties have been
eliminated. The media of communication have been brought under the
control of the Communist party and surveillance networks have become pervasive. These conditions hardly represent the hallmarks of
self-determination.

Many doves have an answer for this too. They simply question
whether these developments are any of our business. Who appointed

us the guardians of other people's interests? Why should we assume that our system of government is appropriate for other people?

Of course, we cannot presume to tell other people what's good for them. But we can determine what's good for us. If the choices inflicted on other people threaten to extinguish *our* ability to choose, I see no reason why we cannot act to protect ourselves. For these purposes, I question why we are obliged to wait until our own territory is under direct attack. If we have substantial grounds to anticipate that the extinction of our freedom is a long-term goal of hostile and resourceful adversaries, where is the virtue in self-inflicted paralysis?

Moreover, like all other values, even self-determination is not an absolute. Circumstances arise in the context of the jungle where competing values must prevail. Indeed, sometimes the situation is so cruel that there is a conflict of self-determinations: the enjoyment of it by one country will endanger it in other countries.

Suppose, for example, that the Western allies had attempted to depose Hitler's Nazi regime before it invaded any other country, but at the point when it began in a serious way to brutalize its own people? To the extent that Hitler had come to power through legal means, it might be said that his regime validly expressed the self-determination of the German people at that time. Nevertheless, an intrusion on that self-determination could have preserved the self-determination and indeed the lives of millions of others throughout the rest of Europe. To what extent would such an intervention have been justified on the basis of Nazi brutality, rearmament, and Hitler's stated intention to engage in further brutality and aggression? No doubt there is something dangerous in adopting hindsight from one situation as foresight for another situation. No doubt such arguments increase the dangers of wholly improper intrusions on the self-determination of nations. But we live in a dangerous world. Only in the fantasies of redemptivists can dangers be eliminated. Sometimes the failure to engage in such an intervention is infinitely more dangerous than not doing so.

Alternatively, might intervention against someone like Hitler have been justified even if his regime had not been seen as potentially expansionist? In a situation of particular cruelty or repression where the people have no reasonable hope of changing things, could an argument sometimes be made for intervention on essentially humanitarian grounds? Again, the implications are certainly dangerous. But it's hard to rule out intervention *a priori*. In a world without absolutes, moral values do not descend upon us from Mount Olympus; they are balanced against other values here on earth. Perhaps there are some circumstances in which the decision for or against intervention should depend upon balancing the magnitude of the dangers against the intensity of the suffering. How can a sensible morality irrevocably foreclose on such an exercise?

Apart from such considerations, the question of intervening for or against insurrections in other countries becomes an empirical as well as a moral matter. At any given time, the issue is whether the conflict threatens our legitimate interest in preserving our own political democracy. To what extent is the victorious government likely to be totalitarian? To what extent is it likely to be dominated or influenced by the expansionist designs of hostile major powers? To what extent is it likely to contribute significant resources to such expansion? And to what extent will intervention relieve or compound the short- and long-term suffering of innocent civilians? In sum, how far do the benefits of intervention, morally *and* factually, justify its costs?

This is not a book on foreign policy. This, therefore, is not the place to try to answer these questions in the context of the issues currently facing the Western world. Such questions involve enormous complexity. Even if our answers to the above questions were to indicate a potential danger in some country which morally justified intervention, there might be a host of practical inhibitors to action. Practical wisdom might dictate intervention in some places but not in others. There would also be questions about the methods of intervention. Should it take the form of training personnel, providing logistical support, supplying military equipment, or even dispatching troops? I leave these questions to forums more appropriate than this and to commentators more expert than I. My concerns here are limited to the moral questions surrounding intervention and the analytical shortcomings of the North American debate.

At the time of the Vietnam war, it was fashionable in many dovish circles to pooh-pooh the idea that the fall of Vietnam was likely to precipitate the fall of other countries. Despite my own qualms about the magnitude of the American mission in Vietnam, I have worried for a long time that many doves may have underestimated the consequences of an American defeat. During the period of the Communist take-over of South Vietnam, Laos and Cambodia also fell to the Communists. In the aftermath of Vietnam, Cuba began to send thousands of combat troops to Africa, where they became involved in countries as far apart as Angola on the one hand and South Yemen and Ethiopia on the other. And shortly after that, Soviet troops moved massively into Afghanistan.

It is impossible to say that these things would not have happened anyway. It is fair to say, however, that yesterday's defeats make tomorrow's encroachments more likely. This is a commentary, not on the precise details of these world events, but on the human condition in general. Those who exercise dictatorial power are more likely than not to be emboldened by the failure of an adversary to defend its proclaimed self-interest. Another factor that could have influenced Communist activity in the post-Vietnam era is how the loss of credibility had reduced America's retaliatory options. It had become more difficult for the United States to exert believable threats and pressure to counter these Communist encroachments.

Indeed, even the earlier history of the Cold War era might sustain a similar interpretation of events. The 1948 Communist coup in Czechoslovakia followed on the heels of the Soviet engulfment of Eastern Europe. The 1950 invasion of South Korea by North Korea followed by a few months the Communist revolution in China. Again, it is not possible to prove that these situations were causally related. But, in view of what we know about human behaviour, such an inference must be seen at least as reasonable. In any event, it is fair to insist that those who oppose these Western interventions virtually *in principle* be called upon to eschew their dogmatizing. Each situation has to be evaluated, morally and strategically, on its own merits and on the basis of the kind of considerations outlined above.

Sometimes certain doves simply ignore unpleasant evidence. In an article outlining why Canadians should support the Sandinistas in Nicaragua, Dr. John Foster, former chairperson of the Inter-Church Committee on Human Rights, extolled the alleged virtues of the regime's social programs. But, except for the general observation that independence from the U.S. often provokes accusations of being pro-Communist and that many groups including Marxists were making common cause in Nicaragua, this article nowhere attempted to assess the charges of Communist domination.

While some attention was paid to the positive activities of the local neighbourhood committees which the Sandinistas had established, the article neglected any reference to the power these committees were supposed to exercise over the Nicaraguan people. There was no mention of the charge that some of these committees resorted to food rationing and withholding other benefits as an instrument of political control. There was no discussion of the allegation that some of the committees developed a system of neighbourhood informers similar to that which Somoza had employed.

Foster failed also to mention the complaints of Sandinista interference with the labour movement. There was not one word responding to the charges made by the International Confederation of Free Trade Unions and the Canadian Labour Congress that the Sandinistas had initiated a pattern of harassment and even arrests and jailings of legitimate trade union leaders. Foster's article ignored completely the accusation that the Sandinistas have used *turbas*, or gangs of ruffians, to stage attacks on independent organizations in Nicaragua. The *turbas* have reportedly vandalized the homes and offices of opposition politicians and labour leaders. They have allegedly humiliated priests and attacked the meeting places of many religious sects. Similarly, Foster's article said nothing about the alleged harassment of the leaders of Nicaragua's Permanent Commission on Human Rights and the party-to-party agreement the Sandinistas signed with the Communist Party of the Soviet Union.

The only mention his article made of press censorship was a cryptic acknowledgement that a "limited" amount was being exercised because of threats from abroad. But he managed to avoid any specific reference to the most important acts of press censorship committed by the Sandinistas: the harassment and closing of the major opposition newspaper, *La Prensa*.

I hasten to point out that, in the context of this book, I make no attempt to assess definitively the validity of these allegations or to determine how far, if at all, they justify an inference that Nicaragua has been sliding into the Soviet bloc. My point simply is that such allegations have been made by reputable sources and they must be considered at least *relevant* to a proper evaluation of the Sandinista regime. Does Dr. Foster affirm or deny that these things have been happening under the Sandinistas? To whatever extent he affirms them, what, in his view, is their significance? Does he believe that the Sandinistas deserve our support in any event? It is not enough to acknowledge in a vague way that there have been excesses. People who believe in human rights, self-determination, and democracy cannot afford to ignore the concomitants of communization.

Dovish critics frequently argue that American hostility is the critical factor propelling Third World revolutionaries into the Soviet orbit.

Former United Church Moderator The Right Reverend Robert Smith, for example, accused the United States of creating a "self-fulfilling prophecy" in Nicaragua. According to Smith, "the U.S. ended all aid (in 1981) and then expresses [*sic*] surprise when the Soviets and Cubans exploit that situation". But this argument fails even to acknowledge the claim that, in its first eighteen months in power, the Sandinista government received more economic aid from the United States than the Somoza regime had received in the preceding four years; indeed, the United States may have provided the Sandinistas with more aid than did any other country. Yet during the same eighteen-month period, a Sandinista delegation in Moscow participated with the Soviet Communists in a joint communiqué which endorsed a whole range of Kremlin foreign-policy positions including a defence of the Soviet encroachment on Afghanistan. Significantly, this communiqué was issued as early as March of 1980, several months before American aid was cut off. Indeed, this all occurred several months before Ronald Reagan was even nominated for president, and during the very time when the Carter administration was actively courting the Sandinistas with money, technical assistance, and large amounts of food and medicine. In short, many doves have trouble coming to grips with the fact that, out there in the jungle, the democracies may have some implacable enemies who cannot be influenced by Western goodwill.

Perhaps Reverend Smith disputes the accuracy of these reports; perhaps he draws different inferences from them. While this is not the place to resolve the correctness of the contesting positions, it is the place to urge that the advocates of such positions at least *address* the disconcerting allegations against their point of view.

The Neglected Alternatives

One of the saddest consequences of this dogmatizing about intervention is the fate of the progressive democrats in the Third World. In a number of those countries, there were popular leaders who were opposed to both the right-wing autocracies in power and the Communist revolutionaries who sought to replace them. The tragedy is that these elements have rarely had advocates in the North American foreign-policy debates. The dovish opponents would deny all sides American backing; the hawkish supporters would back the wrong side. The doves shrink from approving any force; the hawks approve it indiscriminately. The Third World's progressive democrats have often been lost in the shuffle.

At the time of the Bay of Pigs, much of the North American debate focused on whether it was morally permissible for the United States to help Cuban rebels to overthrow the Castro regime. As a result of that preoccupation, too little attention was paid to the possibility that the Americans might have been helping the wrong group of Cuban rebels. The Cuban invasion force that landed at the Bay of Pigs was led by a bunch of right-wing hacks from the ousted and discredited Batista regime.

At the time, there were other anti-Castro Cubans who were virtually ignored by the United States: an underground operating on the Cuban mainland and an exile force in North America which was led by former cadres of Castro's 26th of July Movement. Many of these were democratic social reformers who had participated with Castro in the revolution to oust the corrupt Batista government. They had supported the economic reforms that Castro initiated, but they broke with him when he embraced totalitarian Communism. One of the most prominent of their leaders was Manuel Ray, the minister of public works in the first Castro government. There is some indication that, despite his clear opposition to Castro, Ray might have been considered too much of a "socialist" for the CIA.

There were few audible voices in North America who championed the cause of Castro's democratic opposition. The CIA and its ideological confrères apparently preferred to deal with the right-wing Cubans. The dovish opposition was too busy denouncing the principle of intervention. Little fuss was made about the savage prison terms Castro imposed upon his former co-revolutionaries: twenty years for Regional Governor Huber Matos and thirty years for trade union leader David Salvador. In the result, Castro consolidated his hold on the country and his opposition effectively dried up.

A similar phenomenon plagued the debate over America's policy in Vietnam. Once again the United States was backing a succession of governments that were reactionary, corrupt, or just plain incompetent. And once again there appeared to be some alternatives: indigenous leaders who were opposed both to the autocrats in government and the Communists who were seeking to expel them. These were reformers such as moderate socialist and nationalist Dr. Phan Quang Dan, who spearheaded significant opposition to the Diem government. Others included certain leaders of the Buddhist clergy, such as Thich Tri Quang, who enjoyed substantial popularity among the Vietnamese people. Had such reformers been in positions of government power, they might have been able to supply the crucial missing link in the whole counter-insurrectionary effort: popular support. Instead, at critical points, a number of them wound up in South Vietnamese jails—the victims of right-wing repression.

Today I worry about a possible replay of essentially this scenario in the conflict over Nicaragua. Ronald Reagan and his allies in both the United States and Canada back the Contra movement, much of which is right-wing and many of whose elements were involved in the discredited Somoza government. Many doves and their allies continue to insist that the United States should stay out of this region, unless it supports the incumbent Sandinista regime. Again, it is hard to find anyone in North America who will take up the cudgels for those Nicaraguans opposed to both the Communists among the Sandinistas and the authoritarians among the Contras.

Hardly anyone now mentions Nicaraguans such as Edén Pastora, Alfonso Robelo, and Arturo Cruz. These men played a prominent role in the movement to dethrone Somoza and in the early stages of the Sandinista government. But they fell out with their Sandinista comrades because of what they perceived as the growing communization of the country. The politics of these men ranges from social democratic to the moderate middle of the road.

I have no idea whether any of them would be capable of providing the kind of leadership that the situation demands. The making of such judgments requires a lot more expertise than I happen to have. What bothers me, however, is that virtually none of the participants in the North American debates is even *asking* such questions.

We know that Pastora has been very popular in Nicaragua; he was a hero of the revolution against Somoza. Until recently, he headed up a separate band of about 7,000 anti-Sandinista guerrilla fighters along Nicaragua's border with Costa Rica. We also know that, until recently, Cruz and Robelo participated in the civilian leadership of the main Contra movement. Now they are all out of the picture.

Because of Pastora's refusal to collaborate with pro-Somoza elements among the Contras, the CIA denied him the military aid he sought for his separate operations. There has even been a report that conservative Contras, with the knowledge of American officials, planned to assassinate Pastora. Republicans rejected him and Democrats neglected him. In the wake of quarrels with their right-wing colleagues, Cruz and Robelo resigned from their leadership positions in the Contra movement. Does their passing from the scene exhaust the hope for the early emergence of a more democratic leadership? Unfortunately, this question isn't even being adequately discussed.

Again, it is not my function here to make the case for one foreign-policy option over another. Such determinations require a careful assessment of many factors that I have only touched upon. For present purposes, I seek only to make the point that Western foreign-policy debates have often been enmired in intellectual sterility. They have been excessively dominated by critics who regard intervention as immoral and supporters who regard intervention as sufficient. Time and again, the debate over intervention has ignored the existence of political alternatives in the countries at issue. The hawks have ignored them out of political insensitivity or economic self-interest or perhaps even a measure of each. The doves have ignored them because they absolutized the principle of non-intervention. As long as our politics continues to suffer from these traditional disabilities, we will find ourselves increasingly less able to preserve the twin prerequisites of civilized life: democracy and peace.

Hawkish Cynicism: A Domestic Caveat

Just as certain doves are weakening the defence of democracy abroad, so are certain hawks weakening the basis for democracy at home. The structural defect of the dovish constituency is its failure to recognize the jungle character of the international arena. The structural defect of the hawkish constituency is its attribution of a jungle character to all human relations, including those in the domestic arena.

Consider, for example, the view of *Toronto Sun* columnist Mackenzie Porter on the issue of taking action against terrorists.

> For more than twenty years, I have spread censorious sneers across weak and artful left-lib faces by advocating the hunting down and execution of terrorists anywhere in the world by secret agents of the democratic capitalist powers.... Left-lib prattlers on both sides of the Atlantic oppose the summary execution of known terrorists by Western secret agents on the grounds that such action is not democratic. So insistent is this dubious argument that its proponents must be suspected of sympathy for the terrorist cause.

Remarkably, Porter made no distinction among the countries where the terrorists might be found. In explicit terms, he applied his policy "anywhere in the world". Perhaps Porter might have an argument to the extent that terrorists sought refuge in a dictatorial country like Iran or a political vacuum like Lebanon. A few years ago, for example, Israeli agents in Lebanon reportedly gunned down a couple of PLO operatives who had participated in the 1972 Munich massacre of Israeli athletes. Since the rule of law could not then operate in Lebanon, there would have been no point in apprehending the terrorists and bringing them to Lebanese justice. In the context of the jungle, self-help is arguably permissible.

Suppose, however, the Israelis had found their intended targets in a functioning democracy where the rule of law can and does operate. If the Israelis had committed the same assassination in such a place, I think it would have been appropriate to consider them legally and morally guilty.

Where the rule of law does work, it is repugnant to by-pass it. The rule of law makes possible some semblance of civility and community in human relationships. It means we can conduct our domestic affairs with some confidence that we are not likely to be killed, robbed, or beaten. If Mackenzie Porter's policy were to become the policy of the Western world, the rule of law—the very underpinning of our civilization—would be imperilled.

Porter failed to make it clear whether all Western nations would be equally free to "execute" this policy in all other Western nations. For example, would it be permissible for Israeli, American, or French agents to gun down a terrorist who had sought sanctuary in Canada? May we, in turn, do likewise in their countries? Mackenzie Porter's policy is a mandate for undermining both the territorial integrity and the democratic institutions of the very Western democracies he purports to defend. Nor is there sufficient basis to deny even suspected terrorists the concomitants of a fair trial.

The problem is that, to a large segment of the hawkish constituency, many of the fundamental freedoms and safeguards of the democratic system are indulgences of "left-lib prattlers" which are forfeitable the moment we face some unpleasant pressure. Convinced as they are that so much of human life is irreparably decadent, many hawks rely essentially on what can be accomplished by the use of force.

This probably explains why many of them have opposed almost every civil liberties reform in the law and order area. From the abolition of capital punishment, to bail reform, to the exclusion of certain unconstitutionally obtained evidence, to greater rights for prisoners, the hawkish element has mounted the barricades in opposition. And, to whatever extent our society suffers any increase in violent crime, the blame is put on social democrats, liberals, and civil libertarians for their alleged failure to see the human condition as it really is—a jungle.

The hawkish constituency simply fails to appreciate what profound changes in human society have been produced in those situations where there has been an enforceable rule of law. Throughout our domestic life, it requires only a little force to create a widespread amount of peace and tranquillity. A combination of law, order, custom, and consensus has rendered it possible to govern most Western democracies without recourse to excessive force or surveillance. Such conditions explain the pragmatic basis for the commitment of many Western democracies to the whole panoply of fundamental freedoms and safeguards which they espouse. On the one hand, it is believed that such safeguards are necessary to protect the individual from injustice at the hands of an all-powerful state. On the other hand, it is believed that such safeguards do not unduly disable the state from producing an adequate level of peace and tranquillity. Thus, we have freedom of speech, the presumption of innocence, and the protection of proof beyond a reasonable doubt even for the most detestable elements of our society.

Recently Canada underwent a revival of the bitter controversy on capital punishment. A number of police killings sparked a renewed outcry to restore the death penalty, which had been abolished in 1976. In late 1984, the Toronto *Sun* ran an editorial on its front page.

> How many more policemen have to die?... How long do we have to wait? How much more blood must spill over our streets, staining pride, community and the value we place on our citizens' safety?... It's up to you, Prime Minister Mulroney. You promised us a free vote on the return of capital punishment.

Invoking some well-worn hyperbole, the *Toronto Sun* assumed (without demonstrating) that there was a causal relationship between the raft of police murders and the absence of capital punishment. Conversely, the newspaper implied that public safety would significantly improve if the power to execute were restored.

But the facts simply don't support the hawkish hypothesis. Yes, 1984 was a bad year for police killings. As many as six police officers were murdered on duty that year. But look at 1962, the last year that anyone was executed in Canada. Eleven police officers were murdered then. In 1982—six years after capital punishment was finally abolished for the killers of police officers and prison guards—only one police officer was murdered.

The situation concerning the murder of ordinary citizens is essentially no different. In 1967 capital punishment was abolished for the murderers of anyone except police officers and prison guards. Admittedly, there has been a steady increase in Canada's murder rate since then, and since 1962, the year of our last execution. But it would be impossible to discern the key developments merely from looking at the murder rate. In 1962 there were 1.17 murders for every 100,000 people, and in 1967 the rate was 1.38. In 1982 the figure had risen to 2.53. But there were also many fluctuations in between. The highest recorded murder rate in Canadian history occurred in 1975: 2.8. Yet that was the year *before* capital punishment was finally abolished for police officers and prison guards. Since 1976 the murder rate has not increased. While there have been fluctuations, the general trend has been downward.

Unfortunately, these hawks have often managed to convince the public at large that their perception of our society is accurate. And, to the extent that the public misperceives our society as a jungle, it has been prepared to support increasingly repressive measures.

A Gallup survey conducted in 1982 demonstrated a sizeable gap between hawkish perception and objective reality. Despite the overall decline in murder rates since the final abolition of capital punishment in 1976, almost two-thirds of those surveyed believed that the murder rate had increased since that time. Almost three-quarters said that at least 30 per cent of all crimes committed in Canada involved violence, and many believed that the figure was much higher. On the basis of the official statistics for the year 1981, violent offences represented less than 10 per cent of the total reported to the police. Almost two-thirds of those surveyed believed that at least 40 per cent of the people released on parole commit violent crimes within three years of their release, and many believed that the number was much higher. The official figure is closer to 13 per cent.

These misperceptions explain the frequent public clamour to "get tough" in our criminal justice system. In addition to the demand for the return of capital punishment, there have been many pressures to expand police powers, increase jail sentences, and curb parole. Small wonder. If you really believe that you are living on the edge of a jungle, your tolerance level for civil liberties reform is likely to be rather low.

As a matter of fact, however, the criminal justice system in Canada is not particularly liberal. Here too there is a disquieting gulf between how the system behaves and how it is perceived. The overwhelming number of respondents in the survey did not believe that the imprisonment rate for robbery reached as high as 80 per cent. In fact, the rates are between 85 and 90 per cent. More than half of the respondents thought that break-and-enter convictions produced less than 30 per cent imprisonment. The official figure is 55 per cent. Almost two-thirds of those surveyed believed that at least 60 per cent of all prisoners were released on parole before the expiry of their sentences. The official figure is less than 40 per cent.

Lest I be considered inconsistent, I hasten to point out that these statistics need not imply any redemptive hope for our society. They simply challenge the assumptions of the hawkish constituency. Even if the domestic arena is not potentially celestial, there is no reason to regard it as essentially a jungle. In short, the harangues of the *Toronto Sun* and its fellow travellers are factually misconceived. Our society is not so unsafe; our justice system is not so lenient. The greater danger is likely to come from the hawks themselves. In continuing to exaggerate so grossly, these hawks could well create a permanent and sizeable constituency for the needless erosion of our civil liberties. While we are still a long distance from anything resembling a police state, we know from history that complacency is a dangerous phenomenon. Democracy is no less susceptible to erosion from within than to invasion from without.

In their failure to recognize the jungle character of the international arena, certain doves would undermine our ability to defend democracy against danger from abroad. In their failure to recognize the non-jungle character of the domestic arena, certain hawks would undermine our ability to defend democracy against danger from within. Such doves would use too little force against our enemies from abroad. Such hawks would use too much force against our enemies from within. To identify such defects in analysis is, I hope, to take an important step towards correcting them.

Chapter Fourteen

TOWARDS A SENSE

OF PERSPECTIVE

If nothing else, the foregoing chapters should provide some sense of the many threats to civil liberties and democracy. Such threats emanate from adjudicators as well as legislators, from health providers as well as law enforcers, from welfare bureaucrats as well as business plutocrats, from those who are less advantaged as well as those who are more advantaged, and from doves as well as hawks. The defence of democracy requires the willingness and ability to confront all of these threats. Democrats cannot afford to indulge themselves in the dubiousness of double standards. But to acknowledge this multitude of threats is not to accord to all of them the same weight. Some threats are worse than others. Some will require more of our energy for longer periods of time. What is needed, therefore, is a sense of perspective—some way of comparing and assigning priorities to the various threats we face. While this chapter cannot adequately delineate such priorities, it can identify some of the guideposts and difficulties along the way.

A critical factor in the development of perspective is the issue of language. Since not all threats are equal, they should not all be described in the same language. Unfortunately, linguistic distortion is a very prevalent phenomenon. Critics of various practices in the democratic countries often employ the language of totalitarianism to describe the targets of their dislike. Consider, for example, those gay rights activists who compared Toronto's 1981 bathhouse raids to *Kristallnacht*. As I indicated earlier, there is no question that the bathhouse raids represented an unacceptable abuse of police power. But how can they be mentioned in the same sentence as the nation-wide reign of terror that the Nazis visited upon the Jews of Germany during that unforgettable night back in 1938?

At the time of the Israeli invasion of Lebanon, talented playwright and columnist Rick Salutin invoked the memory of the Warsaw Ghetto to describe the siege of West Beirut. While acknowledging that "Israel is not Nazi Germany" and "Begin is not Hitler", Salutin argued that "it becomes increasingly difficult to look on this State and its leader and not think of such images". Salutin went on to flesh out those "images".

> Someone, for instance, who knows the woeful heroic tale of the Warsaw Ghetto might have found it hard not to conjure up that image during the siege of West Beirut—food, water and electricity cut off, the defenders retreating from house to house, prepared to die rather than suffer further indignities to their people.

It is not necessary to be in favour of that military operation in particular, the Israeli invasion in general, the Begin government, or even Zionism itself in order to take issue with Salutin's analogy. The purpose of the Nazi siege of the Warsaw Ghetto was to exterminate its entire civilian population. The purpose of the Israeli siege of West Beirut was to disgorge the PLO *without* harming the civilian population. By all means, criticize the risks the Israelis created for innocent Lebanese people. But to perceive, in this situation, "images" of the Warsaw Ghetto is to reveal a regrettable loss of perspective.

During the hearings accompanying the 1981 enactment of a revised Human Rights Code for Ontario, the dedicated and able civil liberties lawyer Clayton Ruby urged the inclusion of protections for homosex-uals. The following statement appeared in his testimony before the legislative committee: "I am sorry if I am getting a little angry. You see, as somebody who is Jewish, this is not remote from me because there were committees like this in Germany before the rise of Hitler that had an opportunity to do something, but sat with their arms folded and did nothing." The "committees" in pre-Hitler Germany failed to protect Jews from physical annihilation. The committee in Ontario failed to protect homosexuals from economic discrimination. In pre-Hitler Ger-many, there was a growing Nazi Party that wanted the state to harm Jews. In Ontario, no one was particularly seeking for the state to harm gays. The only issue was how far the state should intrude to help them. In view of all the other groups that the Ontario legislature was prepared to help, Ruby had a real argument that it was unwarrantedly discriminatory to stop at homosexuals. But the usual calibre of his advocacy was marred by the questionable nature of his hyperbole.

So compelling is the imagery of the Holocaust in our collective consciousness that it is invoked even outside of the political arena. Note, for example, the argument employed by University of Toronto sociology professor John Lee against forcing an entire class of students to write an examination against their will. According to the *Varsity* newspaper's representation of Lee's remarks, such an application of university policy "would be exercising the same kind of blind obedience that created the Holocaust".

These questionable analogies have emanated not only from left-wing sources but also from right-wing ones. Criticizing the power of human rights commission investigators to enter business places and demand to see business files, right-wing Tory MPP James Taylor said, "it conjures up in one's mind the sound of jackboots". *Toronto Sun* columnist Claire Hoy labelled these investigators "stormtroopers".

"Dreadful" and "monstrously evil" were the words used by *Toronto Sun* columnist Barbara Amiel to describe Judge Rosalie Abella's 1984 report on employment equity. Abella had recommended the mandatory collection of records showing the job progress made by certain disadvantaged groups. And, in the event that the progress of such groups appeared slow anywhere, the judge called for attempts to identify systemic barriers and, where they were found, she proposed the adoption of certain affirmative measures aimed at removing them. For Barbara Amiel, such proposals revived the images of Nazism. She accused Abella of recommending "an institutionalized racism that makes the Nuremberg race laws of Adolf Hitler appear amateur". It isn't necessary to embrace the Abella report as the last word on equality in employment in order to condemn the Amiel invective as the epitome of fatuity. Criticize, if you like, Abella's affirmative proposals for redress. But when you compare this to what Hitler's Nuremberg laws did to the Jews of Germany, you forfeit any reasonable claim to credibility.

In the early 1980s, all three political parties in the federal House of Commons collaborated to produce a quick amendment to the Canada Election Expenses Act. The amendment provided that, during election campaigns, only authorized parties could spend money to support or oppose candidates. This amendment elicited from Claire Hoy the following comment: "These goofballs would make Hitler proud; he didn't tolerate dissent either." It's one thing to attack the election-expenses amendment as an overbroad restriction on the right to participate in the political process. But it's another thing entirely to compare it with Nazism. Hitler's aim was to suppress all points of view except his own. The aim of the election-expenses amendment was to curtail spending so that money could not buy an election. By all means, criticize the amendment for its overbreadth. But, when you compare it to Nazism, you contaminate communication.

When former prime minister Pierre Trudeau decided to appoint Ed Schreyer, former New Democratic Party premier of Manitoba, as governor general, the monarchists at the *Toronto Sun* went bonkers. An editorial reacted to the appointment in the following terms: "It's more evidence that Trudeau seeks to wreck our system with a Hitler-in-the-bunker mentality."

Of course, as the Soviets replace the Nazis on our list of international enemies, they too appear in the metaphors of domestic polemics. I recall, for example, a television reporter asking me whether Canada's proposed new security agency, CSIS, was likely to become another KGB. Despite the fact that I was then heavily enmeshed in the campaign of the Canadian Civil Liberties Association against the excesses of the federal government's security bill, I felt obliged to tell the reporter that his metaphor was repugnant. Without question the RCMP Security Service had committed some unacceptable encroachments. Without question the government's proposed replacement represented additional threats to civil liberties. But how could any of this be compared to the systematic and comprehensive repression practised by the Soviet secret police?

You'd think that our virulent right-wing anti-Communists would be especially careful to save their harshest rhetoric for the Soviets themselves. But not *Toronto Sun* columnist Claire Hoy. In the course of objecting to an allegedly secret plan by the Ontario government to turn over certain lands to the Indian people, Hoy rhetorically asked, "Whose interests are being protected with that kind of Soviet bloc mentality?"

And there are situations in which both of these totalitarian monstrosities have been used as polemical fodder. Consider, for example, the posture struck by Reverend Robert J. Davis, president of the Niagara Falls Evangelical Fellowship. He labelled an attempt to take religious education out of the public schools as "the first step to turning Canada into Nazi Germany or the Soviet Union". In this connection, it's useful to consider exactly what the issue was about. The opponents of Ontario's religious education program had said time and again that they had no objection to having the schools promote *knowledge about* many of the religions in our society. What they objected to was the schools' promoting a *belief in* Protestant Christianity or any other particular religion. *This* is what the evangelical minister saw as the harbinger of totalitarianism.

Inevitably, there will be a temptation to dismiss as academic these admonitions about language. This is a temptation we would be wise to resist. If our various grievances with Western democracy are described in the same terms as those caused by Nazism or Communism, what incentive would we have to resist the aggressions of the totalitarians? Consider, for example, what is probably the most outrageous violation of civil liberties this country has experienced—the Second World War internment of the Japanese Canadians. If that misdeed had been described in the same language as the genocide at Auschwitz, democrats in Canada and the West would have had much less reason to fight the Nazis. Why risk life and limb in the defence of something that is essentially no different? If this is true of the worst of our injustices, it has to apply to the less bad ones as well.

Thus, we cannot afford to blur the distinctions among the injustices we face. Of course, we must vigorously fight injustice in this country. But the rhetoric we use has to be tailored to the evil involved. Above all, we must observe the difference between democracy and dictatorship.

Beyond the issue of language, the quest for perspective requires some assessment of the methods by which we protect our civil liberties. Increasing attention is being focused on the Charter of Rights and Freedoms. Despite the qualms that a number of civil libertarians have about the inclusion of the Charter in the Canadian Constitution, they would be wise to use it as a weapon for the promotion of their values. Like it or not, the Charter is there. Better to use it in wise ways than to allow others to use it in unwise ways. There is also a companion message here for the pro-Charter civil libertarians. They should not make the mistake of regarding the Charter as the last word on civil liberties. No matter what the drafters intended or the judges proclaim, civil libertarians should still push for the kinds of laws and practices *they* believe are in the interests of Canadian democracy. This means they must avoid putting all their eggs in the judicial basket; they must continue to operate, at least as much as ever, in the political and legislative arenas as well.

Throughout this book, I have argued that the conscious goal of our efforts should be the adoption of the least bad of the available alternatives. Most often, this means the acceptance of fragmentary and inadequate solutions to the problems we face. My justification for this approach stems from my conviction that more comprehensive solutions will require too often the payment of an unacceptable price.

Perhaps one of the most poignant modern illustrations of this quest for total solutions is the decision made by the Communist Party of Weimar Germany when it faced the prospect of Hitler's Nazis coming to power. The Communists rejected the pleas of the Social Democrats for a "united front" to stop Hitler. The Communists were not interested in such "Band-Aid" solutions. They were too concerned about their ultimate aim of a proletarian utopia. If there had to be some suffering under Nazism in order to raise the revolutionary consciousness of the working class, so be it. On the strength of such an analysis, the Communists refused the proposed alliance with the Social Democrats and the way was paved for Hitler's Nazis to assume power. The rest, of course, is history. The utopian aspirations of the German Communists contributed significantly to one of the most monstrous episodes the human species has ever known.

It is important to extract the right lessons from such experiences. I am not suggesting that the long term should always be sacrificed to the short term or that the broader vision should always be subordinated to the narrower one. I am saying simply that we should be wary of *utopian* solutions and conscious of the costs of all solutions. Among the prophetic insights that inspire our lives, we should include the words of the great American philosopher John Dewey, "The best is the enemy of the better."

At a conference a number of years ago, I heard a radical professor attack a liberal lawyer as a "disjointed incrementalist." Significantly, the lawyer was a committed advocate of sizeable and even costly legal reforms. But to the professor, his approach was too piecemeal— it lacked the coherence of an all-encompassing theory. Although the professor's rhetoric was compelling, his analysis was not. The more I reflected on their exchange, the more I came to view "disjointed incrementalism" as a largely sensible approach to human affairs. When we adopt solutions incrementally or piecemeal, we are able to see and address more effectively the countervailing considerations. The more comprehensive we try to be at any one time, the less we are able even to perceive the costs. When we move disjointedly, we increase the likelihood that our priorities will respond to the needs of real people. Conversely, the more attached we are to theories and doctrines, the less sensitive we are likely to be to the needs of the people who will be affected by them.

Remember too, that what might be incremental from the standpoint of recorded history could nevertheless be quite substantial from the standpoint of the affected people. Government health insurance may not look mammoth in the sweep of history, but, to the affected doctors and patients, it is a matter of great importance. In any event, incremental measures often produce a cumulative impact way out of proportion to their individual effects. Many welfare-state reforms that have been enacted within this century may have made only small changes in the totality of our social order. But the cumulative impact of all these reforms has been a veritable revolution in the capitalist system.

In the result, many Western democracies have increased production, reduced unemployment, levelled out the booms and the busts, provided free education, universal health care, increasing supplies of low cost public housing, and financial assistance for those in need. This is not to be complacent about the severe injustices that remain in Western society. It is simply to evaluate the substantial progress that has been possible without causing discernible damage to the institutions of political democracy. By contrast, there was a staggering price paid for the social and economic reforms that were adopted in the Communist countries of the Eastern bloc. As far as the foreseeable future was concerned, they lost any reasonable hope of enjoying the benefits associated with political democracy.

Again, this is not to advocate "disjointed incrementalism" for all circumstances and all occasions. It is simply to say that this approach has received an unwarrantedly bad press. It has often demonstrated a superiority to the available alternatives. All I ask, therefore, is that disjointed incrementalism be accorded a position of intellectual respectability.

At the same time, we must resist the kind of cost-consciousness that invariably dampens the ardour for social reform. This means reminding ourselves that *everything* has its price, including the preservation of the status quo. Indeed, the injustices we encounter every day—from the plight of the poor to that of the aged and the homeless—serve to impress upon us just how costly the status quo can be to human welfare and the values we cherish. Our posture, therefore, should be one of openness to the idea of social reform. Consciousness of cost must coexist with a willingness to change.

Finally, a sensible balance must be struck between thinking and acting. From the days of Edmund Burke through to all the horrors of the twentieth century, we have been admonished to remember that the best way to ensure the triumph of evil is for decent people to do nothing. At the same time, however, a decent intent will not necessarily produce a decent result. When such intentions spawn faulty analysis, the results can be disastrous. Unfortunately, we will rarely have all the facts. There is usually no alternative but to act on the basis of inadequate information. The challenge is to know as best we can in what situations more adequate information might soon be available and in what situations the wait for it would be unacceptably destructive.

The best we can do is to fasten our vision on the concomitants of the human condition. We are finite mortals who cannot avoid the exercise of tragic choice. Whatever we want or wish to avoid generally requires the surrender or acceptance, respectively, of something else we want or wish to avoid. The best tool we have is our intelligence, the ability to seek evidence and draw rational inferences from it. In the course of applying our intelligence, we must be careful to avoid the recurring fallacies that bedevil analysis. Remember, for example, the power-hoarding, packaging, either-or, and Pollyanna fallacies. In particular, we must bear in mind that there are no absolutes upon which we can reasonably rely to rescue us from the pain of tragic choice. And there is no ultimate vision or utopian aspiration which we can reasonably invoke to redeem the pain we cannot avoid.

Instead, we must develop, in addition to our intelligence, both our courage and our sense of humour. Courage, as Churchill noted, is the prerequisite of all other virtues. Without it, we might know what we should do but we could not be counted on actually to do it. Humour is the prerequisite for reducing the inevitable pain of the difficult decisions we must inevitably make. Laughter cannot solve problems but it can help us to face them. With intelligence, courage, and humour, we stand a chance to preserve and perpetuate the precious institutions of political democracy—the only system this world has known that can generate an acceptable level of dignity and decency.

NOTES

PREFACE

Pages iv–v

For more about Pinochet's Chile, Khomeini's Iran, and Zia's Pakistan, respectively, see the following Amnesty International documents: *Chile—Torture Continues: The Cases of Ricardo Campus, Luis Tricot and Jorge Martinez*, November 1987 (AMR 22/50/87), pp. 5–6; "Amnesty International calls for Iran to abandon cruelty and abide by international human rights treaties", news release, May 13, 1987; "Memo to all medical groups re: floggings, amputations & deaths in police custody in Pakistan", November 4, 1980 (ASA 33/07/80).

Pages iv–vi

Within the framework of this book, the limitations of space do not permit a more comprehensive defence of the democratic system. I hope, however, that I have plausibly explained at least some of the factors that impel me to accord to democracy such a high priority in my set of values. Spelling out my ideas in this way was designed, as the younger generation would say, to tell the reader "where I'm coming from."

Page viii

A number of pieces I have written in the past were useful in the writing of this book. Parts of the following chapters appeared in somewhat different form elsewhere: Chapter 2, as "Freedom of Expression: Some Recurring Impediments", in R. Abella and M. Rothman, eds., *Justice Beyond Orwell* (Montreal: Editions Y. Blais, 1985); Chapter 4, as "The Powers of the Police and the

Freedoms of the Citizen", in R.St.J. Macdonald and John P. Humphrey eds., *The Practice of Freedom* (Toronto: Butterworths, 1979); Chapter 6, as "Such probes justified, with guidelines", *Toronto Star*, May 19, 1984, p. D6, and "Should the right to a fair trial limit freedom of speech?", *Sunday [Toronto] Star*, January 15, 1984, p. F2; Chapter 12, as "New rights bill is not 'police state', lawyer says", *Toronto Star*, December 2, 1985, p. A8, and "When dues are paid to fight political battles", *Toronto Star*, October 1, 1981, p. A11; and Chapter 14, as "Orwell would have condemned misuse of Big Brother tag", *Toronto Star*, January 21, 1984, p. B2.

CHAPTER ONE

Page 1

The government of Canada invoked the War Measures Act, RSC 1970, c. W-2, in peacetime by proclamation of the Governor-in-Council, in Public Order Regulations, 1970, SOR/70-444, October 16, 1970. The proclamation was revoked by enactment of the Public Orders (Temporary Measures) Act, SC 1970–71–72, c. 2 (incorporating the Public Order Regulations in somewhat varied form), which expired in April 1971. Public-opinion polls conducted shortly after the invocation of the War Measures Act indicated that a large majority of Canadians supported the measures adopted by government. See the discussion of public reaction in J. Saywell, *Quebec 70* (Toronto: University of Toronto Press, 1971), pp.93–99, 118. For a review of some of the forms of harassment perpetrated against unpopular minorities in October 1970, see A. Borovoy, "Liberty Suspended: Canada in Crisis", in *Civil Liberties*, March 1971, p. 7 (a publication of the American Civil Liberties Union).

Pages 1–2

Revelations regarding the misconduct of the RCMP Security Service and Criminal Investigation Branch were made public in testimony before the McDonald commission and are chronicled in its reports: Canada, Commission of Inquiry Concerning Certain Activities of the RCMP, *Freedom and Security Under the Law*, Second Report, and *Certain RCMP Activities and the Question of Governmental Knowledge*, Third Report (Ottawa: Supply and Services, 1981).

Page 2

For some of the proceedings against RCMP officers in Quebec arising out of illegal acts during the 1970s, see *R. v. Daigle* (1982), 32 CR (3d) 388, 1 CCC (3d) 477 (Que. SC), and *R. v. Vermette*, unreported, Supreme Court of Canada, No. 18919, May 26, 1988, reversing (1984), 45 CR (3d) 341, 16 CCC (3d) 532 (Que. CA) and (1982), 30 CR (3d) 129 (Que. SC). Following the decision of the Supreme Court of Canada to lift the stay of proceedings imposed by Quebec courts in *Vermette*, the Quebec justice minister has announced that ten former and current RCMP officers will face trial on charges that they stole a Parti Québécois membership list some fifteen years ago. See "10 Mounties to face trial over PQ list", *Globe and Mail*, June 13, 1988, p. A4.

For the discriminatory provisions against Indian women, see the Indian Act, RSC 1970, c. I-6, s. 12 (1) (b). Parliament repealed the section in question and provided for the restoration of Indian status to the affected women and children in An Act to Amend the Indian Act, SC 1985, c. 27, s. 4. For a comprehensive review of the issues, see Kathleen Jamieson, *Indian Women and the Law in Canada: Citizens Minus* (Ottawa: Supply and Services, 1978).

Pages 2–3

The *Body Politic*, a gay community newspaper, published an article entitled "Men Loving Boys Loving Men" in its year-end issue of 1977. This led to a criminal prosecution for having used the mails to deliver "obscene, indecent, immoral or scurrilous" material (Criminal Code, RSC 1985, c. C-46, s. 168). The accused were acquitted at trial and then again on appeal. See *R.* v. *Popert et al.* (1981), 58 CCC (2d) 505 (Ont. CA), affirming 51 CCC (2d) 485 *sub nom. R.* v. *Pink Triangle Press et al.* (Ont. Co. Ct.).

Page 3

An account of the attempt to ban publication of the controversial article explaining how to build a hydrogen bomb can be found in "Judge bars newspaper on coast from using letter about H-Bomb", *New York Times*, September 16, 1979, p. 1, and "U.S. drops efforts to bar publication of H-Bomb articles", *New York Times*, September 18, 1979, p. 1.

Philosopher Sidney Hook's views on the nature of human conflict can be found in his essay "Pragmatism and the Tragic Sense of Life", published in his book of the same title (New York: Basic Books, 1974), pp. 3–25.

Page 4

The comments of Mr. Justice Oliver Wendell Holmes on free speech and danger appeared in *Schenck* v. *U.S.* (1919), 249 US 47, 39 S. Ct. 247, p. 249 (USSC).

Page 7

The Ontario statute on free speech of civil servants is the Public Service Act, RSO 1980, c. 418, s. 14. For a critique of this and similar legislation, see Ontario Law Reform Commission, *Report on Political Activity, Public Comment and Disclosure by Crown Employees* (Ontario: Ministry of the Attorney General, 1986).

Page 8

At the time of writing, a replacement to the War Measures Act, RSO 1970, c. W-2, had been passed by Parliament. See Bill C-77, the Emergencies Act, 33rd Parl., 2nd Sess., 1986–87–88.

318   *A. Alan Borovoy*

Pages 8–9

Regarding the problem of soliciting for prostitution, see An Act to Amend the Criminal Code (prostitution), SC 1985, c. 50, s. 1 (Criminal Code, RSC 1985, (1st Supp.) c. 51). The law has been challenged in several provinces on the grounds that it offends the free-speech guarantees contained in s. 2(b) of the Charter. See, for instance, *R.* v. *Jahelka and A.G. of Canada*; *R.* v. *Stagnitta and A.G. of Canada* (1987), 58 CR (3d) 164 (Alta. CA), where the law was upheld; and *R.* v. *Skinner* (1987), 58 CR (3d) 137 (NSCA), where the law was struck down. Appeals in both of these decisions will be heard by the Supreme Court of Canada (S.C.C. *Bulletin*, October 2, 1987, pp. 465–66).

Page 12

On Stalin's starvation of the Kulaks, see D.G. Dalrymple, "The Soviet Famine of 1932–34", in *Soviet Studies*, January 1964, p. 261; and for Stalin's justification, see *History of the Communist Party of the Soviet Union/Bolsheviks/Short Course* (Moscow: Progress Publishers, 1945), p. 305, both cited by Robert C. Tucker, in *Political Culture and Leadership in Soviet Russia* (New York and London: W.W. Norton, 1987), ch. 5. See also Robert Conquest, *Harvest of Sorrow* (Edmonton: University of Alberta Press, 1986).

CHAPTER TWO

Page 18

For more on how the fall 1981 constitutional accord offended women and natives, see "Indians, women are outraged at agreement", *Toronto Star*, November 6, 1981, p. A1. For the reaction to the compromise that was subsequently reached, see "Constitution pact doesn't go far enough, groups say", *Toronto Star*, November 24, 1981, p. A1; and David Milne, *The New Canadian Constitution* (Toronto: James Lorimer & Company, 1982), pp. 155–60.

Page 20

The reference to the right of dissent as democracy's "grievance procedure" was told to me by my friend Terry Meagher, long-time CCLA secretary and former secretary-treasurer of the Ontario Federation of Labour.

Pages 21–22

A summary of the events at the Gainer's plant during the summer of 1986 is conveniently provided by Mr. Justice Cavanagh of the Alberta Court of Queen's Bench in *Gainer's Inc.* v. *U.F.C.W. et al.* (1986), 73 AR 35, pp. 37–39. Regarding the standard of living for Gainer's employees, see "The battle for pork jobs", *Western Report*, Vol. 1, No. 21 (June 16, 1986), p. 22.

Page 23

For the full text of the Supreme Court majority judgment upholding Montreal's anti-demonstration by-law, see *Attorney General for Canada* v. *Dupond,* [1978] 2 SCR 770, p. 797 (Mr. Justice Beetz). In pre-Charter cases, the concept of free speech was not usually seen as an independent constitutional value, but was sometimes used to assist in determining which of the legislative authorities could pass the enactment in question.

Pages 23–24

The rally against high interest rates was organized by the Canadian Labour Congress. See "CLC is exhilarated by Ottawa protest", *Globe and Mail,* November 23, 1981, p. 1.

Page 24

Section 1 of the Canadian Charter of Rights and Freedoms makes all the guarantees of rights and freedoms set out in the Charter "subject only to such reasonable limits prescribed by law as can be demonstrably justified in a free and democratic society."

On the permissible limits of picket-line behaviour, I have quoted from the judgment of the late Mr. Justice Ivan Rand, speaking for a majority of the Supreme Court of Canada, in *Williams et al.* v. *Aristocratic Restaurants,* [1951] SCR 762, p. 784. The court was construing the "watching and besetting" section of the Criminal Code (now RSC 1985, c. C-46, s. 423).

Page 25

Instances where Canadian courts have issued injunctions restricting the numbers of pickets will be found in *Lever Bros.* v. *Briggs et al.* (1957), 10 DLR (2d) 758 (Ont. HCJ) 536; *Re Tilco Plastics Limited* v. *Skurjat et al.,* [1966] 2 OR 547 (Ont. HCJ); *Weyerhauser* v. *Renald et al.,* unreported, Ontario High Court, No. 103/64, March 12, 1964; and more recently in *Gainer's Inc.* v. *U.F.C.W. et al.* (1986), 73 AR 35 (Alta. QB).

As examples of legislation confining the use of injunctions in labour disputes, see the Ontario Judicature Act, RSO 1980, c. 223, s. 20 (3), and the Manitoba Queen's Bench Act, SM 1970, c. 79, s. 2 (now s. 60.2).

Page 26

The leading Ontario case regarding secondary picketing is *Hersees of Woodstock Ltd.* v. *Goldstein et al.,* [1963] 2 OR 81 (Ont. CA). (The quote referred to will be found on page 86.)

The situation appears to be different in Manitoba as a result of the Manitoba Queen's Bench Act. See *Channel Seven Television Ltd.* v. *NABET* (1971), 21 DLR (3d) 424, where the Manitoba Court of Appeal refused to grant an injunction to prevent secondary picketing.

Page 27

For the comments of the Quebec Superior Court on farm-worker picketing, see *Dominion Stores Ltd.* v. *United Farm Workers et al.*, unreported, Quebec Superior Court, Mtl. No. 500-05-006668-758, May 30, 1975.

Pages 27–28

The Ontario grape-boycott case referred to is *Darrigo's Grape Juice Ltd.* v. *Masterson* (1971), 21 DLR (3d) 660 (Ont. HCJ). I have referred to the comments of Mr. Justice Keith, pp. 661–62.

Page 28

The British Columbia secondary-picketing case mentioned here is *Dolphin Delivery Ltd.* v. *Retail, Wholesale and Department Store Union, Local 580, et al.* (1984), 10 DLR (4th) 198, p. 213. The British Columbia Court of Appeal quoted with approval the words of Yale professor of law Thomas Emerson in his book *The System of Freedom of Expression* (New York: Random House, 1970), p. 445. This decision was affirmed on appeal by the Supreme Court of Canada. See *R.W.D.S.U.* v. *Dolphin Delivery Ltd.* (1986), 33 DLR (4th) 174, [1986] 2 SCR 573. It is curious that the Charter guarantees of freedom of "expression" and "association" were argued in this case, but that the Charter guarantee of "freedom of peaceful assembly" did not emerge as an issue. It might be that picket lines, like demonstrations, qualify as an "assembly". Although the Supreme Court of Canada held that the Charter did not apply in this case in any event, the issue of assembly may emerge as an important consideration in later Charter cases.

Page 29

For more detail on the police blockade of the peace protest at Litton Industries, see "Peace protesters kept from Litton," *Globe and Mail*, November 12, 1982, p. 5.

Page 30

For an elaboration of the proposal that police should need authorization from an independent agency to keep demonstrations from the vicinity of the targeted premises, see a letter dated April 19, 1983, from the Canadian Civil Liberties Association to the Honourable Roy McMurtry, Attorney-General of Ontario. The letter also acknowledges the need for unilateral police action, subject to safeguards, in exigent circumstances.

Page 31

The group that was denied a Yonge Street parade permit was the Vietnam Mobilization Committee. The intended parade date was October 26, 1968.

The writer I have paraphrased on freedom of speech and soliloquy is Barbara Wootton, from her *Freedom Under Planning* (Chapel Hill: University of North Carolina Press, 1945), p. 27.

The by-law in question was By-law 12 of the Metropolitan Toronto Board of Commissioners of Police, s. 12, which has since been changed.

Pages 31–32

The Vietnam war protest scheduled for Richard Nixon's second inauguration went ahead as planned but without an opportunity to march down busy Yonge Street. See "Look to local 'wars'...", *Toronto Star*, January 22, 1973, p. 23.

Pages 32–33

The provision on sedition can be found in the Criminal Code, RSC 1985, c. C-46, s. 61. See also the Supreme Court of Canada decision in *Boucher* v. *The King*, [1951] SCR 265, and Walter Tarnopolsky, *The Canadian Bill of Rights*, The Carleton Library No. 83, 2nd ed. (Toronto: McClelland and Stewart, 1975), p. 185.

Page 34

Lawyer Harry Kopyto's remarks regarding the court system were published in "Ex-RCMP officers only doing job, Ontario judge decides", *Globe and Mail*, December 18, 1985, p. A17. Kopyto was charged with, and convicted for, making statements "calculated to scandalize the court and to bring the administration of justice into disrepute." See *R.* v. *Kopyto*, unreported, Ontario Divisional Court, October 17, 1986, Montgomery, J. On appeal, the Ontario Court of Appeal acquitted Kopyto by invoking the guarantee of freedom of expression in the Charter. See *R.* v. *Kopyto* (1987), 61 CR (3d) 309, 62 OR (2d) 449 (Ont. CA).

This RCMP "dirty trick" of fomenting a split within the Trotskyist organization was part of its "Operation Checkmate". This particular tactic was disclosed in testimony before the Krever Commission into the Confidentiality of Health Records in Ontario and the McDonald Commission of Inquiry Concerning Certain Activities of the RCMP. See Ontario, *Report of the Commission of Inquiry into the Confidentiality of Health Information*, Volume II (Ontario: Queen's Printer, 1980), pp. 38–48, and *Freedom and Security Under the Law*, Second Report, Volume 1 (Ottawa: Supply and Services, 1981), pp. 271–73 respectively.

Page 35

For the scandalizing charge and conviction of the New Brunswick student, see *R.* v. *Murphy* (1969), 4 DLR (3d) 289 (NBSC App. Div.).

Regarding the court's power to sentence persons found guilty of contempt to imprisonment for no set term until they purge their contempt, see *In the Matter of a Special Reference from the Bahama Islands*, [1893] AC 138 (Privy Council), pp. 143 (exchange between the court and the attorney-general), 149. See also Gallagher's case discussed in Great Britain, *Parliamentary Debates*, Vol. 185 (March 10, 1908), p. 1400, and *Cann* v. *Cann* (1954), 28 ER 332.

For the quote on the impermissibility of invective in commenting on court judgments, see the judgment of Chief Justice Wood in *R*. v. *Amos Rowe* (1880), Man. R. Temp. Wood 309 (Man. Q.B.), pp. 322–23.

Former Osgoode Hall law dean and now York University President Harry Arthurs made the quoted comments in response to the 1976 contempt-of-court conviction of then federal urban affairs minister André Ouellett. See Alan Borovoy, "To Judge a Judge", *The Canadian* magazine, October 29, 1977, p. 30, and *Re Ouellet (Nos: 1&2)* (1976), 32 CCC (2d) 149 (Que. CA).

Page 36

The British House of Commons in 1906, and again in 1908, resolved that the "jurisdiction of judges in dealing with contempt of court is practically arbitrary and unlimited...." See Great Britain, *Parliamentary Debates*, Vol. 155 (April 4, 1906), p. 614, and Vol. 185 (March 10, 1908), p. 1434. See also Jessel, M.R., in *Re Clements and the Republic of Costa Rica* v. *Erlanger* (1877), 46 LJ Ch. 375 (CA), p. 383.

These same powers were perpetuated in section 8 of the Criminal Code (now RSC 1985, c. C-46, s. 9).

For the case in which contempt convictions were imposed for a newspaper article that described a capital trial as murder, see *R*. v. *Nicol*, [1954] 3 DLR 690 (BCSC).

The invective against Mr. Justice Higgins was published in *The Mercury* (April 7, 1911) of Hobart, Tasmania, Australia. The author was acquitted of the charge of "contempt by scandalizing the Court" in *The King* v. *Nicholls* (1911), 12 Comm. Law Rep. 280 (High Court of Australia).

Page 37

American courts appear to have abandoned the offence of scandalizing the courts. They have held it to be an infringement of the First Amendment protection for freedom of speech. See, for example, *Bridges* v. *California* (1941), 62 S. Ct. 190, 314 US 252 (USSC). See the discussion of American law in this regard by Mr. Justice Cory in *R*. v. *Kopyto* (1987), 62 OR (2d) 449 at pp. 466 ff.

Page 38

The neglected contempt-of-court decision of the Judicial Committee of the Privy Council is *McLeod* v. *St. Aubyn*, [1899] AC 549. (The quote is on page 552.) It is interesting to note that the Privy Council, while finding the offence of contempt by scandalizing had become obsolete in Britain, considered it very much alive in the colonies where backward social conditions required special measures to preserve respect for the administration of justice. This rationale has sometimes provoked me to argue that any attempt to apply the offence in modern Canada must be seen as an offensive commentary on the state of Canadian civilization.

The defamatory libel conviction for the "Pontius Pilate" award can be found in *R*. v. *Georgia Straight Publishing Ltd. et al.* (1970), 4 DLR (3d) 383, [1970] 1 CCC 94 (B.C. Co. Ct.). The offence is contained in section 264 of the Criminal Code (now RSC 1985, c. C-46, s. 300).

The history of the offence of defamatory libel is outlined in Law Reform Commission of Canada, *Defamatory Libel* (Working Paper 35) (Ottawa: Supply and Services, 1984), pp. 3–5. On page 61 of the Working Paper, the authors reached a similar conclusion to my own: the offence should be repealed.

Page 39

The civil defamation judgment from which I have quoted is the trial judgment of Munro, J., in *Vander Zalm* v. *Times Publishers*, [1979] 2 WWR 673 (BCSC), p. 676. The defendants were relieved of liability in the appeal. See *Vander Zalm* v. *Times Publishers*, [1980] 4 WWR 259 (BCCA).

Page 40

The quote attributed to former U.S. president Harry Truman can be found in his *Mr. Citizen* (New York: Bernard Geis Associates, 1960), p. 229.

The U.S. Supreme Court has ruled that a public official cannot recover damages for defamation when the falsehood relates to official conduct, unless it is shown that the falsehood was made with "actual malice". See *The New York Times Company* v. *Sullivan* (1964), 84 S. Ct. 710, 376 US 254. Admittedly, even this standard may not be without its problems. See Lyle Denniston, "The Burger Court and the Press", in Herman Schwartz, ed., *The Burger Years* (New York: Elisabeth Sifton Books, 1987), pp. 23 ff.

For more detail on the Zundel and Keegstra trials, see "Holocaust survivor is accused of lying by Zundel lawyer", *Globe and Mail*, January 25, 1985, p. M4; "View of Belsen was propaganda, trial told", *Globe and Mail*, February 8, 1985, p. M1; Steve Mertl and John Ward, *Keegstra: The Trial, The Issues, The Consequences* (Saskatoon: Western Producer Prairie Books, 1985), pp. 92 ff.

Pages 40–41

For the Ontario Court of Appeal judgment, see *R*. v. *Zundel* (1987), 56 CR (3d) 1, 58 OR (2d) 129 (Ont. CA). The second Zundel trial took place during the winter and spring of 1988. In mid-May he was convicted again and sentenced to nine months in jail. A second appeal has since been launched. See "Jailed nine months, Zundel files appeal", *Globe and Mail*, May 14, 1988, p. A1.

Page 41

For the judgment of the Alberta trial court, see *R.* v. *Keegstra* (1984), 19 CCC (3d) 254 (Alta. QB). The Alberta Court of Appeal has ruled that the hate law violated the Charter guarantee of freedom of speech and has overturned Keegstra's conviction. See *R.* v. *Keegstra*, Alberta Court of Appeal, No. 17699, June 6, 1988. During July, however, the Ontario Court of Appeal in another case upheld the constitutionality of the anti-hate law. Appeals have been launched to the Supreme Court of Canada. See *R.* v. *Andrews and Smith*, Ontario Court of Appeal, Nos. 1010/85, 1047/85, July 29, 1988.

Page 42

Martin Luther King, Jr., talked about "constructive nonviolent tension" in his famous "Letter from Birmingham City Jail", reproduced in James Melvin Washington, ed., *A Testament of Hope: The Essential Writings of Martin Luther King, Jr.* (San Francisco: Harper & Row, 1986), 289, p. 291.

For more on the "Yankee Go Home" incident, see "Hate literature charges against 3 to be dropped", *Globe and Mail*, July 4, 1975, p. 1, and its editorial "A law full of dangers", July 2, 1975, p. 6.

The case involving the anti-French literature is *R.* v. *Buzzanga and Durocher* (1979), 49 CCC (2d) 369 (Ont. CA).

Page 43

Regarding the questionable investigations the anti-hate law has provoked, see "Library won't ban Leon Uris book that Arab groups have called racist", *Toronto Star*, September 26, 1984, p. A6; "Mandela film is screened for possible hate content", *Globe and Mail*, December 24, 1986, p. A14; and "U.S. movie incites hatred lawyer charges", *Sunday [Toronto] Star*, September 2, 1984, p. A17.

The words of Mr. Justice Quigley can be found in *R.* v. *Keegstra* (1984), 19 CCC (3d) 254 (Alta. QB), pp. 259-60.

Pages 43-44

The words quoted from the publication of the Law Reform Commission of Canada can be found in its *Hate Propaganda* (Working Paper 50) (Ottawa: Law Reform Commission of Canada, 1986), pp. 30, 31, and 39, respectively.

Page 44

See the "Brief of the Canadian Jewish Congress on Bill S-21 (Hate Propaganda) to the Senate Standing Committee on Constitutional and Legal Affairs", Ottawa, February 25, 1969. (The quote referred to will be found on pages 14–15.) The sole reference in the brief to the effect of such a law on non-Nazi speech is to the conviction of British black Muslim leader Michael X under the British Race Relations Act for publicly stirring up hatred against whites. Even assuming the Congress was right in describing that case as "a call to violence", it did not consider if such a law could be applied to groups like black power advocates where there was no such call to arms. See pp. 5–6 of its brief, and see "Bitter Attacks on Whites", *The [London] Times*, July 25, 1967, p. 1, and "Michael X Gets 12 Months", *The [London] Times*, November 10, 1967, p. 3.

Page 45

Because of the central flaw concerning the vagueness of the word "hatred", I did not specifically deal in the text with the provision that forbids the public communication of hatred in situations "where [it] is likely to lead to a breach of the peace" [Criminal Code, RSC 1985, c. C-46, s. 319 (1)]. The additional problem created by this provision is that it is broad enough to catch speakers not only for inciting their followers to violence against others but also for attracting the violence of others against themselves. There is a dangerous message here. The way to stop certain speakers is to threaten them with violence. If they decide to brave your threats, *they* might be guilty of an offence. Freedom of speech must not be allowed to rest on the fragile foundation of the "heckler's veto". See Henry Kalven Jr., "Trespass and the First Amendment", in his *The Negro and the First Amendment* (Chicago and London: University of Chicago Press, 1965), pp. 140 ff.

The view that Parliament delete "wilfully" from the Criminal Code, RSC 1985, c. C-46, s. 319 (2), was contained in the recommendations of a parliamentary committee. See Canada, House of Commons, *Minutes of Proceedings and Evidence of the Special Committee on Participation of Visible Minorities in Canadian Society*, No. 4, *Equality Now* (Ottawa: Queen's Printer, March 8, 1984), p. 70. The proposal was subsequently adopted by then Liberal justice minister Mark MacGuigan, who announced his intention to introduce such an amendment. See "Measures proposed to discourage spread of hate propaganda", *Globe and Mail*, June 2, 1984, p. 17.

Page 46

Regarding my hypothetical example of the native speaker who accuses whites of exploitation, contrary to the views of some, I am not persuaded that the native speaker could rely on the Criminal Code defence that "in good faith, he intended to point out, for the purpose of removal, matters producing or tending to produce hatred towards an identifiable group." In this example, the speaker's object is not the elimination of intergroup hatred, but the elimination of economic exploitation.

Amendments to the Criminal Code, removing the religious subject defence to a charge of promoting hatred, in RSC 1985, c. C-46 s. 319 (3) (b), have been advocated by a committee of the Canadian Bar Association and former Ontario attorney- general Roy McMurtry. See Canadian Bar Association, *Report of Special Committee on Racial and Religious Hatred*, July 1984, p. 13; "Give hate law some teeth, lawyer's committee urges", *Globe and Mail*, August 27, 1984, p. M1; and "Tough new laws needed to stop hate literature, McMurtry says", *Toronto Star*, August 28, 1984, p. A11. Even without this change, the anti-hate law might imperil groups like the Jehovah's Witnesses; with the change, the risk of conviction would increase for the kinds of anti-Catholic material they used to publish.

The Supreme Court of Canada dismissed the seditious libel charges against a Jehovah's Witness in *Boucher* v. *The King* (1950), 99 CCC 1, [1951] SCR 265. Praise for this decision will be found in F.A. Brewin, "Case Comment", (1951) 29 *Canadian Bar Review* 194, p. 202.

The parliamentary committee on visible minorities recommended that Parliament delete s. 281.2 (b) of the Criminal Code [now RSC 1985, c. C-46, s. 319 (b)], which requires the consent of a provincial attorney-general in order to institute a prosecution for promoting racial hatred. See its *Equality Now*, p. 70. This proposal was also adopted by then Liberal justice minister Mark MacGuigan, who announced his intention to introduce such an amendment. See "Measures proposed to discourage spread of hate propaganda", *Globe and Mail*, June 2, 1984, p. 17.

Regarding my example where hate charges are laid against Canadian Zionists, it should be acknowledged that a provincial attorney-general would have the power to stay such a charge. However, the mere laying of the charge can cause considerable anxiety, particularly if a lot of time elapses before the attorney-general acts, if indeed the attorney-general acts at all.

Page 47

The quotes from the Law Reform Commission of Canada will be found in its *Hate Propaganda* (Working Paper 50), p. 32.

Page 48

During the course of an exchange with me on CBC radio's "As It Happens" (June 1988), the able University of Calgary law professor Kathleen Mahoney argued that all the rights and freedoms in the Charter should be ranked equally; freedom of expression should not enjoy a priority position. On this basis, she argued for the constitutional validity of the anti-hate law despite the consequent infringements on free speech. In her view, the equality sections of the Charter should be entitled to no less deference than the sections on free speech. The trouble with her argument is that it ignores the strategic function that free speech plays in a democratic society. For the reasons I have indicated, *all* our rights and freedoms depend upon the existence of an effective right of dissent. Indeed, even the minorities whose interests Professor Mahoney properly champions are better served by having a viable right of protest than by not having one. Denying free speech its strategic role risks exposing everyone, including the vulnerable minorities, to repressive restrictions at the hands of a too-powerful state.

The comment of Rabbi W. Gunther Plaut can be found in "Prosecution in Zundel trial faced long odds", *Globe and Mail*, March 1, 1985, p. 15, as can be found the claim, in the testimony of Ditlieb Felderer, a so-called revisionist, that Auschwitz was recreational in character.

Royal Bank of Canada Vice-President John Burnett gave testimony for the Crown in the trial of Ernst Zundel, denying he was part of a Jewish conspiracy directing international Communism. See "Banker bemused at examination in Zundel trial", *Globe and Mail*, January 30, 1985, p. M1.

Mr. Zundel has been so pleased with the publicity his trial attracted that he is reported to be considering involvement in politics. See "Zundel plots his comeback and another run at politics", *Globe and Mail*, January 24, 1987, p. A10.

Page 49

The quotes referred to in the Cohen committee report can be found in Canada, House of Commons, *Report of the Special Committee on Hate Propaganda in Canada* (Ottawa: Queen's Printer, 1966), pp. 24 and 59, respectively.

Mr. Justice Quigley's approval of the Cohen committee analysis is in his judgment in *R.* v. *Keegstra*, (1984), 19 CCC (3d) 254, at p. 272.

The statement of Dr. Daniel G. Hill appeared in his testimony before a committee of Parliament. See Canada, House of Commons, *Minutes of Proceedings and Evidence Before the Standing Committee on External Affairs*, No. 36 (February 25, 1965), pp. 1746 ff.

Pages 49–50

The analysis of the state of Alberta's Social Credit Party is derived from 1984 federal election results published in "How Canada voted", *Globe and Mail*, September 5, 1984, p. 14.

Page 50

The background information on pre-Hitler Germany can be found in Ambrose Doskaw and Sidney Jacoby, "Anti-Semitism and the law in pre-Nazi Germany", *Contemporary Jewish Record* (1940), pp. 498–509, and Donald Niewyk, "Jews and the Courts in Weimar Germany", *Jewish Social Studies* (1975), pp. 99–113. At page 104 Niewyk discusses how some of the trials were used as platforms for the Nazi cause.

My opinion of this country's relative immunity to extremists is fuelled, at least in part, by a study conducted after the Zundel trial. See Gabriel Weiman and Conrad Winn, *Hate on Trial: The Zundel Affair, The Media, and Public Opinion in Canada* (Oakville, Ont.: Mosaic Press, 1986). Unfortunately, the authors attribute to me a position that I do not hold. Contrary to their impression, my objection to the Zundel and Keegstra trials did not include any fear that the hate-mongers would significantly increase their constituency. In addition to my concerns about the dangers to freedom of speech, the grounds on which I opposed the trials were that they amounted to a gratuitous obscenity, unworthy of public expense. See, for example, my article "Law used to prosecute Keegstra is 'dangerously vague'," *Toronto Star*, July 29, 1985, p. A8.

The Ontario Court of Appeal upheld the constitutionality of the false news section of the Criminal Code in *R.* v. *Zundel* (1987), 56 CR (3d) 1 (see especially pp. 28–29).

Page 52

The case in which a Jehovah's Witness was accused of spreading false news is *R.* v. *Carrier* (1951), 104 CCC 75 (Que. KB).

The case of the American who was convicted under the false news section is *R.* v. *Hoaglin* (1907), 12 CCC 226 (SC of NWT).

Page 53

For additional examples of arguments against our anti-hate laws, see the submission of Harry Arthurs before the Senate Standing Committee on Legal and Constitutional Affairs reprinted in "Hate Propaganda—an Argument against Attempts to stop it by legislation", (1970) 18 *Chitty's Law Journal* 1, and Walter Tarnopolsky, "Freedom of Expression v. Right to Equal Treatment", (1967) *U.B.C. Law Review* 43.

For a review of the events leading up to the dismissal of Jim Keegstra from his teaching post and subsequent loss in the mayoralty race, see Mertl and Ward, *Keegstra: The Trial, The Issues, The Consequences*, and David J. Bercuson and Douglas Wertheimer, *A Trust Betrayed: The Keegstra Affair* (Toronto: Doubleday Canada, 1985). It is important to note that Keegstra was dismissed from his teaching post in December 1982, before the case had gained any publicity, and that he lost his post as mayor of Eckville on October 17, 1983, before charges were laid on January 11, 1984.

Pages 53–54

Mary Brown's remarks were reported in "Censor attacks popular films for undermining social values", *Globe and Mail*, February 7, 1983, p. A5.

Page 54

The film *Last Tango in Paris* was the subject of a criminal prosecution in the Manitoba case of *R. v. Odeon Morton Theatres Ltd. and United Artists Corp.* (1974), 16 CCC (2d) 185 (Man. CA), and the children's educational book *Show Me* in the Ontario case of *R. v. Macmillan of Canada Ltd.* (1976), 31 CCC (2d) 286, 13 OR (2d) 630 (Ont. Co. Ct.).

Pages 54–55

Lady Chatterley's Lover was at issue in the case of *R. v. Brodie; R. v. Dansky; R. v. Rubin* (1962), 32 DLR (2d) 507, 132 CCC 161, [1962] SCR 681 (SCC), reversing [1961] Que. QB 610, and *Fanny Hill* was the subject of *R. v. C. Coles Co. Ltd.,* [1965] 1 OR 557 (Ont. CA), reversing (1964), 42 CR 368 (Ont. Co. Ct.).

Page 55

In fact, even when a distributor gets approval from the Prohibited Importations Branch of Canada Customs to import a particular item, this will not, by itself, bar a prosecution for distributing obscene material. See *R. v. Metro News Ltd.* (1986), 56 OR (2d) 321 (Ont. CA) [leave to appeal to SCC refused November 6, 1986, 57 OR (2d) 638].

Pages 55–56

The legislation extending the definition of obscenity beyond sex was Bill C-51, An Act to Amend the Criminal Code, the Canada Evidence Act, and the Parole Act, 30th Parl., 3rd Sess., s. 18, introduced for first reading by former Liberal justice minister Mark MacGuigan on May 1, 1978. He later introduced a bill with a similar provision, Bill C-19, An Act to Amend the Criminal Code, 32nd Parl., 2nd Sess., s. 36, introduced for first reading on February 7, 1984.

Page 56

See "Brief to the Special Committee on Pornography and Prostitution from the Executive of the National Action Committee on the Status of Women", February 1984, p. 3.

Page 57

See Ayn Rand's *The Fountainhead* (New York: New American Library, 1943), pp. 209 ff.

For more on the criminal law maxim that people are presumed to intend the natural consequences of their acts, see Glanville Williams, *The Criminal Law: The General Part* (London: Stevens & Sons Limited, 1953), pp. 705–06.

Page 57–58

The Lorenne M.G. Clark quote will be found in her testimony on behalf of the National Action Committee on the Status of Women, in Canada, House of Commons, *Minutes of Proceedings and Evidence of the Standing Committee on Justice and Legal Affairs*, No. 15 (March 7, 1978), p. 15:7. See also her article "Pornography's Challenge to Liberal Ideology", *Canadian Forum*, March 1980, pp. 9–12.

Page 58

The Susan G. Cole quote can be found in "In Bed with Whom?", *Broadside*, Vol. 3, No. 4 (February 1982), p. 5.

The Lynda Hurst quote will be found in "Time to regulate those who pollute minds", *Toronto Star*, January 27, 1984, p. B1.

Pages 58–59

Fortunately, the kind of material described here does not exhaust the feminist response to pornography and censorship. A number of feminists have argued persuasively and vigorously against the use of censorship. See, for example: Varda Burstyn, ed., *Women Against Censorship* (Vancouver and Toronto: Douglas & McIntyre, 1985); Varda Burstyn, "Porn Again", *Fuse*, Vol. X, No. 6 (Spring 1987), pp. 10–18; Thelma McCormack, "Comment on Pornography and Prostitution in Canada. Report of the Special Committee on Pornography and Prostitution", *Atlantis,* Vol. 13, No. 1 (Fall 1987), pp. 160–63; and Thelma McCormack, "The Censorship of Pornography: Catharsis or Learning?", *American Journal of Orthopsychiatry* (1988), in press.

Pages 59–60

For the relevant sections of the Fraser committee report, see Canada, *Report of the Special Committee on Pornography and Prostitution: Pornography and Prostitution in Canada* (Ottawa: Supply and Services, 1985), Volume 1: pp. 276–77, and Volume 2: p. 635.

Page 60

The first pornography bill from the Mulroney Conservative government was Bill C-114, An Act to Amend the Criminal Code and the Customs Tariff, 33rd Parl., 1st Sess., 1986, introduced for first reading on June 10, 1986, by then justice minister John Crosbie.

Page 61

The successor pornography bill was Bill C-54, An Act to Amend the Criminal Code and other Acts in consequence thereof, 33rd Parl., 2nd Sess., 1986–87, introduced for first reading on May 5, 1987, by Justice Minister Ray Hnatyshyn.

For a further elaboration of the definitions contained in Bill C-54 and the kinds of material that could be caught under them, see my article "Librarians have cause for porn bill concern", *Toronto Star*, November 21, 1987, p. 2.

Some of the classics that could run afoul of Bill C-54 include Aristophanes' speech in Plato's *The Symposium*; the tenth tale of the third day of *The Decameron* by Giovanni Boccaccio; and the *Satyricon of Petronius*. The books by modern-day clinicians that might be caught by Bill C-54 because they encourage masturbation by persons under eighteen include: Dr. Benjamin Spock, *Baby and Child Care*; rev'd. ed. (New York: E.P. Dutton, 1985); John V. Flowers, Jennifer Horsman, and Bernard Schwartz, *Raising Your Child to Be A Sexually Healthy Adult* (Englewood Cliffs, N.J.: Prentice Hall, 1982); and Howard R. and Martha E. Lewis, *Sex Education Begins At Home* (Norwalk, Conn.: Appleton-Century-Crofts, 1983).

I have quoted from senior Department of Justice lawyer Richard Mosley, who stated that it was "extremely unlikely to happen [that librarians would be prosecuted] because the police take direction on what is or is not pornographic from the provincial attorney-general and ultimately the courts." See "Libraries' fear of porn bill 'wrong', Ottawa says", *Toronto Star*, November 17, 1987, p. A2.

Page 62

Regarding the seizure of slides belonging to the Alberta Coalition Against Pornography, see "Anti-porn group target of seizure", *Globe and Mail*, October 17, 1987, p. A6, and "Police drop porn slides probe", *Calgary Herald*, October 21, 1987, p. B1. For more on censorship of *Not A Love Story* by the Ontario Censor Board, see "End film censorship now" [ed.], *Sunday [Toronto] Star*, September 20, 1981, p. C2. For more on the seizure of a film on male masturbation from the State University of New York, destined for the University of Manitoba medical school, see "Medical film ruled not porn", *Toronto Star*, October 26, 1983, p. C18, and *Re University of Manitoba and Deputy Minister, Revenue Canada, Customs & Excise* (1983), 4 DLR (4th) 658 (Man. Co. Ct).

For an account of some of the laboratory-based research on pornography and aggression, see Edward Donnerstein, "Aggressive erotica and violence against women", *Journal of Personality and Social Psychology,* Vol. 39 (1980), pp. 269–77; Neil Malamuth and James Check, "The Effects of Mass Media Exposure on Acceptance of Violence Against Women: A Field Experiment", *Journal of Research in Personality*, Vol. 15 (1981), pp. 436–46.

Page 63

For a study suggesting little relationship between on- and off-ice violence by hockey players, see Michael D. Smith, "Hockey Violence: A Test of the Violent Subculture Hypothesis", *Social Problems*, Vol. 27 (December 1979), pp. 235–47, and Michael D. Smith, *Violence in Canadian Amateur Sport: A Review of Literature* (Report to the Research Subcommittee of the Fair Play Commission, Fitness and Amateur Sport, Government of Canada, August 1987), pp. 29–36.

The comments of University of Toronto psychologist Professor Jonathan Freedman will be found appended to the brief of the Canadian Civil Liberties Association to the Fraser committee (April 6, 1984), p. 19. Professor Freedman has also reviewed lab- and field-research studies into the relationship of television violence on behaviour and has come to a similar conclusion. See "The Effect of Television Violence on Aggressiveness", *Psychological Bulletin*, Vol. 96 (1984), pp. 227–46, and "Television Violence and Aggression: A Rejoinder", *Psychological Bulletin*, Vol. 100 (1986), pp. 372–78.

A similar conclusion was reached by Canadian social scientists H.B. McKay and D.J. Dolff in *The Impact of Pornography: An Analysis of Research and Summary Findings* (Ottawa: Department of Justice Research and Statistics Section, Working Papers on Pornography and Prostitution, Report No. 13, 1984), p. 93. See also Thelma McCormack, "Making Sense of the Research on Pornography", in Varda Burstyn, ed., *Women Against Censorship*, pp. 181–205.

The 1986 U.S. Attorney General's Commission on Pornography, widely known as the Meese commission, on a budget a fraction the size of that enjoyed by the 1970 U.S. Presidential Commission on Obscenity and Pornography, concluded that pornography was "harmful" and should be outlawed. In order to arrive at this finding, the 1986 commission relied, in part, on the laboratory-based studies of Edward Donnerstein. See *Final Report of the Attorney General's Commission on Pornography* (Nashville: Rutledge Hill Press, 1986), ch. 18, and Hendrick Hertzberg, "Big Boobs", *The New Republic*, Vol. 195, Nos. 2, 3 (July 14 and 21, 1986), pp. 21–24. Donnerstein himself has stated that the commission's interpretation of the evidence seems "bizarre". For his comments, see "Researchers dispute pornography report on its use of data", *New York Times*, May 17, 1986, p. 1; Edward Donnerstein and Daniel Linz, "The Question of Pornography", *Psychology Today*, December 1986, pp. 56–59; and Edward Donnerstein, Daniel Linz, and Steven Penrod, *The Question of Pornography* (New York: The Free Press, 1987). See also Berl Kutchinsky, "Deception and Propaganda", *Society*, July/August 1987, pp. 21–24.

The Edward Donnerstein quote on attitudes and behaviour will be found in "The War Against Pornography", *Newsweek*, March 18, 1985, p. 62.

Page 64

Recommendations regarding the public display of pornography will be found in Canada, Law Reform Commission of Canada, *The Limits of Criminal Law Obscenity: A Test Case*(Working Paper 10) (Ottawa: Queen's Printer, 1979). The law could also appropriately regulate access to such material by children. While there could still be difficulties of definition even in regulating public display and access by children (and therefore issues of free speech could arise), they would not create the kind of problems involved in outright prohibition.

Irving Howe's views and quotes will be found in his comments on Murray Hausknecht, "The Problem of Pornography", *Dissent*, Spring 1978, 193, p. 205.

"Snuff" films are reportedly produced in South America and made available to select audiences at a high price. See Maureen O'Hara, "Rape Crisis Centres: Supporting and Informing", *Upstream*, Vol. 3, No. 3 (February 1979), p. 7.

Regarding the production and distribution of child pornography in Canada, see the Fraser committee, *Pornography and Prostitution in Canada*, Volume 2, p. 569. The committee found no evidence that child porn was being produced in Canada but it was making its way into Canada through direct-mail and regular-import channels. The U.S. Meese commission found that federal and state restrictions on child pornography had "effectively halted" its commercial production and "drastically curtailed its public presence" in the United States. See United States, *Final Report of the Attorney General's Commission on Pornography*, p. 134.

Page 65

Prior-restraint censorship exists in several provinces in Canada, including Ontario. See the Theatres Act, RSO 1980, c. 498, s. 35, as amended by SO 1984, c. 56, s. 13. The existence of prior-restraint censorship was recently challenged in Ontario but, having rescinded the decision of the Ontario Censor Board in the particular case, the Ontario Divisional Court declined to rule on the constitutionality of the legislation. See *Re Ontario Film and Video Appreciation Society and Ontario Film Review Board et al., Canadian Civil Liberties Association, Intervenor* (1986), 57 OR (2d) 339 (Ont. Div. Ct.).

Page 66

The "decline in U.S. tobacco consumption can be dated from 1964–65...the years immediately following the U.S. Surgeon General's first Smoking and Health report.... The beginning of a decline in tobacco consumption in Canada appeared in 1966–67." See Byran Rogers, Gordon Myers, and Neil E. Collishaw, "Trends in Tobacco Consumption in Seven Countries, 1950–84", in *Proceedings of the 34th International Congress on Alcoholism and Drug Dependence*, August 4–10, 1985, p. 521.

Donnerstein, Linz, and Penrod write that "exposure to violent materials coupled with debriefings will produce significant reductions in rape-myth acceptance...not only immediately, but the effects will remain 6 months later". See *The Question of Pornography*, p. 185.

CHAPTER THREE

Page 67

For a review of the events leading up to the sensational resignation of CSIS director Ted Finn, see "Security Chief resigns his post under pressure", *Globe and Mail*, September 12, 1987, p. A1.

Pages 67–68

I have quoted from the Security Intelligence Review Committee, *Annual Report, 1986–87* (Ottawa: Supply and Services, 1987), pp. 37, 39, and 40, respectively.

Page 68

Marc Boivin was strike organizer for Quebec's Confederation of Trade Unions (CNTU) for some fourteen years before it was disclosed that he was an RCMP and CSIS informer. For more on the charges against him and his guilty pleas, see "Unions resent infiltration by CSIS informers", Ottawa *Citizen*, October 3, 1987, p. B4; "CSIS not spying on unions, watchdog committee says", *Globe and Mail*, March 30, 1986, p. A4; and SIRC, *Section 54 Report to the Solicitor General of Canada on CSIS' Use of Its Investigative Powers with Respect to the Labour Movement*, March 25, 1988.

The illegal activities of the RCMP Security Service were chronicled in great detail by the McDonald commission and documented in its reports: Canada, Commission of Inquiry Concerning Certain Activities of the RCMP (the "McDonald commission"), *Freedom and Security Under the Law*, Second Report, and *Certain RCMP Activities and the Question of Governmental Knowledge*, Third Report (Ottawa: Supply and Services, 1981); and in Jeff Sallot, *Nobody Said No* (Toronto: James Lorimer & Company, 1979).

The following represent some of the sources of the information regarding the targets of RCMP surveillance: for the Canadian Union of Public Employees ("RCMP hired people to spy on unions, leaders in 1960's, CLC charges", *Globe and Mail*, January 19, 1978, p. 3); for the former Waffle faction of the New Democratic Party ("RCMP probed NDP for communist infiltration", *Globe and Mail*, August 25, 1977, p. 1, and McDonald commission, *Freedom and Security Under the Law*, Second Report, Volume 1, pp. 478–84); for the Parti Québécois (McDonald commission, *Transcripts*, Vol. 100 [March 15, 1979], pp. 15970–73, and *Freedom and Security Under the Law*, Second Report, Volume 1, pp. 453–65); for the National Farmers Union (McDonald commission, *Transcripts*, Vol. 116 [April 5, 1979], pp. 17893–94); for the National Black Coalition (McDonald commission, *Transcripts*, Vol. 115 [April 4, 1979], p. 17773). I have quoted from the McDonald commission testimony of former solicitor-general Warren Allmand in which he also confirms that he turned over to the commission the names of a number of RCMP targets he considered inappropriate (McDonald commission, *Transcripts*, Vol. 115 [April 4, 1979], pp. 17765–66, and Vol. 116 [April 5, 1979], p. 18009, respectively).

Pages 68–69

The infiltration and disruption tactics employed by the American Federal Bureau of Investigation (FBI) against American citizens involved in legal and peaceful political activities are reported in detail in U.S. Senate, Select Committee to Study Governmental Operations with Respect to

Intelligence Activities, *Final Report, Book II: Intelligence Activities and the Rights of Americans* (Washington, D.C.: U.S. Government Printing Office, 1976). The same report documents the FBI's "neutralizaton" campaign against Dr. Martin Luther King (pp. 219–23).

Page 69

Regarding the revelations that Britain's national security agency, M.I.5, had attempted to "sabotage" the Labour government of Prime Minister Harold Wilson, see "Pressure grows in U.K. for spy agency inquiry", *Globe and Mail*, May 5, 1987, p. A10. Regarding Australia, see the Royal Commission on Intelligence and Security, *First Report, Second Report, Third Report: Abridged Findings and Recommendations*, and *Fourth Report* (2 vols.) (The Hon. Mr. Justice R. M. Hope, Commissioner) (Canberra: Australian Government Publishing Service, 1976 and 1977). Regarding the findings that the Israeli security service, Shin Bet, had obstructed justice, see "Scandal rocks Israeli secret service", *Toronto Star*, May 26, 1987, p. A3. See "France admits agents sank Greenpeace ship", *Toronto Star*, September 23, 1985, p. A1, regarding French secret-service activities against Greenpeace.

Following, in part, upon the recommendations of the McDonald commission, the Canadian Parliament passed into law the Canadian Security Intelligence Service Act, RSC 1985, c. C-23.

Page 70

For a discussion of the lack of "civilianization" in CSIS, see SIRC, *Annual Report: 1986–87*, pp. 42 ff.

See the comments of Professor Peter Russell in "Reported switching of ministers blamed for security tensions", *Toronto Star*, September 16, 1987, p. A13. His remarks were made in the context of a discussion regarding the tensions between CSIS and the RCMP. There were allegations that the RCMP would not grant CSIS access to the Canadian Police Information Centre and that CSIS was not quickly enough turning over to the RCMP evidence of unlawful acts. This could qualify as yet another of the controversies plaguing the new agency. For more on this, see SIRC, *Annual Report: 1986–87*, pp. 14–15 and 27–29.

Page 71

The source of the quotation on terrorism and the need for an early warning is Paul Wilkinson, *Terrorism and the Liberal State* (Toronto: Macmillan of Canada, 1977), p. 135. It was quoted by the McDonald commission in *Freedom and Security Under the Law*, Second Report, Volume 1, p. 436.

Page 72

For the SIRC quote on the Quebec CSIS informant, see *Section 54 Report to the Solicitor General of Canada on CSIS's Use of its Investigative Powers with Respect to the Labour Movement*, March 25, 1988, p.14.

Page 73

Former RCMP commissioner Robert Simmonds testified before the McDonald commission that, although for administrative and disciplinary purposes the security service was subject to the control of divisional commanders, security service operations were centralized and split from the rest of the force. See *Freedom and Security Under the Law*, Second Report, Volume 2, p. 684.

The statement attributed to a former FBI director was made by Clarence Kelly and is quoted by John T. Elliff in *The Reform of FBI Intelligence Operations* (Princeton, N.J.: Princeton University Press, 1979), p. 77.

The FBI scandals that emerged some seven years after the reform of its intelligence operations involved certain dubious investigations of groups sympathetic to the rebels in El Salvador. From preliminary reports, it appears that the investigations involved informants, rather than techniques such as wiretapping, which American law may well not permit in these circumstances. While I suggest that the FBI compares favourably to CSIS in a number of respects, the situation in the United States is nevertheless less favourable in others. Unlike the provisions for CSIS, the FBI mandate is not now statutory. Thus, it can be (and has been) readily changed by presidential or attorney-general directive. Under President Reagan, the FBI guidelines became broader than they had been under presidents Carter and Ford. The guidelines under which the above investigations were conducted are in the counter-intelligence rather than in the domestic arena and are partly classified. Moreover, the congressional committees that monitor the FBI do not have as much access to secret material as SIRC does in the case of CSIS. Although the FBI is far from what it should be, it appears to be functioning better (or less badly) than it did before the reforms of the 1970s. See "FBI again called lax on liberties", *New York Times*, January 31, 1988, p. E5; "FBI's chief says surveillance was justified", *New York Times*, February 3, 1988, p. 1; and Jerry Berman, "FBI spies on Central American protestors", *Civil Liberties* No. 363 (March 1988), p. 1. For more on the standards for FBI domestic security investigations, see John T. Elliff, "The Attorney General's Guidelines for FBI Investigations", (1984) 69 *Cornell Law Review* 785.

Pages 75-76

I have referred consecutively to sub-sections 2 (b), (c), and (d) of the CSIS act, defining "threats to the security of Canada."

Page 76

I have quoted from SIRC, *Annual Report: 1986–87*, p. 37.

The advisory team established by the government on the heels of SIRC's 1986–87 report concluded, after studying CSIS counter-subversion operations, that "the service applies too many resources in this area". The team suggested that the counter-subversion branch be discarded. See Report to the Solicitor General by the Independent Advisory Team on CSIS, *People and Process in Transition* (Ottawa: Solicitor General of Canada, 1987), p. 23. The solicitor-general accepted these recommendations, eliminating the counter-subversion branch and assigning its activities to either the counter-intelligence or counter-terrorism branches of CSIS. See "Spy service to undergo major shakeup," *Globe and Mail*, December 1, 1987, p. A1.

Page 77

The quotation from the GAO audit of the FBI is found in U.S. Senate, Select Committee to Study Governmental Operations with Respect to Intelligence Activities, *Final Report, Book II: Intelligence Activities and the Rights of Americans*, p. 19, fn. 108. The GAO audit can be found in U.S. Senate, Report to the House Committee on the Judiciary by the Comptroller General of the United States, *FBI Domestic Intelligence Operations—Their Purpose and Scope: Issues That Need to Be Resolved* (Washington, D.C.: GAO, February 24, 1976), pp. 138–47.

The confirming quote attributed to a member of the U.S. Senate Intelligence Committee can be found in the "Additional Views of Senator Philip A. Hart", U.S. Senate, Select Committee to Study Governmental Operations with Respect to Intelligence Activities, *Final Report, Book II*, p. 359.

The confirming quote attributed to a former White House official appeared in the testimony of Joseph Califano before the U.S. Senate Intelligence Committee and is cited in U.S. Senate, Select Committee to Study Governmental Operations with Respect to Intelligence Activities, *Final Report, Book II*, p. 19.

For the reference to the U.S. bugging power against foreign influences, see the Foreign Intelligence Surveillance Act of 1978, 50 U.S.C. §1801, 101 (b) (2) (B). For a somewhat less stringent (but still demanding) standard against other foreign threats, see §1801 (b)(2)(B). See also John T. Elliff, *The Reform of FBI Intelligence Operations*, pp. 155–56.

It was in *United States v. United States District Court* (1972), 407 U.S. 297 (commonly referred to as the *Keith* decision) that the U.S. Supreme Court invited the U.S. Congress to consider legislating broader bugging powers for domestic intelligence purposes than those available for criminal law purposes. Since this case, electronic bugging against domestic security threats has been conducted entirely under the authority of the regular criminal law in title III of the Omnibus Crime Control and Safe Streets Act, 18 U.S.C. §2516 (1968).

Page 78

It has been argued with some persuasiveness that CSIS should be allowed to use intrusive surveillance to investigate certain forms of foreign-influenced activities even if illegality is not in evidence. The proponents of this position point, for example, to the attempts of the Soviet Union and other hostile powers to influence developments in the democracies through the deployment of clandestine agents whose conduct might well be lawful but is nevertheless harmful.

The Americans have resolved this problem through the enactment of legislation that requires agents of foreign powers to register with the U.S. government. In this way, these agents are denuded of their clandestine character. On the basis of this provision, some civil libertarians might be persuaded to accept intrusive surveillance of foreign agents who failed to register. While I have not yet resolved whether I am in favour of such compulsory registration, I am reluctant to render Canadian citizens and permanent residents vulnerable to intrusive surveillance on the basis of the definitions of "foreign influence" in the CSIS Act. This definition creates too great a risk of exposing our citizens and permanent residents in situations where no real security threats are involved. In any event, if conduct is not considered sufficiently adverse to our interests to warrant a legal prohibition, there is a real question whether it should suffice to trigger intrusive surveillance. For the American legislation, see the Foreign Agents Registration Act of 1938, 22 U.S.C. §611–21.

Professor Ira S. Shapiro in "Foreign Intelligence Surveillance Act: Legislative Balancing of National Security and the Fourth Amendment", (1977) 15 *Harvard Journal on Legislation* 119, p. 173, reports that both former U.S. attorney- general Griffin Bell and former FBI director Clarence Kelly have noted that, in the U.S., significantly higher proportions of foreign visitors than Americans are involved in spying activities on behalf of foreign powers.

Page 79

I have referred to the conflicting recommendations of the Pitfield committee. See Senate of Canada, Report of the Special Committee of the Senate on the Canadian Security Intelligence Service, *Delicate Balance: A Security Intelligence Service in a Democratic Society* (Ottawa: Supply and Services, 1983), pp. 22 and 19, respectively. See also McDonald commission, *Freedom and Security Under the Law*, Second Report, Volume 1, p. 580, where the commission had earlier declined to adopt such a distinction.

Pages 79–80

The American statistics on electronic bugging were computed by Herman Schwartz from data supplied by the U.S. Justice Department. See Herman Schwartz, *Taps, Bugs, and Fooling the People* (New York: The Field Foundation, 1977), p. 38.

For comparable Canadian material, see Solicitor General of Canada, *Annual Report as Required by the Criminal Code of Canada Section 178.22, 1978*, p. 4, and *Annual Report as Required by the Criminal Colde of Canada Section 178.22, 1983*, p. 4; Solicitor General of Canada, *Annual Report Required by Section 16 (5) of the Official Secrets Act, 1978*, p. 1, and *Annual Report Required by Section 16 (5) of the Official Secrets Act, 1983*, p. 1, respectively.

Page 80

The statement attributed to Morton Halperin was made on April 24, 1974, before a House of Representatives judiciary sub-committee and reported in the Prepared Statement of Congressman Robert F. Drinan before the U.S. Senate Select Committee on Intelligence. See U.S. Senate, Subcommittee on Intelligence and the Rights of Americans of the Select Committee on Intelligence, *Hearings: Electronic Surveillance Within the United States for Foreign Intelligence Purposes*, 94th Cong., 2nd Sess. (Washington, D.C.: U.S. Government Printing Office, 1976), p. 113.

Former U.S. attorney-general Ramsey Clark made his statement on electronic surveillance in 1972, at hearings on warrantless surveillance before the U.S. Senate Administrative Practices and Procedures Subcommittee. I first saw this quote in Schwartz, *Taps, Bugs, and Fooling the People*, p. 39. See also U.S. Senate, *Hearings: Electronic Surveillance Within the United States for Foreign Intelligence Purposes*, p. 160.

The quote attributed to FBI director J. Edgar Hoover (actually, his comments were found scribbled in the margin of a 1965 memorandum regarding a U.S. Senate subcommittee investigation) is reproduced in John T. Elliff, *The Reform of FBI Intelligence Operations*, p. 41.

Pages 80–81

The recommendation by the late William F. Sullivan, former assistant to J. Edgar Hoover for Intelligence, is cited by Schwartz in *Taps, Bugs, and Fooling the People*, p. 40, as is the quote attributed to Richard Nixon, while talking to John Dean on February 28, 1973 (p. 39).

Page 81

The reference to the ordinary Canadian law on electronic bugging can be found in the Criminal Code, RSC 1985, c. C-46, ss.183–188.

Page 82

For the mail opening power, see the CSIS Act, s. 21(3). For the McDonald commission view about the "marginal" value of RCMP mail opening, see *Freedom and Security Under the Law*, Second Report, Volume 1, p. 575.

Page 84

For the power in government agencies to disclose personal information to other government agencies, see the Privacy Act, RSC 1985, c. P-21, s. 8 (2) (e). This provision is subject to the confidentiality provisions in statutes such as the Unemployment Insurance Act, RSC 1985, c. U-1, s. 96, and the Income Tax Act, S.C. 1970–71–72, c. 63, s. 241.

The CSIS Act, s. 21, authorizes the issuance of a judicial warrant to penetrate the sanctuaries of confidential information. But it does not apply to census information (see section 21(3) of the CSIS Act, which is subject to the Statistics Act, RSC 1985, c. S-19. This exemption followed upon the recommendations of the McDonald commission in *Freedom and Security Under the Law*, Second Report, Volume 1, p. 587).

Until the CSIS Act, there was no access to tax information unless it was needed to enforce the Income Tax Act itself or for certain court proceedings. At least in the latter case, I believe that tax-payers should have some opportunity to challenge the invasion of their records. See the Income Tax Act, s. 241 (3) (6).

For more on how the RCMP avoided the tax laws, see McDonald commission, *Freedom and Security Under the Law*, Second Report, Volume 1, pp. 222–35, 253–60.

Page 85

Sara Jane Moore was an FBI informer; she also attempted to assassinate former U.S. president Gerald R. Ford. See Christine M. Marwick, "The Government Informer: A Threat to Political Freedom", *First Principles*, Vol. 2, No. 7 (March 1977), p. 4, and see p. 3 for a report of FBI infiltration of the American Communist Party.

Page 86

It was in *Hoffa* v. *U.S.* (1966), 385 U.S. 293, p. 302, that the U.S. Supreme Court noted how the risk of betrayal exists in all conversation.

The McDonald commission explicitly declined to make recommendations allowing covert operatives to commit acts "otherwise criminal". Its position was based in part on the fact that difficult cases could be handled by the subsequent exercise of prosecutional discretion. Unfortunately, the commission made no recommendations regarding *how* such discretion should be exercised. See *Freedom and Security Under the Law*, Second Report, Volume 1, pp. 536–51, 658–64.

Page 87

RCMP informant Robert Toope infiltrated the extremist Western Guard Party and participated in the painting of swastikas on private property. See "Mounties planted him in Western Guard, painter tells jury", *Toronto Star*, November 23, 1977, p. A1, and "Broke law 100 times—informer", *Toronto Star*, November 24, 1977, p. A3. The case is discussed in Stanley Barrett, *Is God a Racist?* (Toronto: University of Toronto Press, 1987), p. 89.

The defence of entrapment has developed an extensive jurisprudence in the United States. See, for example, the decision of the U.S. Supreme Court in *Sorrells* v. *United States* (1932), 287 U.S. 435. For the Canadian situation, see Canada, Report of the Canadian Committee on Corrections, *Toward Unity: Criminal Justice and Corrections* (Ottawa: Queen's Printer, 1969), pp. 75–80, and McDonald commission, *Freedom and Security Under the Law*, Second Report, Volume 2, p. 1053. See also the dissent of Estey, J., in the Supreme Court of Canada case *Amato* v. *The Queen* (1982), 69 CCC (2d) 31, pp. 41 ff.

There has been some suggestion that a defence of entrapment may be contained in section 7 of the Charter. See the cases cited and discussion by Michael Stober, *Entrapment in Canadian Law* (Calgary: Carswell Legal Publications, 1985), pp. 190–91.

Page 88

For more on the number of security files, see McDonald commission, *Freedom and Security Under the Law*, Second Report, Volume 1, p. 521, and SIRC, *Annual Report: 1986–87*, pp. 22–23.

The quote on the dangers of government controlling personal information is in the American Civil Liberties Union submission on the National Intelligence Reorganization and Reform Act (s. 2525) presented to the U.S. Senate Committee on Intelligence, July 18, 1978, p. 37.

Page 89

The 1975 RCMP mandate referred to is the cabinet directive dated March 27, 1975. It is reproduced in McDonald commission, *Freedom and Security Under the Law*, Second Report, Volume 1, p. 75.

Operation Bricole, the RCMP Security Service break-in at the APLQ offices, was seen by the Mounties as an opportunity to disrupt one of the FLQ's allied groups, the Movement for the Defence of Political Prisoners of Quebec. See Sallot, *Nobody Said No*, p. 24.

In 1971 a superintendent of the RCMP Security Service drafted a communiqué in the name of the fictitious Minerva Cell of the FLQ, deriding Pierre Vallières's call to join the Parti Québécois. The officer's testimony regarding this incident can be found in McDonald commission, *Transcripts*, Vol. 65 (July 18, 1978), pp. 10593 ff. (regarding Exhibit D-26), and in "Faked note to keep terrorists out of PQ...", *Globe and Mail*, July 19, 1978, p. 9.

The RCMP "dirty trick" against the Trotskyists was disclosed in testimony before the Krever Commission into the Confidentiality of Health Records in Ontario and the McDonald commission. See Ontario, *Report of the Commission of Inquiry into the Confidentiality of Health Information*, Volume II, pp. 38–48, and "Security Service used secret medical data to write disruptive letters—Mountie to Krever", *Globe and Mail*, March 10, 1979, p. 1. See also McDonald commission, *Freedom and Security Under the Law*, Second Report, Volume 1, pp. 271–73.

Page 90

For the failure of FBI investigations to uncover criminal conduct among the Trotskyists, see U.S. Senate, Select Committee to Study Governmental Operations with Respect to Intelligence Activities, *Final Report, Book II*, p. 8.

American Trotskyists have since successfully sued the FBI and have been awarded $264,000 in damages. See "Target of FBI for 35 years, Marxists win damage suit", *Globe and Mail*, August 26, 1986, p. A11.

For confirmation that the RCMP officer and former solicitor-general Warren Allmand continued to endorse those dirty tricks, see McDonald commission, *Transcripts*, Vol. 65 (July 18, 1978), p. 10720, and Vol. 117 (April 6, 1979), p. 18281, respectively.

The internal RCMP memorandum referring to "disruption, coercion, and compromise" can be found in McDonald commission, *Transcripts*, Vol. 27 (March 6, 1978), p. 4394 (Exhibit D-1).

Page 91

The McDonald commission probed the question of ministerial knowledge of RCMP unlawful acts in its *Certain RCMP Activities and the Question of Governmental Knowledge*, Third Report (Ottawa: Supply and Services, 1981), Pt. III.

The quote of Pierre Trudeau on ministerial supervision of day-to-day police activity is from a press conference on December 9, 1977 (see "Trudeau: Keep politicians ignorant of police actions", *Globe and Mail*, December 12, 1977, p. 7). The transcript of the press conference is reproduced, in part, in J.L.l.J. Edwards, *Ministerial Responsibility for National Security* (Ottawa: Supply and Services, 1981), pp. 94–95.

Page 92

According to SIRC, no applications for judicial warrants have been turned down by the Federal Court, although "searching questions have been asked from the bench and conditions designed to protect individual rights have been imposed in the order granting the warrant." See SIRC, *Annual Report, 1986–87*, p. 9.

Pages 92–93

Regarding the nomination and tenure of SIRC members, see the CSIS Act, s. 34 (1) (2).

CHAPTER FOUR

Page 94

Reports on the Fort Erie drug raid of May 11, 1974, can be found in "115 hotel patrons stripped, searched in drug raid...", *Globe and Mail*, May 28, 1974, p. 1, and "Raid shows wide powers of police", *Globe and Mail*, May 29, 1974, p. 5. Regarding the amount of drugs found and persons charged, see "Sergeant ordered all women stripped in drug search", *Toronto Star*, July 23, 1974, p. A1, and "Man denies seeing drugs at his hotel", *Globe and Mail*, July 30, 1974, p. 1.

The commission's findings of fact and recommendations will be found in Ontario, *The Royal Commission on the Conduct of Police Forces at Fort Erie on the 11th May, 1974* (Toronto: Queen's Printer, 1975). On page 69 of the report, the commission described the raid as "foolish" and "unnecessary" but, on page 57, not unlawful.

Page 96

The cases in which the courts have used the Charter to reduce the police powers of search and seizure include the following: *R.* v. *Rao* (1984), 12 CCC (3d) 97, 40 CR (3d) 80, and *R.* v. *Noble* (1984), 16 CCC (3d) 146, 48 OR (2d) 643 (both Ont. CA).

Pages 96–97

Statistics regarding the number of persons convicted of criminal offences in cases where there was bugging, and the number of conversations bugged, in the United States between 1969 and 1970 will be found in Herman Schwartz, "Reflections on Six Years of Legitimated Electronic Surveillance", in Annual Chief Justice Earl Warren Conference on Advocacy in the United States, *Final Report: Privacy in a Free Society* (Boston: Roscoe Pound—American Trial Lawyers Foundation, 1974) 38, pp. 48 and 45, respectively. I use the years 1969–70 because it is unlikely that there will now be a significant number of additional convictions attributable to investigations conducted during those years. See also Herman Schwartz, *A Report on the Costs and Benefits of Electronic Surveillance—1972* (New York: ACLU Reports, March 1973).

Page 97

The percentage of bugged conversations in narcotics- and theft-related investigations in the United States between 1968 and 1973 that did not yield incriminating evidence will be found in U.S., National Commission for the Review of Federal and State Laws Relating to Wiretapping and Electronic Surveillance, *Electronic Surveillance Report* (Washington, D.C.: U.S. Government Printing Office, 1976), p. 4. See also Herman Schwartz, *Taps, Bugs, and Fooling People* (New York: The Field Foundation, 1977), pp. 26–31.

Among the materials that invoke organized crime to justify electronic bugging is William and Nora Kelly, *Policing in Canada* (Toronto: Macmillan of Canada, 1976), p. 397.

For a review of FBI activities against La Cosa Nostra beween 1966 and 1969, when electronic surveillance was temporarily stopped, see the testimony of former U.S. attorney-general Ramsey Clark in Canada, House of Commons, *Minutes and Proceedings of the Standing Committee on Justice and Legal Affairs*, No. 21 (July 5, 1973), p. 21:10.

The FBI declaration that 1968 was "a year of striking accomplishment against...La Cosa Nostra" will be found in U.S., *FBI Annual Report, Fiscal Year, 1968*, pp. 3–4. It was brought to my attention by Herman Schwartz in his "The Legitimation of Electronic Eavesdropping: The Politics of 'Law and Order' " (1969), 67 *Michigan Law Review* 455, p. 503.

Page 98

For the special tributes paid to New York and Chicago for their efforts against organized crime, see U.S., President's Commission on Law Enforcement and Administration of Justice, *The Challenge of Crime in a Free Society* (Washington, D.C.: U.S. Government Printing Office, February 1967), p. 198. This tribute was paid despite the fact that Illinois Revised Statutes, [1965] c. 38, s. 14-1, prohibited wiretapping at the time. This point was also brought to my attention by Schwartz in "The Legitimation of Electronic Eavesdropping: The Politics of 'Law and Order' ", p. 502.

The statement by one strike-force co-ordinator regarding the usefulness of electronic surveillance is quoted by Schwartz, "Reflections on Six Years of Legitimated Electronic Surveillance", in *Privacy in a Free Society*, p. 48. He was quoting from strike-force co-ordinator Edith Lapidus's *Eavesdropping on Trial* (Rochelle Park, N.J.: Hayden Book Co., 1974), p. 162.

The admission by Robert Blakey will be found in his separate concurring report in U.S., *Electronic Surveillance Report*, pp. 192–93, fn. 30.

See section 178.1 of the Criminal Code (now RSC 1985, c. C-46, s. 183) for the list of offences for which bugging could be authorized.

A telephone call threatening to kill, maim, wound, poison, or injure an animal or bird is an offence under the Criminal Code, s. 331 (now RSC 1985 c. C-46, s. 373). Until recently, that section was included in the list of criminal offences for which a wiretap may be authorized.

Page 98–99

Bill C-51, An Act to Amend the Criminal Code, 30th Parl., 2d Sess., 1976–77, s. 7 (1) (a), introduced for first reading on April 20, 1977, would have authorized a wiretap for any five-year offence. The proposed section was amended and passed to permit bugging for such offences involving an organized "pattern of criminal activity." Although this change was welcome, it does not dispel my concern about the needless expansion of police powers. See the Criminal Code, RSC 1985, c. C-46, s. 183.

Pages 99–100

Section 178.23 of the Criminal Code (now RSC 1985, c. C-46, s. 196) contains the requirement for the police to notify the target of their bugging within ninety days. Former justice minister Otto Lang is quoted in "Senate sends wiretap bill back to MPs, wants change", *Toronto Star*, December 14, 1973, p. 1.

Pages 99–100

Former justice minister Ron Basford introduced Bill C-83, An Act to Amend the Criminal Code, 30th Parl., 1st Sess., 1974–75–76, for first reading on February 24, 1976. Section 10 of the proposed legislation would have repealed section 178.23. The Liberal government then introduced Bill C-51, An Act to Amend the Criminal Code, 30th Parl., 2d Sess., 1976–77, for first reading on April 20, 1977. Section 12 of the bill [now s. 196 (3) (4) of the Criminal Code, RSC 1985, c. C-46] empowered the courts to extend the notification period from ninety days to a period not exceeding three years. Yet section 178.23 (2) (b) of the original wiretap laws empowered the courts to extend the notification period for a "determinate reasonable length of time." For a critique of Bill C-51 and an alternative solution, see the joint submissions of the Canadian Bar Association, Canadian Civil Liberties Association, and Criminal Lawyers' Association, "Amending the Protection of Privacy Act", to the Honourable Ron Basford, Minister of Justice, June 1, 1977.

Page 100

The Charter has been used to facilitate access by the accused to the sealed packet containing the material that authorized the wiretap. See, for example, *R.* v. *Martin* (1986), 32 CCC (3d) 257 (Ont. HCJ). For a contrary view in British Columbia, see *Re Regina and Dersch et al.* (1987), 36 CCC (3d) 435 (BCCA) (appeal pending before the Supreme Court of Canada). See also the pre-Charter case of *Re Zaduk and the Queen* (1979), 46 CCC (2d) 327 (Ont. CA).

Pages 100–01

See *Electronic Surveillance* (Working Paper 47), (Ottawa: Law Reform Commission of Canada, 1986), p. 10, for a comparison of the numbers of Canadian and U.S. wiretap authorizations.

Page 101

Section 178.22 of the Criminal Code (now RSC 1985, c. C-46, s. 195) requires annual reports on the bugging activities of law enforcement authorities.

Page 102

See Commission of Inquiry Concerning Certain Activities of the RCMP (the "McDonald Commission"), *Freedom and Security Under the Law*, Second Report, Volume 1 (Ottawa: Supply and Services, 1981), pp. 203–09, for a detailed review of the RCMP's centralized decision-making for illegal mail opening (code name "Cathedral").

See the comments of then prime minister Pierre Trudeau with respect to "Cathedral," as reported in Jeff Sallot, *Nobody Said No*, (Toronto: James Lorimer & Company, 1979) pp. 131–32.

The mail opening bill was Bill C-26, An Act to Amend the Criminal Code, Crown Liability Act and the Post Office Act, 30th Parl., 3d Sess., 1977–78, introduced for first reading on February 7, 1978.

For the views of Robert Kaplan on mail opening, see "Rights group attacks Kaplan on mail issue", *Montreal Gazette*, April 23, 1980, p. 12. Kaplan also stated, in a letter dated June 6, 1980 to the CCLA that "in principle I am in favour of such [mail opening] power being given to the RCMP."

A broad mail opening power has been proposed in the Police Powers Project of the Ministry of the Solicitor General and the Ministry of Justice, *Powers and Procedures with Respect to the Investigation of Criminal Offences and the Apprehension of Criminal Offenders* (Discussion Paper for Consultation, Government of Canada, September 15, 1986), p. 4. It was proposed that mail opening be permitted for law enforcement purposes, subject to the Criminal Code's search-and-seizure regime.

See also the McDonald commission recommendations in *Freedom and Security Under the Law*, Second Report, Volume 2, p. 1025.

Page 103

The testimony of Chief Inspector T.S. Venner regarding mail opening can be found in the McDonald commission, *Transcripts*, Vol. 18 (February 1, 1978), pp. 2818–19.

Page 104

The case in which the custodial statement revealed the location of the murder weapon is *R. v. Wray*, [1970] 4 CCC 1, [1971] SCR 272, 11 DLR (3d) 673 (SCC).

For a recent development in which it has been suggested that the judgment in the *Wray* case is no longer applicable because of the advent of the Charter, see *R.* v. *Woolley*, Ontario Court of Appeal, No. 986/86, April 5, 1988.

Page 106

For the guarantees of the right to counsel, see s. 2 (c) (ii) of the Canadian Bill of Rights, RSC 1985, App. III, and s. 10 (b) of the Canadian Charter of Rights and Freedoms.

The results of the CCLA surveys into the experience of arrested people can be found in the following CCLA briefs: "Submissions to the Justice Policy Secretariat of Ontario, Re: The Effective Right to Counsel in Ontario Criminal Cases", Toronto, November 13, 1972; "Submissions to Task Force on Policing in Ontario", Toronto, September 21, 1973, p. 4; "Submissions to the Task Force on Legal Aid", Toronto, May 1, 1974, pp. 1–4; and "Submissions to the Royal Commission into Metro Toronto Police Practices", Toronto, January 14, 1976, pp. 9–10.

See *R.* v. *Mannien* (1987), 34 CCC (3d) 385, 76 NR 198, for an important indication of how the Supreme Court of Canada is prepared to vindicate the Charter guarantee of the right to counsel.

Page 107

Statistics regarding the number and result of criminal charges and civil suits against the Metro Toronto Police between 1969 and 1973 can be found in Arthur Maloney, QC, *The Metropolitan Toronto Review of Citizen–Police Complaint Procedure: Report to the Metropolitan Board of Commissioners of Police*, May 12, 1975, pp. 35–42. See also Ontario, *The Royal Commission into Metropolitan Toronto Police Practices* (The Hon. Mr. Justice Donald R. Morand, Commissioner), (Ontario, June 30, 1976), p. 181.

Page 108

Surveys conducted by the CCLA indicating the reluctance of accused people to complain about police misconduct will be found in Canadian Civil Liberties Education Trust, *Due Process Safeguards and Canadian Criminal Justice* (Toronto: CCLET, October 1971), pp. 32 and 74; and in CCLA, "Submission to Arthur Maloney, QC, Re: Metropolitan Toronto Review of Citizen–Police Complaint Procedures", Toronto, October 17, 1974, pp. 5–6.

Recommendations that the investigative function in the complaints process be carried out by police personnel can be found in Arthur Maloney, QC, *The Metropolitan Toronto Review of Citizen–Police Complaint Procedure: Report to the Metropolitan Toronto Board of Commissioners of Police*, May 12, 1975, pp. 211–13; Ontario, *The Royal Commission into Metropolitan Toronto Police Practices* (The Hon. Mr. Justice Donald R. Morand, Commissioner), p. 187; and

Canada, *The Report of the Commission of Inquiry Relating to Public Complaints, Internal Discipline and Grievance Procedure within the Royal Canadian Mounted Police* (Judge René J. Marin, Chairman) (Ottawa: Information Canada, 1976), p. 85.

The investigations for the McDonald commission and the Morand commission were conducted by investigators independent of the RCMP and Metro Toronto Police, respectively. See McDonald commission, *Freedom and Security Under the Law*, Second Report, Volume 1, pp. ix–x, and Ontario, *The Royal Commission into Metropolitan Toronto Police Practices*, p. ix.

Page 109

For a review of the American experience with civilian review boards, see Robert W. Olsen, "Grievance Response Mechanisms for Police Misconduct", (1969) 55 *Virginia Law Review* 909, and Algernon D. Black, *The People and the Police* (New York: McGraw-Hill, 1968).

Civilian complaints regarding the RCMP are governed by the RCMP Public Complaints Commission and in Toronto by the Office of the Public Complaints Commissioner. See An Act to Amend the Royal Canadian Mounted Police Act and other Acts in Consequence thereof, SC 1986, c. 11, s. 15 (Pts. VI & VII), and the Metropolitan Toronto Police Force Complaints Act, 1984, SO 1984, c. 63.

In Manitoba, unlike the federal and Toronto schemes, the new civilian complaints system provides not only for external review but also for external investigation. However, in its first annual report the agency states that it has started out as only a two-person operation, with occasional part-time investigative services provided by the Attorney-General's Law Enforcement Services Branch. See the Law Enforcement Review Act, CCSM, c. L75, and Manitoba, Law Enforcement Review Agency, *Annual Report, 1985* (Winnipeg, Man.), p. 7.

For details on the officer who was "cold shouldered", see "Police ostracized fellow officer who blew whistle, assault trial told", *Toronto Star*, May 30, 1987, p. A3, and "No one forced constable to quit job, officers say", *Toronto Star*, June 26, 1987, p. A2.

Page 110

The statement of the Ontario Crown Attorney will be found in "Police lawbreaking remark not meant, Crown asserts", *Globe and Mail*, December 6, 1979, p. 5.

Several empirical studies in the United States have attempted to assess the deterrent effects of the exclusionary rule on police behaviour. See, for example, Dallin Oaks, "Studying the Exclusionary Rule in Search and Seizure", (1970) 37 *University of Chicago Law Review*, 665; James Spiotto, "Search and Seizure: An Empirical Study of the Exclusionary Rule and Its Alternatives", (1973) 2 *Journal of Legal Studies* 243; Bradley Canon, "Testing the Effectiveness of Civil Liberties Policies at the State and Federal Levels: The Case of the Exclusionary Rule", (1977) 5 *American Politics Quarterly* 57; and Bradley Canon, "Is the Exclusionary Rule in Failing Health? Some

New Data and a Plea Against a Precipitous Conclusion", (1974) 62 *Kentucky Law Journal* 681. Mr. Justice Blackmun, writing for the U.S. Supreme Court in *United States* v. *Janis* (1976), 428 U.S. 433, pp. 450–53, concluded, after reviewing various empirical studies, that the evidence remains inconclusive. But see the views of the late U.S. Supreme Court Justice Potter Stewart in "The Road to *Mapp* v. *Ohio* and Beyond: The Origins, Development and Future of the Exclusionary Rule in Search-and-Seizure Cases", (1983) 83 *Columbia Law Review* 1365, p. 1395. He concluded that the rule has had a "tremendous impact on police practices." That view is shared by Professor Yale Kamisar in "The 'Police Practice' Phases of the Criminal Process and the Three Phases of the Burger Court", in Herman Schwartz, ed., *The Burger Years* (New York: Elisabeth Sifton Books, 1987), pp. 161–62, fn. 87. See also Yale Kamisar, "Does (Did) (Should) the Exclusionary Rule Rest on a 'Principled Basis' Rather Than an 'Empirical Proposition'?", (1983) 16 *Creighton Law Review* 565.

Page 111

For examples of some of the alarmist statements made by law enforcement authorities regarding Canada's adoption of an exclusionary rule in the Canadian Charter of Rights and Freedoms, see Roderick McLeod (then assistant deputy attorney-general of Ontario and spokesperson for the Canadian Association of Crown Counsel), "The pitfalls in Americanizing the Canadian criminal law", *Globe and Mail*, March 11, 1981, p. 7, and Canadian Association of Chiefs of Police, "Press Release Re: The Constitution Act, 1982, Pt. I, Canadian Charter of Rights and Freedoms". On page 3 of the press release, the association expresses its "concern lest the Canadian government blindly follow the American example, and enact legislation so protective of 'civil rights' that crime flourishes, while law enforcement is repeatedly emasculated."

Empirical studies of the costs of the exclusionary rule in terms of lost convictions indicate that the rule affects the outcome of very few prosecutions. A 1977 study of the effects of the rule on federal felony prosecutions conducted by the U.S. General Accounting Office found that only 1.3 per cent of the motions to suppress evidence were successful and, of these, convictions were obtained in one half of them. A total of 0.8 per cent of felony prosecutions were lost as a result of illegal searches, because of either prosecutorial discretion or court dismissal.

Another study looked at the effects of the exclusionary rules on physical evidence, confessions, and identification in 7,500 cases in three states. Professor Peter Nardulli found that successful motions to suppress physical evidence occurred in only 0.69 per cent of the cases, and successful motions to suppress confessions or identifications occurred even less often. Of all the cases, only 46 (less than 0.6 per cent) were lost because of one of the three exclusionary rules, and of these 46, most were in regard to offences attracting less than six months' imprisonment or involving first offenders. See Peter F. Nardulli, "The Societal Cost of the Exclusionary Rule: An Empirical Assessment", (1983) *American Bar Foundation Research Journal* 585. Thomas Davies has concluded that a careful review of these and other empirical studies shows "a fairly consistent picture of the low overall costs of the exclusionary rule." They consistently indicate that "*the general level of the rule's effects on criminal prosecutions is marginal at most.*" See

Thomas A. Davies, "A Hard Look at What We Know (and Still Need to Learn) About the 'Costs' of the Exclusionary Rule: The NIJ Study and Other Studies of 'Lost' Arrests," (1983) *American Bar Foundation Research Journal* 611, p. 622. Nardulli and Davies each summarize the 1977 GAO study, pp. 589 and 659–61, respectively.

For examples of how the exclusionary rule has resulted in certain contentious acquittals in the United States, see *Coolidge* v. *New Hampshire* (1971), 403 U.S. 443 (USSC), and *Brewer* v. *Williams* (1977), 430 U.S. 387 (USSC), both cited by Judge Malcom Wilkey in "The exclusionary rule: Why suppress valid evidence?", *Judicature*, Vol. 62, No. 5 (November 1978), 215, p. 219. Wilkey's article is part of an exchange with University of Michigan law professor Yale Kamisar on the exclusionary rule published in (1978) 62 *Judicature*, Nos. 2, 5, and 7.

See *Collins* v. *The Queen* (1987), 33 CCC (3d) 1, 38 DLR (4th) 508, 13 BCLR (2d) 1, for an example of how the Supreme Court of Canada interprets what would cause "disrepute" to the administration of justice.

Page 112

For examples of judicial reluctance to use the Diefenbaker Bill of Rights for excluding evidence obtained by violating the right to counsel, see *O'Connor* v. *The Queen,* [1966] SCR 619, [1966] 4 CCC 342, 57 DLR (2d) 123, and *Hogan* v. *The Queen* (1975), 18 CCC (2d) 65, [1975] 2 SCR 574, 48 DLR (3d) 427.

Page 112–13

For the way Scottish law protects arrested people, see Hardin, "Other Answers: Search and Seizure, Coerced Confession and Criminal Trial in Scotland", (1964) 113 *University of Pennsylvania Law Review* 165, pp. 171–72, and the following cases: *Chalmers* v. *HMA*, [1954] SLT 177; *Tongue* v. *HMA*, [1982] SLT 506; *Lord Advocates Reference No. 1 of 1983*, [1984] SLT 337.

The conviction rates in Scotland and Canada were favourably compared in Canada, Report of Canadian Commission on Corrections, *Toward Unity: Criminal Justice and Corrections* (Ottawa: Queen's Printer, 1969), p. 153.

Page 113

For some insights into how the *Miranda* case has affected police performance, see the following: R.H. Seeburger and R.S. Wettich, Jr., "Miranda in Pittsburgh: A Statistical Study", (1967) 29 *University of Pittsburgh Law Review* 1; Special Project, "Interrogation in New Haven: the Impact of Miranda", (1967) 76 *Yale Law Journal* 1519; and James W. Witt, "Non-Coercive Interrogation and the Administration of Criminal Justice: The Impact of Miranda on Police Effectuality", (1975) 64 *Journal of Criminal Law and Criminology* 320.

For limits the Supreme Court of Canada has placed on custodial interrogation as a result of the Charter, s. 10 (b), see, for example, *Clarkson* v. *The Queen* (1986), 25 CCC (3d) 207, 26 DLR (4th) 493, and *R.* v. *Mannien* (1987), 34 CCC (3d) 385, 76 NR 198.

Page 113–14

For the limits on an Ontario police officer's right to appeal disciplinary measures, see The Police Act, RSO 1980, c. 381, and RRO 1970, Reg. 680, s. 16 (15) and s. 20 (3).

CHAPTER FIVE

Page 115

Reports of the simultaneous raids of four downtown Toronto steambaths on the night of February 5, 1981, will be found in "Police arrest hundreds in steambaths", *Toronto Star*, February 6, 1981, p. 1. As a result of the raids, more than three hundred men were arrested as "found-ins" and fewer than twenty-five were charged with keeping a bawdy house.

For some details on the press conferences, demonstrations, meetings, and rallies, see "Protests mount over police raids on homosexuals", *Toronto Star*, February 10, 1981, p. A3, and "Meeting on police raids ends noisily", *Toronto Star*, February 13, 1981, p. A3.

The Canadian Civil Liberties Association wrote to Attorney-General and acting Solicitor-General Roy McMurtry (letter dated February 9, 1981), asking that he set up an independent inquiry into the raids. See "Independent inquiry sought on bath raids", *Globe and Mail*, February 10, 1981, p. 5. The CCLA followed up this request with a delegation to the solicitor-general on February 24, 1981.

The Toronto City Council passed a supporting motion, eleven votes to nine, calling on the solicitor-general to set up an independent inquiry into the bathhouse raids. See "Toronto Council wants probe of police raids on bathhouses", *Globe and Mail*, February 27, 1981, p. 1.

The Metro Police Commission refused to pass a similar motion and ultimately the solicitor-general refused. See "Inquiry on bathhouse raid rejected amid accusations", *Globe and Mail*, February 13, 1981, p. 1. The Toronto City Council followed up with a study of the gay community's problems with the police. See Arnold Bruner, *Out of the Closet: Study of Relations Between the Homosexual Community and the Police* (Toronto: City of Toronto, 1981).

Pages 115–16

The McMurtry explanation for the low conviction rate of bathhouse found-ins can be found in Ontario, Legislative Assembly, *Debates,* No. J-11 (October 20, 1983), p. J-256.

Page 116

The reported convictions resulting from the bathhouse raids will be found in "Toronto's bath-house raids leave legacy of bitterness", *Toronto Star*, January 20, 1983, p. A21.

Page 117

Statistics regarding the number of men arrested in Ontario by washroom video surveillance are derived, in part, from "St. Catharines: indecent exposure", *Body Politic*, March 1985, 7, p. 9. For a review of the types of local newspaper accounts the arrests and convictions attracted, see "Mall washroom blitz nets 33 arrests", *Body Politic*, March 1984, p. 13, and "Naming 'Names' ", *Body Politic*, March 1985, p. 9. For a discussion of how these mass arrests destroyed the lives of many of the individuals involved, see "It's hell, say their families", Kitchener-Waterloo *Record*, October 19, 1985, p. E1, and Kevin McMahon, "Tea for Thirty-Two", *This Magazine*, Vol. 19, No. 2 (June 1985), p. 26. In St. Catharines, a forty-two-year-old salesman committed suicide after being charged for a second time. See "Model citizen was a victim of his secret life", *Globe and Mail*, January 11, 1985, p. M1.

Typical of the reaction of certain police authorities at the time was that attributed to a community relations officer for the Guelph police: "When a criminal offence is committed, the law says we have to act on that." See "High-tech sex cops strike again", *Body Politic*, August 1985, p. 17.

Page 118

The investigation of Dudley Laws's speech is reported in "Police upset school, board", *Globe and Mail*, December 11, 1979, p. 5.

The quoted explanation for the investigation of Dudley Laws's speech is contained in a letter, dated February 1, 1980, from Mr. R.M. Parker, legal counsel to the Municipality of Metropolitan Toronto, to myself, on behalf of the Canadian Civil Liberties Association. The letter is appended to the CCLA's "Submission to the Metropolitan Toronto Board of Commissioners of Police", March 2, 1980.

Page 119

For details on the police press conference regarding the bombings, see "Daring ruse caught Litton suspects cold", *Toronto Star*, January 22, 1983, p. A1, and "5 charged in bomb attacks", *Vancouver Sun*, January 21, 1983, p. A1.

The mid-trial statement made by Ontario Attorney-General Roy McMurtry appears in "Nothing that I would not say again...", *Globe and Mail*, November 20, 1982, p. A5.

Pages 119–20

For more on the tensions arising from the Boise Cascade strike in the Kenora–Fort Francis area, see "Fort Francis police demoralized after a year of charging strikers", *Globe and Mail*, July 5, 1979, p. 48.

Page 120

Many of the Boise Cascade incidents were reported in detail to Roy McMurtry in a letter from the CCLA, dated August 15, 1979. The exchange of letters occurred between September 1979 and March 1980.

Page 121

Chrétien decided not to prosecute RCMP law-breakers and informed Solicitor- General Robert Kaplan of his decision by letter (dated July 20, 1982). That decision did not become public until some four months later. See "Ottawa quietly drops prosecution against Mounties", *Globe and Mail*, November 20, 1982, p. 1.

Page 122

Prosecutions of civilians for offences under the Income Tax Act have been based on events as old as the Mounties' misconduct. See *R. v. Plotnick* (1954), 55 DTC 1008, where the accused was charged with making a false statement in his income tax return twelve years earlier. Mr. Justice Theberge, at p. 1012, even cites an English prosecution in 1863 for the theft of a page from a parish register sixty years earlier.

For the material impugning the alleged legitimacy of RCMP mail opening, see Commission of Inquiry Concerning Certain Activities of the RCMP, *Freedom and Security Under the Law*, Second Report, Volume 1 (Ottawa: Supply and Services, 1981), pp. 203–09, and Jeff Sallot, *Nobody Said No* (Toronto: James Lorimer & Company, 1979), Ch. 7.

On the government action against CUPW President Jean Claude Parrot for defying the 1978 back-to-work law, see "Parrot ordered to recant on postal strike order", *Globe and Mail*, October 7, 1978, p. 1.

For the Ledain recommendation, see *Final Report of the Commission of Inquiry into the Non-Medical Use of Drugs* (Ottawa: Information Canada, 1973), p. 129. Despite the report's recommendations, more than 47,000 charges for simple possession of cannabis were laid in 1981 and more than 25,000 in 1986. See Statistics Canada, *Crime and Traffic Enforcement Statistics, 1981* (Canada: Supply and Services, 1982), p. 7, and Statistics Canada, *Canadian Crime Statistics, 1986* (Canada: Supply and Services, 1987), p. 7.

Page 123

The text of the November 1977 letter from the CCLA to Prime Minister Trudeau was published as a full-page advertisement in the *Globe and Mail*, November 19, 1977, p. 14. Trudeau replied by letter, dated December 9, 1977.

The Basford quote on RCMP wrongdoing and the McDonald commission will be found in Canada, House of Commons, *Debates*, January 31, 1978, p. 2384.

McGuigan expressly refused to prosecute RCMP wrongdoers in response to a delegation from the CCLA on January 25, 1983. See "Call for Watergate-style hearing into RCMP rejected", Ottawa *Citizen*, January 26, 1983, p. 4, and "Cover-up?", *Cape Breton Post*, January 31, 1983.

Pages 123–24

The Department of Mines and Resources for the Province of Manitoba, with the active concurrence of federal officials, sought to exempt Manitoba Indians from the operation of the Migratory Birds Convention Act, RSC 1970, c. M-12. A special "no-prosecution" policy was ultimately communicated in 1968 by the director of the Canadian Wildlife Service to his Manitoba counterpart, to the wildlife field staff, and to the vice-president of the Manitoba Indian Brotherhood. Notwithstanding this stated policy, the Crown successfully prosecuted a Manitoba Indian seven years later for an offence under the Migratory Birds Convention Act. This background information is contained in *R.* v. *Catagas* (1977), 38 CCC (2d) 296, reversing [1977] 3 WWR 706 (Man. CA).

Page 124

Disruptive tactics, such as the leaking of confidential psychiatric information about a leader of Canada's Trotskyist movement, were conducted under the RCMP code name "Operation Checkmate". These activities were disclosed in evidence before the Ontario Royal Commission of Inquiry into the Confidentiality of Health Records in Ontario and the McDonald commission. See Ontario, *Report of the Commission of Inquiry into the Confidentiality of Health Information*, Volume II (Ontario: Queen's Printer, 1980), pp. 38–48, and the McDonald commission, *Freedom and Security Under the Law*, Second Report, Volume 1, pp. 271–73.

The McMurtry quote regarding Dr. Henry Morgentaler can be found in Ontario, Legislative Assembly, *Debates*, No. J-15 (December 9, 1982), pp. J-311 and J-312.

124–26

The Ontario attorney-general's reasons for directing a stay of prosecution against the RCMP officers will be found in "Information Provided by Counsel for the Attorney General of Ontario to His Worship Justice of the Peace Allen", by M.G. Black, Crown counsel and agent of the attorney-general for Ontario, on October 30, 1980. He also directed a similar stay of proceedings on January 19, 1981, in respect of a prosecution launched by the Praxis Corporation against members of the RCMP. It was alleged that Mounties were in wrongful possession of materials from Praxis offices. See "Protection of police assailed", *Globe and Mail*, January 10, 1981, p. 5.

Page 126

The relevant declarations of the Nuremberg court can be found in *Judgment of the International Military Tribunal for the Trial of Major War Criminals, Nuremberg, 1946* (London: Cmd. 6964), pp. 3, 38.

Regarding the CLC's refusal to back the unlawful CUPW strike and the internal controversy it created, see "CLC faces showdown", *Toronto Star*, November 10, 1978, p. A1.

Page 128

Following upon a delegation from the CCLA to the Ontario solicitor-general on March 6, 1986, the Ontario Police Commission issued guidelines on washroom surveillance which achieve some of the objectives I advocate here. See a memorandum dated June 3, 1986, from Shawn McGrath, chairman of the Ontario Police Commission, to all chiefs of police, "Re: Video Surveillance of Public Washrooms to Apprehend Sexual Offenders". As well, the British Columbia Police Commission has urged the federal government to enact legislation to control the use of video surveillance. See "BC police body urges Ottawa to regulate video surveillance", *Globe and Mail*, January 14, 1987, p. A4. For judicial consideration of washroom video surveillance, see *R.* v. *Lofthouse* (1988), 62 CR (3d) 157, (Ont. CA), affirming (1986), 27 CCC (3d) 553 (Ont. Dist. Ct.).

For an interesting and more elaborate discussion of the whole issue of government discretion, see Kenneth Culp Davis, *Discretionary Justice* (Urbana: University of Illinois Press, 1971).

CHAPTER SIX

Page 131

Canada has taken an important step by enshrining in the Charter a provision that protects witnesses who provide self-incriminating evidence in one proceeding from having that evidence used against them in any other proceeding, "except in a prosecution for perjury or for the giving of contradictory evidence" (s. 13). It was thought at one time that this protection extended beyond prosecutions to even professional and employment discipline [see, for example, *Re Donald and the Law Society of British Columbia* (1983), 2 DLR (4th) 385 (BCCA)], but the Supreme Court of Canada has held that, for the purposes of police employment discipline, the Charter protection has no application (see *R.* v. *Wigglesworth* [1987], 60 CR [3d] 193 [SCC]). Regarding the application of this Charter protection in criminal proceedings, see *R.* v. *Mannien* (1986), 28 CCC (3d) 544,

31 DLR (4th) 712 (SCC). This type of protection is also available in a number of statutes, such as the Canada Evidence Act, RSC 1985, c. C-5, s. 5, and the Ontario Public Inquiries Act, RSO 1980, c. 411, s. 9.

Nurse Susan Nelles was charged with four counts of first-degree murder on March 25 and 27, 1981. On May 21, 1982, the Ontario Provincial Court ruled, after a lengthy preliminary hearing, that there was insufficient evidence to proceed to trial and discharged Ms. Nelles. See *R. v. Nelles* (1982), 16 CCC (3d) 97.

Pages 131–32

Mr. Justice Samuel Grange was appointed on April 23, 1983, to head up the Ontario Royal Commission of Inquiry into Certain Deaths at the Hospital for Sick Children. His terms of reference can be found in Ontario, Orders-in-Council 1076/83, dated April 21, 1983, and 1412/84, dated May 24, 1984.

Page 132

For a number of criticisms of the Grange commission, see the comments of the Canadian Civil Liberties Association as reported in "Baby probe is accused of ruining reputations", *Globe and Mail*, February 27, 1984, p. 1; Orland French, "Hearing gives one the shakes", *Globe and Mail*, February 14, 1984, p. 7; Dennis Braithwaite, "Probe nails nurses", *Toronto Sun*, April 15, 1984, p. 11; "Pointing fingers" [ed.] , *Toronto Sun*, February 15, 1984, p. 10; and "Toronto infant death inquiry stirs concern", *New York Times*, April 8, 1984, p. 21.

The judgment of the Ontario Court of Appeal precluding the commissioner from naming the responsible parties is contained in *Nelles et al.* v. *Hon. Mr. Justice Grange* (1984), 46 OR (2d) 210. This reversed the judgment of the Ontario Divisional Court, dated January 30, 1984. See also "Court rules Grange can't name names", *Globe and Mail*, April 13, 1984, p. 1.

Page 133

McMurtry's statement to the Ontario legislature regarding the appointment of the Grange commission will be found in Ontario, Legislative Assembly, *Debates*, No. 4 (April 22, 1983), pp. 92–98, and is reproduced, in part, in the Ontario Court of Appeal decision at (1984), 46 OR (2d) 210, p. 215.

Page 135

For the attempt of Mr. Justice Grange to clear Susan Nelles by recommending compensation be paid for her legal costs in defending the criminal charge against her, see Ontario, *Report of the Royal Commission of Inquiry into Certain Deaths at the Hospital for Sick Children* (December 29, 1984), pp. 221–22.

Page 136

For examples of the contentious testimony at the Grange inquiry, see "Nurse injected unidentified drug", *Globe and Mail*, February 8, 1984, p. 1, and "Threatening voice on phone sounded like Nelles, nurse says", *Toronto Star*, March 2, 1984, p. A1.

Pages 136–37

The CCLA attempted to gain standing and be represented by counsel at the McDonald commission of inquiry into the RCMP. That request was denied by the commission. See Commission of Inquiry Concerning Certain Activities of the RCMP, *Freedom and Security Under the Law*, Second Report, Volume 2 (Ottawa: Supply and Services, 1981), Appendix "E" (Reasons for Decision of the Commission, December 8, 1977), pp. 1169 ff.

Page 137

During the course of the hearings, counsel for the attorney-general for Ontario, supported by counsel for some of the nurses, moved that closing arguments relating to phase one of the inquiry be heard in camera, in order to avoid the inflammatory press reports that would likely follow the naming of names in argument. Commissioner Grange rejected the motion. See "Statement of Commissioner with Regard to Application to Hear Argument *In camera*", June 4, 1984, and "Not on a witch hunt, Grange lawyer says", *Toronto Star*, June 5, 1984, p. A2.

Page 138

The McDonald commission recommended that those parts of its report implicating members of the RCMP should be withheld from publication until there was a decision not to prosecute or proceedings against them had been concluded. See McDonald commission, *Certain RCMP Activities and the Question of Governmental Knowledge*, Third Report (Ottawa: Supply and Services, 1981), Part VIII, "Recommendations Concerning Publication of this Report", pp. 517 ff.

Page 138–39

Regarding the law of contempt of court *sub-judice*, see, for example, *A.G.* v. *Times Newspapers Ltd.*, [1973] 3 A11 ER 54 (H.L.).

Page 139

The Criminal Code, RSC 1985, c. C-46, s. 539, requires a court to order, upon application by an accused, a publication ban with respect to evidence taken at the preliminary inquiry.

Former Conservative MP Paul Dick introduced private bills before the House of Commons calling for amendments to the Criminal Code to ban the publication of the names of accused persons who are awaiting or undergoing trial, or have been acquitted, or have received an absolute discharge or pardon. See Canada, House of Commons, *Debates*, May 27, 1980, pp. 1458 ff., and *To Name or Not to Name* (Revised) (Ontario Press Council, 1981), pp. 21–26.

For the exchange between Lawrence Greenspon and Chief Justice Laskin, see "Supreme Court to consider argument...", *Globe and Mail*, December 21, 1983, p. 1.

Page 140

Regarding some of the rules of evidence in constitutional cases, see Brian G. Morgan, "Proof of Facts in Charter Litigation", in Robert J. Sharpe, ed., *Charter Litigation* (Toronto and Vancouver: Butterworths, 1987).

The Ontario Press Council forum "Trial by Media" was held on October 13, 1983. I was one of the panelists who received a copy of the lawyer's letter.

Page 141

The press conference convened by the accused alderman was reported in "...sex arrest made too hastily, supporters say", *Toronto Star*, September 21, 1983, p. A6.

Page 144

Regarding the investigation by Metropolitan Toronto police of a speech by Dudley Laws, see "Police upset school, board", *Globe and Mail*, December 11, 1979, p. 5.

The police raid of the Toronto Scientology centre is reported in "100 officers raid Scientology centre", *Globe and Mail*, March 4, 1983, p. 1. See also *R. v. Scientology; R. v. Zaharia* (1987), 30 CRR 238 (Ont. CA).

Pages 144–45

Regarding alleged RCMP surveillance of lawyer Clayton Ruby, see "Ruby's civil rights legal work led to RCMP surveillance", *Globe and Mail*, November 16, 1977, p. 5, and regarding surveillance of National Farmer's Union President Roy Atkinson, see McDonald commission, *Transcripts*, Vol. 116 (April 5, 1979), p. 17894. Regarding the other surveillance targets mentioned, see the note to Ch. 3, p. 68.

Pages 145–46

See my exchange with former justice Tom Berger regarding the government employment of members of the Communist party in A. Borovoy, "The Plight of Minorities", *Canadian Forum*, Vol. 62, No. 717 (April 1982), pp. 28–30; T. Berger, "The Constitution, The Charter and 'Fragile Freedoms' ", *Canadian Forum*, Vol. 62, No. 719 (June/July 1982), pp. 8–14; and A. Borovoy, "A Rejoinder to Mr. Justice Berger", *Canadian Forum*, Vol. 62, No. 720 (August 1982), pp. 6–7.

Page 146

Regarding the Alberta couple charged with child abuse at their Cremona Valleyview Children's Home, see "Punishment for parental punishing", *Alberta Report*, Vol. 10, No. 41 (October 3, 1983), pp. 28–30.

Pages 146–47

See Law Reform Commission of Canada, *Public and Media Access to the Criminal Process* (Working Paper 56) (Ottawa: LRC of Canada, 1987), pp. 50 and 64, where it is recommended the courts be empowered to ban publication, in certain circumstances, of the name of an accused or the name of a person who is the subject of a search warrant.

CHAPTER SEVEN

Page 149

Representative of the political philosophy that equates property rights with freedom are the proponents of the "Chicago school" of economics. See, for example, Milton Friedman, *Capitalism and Freedom* (Chicago and London: University of Chicago Press, 1962) and Friederich Hayek, *The Road to Serfdom* (Chicago and London: University of Chicago Press, 1944).

For more on working and living conditions of working-class Canadians prior to the enactment of modern labour legislation, see the Report and Testimony of the 1889 Royal Commission on the Relations of Labour and Capital, reproduced in abridged form in Greg Kealey, ed., *Canada Investigates Industrialism* (Toronto: University of Toronto Press, 1973). For a comparison of mortality rates during this period, see the Montreal death rate, 1872–1920, in M.C. Urquhart and K.A.H. Buckley, eds., *Historical Statistics of Canada* (Toronto: The Macmillan Company of Canada, 1965), p. 43.

Page 150

Representative of the laws restricting employer freedom in the workplace are the Ontario Employment Standards Act, RSO 1980, c. 137; Worker's Compensation Act, RSO 1980, c. 539; Labour Relations Act, RSO 1980, c. 228; and the Canada Unemployment Insurance Act, RSC 1985, c. U-1.

Page 151

For some corroboration of my claim that the marketplace has always been governed by rules and regulations, see E. Merrick Dodd, "From Maximum Wages to Minimum Wages: Six Centuries of Regulation of Employment Contracts", (1943) 43 *Columbia Law Review* 643, p. 654, cited by

David Beatty, *Putting the Charter to Work: Designing a Constitutional Labour Code* (Kingston and Montreal: McGill-Queen's University Press, 1987), p. 36, fn. 17.

For an enunciation of the common-law maxim *caveat emptor*, or "let the buyer beware", see *Janes* v. *Just* (1868), LR 3 QB 197, p. 202.

Page 152

For an example of a law that regulates the preparation of food sold in the marketplace, see the Ontario Health Protection and Promotion Act, 1983, SO 1983, c. 10. For broader protections of consumers, see, for example, the Ontario Consumer Protection Act, RSO 1980, c. 87, s. 38, and the Manitoba Consumer Protection Act, CCSM, c. C200.

At common law, there was no general implied warranty of fitness for habitation in a lease for a house even if the house was destroyed by fire [*Monk* v. *Cooper* (1737), 92 ER 460] or overrun by a swarm of nasty insects [*Hart* v . *Windsor,* [1843–60] A11 E. R. Rep. 681 (Ex. Ct.)]. This rule has been abrogated by such laws as the Ontario Landlord and Tenant Act, RSO 1980, c. 232, s. 96 (1).

Page 153

I have quoted from the second inaugural address of Franklin Delano Roosevelt. See "The second inaugural address", *New York Times*, January 21, 1937, p. 1.

The Canadian government has encouraged low-cost housing through such legislation as the Canada Mortgage and Housing Corporation Act, RSC 1985, c. C-7, and the National Housing . Act, RSC 1985, c. N-11.

Provincial governments have regulated rent prices through such legislation as the Ontario Residential Rent Regulation Act, 1986, SO 1986, c. 63, and the delivery of medical services through such legislation as the Ontario Health Insurance Act, RSO 1980, c. 197.

Page 155

An example of right-wing literature advocating voluntary taxes is Ayn Rand's "Government Financing in a Free Society", in her *The Virtue of Selfishness* (New York: Signet, 1969), p. 116.

Pages 155–56

The activities of private welfare agencies in Canada proved insufficient to meet the needs of an ever-increasing urban and industrial society. As a result, responsibility for their activities shifted to the public sectors. In Quebec, for example, government assisted private charity through the Bureau of Public Charities. In Manitoba, when the Associated Charities of Winnipeg could not get sufficient private funds to meet public needs, they were transformed into the publicly funded

Social Welfare Commission. See Esdras Minville, *Labour Legislation and Social Services in the Province of Quebec* (A Study Prepared for the Royal Commission on Dominion-Provincial Relations, Appendix 5), (Ottawa: King's Printer, 1939), pp. 55 ff; Canada, House of Commons, Select Standing Committee on Industrial and International Relations, *Report, Proceedings and Evidence* (Ottawa: King's Printer, 1928), p. 83; and John S. Morgan, "Social Welfare Services in Canada", in Michael Oliver, ed., *Social Purpose for Canada* (Toronto: University of Toronto Press, 1961), 130, pp. 144–45. For the similar trend in the United States, see Ralph M. Kramer, *Voluntary Agencies in the Welfare State* (Berkeley: University of California Press, 1981), pp. 64–65.

Page 156

For conditions of depression-era Saskatchewan, see *A Submission by the Government of Saskatchewan to the Royal Commission on Dominion-Provincial Relations* (Canada, 1937), pp. 290–91. Under the circumstances there described, "direct relief quickly became necessary if starvation was to be averted, though the standard of living was often actually lower for the very large marginal group that managed to avoid relief or for those who were just about to be pushed on to relief" (p. 291).

Since the beginning of this transition, public-sector expenditures have far out-distanced private-sector contributions in both Canada and the United States. See Samuel A. Martin, *Financing Humanistic Service* (Toronto: McClelland and Stewart, 1975), pp. 23–25; Kramer, *Voluntary Agencies in the Welfare State*, p. 67; and Frank G. Dickinson, *The Changing Position of Philanthropy in the American Economy* (NBEC Occasional Paper 110) (New York: Columbia University Press, 1970).

Economist Milton Friedman, for example, advocates a flat-rate tax system. See *Capitalism and Freedom*, p. 174.

Page 157

Milton Friedman acknowledges that his proposed flat-rate tax system would only apply to income above an exemption and that this could be instituted together with a system of subsidies for the poor to ensure that income did not fall below a certain level. See *Capitalism and Freedom*, pp. 174 and 192.

Page 158

The shifting onus of proof was struck down in *R*. v. *Oakes* (1986), 26 DLR (4th) 200, [1986] 15 SCR 103 (SCC), and the power of general search under a writ of assistance was upset in *R*. v. *Noble* (1984), 16 CCC (3d) 146, 48 OR (2d) 643 (Ont. CA).

CHAPTER EIGHT

Page 160

Although most of the material in this chapter comes from Ontario, there is a remarkable similarity in welfare practices and problems across the country. Conversely, it should be appreciated that the Ontario situation is now in some flux. Within the past couple of years, there has been a review of the system and, even more recently, a substantial change of personnel in the appeal tribunal (the Social Assistance Review Board).

The material discussed in this chapter continues, at least in general, to describe many of the recurring welfare issues both in Ontario and in other jurisdictions.

Pages 160–61

The affidavit sworn by the separated mother on welfare is reproduced in part in the Canadian Civil Liberties Education Trust, *Welfare Practices and Civil Liberties—A Canadian Survey* (Toronto: CCLET, 1975), pp. 24–25.

Page 162

I was advised of the 1987 Toronto case by a clinic lawyer who chooses to remain anonymous.

Page 163

For some insight into how welfare departments have treated women who are reluctant to sue their husbands for support, see *Welfare Practices and Civil Liberties—A Canadian Survey*, pp. 10–12. See also Simon Fodden, "Dependent Wives and the Requirement to Sue", *Bulletin of Canadian Welfare Law*, Spring 1974, p. 22. David Draper, a lawyer at Parkdale Community Legal Services Clinic in Toronto, reports that his impressions of current practice coincide generally with what I have written in the text. Mr. Draper has been in his present position for three and a half years and has regular contact with counterpart clinics all over Ontario.

The law imposes a general requirement on spouses to support each other and their children. See, for example, the Ontario Family Law Act, SO 1986, c. 4, s. 30. For more on the growing numbers of women facing poverty, see the National Council of Welfare, *Poverty Profile 1988* (Ottawa: Supply and Services, 1988), pp. 66 ff.

Page 164

The case of the Toronto husband forced to leave the matrimonial home in order that his wife and children could qualify for welfare benefits was reported to the Canadian Civil Liberties Education Trust and described in its *Welfare Practices and Civil Liberties—A Canadian Survey*, p. 17.

Page 165

The case of the wife and two children who were unable to move from the marital home was reported to the Canadian Civil Liberties Education Trust and described in its *Welfare Practices and Civil Liberties—A Canadian Survey*, p. 17. For more on the idea of treating the applicant for welfare as an "individual", see Mary Jane Mossman and Morag MacLean, "Family Law and Social Welfare: Toward a New Equality", (1986) 5 *Canadian Journal of Family Law* 79.

The policy of regarding men and women who live together "as if they were husband and wife" for welfare purposes was codified in the definition of "spouse" in RRO 1980, Reg. 441, s. 1 (p), filed under the General Welfare Assistance Act, RSO 1980, c. 188. It was also found in the definition of "single person" in O. Reg. 424/82, s. 2 (1), filed under the Family Benefits Act, RSO 1980, c. 151.

Page 166

Instances where welfare officials are reported to have looked through the homes of welfare mothers, seeking clues of a male presence, were collected by the Canadian Civil Liberties Education Trust and reproduced in its *Welfare Practices and Civil Liberties—A Canadian Survey*, pp. 22–26. Although we have not heard as many reports of this practice in recent years—particularly from Toronto—Montreal seems to be generating some serious complaints. See "Boubou Macoutes take a beating", *Globe and Mail*, July 23, 1988, p. D2. This is confirmed by McGill professor of social work Jim Torczyner, who, during the past two years, has handled some forty welfare cases in that city.

Some of the cases where review boards have upheld the welfare department's decision to terminate benefits because of a man in the house are documented in *Welfare Practices and Civil Liberties—A Canadian Survey*, p. 26. They are also documented by Professor Robert Kerr, in "Living Together as Husband and Wife", (1978) 1 *Low Income Law* 29, and by the Manitoba Association for Rights and Liberties and the Canadian Civil Liberties Association in their joint "Submission to the Honorable Len Evans, Minister of Employment Services and Economic Security, Re: The Social Allowance Act, Sec. 5 (5): 'The Man in the House' ", 1985.

For a case where an appeal board rejected an applicant woman's evidence, see *Re Burton and Minister of Community and Social Services* (1985), 52 OR (2d) 211 (Ont. Div. Ct.). Both the appellant and her alleged "husband" flatly denied they were living together as husband and wife. The Social Assistance Review Board found otherwise, preferring the evidence of a credit bureau and records at Ontario Hydro and Granada T.V. Rentals. On appeal, the court reinstated the woman's benefits and admonished the board for its "persistent misinterpretation" of previous court decisions in this area. Similarly, see *Re Dowlut and Director of Family Benefits Branch of the Ministry of Community and Social Services* (1985), 11 *Admin. Law Reports* 54 (Ont Div. Ct.).

The case that held that money, not sex, is the central factor in the "spousal" relationship is *Re Proc and Minister of Community and Social Services* (1974), 6 OR (2d) 624, 53 DLR (3d) 512 (Ont. Div. Ct.) (appeal dismissed, without reasons, Ontario Court of Appeal, April 1, 1975).

The 1985 case is *Re Pitts and Director of Family Benefits Branch of the Ministry of Community and Social Services* (1985), 51 OR (2d) 302 (Ont. Div. Ct.), p. 314.

Page 167

For an example of the laws that require a person to provide support to their marriage partner or common law spouse, see the Ontario Family Law Act, SO 1986, c. 4, s. 30.

Page 168

The CCLA "spouse in the house" delegation to the Ontario Minister of Community and Social Services occurred on March 25, 1986. Reports of the LEAF Charter Challenge can be found in "Ontario kicks snoops out of bedroom in single-parents' welfare rules reform", *Toronto Star*, September 19, 1986, p. 1. The subsequent change of policy by the Ontario government can be found in Ont. Reg. 589/87, s. 1 (FBA), and Ont. Reg. 590/87, s. 1 (GWA).

The "man in the house" rule continues in other parts of the country. For example, it will be found in the Saskatchewan Assistance Act, RSS 1978, c. S.8, and Sask. Reg. 78/66, s. 10 (2); the Nova Scotia Family Benefits Act, SNS 1977, c. 8, S.5 (3) (b); and the Quebec Social Assistance Act, RSQ, c. A-16, ss. 1, 15. Regarding the application of the Quebec law, see Miriam Raymond, *La Vie Maritale sous la loi d' aide Sociale* (Montreal: La Ligue des Droits et Libertés, January 1988).

Although my proposals for changing the "man in the house" rule rely somewhat on the provisions of our family law statutes, this should not necessarily be taken as an endorsement of the financial obligations that the family law currently imposes upon people who live together outside of marriage. This subject raises difficult issues beyond the scope of our present discussion.

Page 169

For more on the attempts of welfare authorities to learn the identity of putative fathers, see *Welfare Practices and Civil Liberties—A Canadian Survey*, pp. 28–33.

The case in which the Ontario Divisional Court upheld the denial of welfare assistance to a woman who did not identify the father of her children is *Re Clifton and Director of Income Maintenance Branch, Ministry of Community and Social Services* (1985), 53 (OR) (2d) 33 (Ont. Div. Ct.). I have quoted from page 36 of that decision. It is also cited, and some background information is provided, by Judy Parrack, "The Interrelationship between Social Assistance and Family Law" (paper prepared for the Ontario Social Assistance Review Committee, April 1987), p. 56.

Page 170

Intrusions on the residential privacy of welfare claimants are authorized by laws such as Ont. Reg. 709/84, s. 10, filed under the Family Benefits Act, RSO 1980, c. 151. The regulation authorizes home visits "for the purpose of inquiring into the living conditions and financial and other circumstances of the applicant" and dependants.

For some indication of welfare-department practices concerning home visits, see *Welfare Practices and Civil Liberties—A Canadian Survey*, pp. 34–39.

A 1987 report by the National Council of Welfare notes that home visits "are sometimes carried out in the manner of an investigation." See its *Welfare in Canada—The Tangled Safety Net* (Ottawa: Supply and Services, November 1987), p. 88.

The home-visit blitz in Quebec is reviewed in the same National Council of Welfare report (pp. 89–90). The denunciation of Quebec's "welfare police" will be found in "Rally in Quebec assails 'welfare squad' probes", *Globe and Mail*, May 7, 1987, p. A8.

The Charter and the canons of statutory interpretation would likely restrict the intrusions on the residential privacy of welfare recipients, which welfare workers could demand as a condition of granting assistance. But the language in the applicable law is so general that it does not give the workers an adequate sense of the limits they must observe or the recipients an adequate sense of the rights they may enjoy. In view of their dependent relationship, this situation hardly inspires confidence that legal rights and duties will be adequately respected.

Page 171

For an example of the requirement that welfare recipients seek and accept work, see RRO 1980, Reg. 441, s. 3 (1), filed under the Ontario General Welfare Assistance Act, RSO 1980, c. 188.

The case of the woman who would not undergo medical treatment is Case No. 256224, before the Ontario Social Assistance Review Board in April 1974.

Page 172

The case of the young man who refused to cut his hair in order to get a job as a security guard is Case No. 253568, before the Ontario Social Assistance Review Board in September 1972.

Pages 172–73

The case of the man who refused to do roof work is Case No. 252680, before the Ontario Social Assistance Review Board in 1973.

Page 173

The Simcoe policy on what constitutes "reasonable efforts" to find employment is found in *Champagne and the Administrator, Department of Social Services, County of Simcoe*, unreported, Ont. Div. Ct., No. 764/85, April 24, 1986.

The comments of some welfare administrators regarding the ineligibility of striking workers for income assistance were related to the Canadian Civil Liberties Education Trust and published in *Welfare Practices and Civil Liberties—A Canadian Survey*, pp. 48–49.

Legislation such as the Ontario Labour Relations Act, RSO 1980, c. 228, preserves certain rights of striking workers. The Act expressly provides that striking employees shall continue to be considered "employees" for the purposes of the Act [s. 1 (3)]. See also Jeffrey Sack and C. Michael Mitchel, *Ontario Labour Relations Board Law and Practice* (Toronto and Vancouver: Butterworths, 1985), pp. 54–55, 122–23.

Page 174

In Case No. 254967, before the Ontario Social Assistance Review Board in April 1973, the board ruled that a striker's unemployment was as a result of the striker's voluntary act. This policy is perpetuated in a July 21, 1980, directive in the *Ontario General Welfare Assistance Act Policy Manual*. See also *Alden* v. *Gaglardi et al.* (1972), 30 DLR (3d) 760 (SCC), and for a more enlightened approach to a similar problem under unemployment insurance laws, see *Hills et al.* v. *Attorney General of Canada*, unreported, S.C.C. No. 19094, March 24, 1988.

Pages 174–75

Freedom of movement across provincial boundaries is guaranteed by the Canadian Charter of Rights and Freedoms, s. 6.

Page 175

Trusteeship provisions can be found in the Ontario Family Benefits Act, RSO 1980, c. 151, s. 10 (2), and in RRO 1980, Reg. 441, s. 14 (2), filed under the Ontario General Welfare Assistance Act, RSO 1980, c. 188.

For an example of the trusteeship provisions in non-welfare situations, see the Ontario Mental Incompetency Act, RSO 1980, c. 264, as amended, and Gilbert Sharpe, *The Law and Medicine in Canada*, 2nd ed. (Toronto: Butterworths, 1987), pp. 399 ff.

For more on the command appearances at the welfare office and the hardships involved, see *Welfare Practices and Civil Liberties—A Canadian Survey*, pp. 62–63. Mr. Draper verifies that this issue remains very much a component of current practice.

Pages 175–76

There is some indication that these conditions have not improved. See CUPE, Local 79, "Challenging Old Assumptions: A Brief to the Ontario Social Assistance Review Committee", November 27, 1986, pp. 1–3.

Page 176

For more on the requirement of a residence in order to get assistance, see *Welfare Practices and Civil Liberties—A Canadian Survey*, p. 69. Mr. Draper says that, while this problem has been a feature of his experience in Metro Toronto, the situation may now be improving to some extent. He says, however, that clinics in other communities continue to report such problems. I verified this with Mary McCormack, a lawyer who has worked for more than two years at the North Frontenac Community Services Corporation in Sharbot Lake, Ontario.

Pages 176–77

For more on the difficulty of getting access to welfare workers, see *Welfare Practices and Civil Liberties—A Canadian Survey*, pp. 74–76, and "Challenging Old Assumptions: A Brief to the Ontario Social Assistance Review Committee", November 27, 1986, p. 1.

Page 177

For more on the lack of information available to welfare recipients regarding their legal rights, see *Welfare Practices and Civil Liberties—A Canadian Survey*, pp. 77–81. This lack of information was confirmed by Parkdale Community Legal Services in its "Submissions to the Social Assistance Review Committee", November 1986, p. 6. Mary McCormack has said that welfare officials in her area have advised people of their right to appeal. But she is not aware that these officials routinely advise her clients of some of their other claims on the system.

The lawyer who has never known a cancellation of general welfare assistance to be preceded by notice to a client is Joanne Leatch. See her paper "Procedural Fairness in the Social Assistance System" (prepared for the Ontario Social Assistance Review Committee, August 1987), p. 14.

The notice requirement for the denial of family benefits is in the Family Benefits Act, RSO 1980, c. 151, s. 13 (1).

Page 178

The letter advising an applicant of an impending adverse decision was supplied to me by David Draper. This practice is confirmed by lawyer Joanne Leatch in her "Procedural Fairness in the Social Assistance System", pp. 14–15.

The series of cases referred to are, respectively: *Re Burton and Minister of Community and Social Services* (1985), 52 OR (2d) 211 (Ont. Div. Ct.), p. 223; *Re Pitts and Director of Family Benefits Branch of the Ministry of Community and Social Services* (1985), 51 OR (2d) 302 (Ont. Div. Ct.), p. 314; *Willis* v. *Ministry of Community and Social Services* (1983), 40 OR (2d) 287 (Ont. Div. Ct.), p. 293; *Re Dowlut and Director of Family Benefits Branch of the Ministry of Community and Social Services*, (1985) Admin. Law Reports 54 (Ont. Div. Ct.).

Pages 179–80

For the experiences of the Canadian Civil Liberties Association in establishing temporary citizen-advocacy services in a few Toronto welfare offices, see *Welfare Practices and Civil Liberties—A Canadian Survey*, pp. 100–06.

Pages 180–81

I have quoted figures obtained from the Ontario Social Assistance Review Board and cited by Joanne Leatch in her "Procedural Fairness in the Social Assistance System", pp. 47–48.

Page 181

I have also quoted from the results of the Social Assistance Review Board Duty Counsel Pilot Project, conducted by community legal clinics of Metropolitan Toronto from November 1984 to May 1985, and cited by Joanne Leatch in "Procedural Fairness in the Social Assistance System", p. 48.

CHAPTER NINE

Pages 183–83

For the late Mr. Justice Brandeis's statement, see Samuel D. Warren and Louis D. Brandeis, "The Right to Privacy", (1890) 4 *Harvard Law Review* 194, p. 195 (quoting from *Cooley on Torts*, 2nd ed., p. 29) and also *Olmstead et al.* v. *United States* (1928), 277 U.S. 438, p. 478 (Brandeis, J., dissenting).

Pages 183–84

See American Psychiatric Association, *DSM. III: Diagnostic and Statistical Manual of Mental Disorders*, 3rd ed. (Washington, D.C.: APA, 1980), pp. 188–89.

Page 184

The attempt to add serious emotional harm to the commitment criteria can be found in the March 26, 1986, draft of a Uniform Mental Health Act, s. 3 (b) 3.i, by the Uniform Law Conference of Canada.

Page 185

A power to impose a trustee to manage the affairs of an incompetent person can be found in the Ontario Mental Incompetency Act, RSO 1980, c. 264, s. 12.

Some provincial jurisdictions provide for the compulsory institutionalization of persons in circumstances where, in addition to other factors, they are mentally incompetent. See, for example, the Nova Scotia Adult Protect Act, SNS 1985, c. 2, s. 9 (3), and Harvey Savage and Carla McKague, *Mental Health Law in Canada*, (Toronto and Vancouver: Butterworths, 1987), p. 184.

Pages 185–86

The case of the man of Serbo-Croatian descent is provided by Gilbert Sharpe in his unpublished article "Do Mentally Disordered Offenders Have Rights?", prepared for the CCLA, 1986, p. 5.

Page 187

The studies referred to are, respectively: Ralph E. Tarter, Donald I. Templer, and Charlotte Hardy, "Reliability of the psychiatric diagnosis", (1975) 36 *Diseases of the Nervous system* 30–31; Martin M. Katz, Jonathan O. Cole, and Henri A. Lowry, "Studies of the Diagnostic Process: The Influence of Symptom Perception, Past Experience and Ethnic Background in Diagnostic Decisions", (1969) 125 *American Journal of Psychiatry* 397; a 1959 study cited by Rona Cherry and Lawrence Cherry, "The Common Cold of Mental Ailments: Depression", *New York Times Magazine*, November 25, 1973, p. 38; Dorothea D. Braginsky and Benjamin M. Braginsky, "Psychologists: High Priests of the Middle Class", *Psychology Today*, Vol. 7, No. 7 (December 1973), p. 15. These and some of the other studies cited later in the chapter are conveniently summarized in the superb article by Bruce J. Ennis and Thomas R. Litwack, "Psychiatry and the Presumption of Expertise: Flipping Coins in the Courtroom", (1974) 62 *California Law Review* 693, pp. 699 ff.

Pages 187–88

Dr. Spitzer's remarks will be found in Robert L. Spitzer, Jacob Cohen, Joseph L. Fleiss, and Jean Endicott, "Quantification of Agreement in Psychiatric Diagnosis", (1967) 17 *Archives of General Psychiatry* 83, p. 83.

Page 188

On the validity of psychiatric predictions, see J.R. Rappeport, G. Lassen, and F. Gruenwald, "Evaluations and Follow-up of State Hospital Patients Who Had Sanity Hearings", (1962) 118 *American Journal of Psychiatry* 1078.

I have quoted J. Zisken from his *Coping with Psychiatric and Psychological Testimony*, 3rd ed. (Venice, Calif.: Law and Psychology Press, 1981), p. 288.

For more on the maxim by which we prefer to let nine guilty go free than to convict one innocent, see Glanville Williams, *Proof of Guilt*, 3rd ed. (London: Steven & Sons, 1963), pp. 186–87.

Page 189

As to the ineffectiveness of hospitalization and treatment, see Donald G. Langsley, Frank S. Pitman III, Pavel Machotka, and Kalmen Flomenhaft, "Family Crisis Therapy Results and Implications", (1968) 7 *Family Process* 145.

As to the effects of chlorpromazine treatment, see David M. Engelhardt and Norbert Freedman, "Maintenance Drug Therapy: The Schizophrenic Patient in the Community", (1965) 2 *International Psychiatric Clinics* 933, pp. 951–52, and Rappaport et al., "Schizophrenics for whom Phenothiazines May Be Contra-indicated or Unnecessary" (unpublished study on file at *Minnesota Law Review*), p. 9, all of which are cited by Eugene Z. Dubose, Jr., in "Of the Parens Patriae Commitment Power and Drug Treatment of Schizophrenia: Do the Benefits to the Patient Justify Involuntary Treatment?", (1976) 60 *Minnesota Law Review* 1149, pp. 1196 ff. Chlorpromazine is also associated with death from aspiration. See Frederick T. Zugibe, "Sudden Death Related to the Use of Psychotropic Drugs", *Legal Medicine 1980* (Philadelphia: W.B. Saunders, 1980), pp. 75–90, at p. 79.

For studies regarding institutional dependence as a result of drug treatment, see the number of studies cited by Dubose, Jr., "Of the Parens Patriae Commitment Power...", pp. 1195–1202.

Pages 189–90

The side-effects of anti-psychotic drugs are described in Dubose, Jr., "Of the Parens Patriae Commitment Power...", pp. 12025. He also cites the following studies on tardive dyskinesia and agranulocytosis.

Page 190

The symptoms of tardive dyskinesia are described in D.F. Klein and J.M. Davis, *Diagnosis and Drug Treatment of Psychiatric Disorders* (Baltimore: Williams and Wilkins, 1969), p. 99, and the success of its treatment, by George Gardos and Jonathan O. Cole, "Maintenance antipsychotic therapy: Is the cure worse than the disease?", (1976) 133 *American Journal of Psychiatry* 32.

The symptoms of agranulocytosis are described in Jonathan O. Cole and John M. Davis, "Antipsychotic Drugs", in L. Bellack and L. Loeb, eds., *The Schizophrenic Syndrome* (New York: Grune and Stratton, 1969), pp. 529–30.

Pages 191–92

For examples of the type of legislation that sets a higher standard for commitment than that which exists in many provinces, see the Ontario Mental Health Act, RSO 1980, c. 262, s. 9, and the Prince Edward Island Mental Health Act, RSPEI 1974, c. M-9, s. 10. The Uniform Law Conference of Canada has suggested similar criteria in its recent draft of a "uniform mental health act", February 19, 1987. Regarding the standards in other provinces, see the discussion in Harvey Savage and Carla McKague, *Mental Health Law in Canada*, pp. 77–79.

Pages 193–94

Debate centred around amendments to the Ontario Mental Health Act, RSO 1970, c. 269, s. 8. I have quoted the former president of the Ontario Psychiatric Association, Dr. Merville O. Vincent, from a public statement he made at the time of the debate. Also see his "Commentary", (1978) 24 *Canadian Journal of Psychiatry* 334.

Page 194

I have referred to Burton T. Perrin's "Involuntary Commitment to Mental Hospitals: Why?", unpublished Master's thesis, York University, September 1973. See also the following similar studies by S. Page and E. Yates: "Semantics and civil commitment", (1974) 19 *Canadian Psychiatric Association Journal* 413; "Civil Commitment Practices in 1977", (1978) 24 *Canadian Journal of Psychiatry* 329. Some studies have also suggested the possibility that legislative amendments designed to restrict involuntary commitment do not deter psychiatric professionals from continuing to apply old criteria. See, for example, R. Michael Bagby, Irwin Silverman, David Patrick Ryan, and Susan E. Dickens, "Effects of Mental Health Legislative Reform in Ontario", (1987) 28 *Canadian Psychology* 21, p. 28, and R. Michael Bagby and Leslie Atkinson, "The Effect of Legislative Reform on Civil Commitment Rates: A Critical Analysis", (1988) 6 *Behavioral Sciences and the Law* 45.

Pages 194–95

A report of the legal opinions solicited by the CCLA from lawyers Kenneth Howie and John Sopinka will be found in "Studies find 70% of mental patients committed illegally", *Globe and Mail*, February 21, 1977, p. A1. The form used for certificates of committal at the time of the study will be found in RRO 1970, Reg. 576, Form 1. The verbatim texts of certificates of committal quoted are contained in the CCLA's letter, dated February 18, 1977, to the Honourable Dennis Timbrell, minister of health for Ontario. They were found among the two hundred randomly selected certificates obtained by Burton Perrin.

Pages 195–96

See "Mental committals are called unlawful", *Toronto Star*, February 21, 1977, p. 1, regarding the response of the medical community to the CCLA revelations.

Page 197

Recent amendments to sub-section 9 (5) (b) of the Ontario Mental Health Act reduced the duration of emergency committals from 120 to 72 hours. See SO 1986, c. 64, s. 33 (8). Regarding the ability of physicians to extend commitment for up to six months, see the Ontario Mental Health Act, RSO 1980, c. 262, s. 14 (4).

The percentage of certificates of committal reviewed by boards of review is from 1984–85 data compiled by the Ministry of Health for the Working Group to Develop Rights Advisors Programme, February 18, 1985.

Regarding the automatic review process after the six-month period of confinement, see the Ontario Mental Health Act, s. 31 (4). Patients can take the initiative earlier by application to the review board (s. 31) or by application for habeas corpus to the courts.

Pages 197–98

Regarding the authorization of electro-convulsive therapy (ECT) or "shock treatment", see Gerald B. Robertson, *Mental Disability Law in Canada* (Toronto: Carswell, 1987), pp. 401–02. The Ontario government recently issued guidelines for the use of ECT in Ministry of Community and Social Services, "Standards for the Use of Behavioral Training and Treatment Procedures in Settings for the Developmentally Handicapped", August 1986. The Ontario Mental Health Act was subsequently amended to prohibit the administration of ECT on competent involuntary patients against their will and incompetent involuntary patients where the next of kin refused. See SO 1986, c. 64, s. 33.

CHAPTER TEN

Page 203

The U.S. Supreme Court upheld the constitutionality of the forced relocation imposed upon Japanese Americans in *Korematsu* v. *U.S.* (1944), 323 U.S. 214, 65 S. Ct. 193. By contrast, the same court on the same day ordered the release of a Japanese American following a two-year detention after she had been evacuated to a "relocation centre" [*Ex parte Mitsuye Endo* (1944), 323 U.S. 283, 65 S. Ct. 208]. It was held that detention beyond an iterim period was not authorized by the enabling legislation in circumstances where the person was not guilty of disloyalty or subversiveness. Significantly, the court achieved this result *without* recourse to the constitutional protections contained in the U.S. Bill of Rights.

The Smith Act, 54 Stat. 671, 18 U.S.C. §11 (1946 ed.), was held not to violate the First and Fifth amendments of the U.S. Bill of Rights in *Dennis* v. *U.S.* (1951), 341 U.S. 494, 71 S. Ct. 857.

Pages 203–04

For a review of how courts have responded to the curtailment of human rights in periods of national emergency, see G.J. Alexander, "Protection of Human Rights by National Courts During Periods of Emergency", (1984) 5 *Human Rights Law Journal* 1. For a review of the American experience in this regard, see Alan Dershowitz, "Could It Happen Here?", in Irving Howe and Michael Harrington, eds., *The Seventies: Problems and Proposals* (New York: Harper & Row, 1972), pp. 220–35.

Page 204

The U.S. Supreme Court approved "separate but equal" transportation systems for black Americans in *Plessy* v. *Ferguson* (1896), 163 U.S. 537. School segregation was finally outlawed in *Brown* v. *Board of Education* (1954), 347 U.S. 483, 74 S. Ct. 686 (USSC).

The Missouri Compromise, outlawing slavery in the new territories that entered the Union, was struck down in *Dred Scott* v. *Sandford* (1856), 60 U.S. (19 How.) 393.

Sidney Hook writes of *Dred Scott* that "in the opinion of an amazing number of witnesses contemporary to the event, [it] was one of the major causes of the Civil War, or one of the two main proximate causes of that conflict." See his *Paradoxes of Freedom* (New York: Prometheus Books, 1987), p. 92.

Federal legislation prohibiting discrimination in public places was struck down in *The Civil Rights Cases* (1883), 109 U.S. 3, 3 S. Ct. 18.

Page 205

The U.S. Supreme Court outlawed various statutes regulating the economy, under the aegis of the "due process" clause in the Fourteenth Amendment, in a series of cases commencing with *Lochner* v. *New York* (1905), 198 U.S. 45, 25 S. Ct. 539, where a New York statute prohibiting employment in bakeries for more than sixty hours a week or more than ten hours a day was struck down. Subsequently, in *Adkins* v. *Children's Hospital of District of Columbia* (1923), 261 U.S. 525, 43 S. Ct. 394, a District of Columbia law prescribing minimum wages for women was ruled unconstitutional. A law prohibiting interstate commerce in the products of child labour was struck down in *Hammer* v. *Dagenhart* (1918), 247 U.S. 251, 38 S. Ct. 529. In *Coppage* v. *Kansas* (1915), 236 U.S. 1, 35 S. Ct. 240, the court ruled unconstitutional a Kansas law of 1903 prohibiting employers from requiring, as a condition of employment, that employees agree not to join or become members of any labour organization. The same employment practice was prohibited on interstate railroads by federal law, and in *Adair* v. *U.S.* (1908), 208 U.S. 161, 28 S. Ct. 277, that, too, was ruled unconstitutional. A law prohibiting employment agencies from charging employees agency fees was struck down in *Adams* v. *Tanner* (1917), 244 U.S. 590, 37

S. Ct. 662 (see the dissent of Mr. Justice Brandeis for a discussion of the evils this legislation was designed to combat, 244 U.S., pp. 597 ff.). The quotes, in order, are from *Lochner* v. *New York*, 198 U.S., p. 53; *Coppage* v. *Kansas*, 236 U.S., p. 14; *Adair* v. *U.S.*, 208 U.S., p. 175; and *Adams* v. *Tanner*, 244 U.S., p. 597.

In *West Coast Hotel* v. *Parrish* (1937), 300 U.S. 379, 57 S. Ct. 578, the U.S. Supreme Court began a series of judgments effectively reversing these precedents.

The U.S. Supreme Court cases dealing with warrantless entry are *Marshall* v. *Barlows Inc.* (1978), 436 U.S. 307, 98 S. Ct. 1816, and *Wyman* v. *James* (1971), 400 U.S. 309, 91 S. Ct. 381.

Workplace safety inspections, without warrant, were ruled unconstitutional in the former case but distinguished in *Donovan* v. *Dewey* (1984), 452 U.S. 594, 101 S. Ct. 2534, where the U.S. Supreme Court upheld the constitutionality of warrantless inspections under the federal Mine Safety and Health Act. In determining whether such inspections were in violation of the Fourth Amendment to the U.S. Constitution, the Supreme Court articulated a number of criteria, including: whether there is a history of government supervision in the area; whether such legislation fulfils a substantial government interest; whether there is any reasonable expectation of privacy; whether there are neutral criteria and standards for determining when an inspection would be conducted and the manner of that inspection; and whether the scheme permits forcible entry.

But in the case of *Wyman* v. *James* the U.S. Supreme Court upheld the constitutionality of a New York enactment that revoked welfare assistance for recipients who denied welfare officials access to their homes. In determining whether such intrusions on the residential privacy of welfare recipients could be made without warrant, the court did not even consider most of the criteria it subsequently established for permitting warrantless intrusions on business privacy.

Pages 205–06

The California rent-control ordinance case that dealt with mobile homes is *Gregory* v. *City of San Juan Capistrano* (1983), 191 Cal. Rptr. 47 (CA). See also *Hall* v. *City of Santa Barbara* (1986), 797 F. 2d 1493 (U.S. Court of Appeals, 9th Circuit), *Ross* v. *City of Berkeley* (1987), 655 F. Supp. 820 (U.S. District Court), and Notes, "The Constitutionality of Rent Control Restrictions on Property Owners' Dominion Interests", (1986) 100 *Harvard Law Review* 1067.

Page 206

Irish rent-control legislation, in effect in similar form since the First World War, was struck down by Ireland's High Court and Supreme Court in *Blake* v. *The Attorney General*, [1982] IR 117 (the quote is from pp. 125–26), affirmed, [1982] IR 127. The Supreme Court, in this opinion, recognized that removal of rent control would affect thousands of families and expected that new legislation would be "speedily enacted" to fill the statutory void. Heeding this advice, Ireland's

House of Oireachtas passed new legislation that would stagger rental increases to market rates over five years. This legislation was immediately referred to the Supreme Court and, in *The Housing (Private Rented Dwellings) Bill, 1981*, [1983] IR 181, the Supreme Court repeated its reasoning in *Blake*, finding that this legislation, too, constituted an "unjust attack" on property rights.

Page 207

Mr. Justice Lamer, writing for a majority of the Supreme Court of Canada in *Ref. re s. 94 (2) of the Motor Vehicle Act* (1985), 23 CCC (3d) 289, 24 DLR (4th) 536, [1985] 2 SCR 486, pp. 497–98, suggested that the words "fundamental justice", in section 7 of the Charter, may be read substantively. This interpretation of section 7 was approved by some members of the court in *R. v. Morgentaler, Smoling and Scott* (1988), 37 CCC (3d) 449, [1988] 1 SCR 30, at p. 53 (per Chief Justice Dickson).

The Ontario Divisional Court struck down wage-restraint legislation as contrary to the Charter's guarantee of freedom of association in *Re Service Employees International Union, Local 204 and Broadway Manor Nursing Home et al.* (1983), 4 DLR (4th) 231, 44 OR (2d) 392, reversed in part, (1984) 13 DLR (4th) 220, 48 OR (2d) 225 (Ont. CA).

The Saskatchewan Court of Appeal in *Re Retail, Wholesale & Department Store Union & Government of Saskatchewan et al.* (1985), 19 DLR (4th) 609, 39 Sask. R. 193, [1985] 5 WWR 97, came to a similar conclusion [reversed on appeal, (1987), 38 DLR (4th) 277, [1987] 1 SCR 460].

Page 208

The Supreme Court of Canada judgment, effectively overruling *Broadway Manor* and *RWDSU*, occurred in *Reference Re Public Service Employee Relations Act, Labour Relations Act and Police Officers Collective Bargaining Act* (1987), 38 DLR (4th) 161, [1987] 1 SCR 313, and in the related decisions *PSAC et al. v. The Queen in right of Canada et al.* (1987), 38 DLR (4th) 249, [1987] 1 SCR 424; *Gov't. of Sask. et al. v. RWDSU, Locals 544, 496, 635 and 955 et al.* (1987), 38 DLR (4th) 277, [1987] 1 SCR 460.

The case in which an employer sought to use "freedom of association" against the reinstatement of a discharged employee is *CIBC v. Rifou* (1986), 25 CRR 164 (Fed. CA).

The federal government's metrification program was upheld in *R. v. Halpert* (1984), 48 OR 249, 15 CCC (3d) 292 (Co. Ct.), reversing (1983), 9 CCC (3d) 411 (Prov. Ct.). Halpert had argued that the government legislation offended not only the free speech guarantee—section 2 (b) of the Charter—but also sections 7 and 8 of the Charter.

For some cases spelling out the "frozen concepts" theory, see *Robertson & Rosetanni* v. *The Queen*, [1964] 1 CCC 1, 41 DLR (2d) 405, [1963] SCR 651; *Attorney General of Can.* v. *Lavell; Isaac et al.* v. *Bedard* (1973), 38 DLR (3d) 481, [1974] SCR 1349; and *R.* v. *Burnshine* (1974), 15 CCC (2d) 505, 44 DLR (3d) 584, [1975] 15 SCR 693. See also Walter S. Tarnopolsky, "A New Bill of Rights in the Light of the Interpretation of the Present One by the Supreme Court of Canada", in Law Society of Upper Canada, *The Constitution and the Future of Canada* (LSUC Special Lecturers, 1978) (Toronto: Richard De Boo, 1978), pp. 181–91. But see also *R.* v. *Drybones* [1970] 3 CCC 355, 9 DLR (3d) 473, [1970] SCR 282.

Page 209

The results of a breath test obtained in contravention of the Canadian Bill of Rights guarantee for the right to counsel was ruled admissible by the Supreme Court of Canada in *Hogan* v. *R.* (1975), 48 DLR (3d) 427, [1975] 2 SCR 574.

The case that treated sixteen-year-old boys and girls differently was *R.* v. *MacKay; R.* v. *Willington* (1977), 36 CCC (2d) 349 (Alta. CA), reversing (1975), 30 CCC (2d) 349 (Alta. Dist. Ct.).

For some of the ways the Charter is supposed to have improved on the Bill of Rights, see Peter Hogg, "A Comparison of the Canadian Charter of Rights and Freedoms with the Canadian Bill of Rights", in W.S. Tarnopolsky and G.A. Beaudoin, eds., *The Canadian Charter of Rights and Freedoms: Commentary* (Toronto: Carswell, 1982), pp. 10 ff.

The reverse-onus clause, s. 8 of the Narcotic Control Act, RSC 1970, c. N-1, was found to offend s. 11 (d) of the Charter in *R.* v. *Oakes* (1986), 24 CCC (3d) 321, 26 DLR (4th) 200, [1986] 1 SCR 103 (SCC). Section 10 (1) (a) of the same Act authorized warrantless searches of commercial premises. The Ontario Court of Appeal ruled in *R.* v. *Rao* (1984), 12 CCC (3d) 97, 9 DLR (4th) 542, 46 OR (2d) 80, that, in respect of s. 10 (1) (a), it is unconstitutional to bypass the requirement of a warrant, in such circumstances, when it is practicable to obtain one.

Pages 209–10

Quebec's Bill 22, prohibiting the use of any language other than French on commercial signs, was ruled unconstitutional by the Quebec Court of Appeal in *A.-G. of Quebec* v. *La Chaussure Brown's Inc. et al.* (1986), 36 DLR (4th) 374 (the case is currently before the Supreme Court of Canada).

Page 210

The offence of scandalizing the courts was struck down in *R.* v. *Kopyto* (1987), 61 CR (3d) 209, 62 OR (2d) 449 (Ont. CA).

Canada's abortion laws were struck down in *R. v. Morgentaler, Smoling and Scott* (1988), 37 CCC (3d) 449, [1988] 1 SCR 30 (SCC).

The use of the Lord's Prayer as an opening exercise in Ontario public schools was ruled constitutional in *Re Zylberberg et al. and Director of Education* (1986), 55 OR (2d) 749 (Div. Ct.), as was Ontario's course of formal religious education in the public schools in *The Corp. of the Canadian Civil Liberties Association et al. v. The Minister of Education and the Elgin County Board of Education*, unreported, Supreme Court of Ontario, No. 280/86, March 28, 1988.

The hate-propaganda section of the Criminal Code (s. 281.2) was ruled constitutional in *R. v. Keegstra* (1984), 19 CCC (3d) 254 (Alta. QB). The Alberta Court of Appeal ruled the anti-hate law unconstitutional. See *R. v. Keegstra*, unreported, Alberta Court of Appeal, No. 17699, June 6, 1988. And the Ontario Court of Appeal ruled it constitutional in *R. v. Andrews and Smith*, Ontario Court of Appeal, Nos. 1010/85, 1047/85, July 29, 1988. The false-news section (s. 177 of the Criminal Code) was held constitutional in *R. v. Zundel* (1987), 31 CCC (3d) 97, 35 DLR (4th) 338 (Ont. CA).

In *International Fund for Animal Welfare Inc. et al. v. The Queen et al.* (1986), 30 CCC (3d) 80 (FCTD), the federal court upheld regulations restricting access to northern ice floes during the seal hunt. Sometime after May 1, 1988, it was brought to my attention that this decision was overturned by the Federal Court of Appeal Division, No. A-620-86, April 19, 1988.

Workers' compensation laws were challenged because they denied to claimants the right to sue in court. These laws were upheld in Ontario in *Re Terzian et al.* (1983), 148 DLR (3d) 380, 42 OR (2d) 144 (Div. Ct.), and in Newfoundland were struck down at trial in *Piercey* v. *General Bakeries Ltd.* (1986), 31 DLR (4th) 373 (Nfld. SC) but upheld on reference to the Newfoundland Court of Appeal in *Reference Re Workers Compensation Act, 1983* (1988), 44 DLR (4th) 501, 67 Nfld. & P.E.I.R. 16. In Alberta, the law was upheld in *Budge* v. *W.C.B.*, [1985] 1 WWR 437 (Alta. Q.B.), reversed in part, [1987] 1 WWR 83 (Alta C.A.), and struck down on retrial in *Public Trustee for Alta. et al.* v. *WCB et al.*, [1987] 6 WWR 217 (Alta. QB).

Mandatory retirement was unsuccessfully challenged in *Re McKinney and Bd. of Gov's of Univ. of Guelph et al.* (1986), 46 DLR (4th) 193, 63 OR (2d) 1 (Ont. CA), affirming (1986), 32 DLR (4th) 65, 57 OR (2d) 1 (Ont. HCJ), (leave to appeal to Supreme Court of Canada granted April 21, 1988), but successfully challenged in *Connell* v. *University of British Columbia; Harrison* v. *UBC* (1988), 21 BCLR (2d) 145 (BCCA), reversing (1986), 30 DLR (4th) 206, [1986] 6 WWR 7 (BCSC), and in *Stoffman et al.* v. *Vancouver General Hospital et al.* (1988), 21 BCLR (2d) 165 (BCCA), affirming (1986), 30 DLR (4th) 700, [1986] 6 WWR 23 (BCSC).

On the use of conscripted union dues for political purposes, see *Re Lavigne and O.P.S.E.U. et al.* (1986), 55 OR (2d) 449, 86 CLLC para. 14 039 (Ont. HCJ), and *Re Baldwin and B.C.G.E.U.* (1986), 28 DLR (4th) 301, 3 BCLR (2d) 242 (BCSC).

Pages 210–11

The constitutional challenge of the Ontario law banning extra billing by doctors is *Canadian Medical Association et al.* v. *The Attorney General of Canada and The Attorney General of Ontario*, Ontario Supreme Court, Ottawa Reg. No. 1217/85.

Page 211

The override provision in the Charter is section 33. For a discussion of the last-minute negotiations from which it was hatched, see R. Romanow, J. Whyte, and H. Leeson, *Canada Notwithstanding* (Toronto: Carswell/Methuen, 1984), pp. 193 ff.

Page 212

For the applicable material on the various overrides, see the Canadian Bill of Rights, RSC 1985, App. III, s. 2; the Alberta Bill of Rights, RSA 1980, c. A-16, s. 2; the Quebec Charter of Human Rights and Freedoms, RSQ 1977, c. C-12, s. 52; the Saskatchewan Human Rights Code, RSS 1978, c. S-24.1, s. 44 (previously the Saskatchewan Bill of Rights, RSS 1965, c. 378).

The situations in which overrides were involved include: the Public Order (Temporary Measures) Act, SC 1970–71–72, c. 2; An Act to Ensure the Resumption of Services in the Schools and Colleges in the Public Sector, SQ 1983, c. 1, s. 28 (in this connection, see "Overriding of rights called unacceptable", *Montreal Gazette*, February 17, 1983, p. A1); An Act Respecting the Constitution Act, SQ 1982, c. 21 [this blanket invocation of section 33 was ruled invalid by the Quebec Court of Appeal in *Alliance des Professeurs de Montreal et al.* v. *A.-G. of Quebec* (1985), 21 CCC (3d) 273, 21 DLR (4th) 354]; and the SGEU Dispute Settlement Act, SS 1986, c. 111 (in this connection, see "Saskatchewan is the first to declare single law exempt from Charter", *Globe and Mail*, February 12, 1986, p. A1).

Some of the Charter provisions to which the override applies include: the fundamental freedoms of speech, press, and assembly; the legal rights such as presumption of innocence, rights to counsel, and against unreasonable search and seizure; and the equality rights of section 15. There remain, however, residual areas that are not susceptible to the override. These include certain electoral rights, language rights, and a special provision that Charter rights apply equally to men and women.

Page 213

See Canada, Parliament, *Minutes of Proceedings and Evidence of the Special Joint Committee of the Senate and the House of Commons on the Constitution of Canada*, No. 45 (January 26, 1961) and No. 46 (January 27, 1981), regarding the debate and decision to exclude property rights from section 7 of the Charter. Professor John Whyte writes that the "most dramatic aspect of the

Committee's consideration of section 7 was the nearly successful attempt to have 'enjoyment of property' added to the section." The issue "took up most of the three days which were devoted to section 7." See "Fundamental Justice: The Scope and Application of Section 7 of the Charter", in *The Canadian Charter of Rights and Freedoms: Initial Experience, Emerging Issues, Future Challenges* (Montreal: Les Editions Yvon Blais, 1983), p. 24. Two years later, the House of Commons defeated a Conservative motion to entrench property rights in the Charter. See "Liberals defeat property rights motion", *Globe and Mail*, May 3, 1983, p. 1.

Page 216

For a discussion of the scope of commercial speech, see Robert J. Sharpe, "Commercial Expression and the Charter", (1987) 37 *University of Toronto Law Journal* 229.

CHAPTER ELEVEN

Pages 217–18

My radio exchange with Barbara Amiel is contained in a transcript of the CBC program "Morningside" for March 9, 1982. More than four years later, Barbara Amiel acknowledged that "overwhelming policy consideration" might justify "outlawing discrimination on the basis of race." See "The right to discriminate", *Toronto Sun*, November 9, 1986, p. C2. I am not sure how far, if at all, this represents a conversion. If it did, I would be pleased to welcome her to the fold, even retroactively.

Page 219

The quote from John Maynard Keynes appears in his "A Tract on Monetary Reform", in *The Collected Writings of John Maynard Keynes*, Volume IV (London: Macmillan, 1971), p. 65.

For a recounting of the Montgomery bus boycott of 1958, see Martin Luther King, Jr., *Stride Toward Freedom: The Montgomery Story* (New York: Harper & Row, 1958).

For the Saul Alinsky quote, see his *Rules For Radicals* (New York: Vintage Books, 1971), p. 13.

Pages 221–22

Every human rights statute in Canada permits the reaching of a settlement between the parties. Some make conciliation efforts mandatory; some make them discretionary. See Walter S. Tarnopolsky and William F. Pentney, *Discrimination and the Law in Canada*, revised (Toronto: Richard De Boo, 1985), p. 15–18.

Page 222

In some provinces human-rights tribunals can order, and in other provinces can merely recommend, a variety of remedies. See Tarnopolsky and Pentney, *Discrimination and the Law in
Canada*, revised, pp. 15–63 to 15–66.

The quote regarding the powers of boards of inquiry is from the Ontario Human Rights Code,
1981, SO 1981, c. 53, s. 40 (1).

For a comparison of the number of settled cases with the number of boards of inquiry, see
Ontario Human Rights Commission: *Annual Report, 1981–82*, pp. 53 and 56, and *Annual Report,
1983–84*, pp. 26 and 32.

Page 223

The case of the marina owner is reported in "Plan complains of color bar at boat club", *Globe
and Mail*, June 10, 1963, p. 9.

Pages 223–24

The following are some of those who recommend a greater emphasis than there is now on
litigation, as opposed to conciliation, in human rights administration. See "Brief Submission to
the Ontario Human Rights Commission from the Urban Alliance on Race Relations", June 17,
1976, pp. 3–4, 11–12; "Brief Submitted by the Continuing Committee on Race Relations to the
Ontario Human Rights Commission for its Review of the *Ontario Human Rights Code"*, Toronto,
June 17, 1976, p. 4; and the presentation of lawyer Charles Roach, on his behalf and on behalf of
lawyer Harry Kopyto, to the Standing Committee on Resources Development, October 1, 1981,
pp. 13–14. See also Ian Hunter, "Civil Actions for Discrimination", (1977) 55 *Canadian Bar
Review* 106.

Prosecution of human rights offenders is available in Ontario through the Ontario Human Rights
Code, 1981, s. 43. Civil litigation is likely unavailable without an amendment to the code
providing for such litigation. See *Bhadauria* v. *Board of Governors of Seneca College* (1981),
124 DLR (3d) 193, [1981] 2 SCR 181 (SCC), reversing (1979), 27 OR (2d) 142, 105 DLR (3d)
707 (Ont. CA).

On the question of whether there should be more emphasis on prosecution than on conciliation,
studies of deterrence have produced mixed results. In the words of criminology professor E.A.
Fattah, research on deterrence "is in an early stage of development and has a long way to go
before the basic issues are clarified and before major hypotheses are verified." See E.A. Fattah,
"Deterrence: A Review of the Literature", in Law Reform Commission of Canada, *Fear of
Punishment: Deterrence* (Ottawa: Supply and Services, 1976), p. 99.

Page 224

In jurisdictions such as British Columbia, Alberta, Manitoba, Saskatchewan, and Ontario, orders of human-rights tribunals may be filed with a court and enforced as an order of the court. In other jurisdictions—Nova Scotia, for example—the human-rights statute provides for enforcement of the order by the appropriate authority and for penalties for its contravention. See Tarnopolsky and Pentney, *Discrimination and the Law in Canada*, revised, p. 15–66.

Pages 225–26

The results of the Canadian Civil Liberties Association's employment-agency survey in Toronto in 1975 will be found in "11 of 15 job firms show bias study finds", *Toronto Star*, October 28, 1975, p. B1. They were reported to the chairman of the Ontario Human Rights Commission in a letter from the CCLA, dated October 24, 1975.

The results of the 1976 survey in Hamilton, London, and Ottawa will be found in Canadian Civil Liberties Association, "Submissions to the Ontario Human Rights Commission, Re: Review of Ontario Human Rights Code", Toronto, January 1977, p. 7.

Page 226

The results of the 1980 survey were aired on CTV's "W5" television program on December 7, 1980, and were reported to the minister of labour of Ontario in a letter from the CCLA, dated December 8, 1980.

The Ontario Ministry of Labour produced "Employment Agencies and Discrimination: A Discussion Paper", December 1982 [see p. (i)].

The 1983 Calgary Civil Liberties Associaiton survey will be found reported in "Firms fall for whites-only ploy", *Calgary Herald*, February 17, 1983, p. 1.

The 1987 student paper "Fieldwork Project: Private Employment Agencies and the Regulatory Environment" was prepared by Charles J. Zach and Caroline Lee for course credit at Seneca College of Applied Arts and Technology. I have quoted from page 10 of that paper.

I have also referred to the Canadian Recruiters Guild, "A Survey of Employment Discrimination in Canada" (April 1988), p. 6.

The quotes attributed to Canadian employment-agency representatives were extracted from the texts of telephone conversations with CCLA representatives in fall 1980. All of them formed part of the broadcast of the "W5" television program on December 7, 1980.

Page 227

For a review of existing provincial legislation regulating employment agencies see Ontario, Ministry of Labour, "Employment Agencies and Discrimination: A Discussion Paper", pp. 7–8.

The Ontario Health Protection and Promotion Act, 1983, SO 1983, c. 10, s. 40, authorizes the inspection of restaurants for health purposes. For an example of a provision authorizing access to lawyers' trust accounts, see RRO 1980, Reg. 573, s. 13, filed under the Ontario Law Society Act, RSO 1980, c. 233.

Page 228

The 1975 fire-department survey, the 1976 police-department survey, and the 1976 Ontario senior-civil-servant survey will all be found in Canadian Civil Liberties Association, "Submissions to the Ontario Human Rights Commission, Re: Review of Ontario Human Rights Code", Toronto, January 1977, pp. 11, 12, and 13, respectively.

The 1976 *Financial Post* survey was reported to the chairman of the Ontario Human Rights Commission in a letter from the CCLA, dated June 24, 1977.

The 1978 survey of native people in bank positions was reported to the chief commissioner of the Canadian Human Rights Commission, in a letter from the CCLA, dated January 24, 1979.

A 1985 and 1987 survey of the composition of metropolitan and provincial police forces was conducted by McMaster professor Harish Jain and can be found in "An Up-date on the Recruitment and Selection of Visible Minorities in Canadian Police Forces" (McMaster University, Faculty of Business, Working Paper No. 284, October 28, 1987), p. 4. See also his "Recruitment and Selection of Visible Minorities by Selected Canadian Police Forces", *Currents*, Vol. 3, No. 4 (Summer 1986), pp. 13–16.

Page 229

The quote attributed to Barbara Amiel will be found in "Report a blueprint for hate", *Toronto Sun*, November 25, 1984, p. CL3.

The procedure employed by the Toronto Fire Department for hiring firefighters was summarized in a memorandum dated August 23, 1976, from the fire chief to the City of Toronto Executive Committee.

For more on "Canadian experience" as a job specification, see the CCLA survey as reported to the chairman of the Ontario Human Rights Commission, in a letter dated November 24, 1975, and "Call for Canadian job experience cited as a racist device of some employers", *Globe and Mail*, November 26, 1975, p. 5.

The height and weight requirements, and policies preventing the employment of Sikhs in Canadian police forces, are discussed by Jain in "An Up-date on the Recruitment and Selection of Visible Minorities in Canadian Police Forces", pp. 16 and 14, respectively.

In the case of the Jewish woman who was fired because she would not work on a Jewish holiday, the recent amendment to the Ontario Human Rights Code, 1981, s. 10 (2), which requires that employers make reasonable accommodation, may now apply in such circumstances. See SO 1986, c. 64, s. 18 (8).

Page 231

As an example of the debate on affirmative action among civil libertarians, see Debate (Askin/Cohen), "Preferential Admission in Higher Education: Should We Support or Condemn It?", *The Civil Liberties Review*, Vol. 2, No. 2 (Spring 1975), (published by the American Civil Liberties Union), pp. 95 ff.

Page 232

A study of ethnic job segregation in Toronto revealed that men having an occupation in the natural sciences, engineering, and mathematics were 2.7 times more likely than others to be of Chinese origin. See Jeffrey G. Reitz, Liviana Calzavara, and Donna Dasko, *Ethnic Inequality and Segregation in Jobs*, Research Paper No. 123 (Toronto: Centre for Urban and Community Studies, University of Toronto, May 1981), pp. 35–45.

It will be noted that my current opposition to the use of race, ethnicity, or numbers based on them as a factor in hiring applies generally, not universally. At the moment, some possible exceptions occur.

There are some achievements and qualifications that may appear more impressive in certain non-white people than they would in certain white people because the non-whites may have had to overcome the disabilities of colour. Strictly from the point of view of merit, therefore, colour can sometimes be a valid tool of assessment.

As another possibility, it might not be inappropriate to require racial or ethnic numbers where an employer, found guilty of discrimination, plans to hire essentially unskilled workers. The combination of established guilt on the part of the employer and no significant distinctions among the potential employees arguably might justify special measures.

Even apart from such situations, I do not necessarily suggest that the merit principle must always apply. My point is, simply, that exceptions based upon race and ethnicity should be generally impermissible. Conceivably, however, an exception to the merit principle might be created for the disadvantaged. Suppose, for example, a builder won a government contract to build roads and low-cost housing in some depressed area. I see nothing wrong with providing priority access to the new jobs on the basis of the degree of poverty and length of unemployment that candidates may have been suffering. Just as our society lowers the tax rate on the basis of lower income, so might we expand job opportunities on that basis. While certain racial minorities such as native people would likely benefit from such an arrangement, the scheme would nevertheless be colour blind. It would not likely benefit the few native people who happened to grow up in Westmount or Rosedale.

Page 232–33

At present, provision for "contract compliance" can be found in the Canadian Human Rights Act, RSC 1985, c. H-6, s. 23, which provides that the Governor-in-Council "may make regulations respecting the terms and conditions to be included in or applicable to any contract, licence or grant" made by Her Majesty in right of Canada. As of spring 1988, no regulations had been issued. However, Parliament has passed the Employment Equity Act, SC 1984–85–86, c. 31, and a new federal contractor's program of contract compliance; see William F. Pentney, *Discrimination and the Law, Revised,* Cum. Supp. (Toronto: Richard De Boo, 1987), pp. 27–28.

The American evolution of "contract compliance" in government contracts and subcontracts is reviewed by Tarnopolsky and Pentney in *Discrimination and the Law*, revised, pp. 4–51 to 4–55.

Page 233

Beyond those situations involving actual business between the government and private-sector employers, enforceable agreements normally require some exchange of burdens and benefits (the legal term is "consideration"). For such purposes, however, there is no need to be enslaved by the technicalities of contract law. Even in the absence of such consideration, if publicity and pressure are not enough to produce performance, the agreements might be made enforceable by statute.

Page 234

In order to assist in the surveys recommended here, provision might be made for the companies themselves to collect racial and ethnic data on their employees. In order to address the disquiet that such an exercise might create, the material could be transmitted to the commissions without ever entering the companies' records. Moreover, the disclosures of the information could be made voluntary on the part of the employees. Even if co-operation is not one hundred per cent, it is likely to be great enough to be helpful.

For an example of a racial-auditing scheme that does not repose undue trust in its targets, see the CCLA letter to Ontario Ministry of Labour, February 11, 1983.

Page 235

A number of "affirmative-initiative" recommendations similar to mine were proposed by Toronto's Equal Opportunity Division in its "Background Report on Contract Compliance", City of Toronto, March 1983. See also "Toronto urged to demand equal hiring", *Globe and Mail*, July 30, 1983, p. 4.

For details on the policies of the veterinary authorities regarding foreign graduates, see Canadian Civil Liberties Association, "Submissions to the Ontario Human Rights Commission, Re: Veterinary Licensing Practices", Toronto, April 3, 1979, and "Veterinary licence bias alleged by rights group", *Globe and Mail*, April 10, 1979, p. 4.

Page 236

For information on the way the United Kingdom has handled foreign veterinary graduates, see the Royal College of Veterinary Surgeons, "General Information for the Guidance of Candidates" (February 1970), and the Veterinary Surgeons Act (U.K.), 1966, c. 36 s. 6 (1). For comparable U.S. information, see Educational Commission for Foreign Veterinary Graduates, American Veterinary Medical Association, "Information for Graduates of Colleges of Veterinary Medicine outside the United States and Canada", September 1, 1976.

In a speech to the Canadian Medical Association dated June 21, 1967, then minister of manpower and immigration Jean Marchand offered financial assistance to evaluate foreign medical school graduates. See Toronto and District Labour Committee for Human Rights, "Submissions to Committee on the Healing Arts", December 11, 1967, p. 5.

Pages 236–37

The case of the native man who received no advice about the Ontario Criminal Injuries Compensation Board was reported in Canadian Civil Liberties Education Trust, *Indian Life and Canadian Law: A Report on the Ontario North* (Toronto: CCLET, 1973), p. 37.

Page 237

The 1981 case of the woman entitled to a veteran's pension was brought to my attention by Keewaytinok Native Legal Services of Moosonee, Ontario. The case of the previously unredeemed tax refund was brought to my attention in 1983 by Kinna-Aweya Legal Clinic of Thunder Bay, Ontario.

Pages 237–38

Instances where Canadian Civil Liberties Association field-workers have found valid but unfulfilled legal claims were reported in *Indian Life and Canadian Law: A Report on the Ontario North*, pp. 37 ff. The same publication contains information on the problems resulting from lack of low-cost transportation (pp. 9–11).

Pages 238–39

Although generally a private golf club or college fraternity should not be subject to our human rights codes, it should be recognized that sometimes a façade of privacy is used to mask a facility that essentially serves the public. For my purposes here, I refer only to the truly private organization.

Page 239

The B'nai B'rith and UAW responses to racially restricted clubs are reported in A. Borovoy, *Human Rights and Racial Equality—The Tactics of Combat* (Toronto: Ontario Woodsworth Memorial Foundation, 1964), pp. 6 and 7.

Page 240–41

For a review of the extension of human rights beyond race, see Tarnopolsky and Pentney, *Discrimination and the Law,* revised (Toronto: Richard De Boo, 1985), ch. VII to IX.

Page 241

Disrespect for our human rights commissions manifested itself in various ways, including the dismissal of directors and, in British Columbia, its virtual dismantling. See "Not all right", *Globe and Mail*, November 13, 1984, p. M5, and, in British Columbia, the parsimonious Human Rights Act, SBC 1984, c. 22. Regarding the lack of increased funding in, for example, Manitoba, see the article by former executive director of the Manitoba Association of Rights and Liberties Abraham Arnold, "Rights code broadened", *Winnipeg Free Press*, July 22, 1987, p. 17.

The British Columbia case that upheld the right of long-haired people to be served in a pub is *Douglas Oram and Mariam Joan McLaren* v. *Frank Pho*, unreported, B.C. Board of Inquiry, August 8, 1975 (Wood). I have quoted from p. 21 of the judgment.

Page 242

The case of the high school student is reported in "Civil liberties...boy who wouldn't shave wins", *Toronto Daily Star*, October 9, 1968, p. 13.

"Adult only" apartment buildings are prohibited in Ontario because of the Human Rights Code provision outlawing discrimination in accommodations on the basis of "family status". Apartment buildings had been exempt from this provision until a recent amendment. See the Equality Rights Statute Law Amendment Act, 1986, SO 1986, c. 64, s. 18 (12).

The three Ontario parties agreed to this amendment to the code at the committee stage. However, the Conservatives attempted to amend the proposed law at third reading by permitting condominiums to be "adult only". See Ontario, Legislative Assembly, *Debates*, No. 77 (December 9, 1986), pp. 4065 ff.

Former Toronto mayor John Sewell described the now repealed section of the code that permitted landlords to refuse accommodation to families as "one of the more shameful sections in Ontario's so-called Human Rights Code." See "What's Right Is Right", *Globe and Mail*, February 11, 1985, p. 13.

Sometimes, laws such as the one enacted in Ontario to prohibit discrimination against families with children represent a response to a crisis situation. Conceivably, therefore, my proposed mix of carrots and sticks may not provide fast enough relief. In such event, it might be wise to ban discrimination against children for, let us say, a two-year period but permit exceptions in a number of circumstances. Obviously, a senior-citizen building would be one such exception. In addition, the law might exempt those buildings where the landlord could demonstrate the likelihood that the majority of tenants selected the place in the belief that it was reserved for adults. If the landlord had advertised that way, for example, this might be relatively easy to establish. Such exceptions would obviously be repugnant in the case of discrimination against blacks.

CHAPTER TWELVE

Page 245

For the powers of human rights investigators in Ontario to enter places and examine materials, see the Ontario Human Rights Code, 1981, SO 1981, c. 53, s. 32 (3). See also, among other provinces, the Saskatchewan Human Rights Code, RSS 1978, c. S-24.1, s. 28.

For examples of the invective employed to protest the warrantless powers of investigation in the Ontario code, see: "Bill's Bad Bill" [ed.], *Toronto Sun*, June 23, 1981, p. 10 ("totalitarian"); Claire Hoy, "Human wrongs code", *Sunday [Toronto] Sun*, January 27, 1985, p. CL2 ("stormtroopers"), and "Human rights? Humbug!", *Toronto Sun*, December 9, 1981, p. 35 ("fascism", "stormtrooper law"); lawyer Clayton Ruby's comments and those of the Ontario New Democratic Party are reported in "Ontario's code has serious flaws, critics say", *Toronto Star*, July 2, 1981, p. A14 (Ruby: "the kinds of powers they have in totalitarian countries"; Jim Renwick: "immensely sweeping powers").

For some of labour minister Robert Elgie's statements on the warrantless power of entry under the Ontario code, see "Elgie changing human rights proposals", *Globe and Mail*, September 11, 1981, p. 4.

But the Charter is now being used to attack these types of powers. For instance, in Saskatchewan, see *Re Cole and F.W. Woolworth Co. Ltd. et al.* (1985), 22 DLR (4th) 609 (Sask. QB).

Page 246

Examples of powers of inspection and production similar to those contained in the Ontario code can be found in Ontario in the Employment Standards Act, RSO 1980, c. 137, s. 45; the Labour Relations Act, RSO 1980, c. 228, s. 103 (e) (g); and the Canada Unemployment Insurance Act, RSC 1985, c. U-1, s. 95. See also Appendix "A" to the Ontario Court of Appeal decision in *R.* v. *Rao* (1984), 9 DLR (4th) 542, pp. 572-73.

Page 247

For the primary obligation to conciliate complaints, see the Ontario Human Rights Code, 1981, s. 35 (1).

Page 248

For more on the ability of the police to conduct searches of the person, see James A. Fontana, *The Law of Search and Seizure in Canada*, 2nd ed. (Toronto: Butterworths, 1984), pp. 213 ff.

For examples of the reactions to the requirement that sports fans submit to the search of their bags and parcels, see "Booze checks at CNE stadium called unlawful", *Toronto Star*, June 5, 1984, p. A1.

Page 249

The Ontario law empowering the stopping of cars and the taking of breath samples is An Act to Amend the Highway Traffic Act, SO 1981, c. 72, s. 1, as amended.

For examples of press attacks on the new law, see the following editorials: "Spot checks with spot penalties", *Globe and Mail*, December 1, 1981, p. 6; "The court by the curb", *Globe and Mail*, December 23, 1981, p. 6; "Unwise role for the police", *Toronto Star*, December 1, 1981, p. A8, and "Block McMurtry's unwise bill", *Toronto Star*, December 17, 1981, p. A8. See also J. E. Magnet, "Spot checks vs. Charter: roadside injustice", *Globe and Mail*, January 7, 1982, p. 7.

Regarding the objections of the Opposition, see Ontario, Legislative Assembly, *Debates*, No. 124 (December 10, 1981), pp. 4441 and 4454.

Page 250

The Ontario law has been the subject of unsuccessful Charter challenges on the bases, among others, that motorists are arbitrarily detained and are subject to unreasonable search and seizure. See *Hufsky* v. *The Queen*, unreported, Supreme Court of Canada, No. 19028, April 28, 1988, and *Thomson* v. *The Queen*, unreported, Supreme Court of Canada, No. 19516, April 28, 1988.

Other examples of inspections authorized by legislation designed to protect the public safety will be found in the Ontario Health Protection and Promotion Act, 1983, SO 1983, c. 10, s. 40, and the Ontario Occupational Health and Safety Act, RSO 1980, c. 321, s. 28.

Regarding the requirement that lawyers make their books available for inspection, see, for example, RRO 1980, Reg. 573, s. 13, filed under the Ontario Law Society Act, RSO 1980, c. 233.

Page 252

For my testimony on the Ontario stop-and-check law before the relevant committee of the Ontario legislature, see Standing Committee on Administration of Justice, December 15, 1981, pp. 2–5. More recently, the Supreme Court of Canada held that the lack of criteria for the selection of drivers was arbitrary. However, the court found that this arbitrariness was "a reasonable limit" under section 1 of the Charter. See *Hufsky* v. *The Queen*.

Whereas the law at one time would not allow accused people to testify, today it does not oblige them to do so. See section 11 (c) of the Canadian Charter of Rights and Freedoms.

Regarding the history of the right to remain silent, see The Hon. R.E. Salhany, *The Origin of Rights* (Toronto: Carswell, 1986), Ch. 8, and, on its scope in Canada, *R.* v. *Marcoux & Soloman* (1976), 24 CCC (2d) 1, [1976] 1 SCR 763 (SCC).

Pages 252–53

For examples of the initial reaction to the federal law that authorizes breathalyzer tests, see "Breath-analysis test by police under attack", *Fort Williams Times Journal*, May 22, 1969. A recent Charter challenge, which unsuccessfully argued that this law infringed the right against self-incrimination is *R.* v. *Altseimer* (1982), 1 CCC (3d) 7, 38 OR (2d) 783 (Ont. CA).

Pages 254

For more discussion regarding instances where an innocent person may tell the police a false story, see the late Arthur Maloney's address "The Right to Remain Silent" (n.d.).

The compulsory extraction of blood samples from unconscious drivers has been the subject of challenges under section 8 of the Charter, the search-and-seizure section, rather than section 11 (c), the right-of-silence section. See, for example, *R.* v. *Carter* (1982), 2 CCC (3d) 412, 144 DLR (3d) 301 (Ont. CA).

For examples of the duty of police officers to answer the questions of their superiors, see RRO 1980, Reg. 680, Sched. (Code of Offences), s. 1 (ii) (b), filed under the Ontario Police Act, RSO 1980, c. 381, and on the inadmissibility of such answers at civilian complaint hearings, see, for example, the Metropolitan Toronto Police Force Complaints Act, 1984, SO 1984, c. 63, s. 23 (14). According to RCMP rules currently under review, failure to provide a statement could result in the commission of a "major service offence", making an officer liable to imprisonment for up to one year. See Canada, *Report of the Commission of Inquiry Relating to Public Complaints, Internal Discipline and Grievance Procedure Within the Royal Canadian Mounted Police* (Judge René J. Marin, chairman), (Ottawa: Information Canada, 1976), p. 152, and the Royal Canadian Mounted Police Act, RSC 1985, c. R-10, ss. 25, 36.

Pages 254–55

For examples of the duty of employees to answer the questions of their employers regarding an employee's job-related misconduct, see *Re Ford Motor Co. of Canada Ltd. and UAW, Local 432* (1974), 8 LAC (2d) 10 (Williams) and *Re BC Hydro and IBEW, Local 258* (1985), 18 LAC (3d) 113 (Munroe).

Pages 255–56

The recent Supreme Court of Canada ruling may be found in *R. v. Morgentaler, Smoling and Scott* (1988), 37 CCC (3d) 449, [1988] 1 SCR 30 (SCC).

Dr. Morgentaler's trials are briefly reviewed in "Court ruling resolves 20-year-old battle for women's rights", *Globe and Mail*, January 29, 1988, p. A11.

Page 256

Some of the abortion laws of the Western democracies are canvassed by Mr. Justice Beetz in his concurring reasons in *R. v. Morgentaler et al.*, [1988] 1 SCR 30 at p. 127, and see Mary Anne Glendon, *Abortion and Divorce in Western Law* (Cambridge, Mass.: Harvard University Pres, 1987), pp. 13 ff., App. A and B.

Page 257

Although medical advances have improved upon the situation, there remains a risk that pregnant diabetics can develop a retinal disease and, ultimately, blindness. See Dorothy Reycroft Hollingsworth, *Pregnancy, Diabetes and Birth* (Baltimore: Williams and Wilkins, 1984), at pp. 110–12, and Kenneth R. Niswander and Manuel Port, "Abortion Practices in the United States: A Medical Viewpoint", in J. Douglas Butler and David F. Walbert, eds., *Abortion, Medicine and the Law* (New York: Facts on File Publications, 1986) 248, at pp. 251–54.

For a discussion regarding the reliability of psychiatric judgments, see Chapter Nine, pp. 187–88.

Pages 257–58

The analogy of carrying a baby to term to being a good Samaritan has also been made by Judith Jarvis Thomson in "A Defense of Abortion", (1971) 1 *Philosophy and Public Affairs* 1.

Page 258

The Abortion Act (U.K.) 1967, c. 87, s. 4, provides for health-care givers who conscientiously object to exempt themselves from participating in abortion procedures, unless there is imminent danger to the life of the mother and no other reasonable alternative available.

See Margaret A. Sommerville, "Reflections on Canadian Abortion Law: Evacuation and Destruction—Two Separate Issues", (1981) 31 *University of Toronto Law Journal* 1. She argues that the fetus should be saved, if technologically feasible, once removed from the mother. For a discussion of the ability of children to sue for damage caused to them while in the fetal state, see Edward W. Keyserlingk, *The Unborn Child's Right to Prenatal Care*, McGill Legal Studies, No. 5 (Montreal: Quebec Research Centre for Private and Comparative Law, 1984), ch. III.

Page 259

For one of the original articulations of the "dues shop" principle, see the arbitration award by Mr. Justice Ivan Rand reported at 1 CLLR para. 2150. For a more detailed account, see D. Moulton, "Ford Windsor 1945", in Iriving Abella, ed., *On Strike: Six Key Labour Struggles in Canada* (Toronto: James Lorimer & Company, 1974). For examples of how the law deals with these concepts, see Ontario Labour Relations Act, RSO 1980, c. 228, ss. 43, 46; the British Columbia Labour Code, RSBC 1979, c. 212, ss. 10, 29; The [Saskatchewan] Trade Union Act, SS, c. T-17, ss. 32, 36.

Page 260

Virtually all Canadian jurisdictions provide for union certification when a majority of eligible voters in a collective-bargaining unit cast their vote in favour of union representation. See, for example, the Ontario Labour Relations Act, s. 7 (3) and the British Columbia Labour Code, s. 45 (1) (a). Once certified, a union is obliged to represent all employees in the unit for collective bargaining purposes. See, for example, the Ontario Labour Relations Act, s. 50, and the British Columbia Labour Code, s. 46. Labour legislation permits the negotiation of a union shop, and that provision is enforceable during the life of the collective agreement. See, for example, the Ontario Labour Relations Act, s. 46, and the Manitoba Labour Relations Act, CCSM L10, s. 18 (2).

A number of bitter strikes fought over union security are discussed in Irving Abella, ed., *On Strike*.

Page 261

Many Canadian jurisdictions provide recourse to labour relations boards in certain situations if a union acts towards a union member in a manner that is arbitrary, discriminatory, or in bad faith. It is considered a component of the duty of fair representation. See, for example, the Ontario Labour Relations Act, s. 68, and the Manitoba Labour Relations Act, s. 16.

Pages 261–62

For examples of enactments that accommodate the conscientious objection to joining a union or paying union dues, see the Ontario Labour Relations Act, s. 47, and the B.C. Labour Code, s. 11.

For a case under the Ontario act, see *Re Ontario Public Service Employees Union and Forer et al.* (1985), 52 OR (2d) 705 (Ont. CA), overruling (1984), 46 OR (2d) 789 (Ont. Div. Ct.).

Pages 262–63

I have referred to *Re Lavigne and O.P.S.E.U. et al.* (1986), 55 OR (2d) 449, 86 CLLC para. 14 039, and (No. 2) (1987), 60 OR (2d) 486 (Ont. HCJ). For a review of some of the past activities of the National Citizen's Coalition, see N. Fillimore, "The Right Stuff", *This Magazine*, Vol. 20, No. 2, (June/July 1986), p. 4.

Page 263

In the Lavigne case, the trial court declared that non-members of the union could object to the use of their union dues for purposes other than collective bargaining and administration of the collective agreement. (Authority for the conscription of these dues was the Colleges Collective Bargaining Act, RSO 1980, c. 74, s. 53). Lavigne had challenged the use of dues for financial contributions to any political party; to disarmament campaigns, including the campaign against cruise missile testing; for campaigns in favour of free choice in abortion; for opposing the domed stadium in Toronto; to the striking U.K. coal miners; towards the recognition of the PLO; for medical and food aid projects in Nicaragua and a tour in Canada by two Nicaraguan union members. No money was, in fact, expended by either OPSEU or the OFL in support of the PLO. In the result, all of the impugned actual contributions, except for those to striking U.K. coal miners and towards a tour of Canada by two Nicaraguans, were declared objectionable. See *Re Lavigne and O.P.S.E.U. et al.*, 55 OR (2d), p. 461, and (No. 2) (1987), 60 OR (2d), pp. 506–23.

The case is currently being considered by the Ontario Court of Appeal. For counterparts in the U.S. Supreme Court, see *Abood* v. *Detroit Board of Education* (1977), 431 U.S. 209, 97 S. Ct. 1782, *Ellis* v. *Railway Clerks* (1984), 466 U.S. 435, 104 S. Ct. 1883, and *Chicago Teachers Union* v. *Hudson* (1986), 54 LW 4231.

In Ontario car insurance is made mandatory by the Compulsory Automboile Insurance Act, RSO 1980, c. 83, s. 2. Auto insurance companies are free to contribute to the political parties of their choice and to lobby government either individually or through associations such as the Insurance Bureau of Canada, the Insurers Advisory Organization of Canada, and the Association of Canadian Insurers. Imagine the difficulty certain radical socialists would have trying to find an insurance company whose activities would suit their political preferences. There would also be the further difficulty of being able to determine what the companies' political contributions or activites were. Such information is not easily accessible.

Although the monopoly utility Bell Canada appears to make no direct political contributions, Bell's parent corporation and sole shareholder, Bell Canada Enterprises Inc. (BCE), does. BCE conducts its own lobbying of government regarding, for example, tax breaks for research and development. BCE is also a member of the pressure group the Business Council on National

Issues, which makes representations to government regarding a wide variety of business and social policy issues such as free trade. See the Canadian Labour Congress document "Analysis of Corporate Empires and Their Federal Political Donations (1984)"; Michael Salter, "The Power and the Profit", *Report on Business* magazine, Vol. 4, No. 10 (April 1988), 28 at p. 30; Business Council National Issues: "Social Policy Reform and the National Agenda", Ottawa, December 1986; and "The Canada–United States Free Trade Agreement—Submission to the Ontario Select Committee on Economic Affairs", Toronto, January 28, 1988.

Bell Canada subscribers have no redress against this high-powered lobbying, as BCE is not a regulated company.

Pages 263–64

Regarding the role of the trade-union movement in the development of Canadian social policy, see the "Platform of Principles" of the Trades and Labour Congress in *The Fourteenth Annual Session of the Trades and Labour Congress of Canada Held at Winnipeg, Man.*, September 16–20, 1898, p. 2, and reproduced in Desmond Morton with Terry Copp, *Working People* (Ottawa: Deneau & Greenberg, 1980), p. 61. See also Wayne Roberts, "The little movement that grew", in Clancy, Roberts, Spencer, and Ward, *All for One* (Toronto: OPSEU, 1985), p. 61 ff.

Page 264

Regarding the CLC repudiation of the OFL resolution on the PLO, see Wilfred List, "Case puts union's extra-curricular activities on trial", *Globe and Mail*, November 14, 1985, p. B20.

For an opposing viewpoint to mine, see Colin Brown and David Somerville, " 'Opting in' to union political activity", *Toronto Star*, December 3, 1985, p. A15, and David M. Beatty, *Putting the Charter to Work: Designing a Constitutional Labour Code* (Kingston and Montreal: McGill-Queen's University Press, 1987), pp. 127–32.

Page 265

I have quoted Claire Hoy from his article "A tarnished champion", *Toronto Sun*, June 14, 1981, p. 12. I did argue that immunity from judicial review required panels for human-rights boards of inquiry to be chosen more fairly and not case by case by the Ontario Human Rights Commission itself. See my testimony before the Ontario Legislature, Standing Committee on Resources Development, June 11, 1981, pp. 23–24.

The McRuer commission report endorsed a broad legal right of access to the courts from the decisions of administrative tribunals. See Ontario, Royal Commission, *Inquiry into Civil Rights*, Report I, Volume 1, (Ontario: Queen's Printer, 1968), pp. 304–14 and 326–29.

A.V. Dicey is quoted from his *Introduction to the Study of the Law of the Constitution*, 10th ed. (London: Macmillan, 1960), p. 188. For an incisive critique of Dicey's views on this matter, see

H.W. Arthurs, "Rethinking Administrative Law: A Slightly Dicey Business", (1979) 17 *Osgoode Hall Law Journal* 1.

Page 268

The quote attributed to counsel for the Ontario Labour Relations Board in the *Globe and Mail* case can be found in the outline of arguments before the Ontario Court of Appeal in *Re Toronto Newspaper Guild et al.*, [1952] 2 DLR 302, [1952] OR 345, p. 355. The Supreme Court of Canada subsequently affirmed the decisions of the lower courts revoking certification of the Newspaper Guild. See *In Re Ontario Labour Relations Board*, [1953] 2 SCR 18.

Page 269

The "inferior tribunal" quote is from the judgment of Mr. Justice Kellock in *In Re Ontario Labour Relations Board*, [1953] SCR 18, at p. 35. For an interesting critique of this judicial attitude to "privative clauses", see B. Laskin, "Certiorari to Labour Boards: The Apparent Futility of Privative Clauses", (1952) 30 *Canadian Bar Review* 986, p. 992.

For the statutory amendment restoring the power of the Labour Relations Board, which had been overturned by the courts in the *Globe and Mail* case, see An Act to Amend the Labour Relations Act, SO 1954, c. 42, s. 23.

Page 270

The discharge case in which the Supreme Court of Canada overruled the arbitration board is *Port Arthur Shipbuilding Co.* v. *Arthurs et al.* (1968), 70 DLR (2d) 693, [1969] SCR 85 (SCC), affirming (1967), 62 DLR (2d) 342, [1967] 2 OR 49 *sub nom. R.* v. *Arthurs, Ex.p. Port Arthur Shipbuilding Co.* (Ont. CA), reversing (1966), 60 DLR (2d) 214, [1967] 1 OR 272 (Ont. HC). The quote from Mr. Justice Judson can be found at 70 DLR (2d) 693, pp. 696 and 697, and the relevant provisions of the collective agreement can be found on pages 695–96.

Page 271

For the statutory amendment that allowed arbitration boards to substitute lesser penalties for those of discharge, see An Act to Amend the Labour Relations Act (No. 2), SO 1970, c. 85, s. 12 (2).

Page 272

I have referred to the case of *Canadian Car & Foundry Co. Ltd.* v. *Dinham* (1959), 21 DLR (2d) 273, [1960] SCR 3, at p. 9, where the Supreme Court of Canada decided, in *obiter dicta*, that compulsory retirement at age sixty-five was not a violation of the seniority or discharge clause in the collective agreement. Subsequently, in *Bell Canada* v. *Office and Professional Employees Union, Local 131* (1973), 37 DLR (3d) 561, the Supreme Court of Canada held that compulsory retirement was not a form of "dismissal" that would entitle an employee to invoke the grievance procedure. As a tribute to my consistency (or lack of growth) over the years, see the discussion of this issue in my concurring opinion in *Re International Chemical Workers, Local 174 & Dominion Tar & Chemical Co. Ltd.* (1960), 10 LAC 331.

For a discussion of the rationale, or lack of it, in the distinction between compulsory retirement and discharge, see *Bell Canada and Office Professional Employees International Union, Local 131*, unreported (Weiler), in *Labour Relations Law* (Kingston: Industrial Relations Centre, Queen's University, 1981), 341, at pp. 342–43; *Anaconda American Brass* (1963) 14 LAC 52 (Cross); *Re UAW and Libby, McNeil and Libby Ltd.* (1954), 5 LAC 2120 (Roach).

For an example of the criticism levelled at the *Canadian Car & Foundry* case, see J.J. Spector, "Case Comment", (1960) 38 *Canadian Bar Review* 418, p. 423.

Pages 272–73

The Christian Labour Association case is *R. v. Ontario Labour Relations Board, Ex parte Trenton Const. Workers' Assoc., Local 52* (1963), 39 DLR (2d) 593. The quote of Chief Justice McRuer appears on page 607.

Page 274

The 1979 case in which Mr. Justice Dickson noted the value of not intruding on the decisions of labour boards is *Canadian Union of Public Employees, Local 963 v. New Brunswick Liquor Corp.*, [1979] 2 SCR 227, 97 DLR (3d) 417, p. 424.

The case that turned on the labour-board practice of involving more than panel members in discussing policy implications of current cases is *Re Consolidated-Bathurst Packaging Ltd. and International Woodworkers of America, Local 2-69 et al.* (1985), 51 OR (2d) 481 (Ont. Div. Ct.). Mr. Justice Osler, in his dissenting judgment at pages 500–01, reviews the composition and practice of the OLRB. The Ontario Court of Appeal reversed this decision at (1986), 56 OR (2d) 513 [leave to appeal to the Supreme Court of Canada has been granted: (1987), 59 OR (2d) 736].

Pages 274–75

The case involving the Seventh-Day Adventist is *Re Ontario Human Rights Commission and Simpsons-Sears Ltd.* (1983), 23 DLR (4th) 321, [1985] 2 SCR 536 (SCC), reversing (1982), 138 DLR (3d) 133, 38 OR (2d) 423 (Ont. CA), affirming (1982), 133 DLR (3d) 611, 36 OR (2d) 59 (Ont. Div. Ct.), affirming (1980), 2 CHRRD 267 (*sub nom. O'Malley v. Simpson Sears Ltd.*). The quote is from the judgment of Lacourciere, J.A., in the Ontario Court of Appeal, at 138 DLR (3d) 133, pp. 136–37. The Supreme Court of Canada subsequently gave relief to the Seventh Day Adventist employee. In fairness, the judgment of the Supreme Court of Canada is preferable to that of the board of inquiry. They both agreed that, as long as there was a discriminatory effect, establishment of an offence under the code might not require proof of a discriminatory intent. Unlike the board, however, the court said that discrimination could be found even if the commission did not lead evidence as to the failure of the employer to make reasonable accommodation for the complainant's religious convictions. While I think that the judgment of the Supreme Court of Canada is better in these relevant respects than all of the previous judgments, the judgment of the Board of Inquiry was nevertheless superior to those of the Divisional Court and Court of Appeal. Since so few cases reach the Supreme Court of Canada, it is likely that, in most situations, the lower courts will have the last word. Moreover, appeals to our higher courts cost money and precious time. For the sake of having cases heard by some combination of judges, most of whom have been less right than so many boards of inquiry, I don't believe these appeals are worth the money or the time. Many members of minority groups have been particularly critical about the length of time it often takes to resolve human-rights complaints. This is a factor that threatens to undermine public respect for the protections that our human-rights statutes promise.

Page 275

The Ontario Legislature subsequently amended the Human Rights Code, 1981, to give effect to the Board of Inquiry's conclusion in *Simpsons-Sears*. See Equality Rights Statute Law Amendment Act, SO 1986, c. 64, s. 18 (7).

CHAPTER THIRTEEN

Page 278

An account of the Israeli strike will be found in "Israel defiant as attack condemned", *Globe and Mail*, June 9, 1981, p. 1, and in Shlomo Nakdimon, *First Strike* (New York: Summit Books 1987).

Pages 278–79

See the editorial "Begin's dangerous folly", *Toronto Star*, June 9, 1981, p. A8.

Page 279

See the editorial "Terrorism, not policing", *Halifax Herald*, June 10, 1981, p. 6.

Page 280

See the editorial "Begin's big gamble", Ottawa *Citizen*, June 10, 1981, p. 6.

Historian Telford Taylor, in *Munich: The Price of Peace* (New York: Doubleday, 1979), pp. 998–1000, has concluded that, had France intervened to preserve Rhineland demilitarizaion in March 1936, Hitler could have been kept in check without seriously risking a major war. William L. Shirer, in *20th Century Journey: A Memoir of the Life and the Times*, Vol. II: *The Nightmare*

Years, 1930–1940 (Boston: Little Brown, 1984), p. 250, reports Hitler himself admitting that the Western democracies could have brought his regime "tumbling down" if they had intervened in the Rhineland in 1936.

See the editorial "World peace at risk", *Edmonton Journal*, June 10, 1981, p. A2.

Pages 281–82

I have quoted from Gerald Caplan's article "Defence plan reflects outdated dogma", *Toronto Star*, December 20, 1987, p. B3.

Although my remarks criticize Caplan's attack on the assumptions found in the Defence Department's White Paper on Defence, it does not necessarily follow that I am defending the Canadian government's defence policy.

Indeed, if Caplan had simply criticized the magnitude of Canada's defence plans on the basis that the West is already sufficiently armed and, in any event, the Soviet threat has been subsiding in the age of Gorbachev, it is likely that I would not have responded to his column. But Caplan minimized the nature of the Soviet challenge without even mentioning Gorbachev, and he claimed that, in any event, the Americans posed as great a threat to democratic values. Since this characterization of the world has a potential life beyond the limited context in which it was expressed, I thought it important to join issue. It should also be noted that in a subsequent column Caplan movingly described how the Communists have betrayed the ideals of their movement. See "Recalling the Communist Nightmare", *Sunday [Toronto] Star,* August 14, 1988, p. B3.

Page 282

Although Khrushchev did offer to exchange Soviet missiles in Cuba for American missiles in Turkey, he subsequently dropped the matter. Regarding the obsolete nature of the Turkish missiles, see Robert F. Kennedy, *Thirteen Days* (New York and London: W.W. Norton, 1971), pp. 72–73, 86–87, and Thomas J. Schoenbaum, *Waging Peace and War* (New York: Simon & Schuster, 1988), p. 322.

Pages 282–83

Regarding the threat by the Soviet Union, supported by the Warsaw Pact countries, to sign a separate treaty with East Germany, see "Warsaw Pact chiefs meet; Agree on German treaty", *New York Times*, August 16, 1961, p. 1. The Soviets claimed that, if this was signed, the Western alliance would have to make its own arrangements with East Germany regarding access to West Berlin. See General Lucius D. Clay, "Berlin", *Foreign Affairs*, Vol. 41, No. 1 (October 1962), p. 53.

Page 283

For a discussion of the extent of Soviet arms assistance in the Third World, either directly or through intermediaries such as Cuba, see Stephen R. David, *Third World Coups d'Etat and*

International Security (Baltimore and London: Johns Hopkins University Press, 1987), pp. 75 ff.

The quotes attributed to Lenin can be found in Lenin, *Selected Works*, Vol. VIII (Moscow: Foreign Languages Publishing House, 1951), p. 297, and Sidney Hook, *Marx and the Marxists* (Princeton, N.J.: Von Nostrand, 1955), p. 192, respectively.

   Even Stalin's "socialism in one country" apparently did not depart from Lenin's expansionist vision. According to Stalin, "It is a Leninist principle that the final victory of socialism...is only possible on an international scale.... For what else is our country, 'the country that is building up socialism', but the base of world revolution?" (Stalin, *Problems of Leninism*, Vol. I, pp. 60, 63), quoted in Sidney Hook, *Political Power and Personal Freedom* (New York: Collier Books, 1962), p. 153.

Page 284

Throughout his book *Perestroika* (New York: Harper & Row, 1987), Mikhail Gorbachev credits Lenin as the ideological source for his policies (pp. 25–26, 54, 96). At pp. 150–51 he denies that Lenin ever aimed to promote Communism world-wide.

Page 285

For more on the irrevocability of full-fledged Communist regimes, see note to page 292.

Page 286

The report of the band of Soviet dissidents announcing the formation of a new political party may be found in Natan Sharansky, "Glasnost may be Glasnost, but prison is prison", *New York Times*, May 25, 1988, p. 27.

Since my May 1 cut-off date, there have been remarkable developments in the Communist bloc. In late June 1988, the Soviet Communist Party convened a conference that discussed radical reform of the country's government structure. For the first time since the early days of the Bolshevik revolution, party members publicly criticized incumbent leaders. Not long after the conference, there was a report that the Cubans may soon be leaving Angola. The Soviets had already begun to pull out of Afghanistan.

   All this has generated a level of hope that few would have dared to harbour several years ago. Nevertheless, we know that in the best of systems there is usually a wide gulf between promise and performance. In the Soviet system this gulf could be even wider. Reform has to overcome an entrenched culture of Marxist-Leninist ideology and an entrenched practice of totalitarian coercion. While my hopes, like those of many people, have been kindled by these developments, I stand by the main theme of this chapter. Good sense requires democrats to resist both unrepentant hawks for whom legitimate negotiations border on appeasement and redemptive doves who mistake appeasement for legitimate negotiations. Both make poor negotiators: the former because they give too little; the latter because they give too much.

Yet this chapter is concerned less with the details of foreign policy than with the mind-set of those who participate in the debate. What is particularly significant about those I quote is that none of them based their arguments on Gorbachev, *glasnost*, or *perestroika*. In some cases, of course, this is because the quotes pre-date the Gorbachev era. In all cases, this is because of basic misconceptions about the international arena. If the current developments in the Kremlin really achieve a fundamental liberalization of the Soviet system, my admonitions will not matter as much. If such liberalization does not occur, my caveats will prove more timely than ever. In any event, even the diminution of the Soviet threat will not, by itself, divest the international arena of its jungle character.

Unfortunately, there are other threats to peace and democracy—for example, Iran, Libya, and some of their extremist allies. It remains imperative, therefore, that we examine the mind-sets in our society so that the democratic system can more realistically face whatever challenges this uncertain world throws at us.

Page 287

The quotes attributed to Dr. Helen Caldicott are excerpts from an address to the Annual Conference of Operation Dismantle, Ottawa, September 1983, published in *Humanist in Canada*, Summer 1984, No. 69 (Vol. 17, No. 2), 3, at pp. 5 and 4, respectively.

Page 288

For a review of the practical effects of Gorbachev's policies, see Robert C. Tucker, *Political Culture and Leadership in Soviet Russia*, Ch. 7: "To Change a Political Culture: Gorbachev and the Fight for Soviet Reform", pp. 140 ff.

Pages 288–89

Six major Canadian church leaders advocated a nuclear freeze and "no-first-use pledge" in a December 17, 1983, letter to the prime minister of Canada, reproduced in *The Church and Nuclear Disarmament (Rev'd 1985)* (Project Ploughshares Working Paper 85-3), p. 3. On page 1 can be found their conclusion that under no circumstances could the use of nuclear weapons be justified. This point of view was reiterated in an open letter from eleven Canadian church leaders to Prime Minister Mulroney, dated February 1, 1988, and reproduced in *Peace Building: The Church Response to Canadian Defence Policy* (Project Ploughshares Working Paper 88-1), p. 5.

Former United Church moderator Clarke McDonald and former senior minister of Bloor Street United Church Rev. Clifford Elliot each expressed opposition to retaliating in response to a Soviet first-strike. See "Nuclear War: A moral dilemma", *Toronto Star*, November 20, 1982, p. A16. This position echoes that of the Roman Catholic bishops of the United States in their famous pastoral letter: see *The Challenge of Peace: God's Promise and Our Response—Pastoral*

Statement of the National Conference of Catholic Bishops (USA: Daughters of St. Paul, 1983), p. 41.

Pages 289–90

For a contrary account of the role nuclear deterrence has played in contributing to world peace, see Richard Ned Lebow and Janice Stein, "Beyond Deterrence", (1987) 43 *Journal of Social Issues* 5.

Page 292

I do not include Allende's Chile as an example of a full-fledged Communist regime. At the time of the Pinochet coup, there was a sizeable and vocal opposition in the country. Indeed, that opposition had been strong enough to engage in some very disruptive activities, for example, a national truckers' strike. I don't claim sufficient knowledge of the situation to be able to declare with confiddence that the regime was becoming Communist. What I can say is that, even if it was, there was still a distance to go. See, in this regard, Nathaniel Davis, *The Last Two Years of Salvador Allende* (Ithaca and London: Cornell University Press, 1985), Ch. 8.

There is no question that repression has abated in a number of the East European regimes. While some liberalization has taken place in some of those countries, they are still far from democratic. Moreover, these regimes have periodically fluctuated between various levels of liberalism and retrenchment. It is not without signifiance that one of the most liberal regimes in Eastern Europe is Yugoslavia, which has been outside of the Soviet bloc since 1948. But, even there, dissent has been heavily circumscribed. The former second-in-command, Milovan Djilas, for example, spent years in prison for promoting the cause of a democratic and pluralistic socialism. See Milovan Djilas, *Rise and Fall* (John Fiske Loud, trans.) (Orlando, Fla.: Harcourt Brace Jovanovich, 1985).

One can only speculate about what might have happened to Dubčeck's "socialism with a human face" in Czechoslovakia if Soviet tanks had not been deployed there in the summer of 1968. While there were hopeful signs of an evolution towards a more democratic socialism, we cannot foretell what *might* have happened. In any event, I do not discount the possibility that some Communist leaders may have and nourish democratic inclinations. My concern is that in Communist regimes liberal evolution is disproportionately dependent upon the cosmic accident of liberal individuals rising to power. There are too few vehicles by which people outside of the ruling hierarchy can exert their influence on political development. Moreover, even if a more liberal regime were to evolve, it would be vulnerable to the machinations and intrigues of the party's skilled operatives. And, if these don't prove sufficient to curb perceived excesses of liberalism, there has always been the military power of the Soviet Union, which could be exercised at least in countries that are within easy reach of the Red Army.

The foregoing leaves open the possibility of a democratic evolution occurring in a Communist regime that is located in a country or continent far from the Soviet heartland. Indeed, I cannot rule out such a development even in a country closer to the Soviet heartland or, for that matter, in the heartland itself. All I can say is that, *in fact*, no such democratization has occurred since the Second World War in any country that had a full-fledged Communist regime. Moreover, so long as a regime remained Communist, it was likely to foment or promote the establishment of similar regimes among its neighbours.

The one possible exception to this trend might be Afghanistan, where a Communist regime may be on the verge of some power-sharing with its Moslem opponents. But consider the price that was paid to bring about this change—a savage nine-year war involving thousands of refugees and more than one million estimated dead. In this regard, see "In Afghanistan, the opportunities for War are endless", *New York Times*, March 27, 1988, p. E3; "Kabul accepts coalition proposal", *Globe and Mail*, March 30, 1988, p. A10, and Radek Siroski, "Coda to the Russo-Afghan War", *Encounter*, Vol. 71, No. 1 (June 1988) 20 at p. 23 fn. 5.

It is fair to say then that, while Communist regimes may not have proved perfectly invincible, they have been effectively so.

For more on the irrevocability of full-fledged Communist regimes, see the opposing views of Jeane Kirkpatrick, "Dictatorships and Double Standards," *Commentary*, November 1979, p. 34, and Theodore Draper, "Mrs. Kirkpatrick's Theories", in his *Present History* (New York: Vintage Books, 1984), pp. 313–19.

Page 293

Regarding Hitler's strategy of rising to power by legal means, see Alan Bullock, *Hitler, A Study in Tyranny* (Harmondsworth: Penguin Books, 1962).

Pages 294–95

Regarding Cuba's involvement in South Yemen, Ethiopia, and Angola, see William J. Durch, "The Cuban Military in Africa and the Middle East: From Algeria to Angola", *Studies in Comparative Communism*, Vol. XI, Nos. 1 and 2 (Spring/Summer 1978), pp. 34–74.

Page 295

The article by Dr. John Foster is found in "Nicaragua: Now or Never", *Mandate*, March 1984, pp. 21–23. Dr. Foster is past chairperson of the Canadian Inter-Church Committee on Human Rights in Latin America.

Pages 295–96

For examples of the kind of allegations abut the Sandinista regime that Foster's article did not mention, see the following:

Regarding the activities of the neighbourhood committees, Shirley Christian, *Nicaragua: Revolution in the Family* (New York: Random House, 1985), pp. 124, 127, 133, 151, 224, 243, 300, and Juan E. Corradi, "Nicaragua," *Dissent* (Summer 1984), 275, at p. 277.

Pages 296

On the complaints of Sandinista interference with the labour movement, see a letter dated April 14, 1982, to the second secretary of the Nicaraguan Embassy in Ottawa from John Harker, director of international affairs for the Canadian Labour Congress; a letter dated October 10, 1979, to the director general, International Labour Office, from Otto Kersten, general secretary of the International Confederation of Free Trade Unions; a letter dated February 14, 1980, to the Permanent Commission on Human Rights in Nicaragua (CPDH) from Carlos Huembres Trejos, secretary general of the Central Organization of Nicaraguan Workers (CTN); a letter dated February 19, 1980, to the general secretary of the Regional Organization of Interamerican Workers (ORIT) from Jose Espinoza Navas, general secretary of the Confederation for Trade Unity (CUS), the Nicaraguan affiliate of the International Confederation of Free Trade Unions; "First these questions" [ed.], *Globe and Mai*, February 15, 1983, p. A6; and John Harker, "Rhetoric Masking Realities," Ottawa *Citizen*, July 8, 1983, p. 9.

Regarding the activities of the *turbas*, see Shirley Christian, *Nicaragua: Revolution in the Family*, pp. 228–29, 252, 277, 289, 299, 301.

For more on the harassment of Nicaragua's Permanent Commission on Human Rights, see Shirley Christian, *Nicaragua: Revolution in the Family*, pp. 132–34, 280–82, and the International League for Human Rights, *Report on Human Rights Defenders in Nicaragua* (New York: ILHR, July 1986), pp. 34–45 (the league was founded by Roger Baldwin, who previously founded the American Civil Liberties Union).

On the party-to-party agreement between the Sandinista National Liberation Front (FSLN) and the Soviet Communist Party (CPSU), see "Sandinistas, in Moscow, Find Much to Agree On", *Current Digest of the Soviet Press*, Vol. 23, No. 12 (April 23, 1980), pp. 10–11.

Regarding the tribulations of *La Prensa*, see *Annual Report of the Inter-American Commission on Human Rights 1981–82*, pp. 113–19 [cited by the Puebla Institute, *Nicaragua, Civil Liberties, and the Central American Peace Plan* (Washington, D.C.: Puebla Institute, 1988), pp. 51–52]; *Annual Report of the Inter-American Commission on Human Rights, 1982–83*, p. 23 (cited by the International League for Human Rights, *Report on Human Rights Defenders*, p. 133); and Jaime Chromorro, "How 'La Prensa' was Silenced", *Commentary*, Vol. 83, No. 1 (January 1987), p. 39.

For some indication of political imprisonment in Nicaragua, see Amnesty International, *Nicaragua: The Human Rights Record* (London: AI, March 1986), International League for Human Rights, *Report on Human Rights Defenders in Nicaragua*, pp. 143–53, and the Puebla Institute, *Nicaragua, Civil Liberties, and the Central American Peace Plan* , pp. 76–79.

The public record also discloses a number of statements made by Sandinista leaders themselves in which they disclose their intentions, plans, and ideology. See, for example, the statement reportedly made by *commandante* Bayardo Arce, a member of the FSLN directorate, on press freedom: "We support freedom of the press, but, of course, the freedom of the press we support will be a freedom of the press that supports the revolution" (quoted in Shirley Christian, *Nicaragua: Revolution in the Family*, p. 124).

One of the most important members of the Sandinista directorate, Minister of Defence Humberto Ortega, reportedly made the following statement about elections at a ceremony on August 23, 1980: "Remember…[our] elections are to improve the power of the revolution, but they are not a raffle to see who has power, because the people have the power through their vanguard, the Sandinista National Liberation Front and its National directorate." And, on June 23, 1981, at a gathering of Sandinista army and militia officers, Mr. Ortega reportedly made the following statement: "Marxism-Leninism is the scientific doctrine that guides our revolution, the instrument of analysis of our vanguard to understand [the revolution's] historical process and to make the revolution. *Sandinismo* is the concrete expression of the historical development of the struggle in Nicaragua. Without *Sandinismo* we cannot be Marxist-Leninists, and *Sandinismo* without Marxism-Leninism cannot be revolutionary. Thus, they are indissolubly united and thus our moral force is *Sandinismo*, our political force is *Sandinismo* and our doctrine is Marxism-Leninism." From Robert S. Leiken and Barry Rubin, eds., *The Central American Crisis Reader* (New York: Summit Books, 1987), at pp. 229 and 685, respectively.

Most of the foregoing reportedly occurred, and many were reported, before Dr. Foster's article was published in March 1984. Some of it occurred even before the Reagan administration assumed office, when the Carter administration was actively courting the Sandinistas. Since the Foster article, there have been a number of developments.

For reports of food being used by the neighbourhood committees, see the Puebla Institute, *Nicaragua, Civil Liberties, and the Central American Peace Plan*, p. 22.

Regarding reports of the continued imprisonment and harassment of union leaders independent of the government, see the Puebla Institute, *Nicaragua, Civil Liberties, and the Central American Peace Plan*, p. 45.

Regarding reports of *turba* attacks since the signing of the peace plan, see the Puebla Institute, *Nicaragua, Civil Liberties, and the Central American Peace Plan*, pp. 22–23, 45; CPDH de Nicaragua, *Report for January 1988* (Costa Rica: February 1988), pp. 5–6; "Sandinista Supporters Disrupt Opposition Rally", *Washington Post*, March 7, 1988, p. A23; and "Nicaragua Revives Gang Tactics to Block Opposition", *Washington Post*, March 8, 1988, p. A21. See also the reports of a speech by President Daniel Ortega in "Nicaraguan Cardinal Seeks Pledges

Before Mediation Starts", *New York Times*, November 9, 1987, p. A14, and the Puebla Institute, *Nicaragua, Civil Liberties, and the Central American Peace Plan*, pp. 4–5, 27.

For further examples of the Sandinistas' ideology and intentions, see the comments of *comman-dante* Bayardo Arce reproduced in Leiken and Rubin, eds., *The Central American Crisis Reader*, pp. 292–95, and those reported to have been made by President Daniel Ortega in "Sandinistas Warn Opposition Not to Push Too Far", *New York Times*, December 17, 1987, p. A10, and "Ortega Warns the Opposition", *New York Times*, December 14, 1987, p. A12.

Most of these recent developments have been brought to my attention by Nina Shea, Washington director of the Puebla Institute and former program director of the International League for Human Rights.

Page 297

The comments of the Right Reverend Robert Smith can be found in "Canadian observers blast U.S. role in Nicaragua", *Toronto Star*, November 10, 1984, p. A10.

The article is reproduced in the report of the church and human rights delegation (of which Reverend Smith was a member) that observed the 1984 Nicaraguan election. See Canadian Church and Human Rights Delegation, *Nicaragua 1984: Democracy, Elections and War* (Toronto, 1984), p. vii.

Regarding the amount of economic, food, and medical aid provided to the Sandinista regime during its first eighteen months, see U.S., Department of State and Department of Defense, *The Challenge to Democracy in Central America* (Washington, D.C.: June 1986), p. 18; "U.S. accepts Nicaragua regime by agreeing to let ties continue", *New York Times*, July 25, 1979, p. A4; "U.S. envoy goes back to Nicaragua with planeload of aid supplies", *New York Times*, July 29, 1979, p. 2; "U.S. increasing aid to Nicaragua", *New York Times*, August 7, 1979, p. 4; "Congress is warned not to deny aid to Nicaragua", *New York Times*, September 12, 1979, p. A11; and Robert Pastor, *Condemned to Repitition* (Princeton, N.J.: Princeton University Press, 1987), pp. 196, 207, 209, 229.

The major chunk of that aid was a $75-million ecnomic aid program. Fifteen million of that aid remained to be delivered when the program was cut off by President Reagan. See "U.S. halts economic aid to Nicaragua", *New York Times*, April 2, 1981, p. 3.

The joint U.S. Departments of State and Defence document reports that the $118 million in direct aid was "more aid than the United States had provided Somoza in the previous four years" (p. 18). See also Pastor, *Condemned to Repetition*, p. 43, and *U.S. Overseas Loans and Grants and Assistance From International Organizations, 1945–1982* (n.d.), p. 54.

For the Sandinista–Soviet joint communiqué, see note to page 296, "Sandinistas, in Moscow…".

Page 298

For an excellent account of the American failure to encourage the progressive democrats among anti-Castro Cubans, see Theodore Draper, *Castro's Revolution: Myths and Realities* (Boulder, Colo.: Frederick A. Praeger, 1962), pp. 59–113, and his chapter entitled "How *Not* to Overthrow Castro". For an account of the failure to include the democratic opposition within Cuba in the plan to invade at the Bay of Pigs, see "CIA is accused by bitter rebels", *New York Times*, April 22, 1961, p. 1, and "Underground force quits revolutionary group to protest CIA action", *New York Times*, May 24, 1961, p. 1.

In his book, *The Closest of Enemies* (New York: W.W. Norton, 1987), Wayne Smith, a former U.S. State Department official stationed in Cuba, has written that the CIA "tended to distrust" the Cuban underground "because many of its members were too liberal for the CIA's taste." He recalls a conversation with a CIA man in Havana, where he ventured that it might be wise to assist Manuel Ray, the former minister of public works under Castro who had organized a small but efficient opposition force. "Absolutely not," answered the CIA man, Ray "is something of a socialist himself." Smith is of the view that, as a result of the Bay of Pigs fiasco and the CIA's lack of communication with the underground, the anti-Castro underground was destroyed (pp. 71–72).

For a brief discussion of the "show trials" of David Salvador and Húber Matos, see Theodore Draper, *Castro's Revolution*, pp. 25–26 and 66–67, respectively. Salvador was arrested at sea trying to flee Cuba with his family. See "Ex-Aide of Castro Seized In Flight", *New York Times*, November 6, 1960, p. 24. Carlos Rodriguez Quesada in *David Salvador—Castro's Prisoner* (New York: Labor Committee to Release Imprisoned Trade Unionists and Democratic Socialists, 1961), p. 19 (also cited by Draper at p. 26), reports that Salvador was initially charged with carrying illegal currency (US $13,000) and attempting to leave the country by illegal means. At the time of his arrest, the first offence carried only the penalty of confiscation of the currency, while the second violated only "certain bureaucratic procedures." Salvador was subsequently convicted of counter-revolutionary activities and sentenced to thirty years' imprisonment. See also Armando Valladares, *Against All Hope* (A. Hurley, trans.) (New York: Alfred A. Knopf, 1986), p. 27. Draper reports that Matos received a sentence of twenty years' imprisonment for his disloyalty. Matos seved his full sentence and has been released. See Irving Howe, "On Hearing Húber Matos Speak", *Dissent*, Vol. 27, No. 2 (Spring 1980), p. 171.

I refer to Vietnamese such as Dr. Phan Quang Dan, associated with the moderately socialist Vietnam Nationalist Party, who led opposition elements until his imprisonment in 1960. See Chester A. Bain, *Vietnam: The Roots of Conflict* (Englewood Cliffs, N.J.: Prentice-Hall, 1967), p. 99. I have also referred to Thich Tri Quang, a leading Buddhist monk, whose views are described by Irving Howe as "offering a small glimmer of hope. It may indicate a path by which the people of South Vietnam, *acting on their own*, can find a way to avoid the disaster of a prolonged and fruitless war." See "The Buddhist Revolt in Vietnam", *Dissent*, Vol. 13, No. 3 (May–June 1966), p. 227; "Determined Buddhist, Tri Quang", *New York Times*, September 4, 1963, p. 2; "Thich Tri Quang, Jailed 4 Months, is Freed by Saigon", *New York Times*, July 1, 1968, p. 8; and Weldon A. Brown, *Prelude to Disaster* (New York and London: Kennikat Press, 1975), p. 200. There was also Diem's first foreign minister, Dr. Tran Van Do, who was described as "the truly authentic voice of all Vietnam." See Weldon A. Brown, *Prelude to Disaster*, p. 91.

Page 299

Shirley Christian's book *Nicaragua: Revolution in the Family* details the roles played by Eden Pastora, Alfonso Robelo, and Arturo Cruz in the overthrow of Somoza and in the early stages of the Sandinista government. See also two speeches by Eden Pastora and the political program of Cruz's CDN, reproduced in Leiken and Rubin, eds., *The Central American Crisis Reader*, pp. 252–56, 263–64, and 284–88, respectively.

For more on the Contra plot to assassinate Eden Pastora, see "North's liaison man heard plot devised to kill Contra leader", *Globe and Mail*, January 7, 1987, p. A5. In attendance at that meeting was Robert Owen, liaison man to fired White House aide Oliver North. Such an assassination plot was not the first attempt to kill Pastora. A bomb intended for Pastora wounded him and killed at least eight others in June 1984. For a discussion of this assassination attempt and Pastora's conflicts with conservative Contras and the Sandinista government, see Leslie Cockburn, *Out of Control* (New York: Atlantic Monthly Press, 1987), pp. 74 ff.; Charles Krauthammer, "Throwing it Away", *The New Republic*, June 25, 1984, pp. 13–15; and Dennis Volman, "Nicaraguan rebels' cause is to democratize Sandinistas", *Toronto Star*, July 6, 1984, p. 12.

For more on Pastora's withdrawal from the conflict, see "A top Nicaraguan rebel gives up fight", *New York Times*, May 17, 1986, p. 3. Subsequently, Arturo Cruz and Alfonso Robelo each quit the Contra movement. Although Robelo had been a party to the infighting in the Contra movement, he justified his departure on the basis that his residence permit in Costa Rica would be rescinded if he continued to back the Contras. See "Top Contra [Cruz] quits, saying changes were blocked", *New York Times*, March 10, 1987, p. 1; "Key Contra [Robelo] demands reduction of rightist's role", *New York Times*, February 14, 1987, p. 5, and "Contra leader [Robelo] resigning post", *Globe and Mail*, February 6, 1988, p. A10.

Page 300

There is evidence that U.S. administrations have periodically extended some timely support to democratic alternatives, such as Corazon Aquino's efforts against both the right-wing dictator Ferdinand Marcos and the Communist guerrillas in the Philippines. My concern, however, is that there has not been a sufficient political constituency to sustain such an approach. Too many hawks will support *anyone*, including the most right-wing tyrants, simply because they are anti-Communist. Too many doves don't even address the issue because they regard U.S. meddling as immoral *per se*.

The views of columnist Mackenzie Porter will be found in *Toronto Sun*, November 2, 1984, p. 12.

Page 302

The *Toronto Sun* published its front-page editorial regarding capital punishment on September 19, 1984. It is worth noting that the House of Commons, in a free vote, subsequently rejected a resolution favouring the restoration of capital punishment. See "MPs reject death penalty", *Toronto Star*, June 30, 1987, p. 1.

Pages 302–03

Statistics regarding the number of police officers murdered in Canada in 1962 and 1985 can be found in Canadian Centre for Justice Statistics, *Historical Homicide Data and Other Data Relevant to the Capital Punishment Issue*, March 1987, p. 28.

Page 303

Statistics regarding murder rates in Canada will be found in Statistics Canada, *Homicide in Canada 1982, A Statistical Perspective*, p. 57, and in Canadian Centre for Justice Statistics, *Historical Homicide Data and Other Data Relevant to the Capital Punishment Issue*, p. 14.

An analysis of the 1982 Gallup survey regarding the perceptions of Canadians with regard to criminal-justice questions will be found in A.N. Doob and J.V. Roberts, *Crime: Some Views of the Canadian Public* (Toronto: Centre of Criminology, University of Toronto, 1982). See also A.N. Doob and J.V. Roberts, *Sentencing: An Analysis of the Public's View of Sentencing* (Ottawa: Department of Justice, 1983), and Canada, Report of the Canadian Sentencing Commission, *Sentencing Reform: A Canadian Approach* (Ottawa: Supply and Services, 1987), Ch. 4.

CHAPTER FOURTEEN

Pages 305–06

For the comparison of the bathhouse raids to Kristallnacht, see "Rage! Taking It to the Streets", *Body Politic*, No. 71 (March 1981), p. 9. The night of terror in Nazi Germany known as Kristallnacht is described in some detail by historian Martin Gilbert in *The Holocaust* (London: Collins, 1986), pp. 69–75.

Page 306

Rick Salutin's comments regarding Israel's siege of West Beirut will be found in "Hitler's haunting last laugh", *Maclean's*, October 11, 1982, p. 17.

Pages 306–07

Clayton Ruby's comments are extracted from transcripts of his testimony before the Ontario Standing Committee on Resources Development, June 2, 1981, p. 3, considering revision of the Ontario Human Rights Code. See also "Protect sexual rights: Lawyer", *Toronto Star*, June 3, 1981, p. A5.

Page 307

The reference to John Lee will be found in "Students boycott final exam", *The Varsity*, Vol. 104, No. 40, (January 11, 1984) pp. 1–2.

Tory MPP James Taylor is quoted from "Tory MPP calls rights proposal scandalous", *Globe and Mail*, September 16, 1981, p. 4, and columnist Claire Hoy from "The human wrongs code", *Sunday [Toronto] Sun*, January 27, 1985, p. CL2.

Barbara Amiel's invective against Judge Rosalie Abella's report on employment equity will be found in "Report a blueprint for hate", *Toronto Sun*, November 25, 1984, p. CL3. Abella's recommendations will be found in *Report of the Commission on Equality in Employment* (Ottawa: Supply and Services, 1984).

Pages 307–08

Amendments to the Canada Elections Act, RSC 1970, c. 14 (1st supp.), prompted Claire Hoy's column, from which the quote is extracted, "Our freedom: R.I.P.", *Toronto Sun*, January 17, 1984, p. 30. These amendments were subsequently challenged by the National Citizen's Coalition in *N.C.C. et al.* v. *Attorney-General for Canada* (1984), 11 DLR (4th) 481, [1984] 5 WWR 436 (Alta. QB).

Page 308

The *Sun* editorial on the appointment of Ed Schreyer as governor general will be found in "Insult to Queen", *Toronto Sun*, December 8, 1978, p. 1.

Claire Hoy's quote "Soviet bloc mentality" will be found in "Davis' secret sellout", *Toronto Sun*, December 11, 1983, p. 38.

Pages 308–09

The Reverend R.J. Davis quote is in "No religion leads to Nazism: Minister", *Niagara Falls Review*, November 17, 1983, p. 1.

Page 310

For a poignant analysis of the Communist Party's treatment of the German Social Democrats in Weimar Germany and its tragic consequences, see Theodore Draper, "The Ghost of Social-Fascism", *Commentary*, Vol. 47, No. 2 (February 1969), pp. 29–42.

INDEX

411

Pollyanna fallacy, 10–11

Pornography, 53–66 passim; "artistic merit" defence, 59, 60, 61; "community standards", 54; harmful effects, 62–63, 64–66; legislation, 59–61; "undue exploitation of sex", 54–55, 56. *See also* Censorship; Obscenity

Port Arthur Ship Building Company, 269–71

Porter, Mackenzie, 300–01

Power-hoarding fallacy, 7–9, 60, 95, 103

Pre-censorship, 55, 65

President's Commission on Law Enforcement and the Administration of Justice, 98

Pressure groups, 157

Pre-trial publicity, restrictions on, 138, 139–41, 142, 143, 145. *See also* Contempt of court

Privacy, right to, 96

Privacy Act, 84

Property rights, in Charter of Rights and Freedoms, 213

Public inquiries, 108, 130–38; powers, 133–34

"Public interest", 52

Public policy, 6, 10

Quebec Charter of Rights, "notwithstanding" clause, 212

Quebec language laws, and Charter of Rights and Freedoms, 209–10

Quebec Superior Court, on picket lines, 27

Quigley, Frances Hugh, 43, 49

Race relations, and legislation, 11–12

Racism, 41, 217–19, 220; beyond human rights laws, 238–40; in employment agencies, 225–27. *See also* Discrimination; Human rights laws

Rand, Ivan, 24

RCMP Security Service, 68, 73; vs. CSIS, 69–70; mandate, 89, 90; security files, 88; surveillance targets, 68

RCMP wrongdoing, 1–2, 9, 34, 68, 69–70, 73, 89–90, 91, 121; mail opening, 82, 101–02, 103; and tax data, 85; prosecutions for, 121, 124, 125–27. *See also* Royal Commission of Inquiry Concerning Certain Activities of the RCMP

Redemptive fallacy, 11–13

Redemptivism, 11–15

Reid, Robert, 178

Religion in schools, 210, 309

Rhetoric, distorted, 305–09

Rights. *See* Dissent, right to; Due process of law; Freedom of assembly; Freedom of association; Freedom of expression; Freedom of the press; Freedom of speech; Freedom to be left alone; Legal counsel, right to upon arrest; Marketplace, right to freedom in; Privacy, right to; Self-incrimination, right against

Roosevelt, Franklin Delano, 153

Royal Commission into Metropolitan Toronto Police Practices (Morand commission), 108, 130

Royal Commission of Inquiry Concerning Certain Activities of the RCMP (McDonald commission), 69, 73, 88, 93, 108, 121, 130, 138, 139; on confidential files, 84; on mail opening, 82, 102, 103, 122, 123

Royal Commission on the Conduct of Police Force at Fort Erie, 94–95

Royal Commission on the Non-Medical Use of Drugs (LeDain commission), 122

Ruby, Clayton, 145, 306, 307

Rule of law, 301–02